TOURING NORTHERN
Thailand

WARNING

All information in this book was accurate at the time of writing. However, all things change, and in Thailand things are changing rapidly. Fortunately, accommodation standards and roads are generally improving. New hotels are being built and old ones knocked down. A change in management can mean a change in standards. Prices fluctuate – usually upwards. Please bear these points in mind when using this book, and we at Footloose Books would be most grateful if readers would let us know of anything they feel should be added or changed for the next edition.

All place names are given in the most widely accepted transliteration from the Thai language. Spellings in this book, however, may vary from that quoted in other sources.

In 1989 the leaders of Burma altered the name of the country to "Myanmar". Since this change was decreed by a government which has lost a democratic election and refused to give up power, it is not recognised in this book.

TOURING NORTHERN Thailand

by John R. Davies

This book is dedicated to the memory of
my father, David Rowland Davies

TOURING NORTHERN THAILAND
First published November 1991
ISBN 0-9516496-1-2

Published by Footloose Books, 34 Catherine Street, Salisbury, Wiltshire, U.K.
Distributed in the U.K. and the English speaking world by Roger Lascelles,
47 York Road, Brentford, Middlesex

© John R. Davies 1991

All rights reserved. No part of this publication may be reproduced, or
transmitted in any way or by any means (except for brief extracts for review
purposes) without the written permission of the publisher.

The production of this book has involved a huge effort by a large number of
people. I would particularly like to thank the following:
(Research) William Alexander, John and Sue Boyes, Peter Boyes, Fiona Cook,
Bob Diaper, Nicholas Greenwood, Tom Keevers, Graham Osborne,
Dr. Lek Prasert, John Spies, Vacharin Sirichai, Rusty and Marilyn Staff,
David Unkovich, Tommy Wu, Michael Young, The Thai Tourist Authority and
The Hill Tribe Research Institute, Chiang Mai University
(Production) Jo Bond, Charles and Kate Davies of K. B. Graphics,
L. M. Davies, Roger Lascelles, Nicholas Greenwood, Linda Coleman,
Allan Lee, Antony Gray and David Taylor

All photographs by the author
Illustrations by Linda Coleman

Cover photograph: Flower festival, Chiang Mai

CONTENTS

INTRODUCTION   7

HOW TO USE THIS BOOK   9

Chapter 1:
LAND AND PEOPLE   17
Landscape 18, Climate 19, History 21, Culture 25,
The Thai Character 26, Etiquette 27, Social life 28,
Entertainment 29, Language 30, Religion, 31, Temples 32,
Food and drink 35, The Hill Tribes 42, Opium 54,
Natural history 57.

Chapter 2:
PRACTICALITIES   60
Banks and Money 61, Getting There 62, Local Transport 64,
Business hours 64, Telecommunications 65, Administration 66,
The Economy 67, Consulates 67, Visas 67, Time 68,
Weights and Measures 68, Electricity 68, Photography 68,
Health 69, Sanitation 71, Driving 72, Vehicle Rental 74.

Chapter 3:
CHIANG MAI   77
Introduction 81, History 82, Geography 83, Lay Out 83,
Transport 85, Things To See 86, Things To Do 88,
Places To Eat 90, Nightlife 92, Bars 93, Massage 94,
Bookshops 94, Accommodation 96, Around Chiang Mai 101,
Sankamphaeng 104, Doi Sutep and Doi Pui 106, Mae Sa Valley 107,
Lamphun and Pasang 111, Doi Inthanon 113

Chapter 4:
THE GOLDEN TRIANGLE AND THE FAR NORTH   116
Introduction 124, Chiang Mai to Chiang Rai 125,
Chiang Rai to Thaton 127, Thaton To Chiang Mai 129,
Chiang Rai 132, Around Chiang Rai 143, Mae Sai 149,
Chiang Saen 153, Golden Triangle 155, Chiang Khong 157,
Doi Mae Salong 158, Thaton 161, Fang 162,

Chapter 5:
THE WEST 165
Introduction 172, Chiang Mai to Mae Hong Son 173,
Mae Hong Son to Mae Sariang 175,
Mae Sariang to Chiang Mai 177, Pai 180, Soppong 185,
Mae Hong Son 188, Mae Sariang 198

Chapter 6:
THE SOUTH 202
Introduction 209, Lampang to Sukhothai 210,
Sukhothai to Tak 213, Tak to Mae Sot 213,
Mae Sot to Mae Sariang 214, Sukhothai 216, Phitsanulok 222,
Tak 228, Mae Sot 231.

Chapter 7:
THE EAST 235
Introduction 236, Chiang Mai to Lampang 242,
Lampang to Phrae 243, Phrae to Nan 244, Nan to Phayao 245,
Phayao to Chiang Mai 245, Lampang 246, Phrae 254,
Nan 258, Phayao 263.

Appendix 1:
THAI WORDLIST 267

Appendix 2:
LIST OF MAPS 274

INDEX 276

INTRODUCTION

There can be few places in the world which have as much to offer the visitor as Northern Thailand. The scenery is spectacular, the climate perfect for much of the year, the people charming, the food delectable and the culture fascinating - small wonder that over 3 million people a year visit the north.

It is a land of vibrant colours, cultures and contrasts. The tropical light shining on gaudy temples, shimmering green plains and jungle covered mountains produce breathtakingly beautiful scenes at every turn.

The countryside of Northern Thailand, fingers of sharp peaked mountain ranges reaching south into the flat, fertile plains, abounds in waterfalls, caves, torrents, lakes and forests. There is a huge variety of wildlife, from intensely coloured and over large butterflies to gibbons and even the occasional tiger. The National Park of Doi Inthanon alone has over 360 species of birds. Elephants are not just reserved for the tourist - they can be seen used as beasts of burden thoughout the north - although wild elephants are now extremely rare. Orchids, the symbol of Thailand, grow wild in the forests, their incredibly delicate and colourful flowers appearing at the peak of the dry season.

The Thai culture has been compared to a sheet of water, which, although outwardly placid, has great strength and power. It can reflect the world around it, absorb whatever is thrown into it, without changing its underlying nature or direction. True, the modern Thailand has adopted western ways and styles with glee, but retains its Buddhist essence which is very different and unique. Every corporate headquarters and concrete luxury hotel has a spirit house, reverently placed and respected. No Thai would think of driving his new expensive car until it had been blessed and sprinkled with holy water by a monk. The new is added to the old, but the old is never lost or forgotten.

But northern Thailand is not limited to just one culture - there are at least eight more. The hilltribes, although minority groups, have very distinct cultures, with separate languages, religions, customs and economies, and flamboyant costumes, sometimes within an area of a few kilometres. Flooding into Thailand as a refuge from less friendly regimes elsewhere, they have been accepted and helped, their cultures adding to the rich fabric of the north.

The early history of Thailand is little more than folk stories - all records where lost when the Burmese sacked the capital, Ayutthaya, in the 15th century. Undoubtedly, though, the Thais where influenced profoundly by the two great Empires of East Asia, China and India. The cuisine seems to combine the best of both - the piquancy of Indian food and the subtlety of Chinese. The religion, Buddhism, originated in the Indian Empire, but temple design has much in common with that of China.

Until recently, most of Northern Thailand was largely inaccessible. In the last decade, an intensive road building programme has opened up even the most remote areas. Tourism is gradually extending outwards from a few well trodden routes, but most of the north, and many of its most interesting and beautiful sights, are still unknown - until the publication of this book, that is!

Facilities for the visitor to the north are very good. The heavily touristed areas have a huge variety of accommodations and restaurants, tailor made for western needs and tastes. Remoter areas have a smaller choice, and less compromise for the western tourist, but nevertheless one is never too far from a comfortable hotel and good food. Public transport is convenient, punctual and cheap. Prices everywhere in northern Thailand are low, but often ridiculously low where tourists are a rarity.

There is more for the visitor to take away from Thailand than memories. The Thais are skilled craftsmen and artistic designers. Clothing, jewellery, carvings pottery and a wealth of other goods are available at very low prices and often very high quality. It is better to come with plenty of spare luggage capacity, as only the most determined can avoid packing their bags with bargains for the trip home!

A visit to Northern Thailand is a true adventure - for the mind, body and spirit. It is a land of many faces. Keep an open mind, be prepared to slow down and adopt the easy going uncritical manner of the Thais, and your first visit is unlikely to be your last.

HOW TO USE THIS BOOK

In this book Northern Thailand has been divided into 4 regions, with the city of Chiang Mai as the hub. Geographically and culturally these areas are distinct, and the road network makes this the most practical way to organize tours.

North of Chiang Mai "The Far North", includes Chiang Rai and the "Golden Triangle". "The South" region extends into Thailands central plains, and includes the archaeological sites of Sukhothai, the cities of Phitsanulok to the east and Mae Sot on the Burmese border to the west. "The East" region includes Nan, Phayao and the Laos border area. "The West" extends to the towns of Mae Hong Son and Mae Sariang and the Burmese border west and north of Chiang Mai.

Each region in the book begins with a general overview, followed by a series of maps which shows the best possible route through the region. In general, the major roads are used, with suggested side trips to sites within 20 kilometres of this road (side trips are usually on dirt roads, often slow and bumpy). Each series of maps is followed by a kilometre by kilometre description of the route. Accommodations along these routes are marked and described.

NB. All main roads in Thailand have low, white marker posts every kilometre. On the front of each post the kilometre number is shown, distances being from the origination of that road. These numbers are used for reference throughout this book, and are given alongside the route descriptions

Following the route, the towns in each region are described, including all places of interest in and near the town, things to do and where to eat. At the end of each town description is a very full and detailed analysis of accommodations in that town.

ACCOMMODATION CATEGORIES

Throughout this book, lists of accommodations follow town descriptions at the end of each "map guide" section. Accommodations have been categorised into resort, hotel and guest house, and each entry is graded according to the criteria outlined below.

General Map

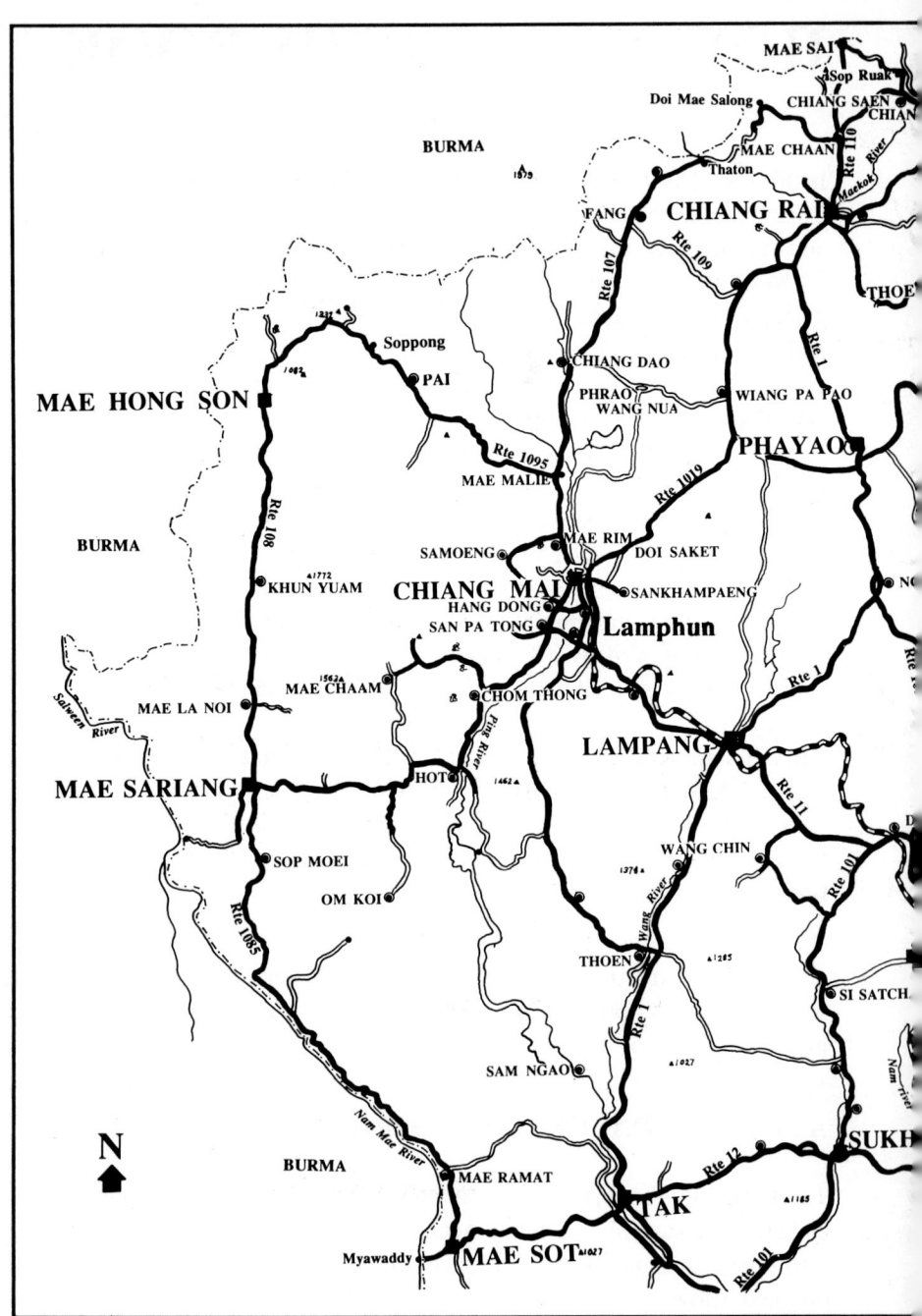

General Map

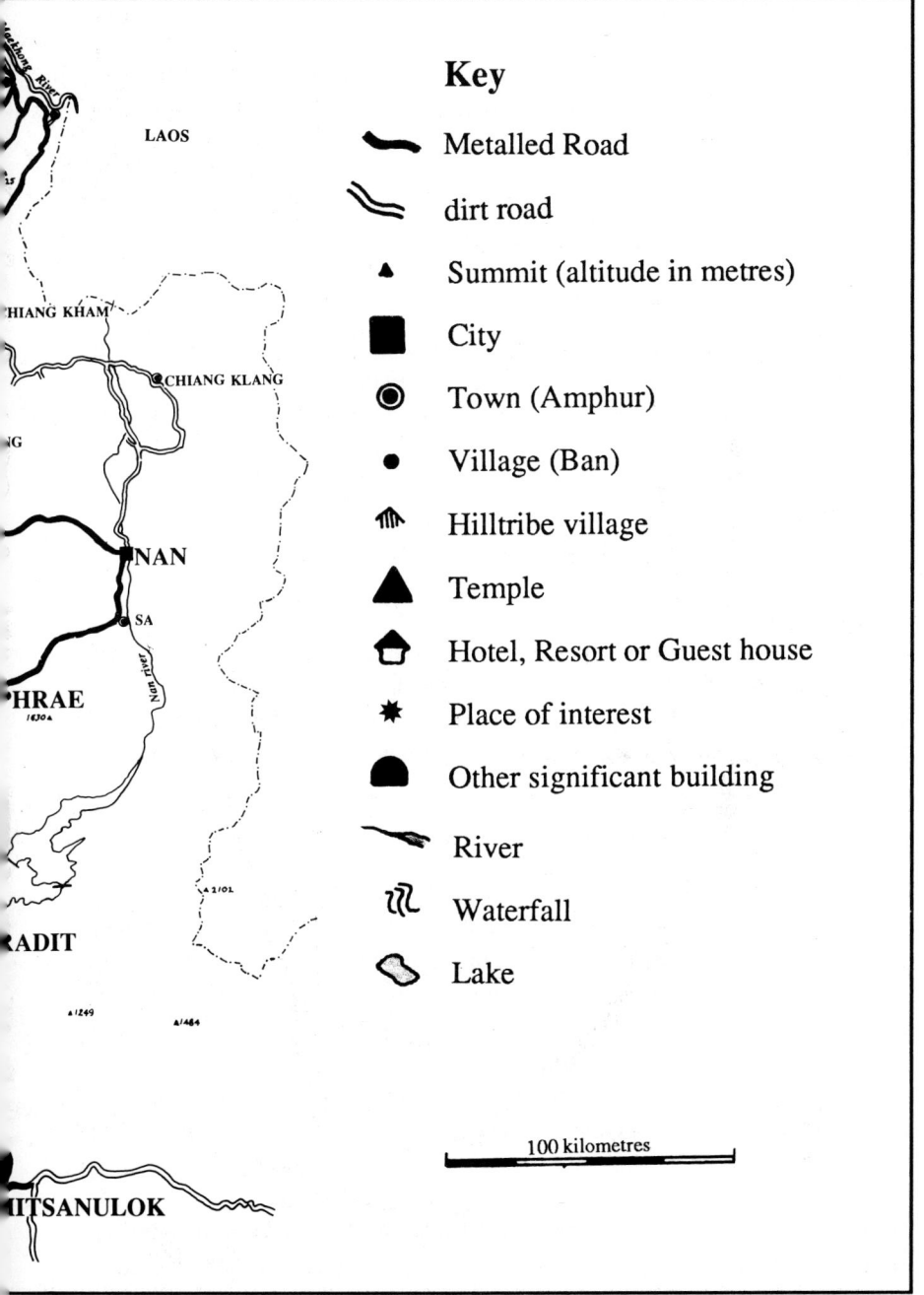

Touring Northern Thailand

There are a great variety of types and standards of accommodations available throughout Thailand. Prices are generally low compared to the west, so value for money at all levels is very good. Typically a room for two people in a cheap but comfortable guest house will cost about 100 *baht* per night, in a luxury hotel about 1000 *baht*. A bungalow in a resort will cost about 500 *baht*.

TYPES OF ACCOMMODATION

INTERNATIONAL HOTELS
These provide an excellent standard of accommodation, equal to anywhere in the world, and are available at most large towns in the north. Thai and western food are available, and typically there will be restaurants, coffee shops, nightclubs and discos. In smaller towns, these hotels are often the centre for the social life of the richer citizens, so the entertainment side of the hotel is likely to be busy and interesting.

THAI HOTELS
Older teak built hotels are pleasant to look at, but often rather dirty and neglected. These have mostly been replaced by rather unattractive but sometimes very comfortable modern concrete constructions, catering mainly to Thai businessmen. Prices vary according to standard, from 70 to 400 *baht*, but they are usually excellent value for money. One problem for tourists is that English is rarely spoken or understood.

RESORTS
Mainly restricted to Northern Thailand, these are landscaped gardens or parks, frequently beautifully designed, catering to the richer Thais who are escaping the heat and bustle of Bangkok and other big cities. The gardens contain cabins, usually of wood and generally well furnished and equipped, and are usually some miles from the nearest town, typically in a jungle clearing. Prices are much lower than luxury hotels, although the facilities are frequently almost of that level, and are good value for money. Little used by tourists at present, they generally provide delightful and romantic places to stay.

GUEST HOUSES
These cater almost exclusively to western tourists. They vary tremendously from cramped and unpleasant rooms to establishments rivalling the best hotels.

At the lower end (below 100 *baht*), their major market is the young backpacker on a very tight budget. No self respecting Thai would stay in these places, though frequently the atmosphere of young people from all over the world exploring Thailand is intimate and fun, making up for the lack of comfort and facilities. Mid price guest houses (100 - 300 *baht*), provide a much higher standard of accommodation. Since the clientele is mainly western, the staff will always have some understanding of English, and the restaurant menus provide a mixture of Thai and western food to suit all tastes.

CATEGORIES

1. OVERALL (FOLLOWING THE NAME OF THE HOTEL)
This is an average of the number of stars given for other categories. This means that a luxury hotel in a poor location may have the same overall rating as a lesser hotel in a better location.

2. PRICE RANGE
Unless otherwise stated, the price range is for a room for two persons, from the cheapest to the most expensive. What is termed a "single" room has one double bed, a double room has twin beds. A single room for one person can usually be rented for a discount of 25-30%. "Dorm" prices are common in guest houses and resorts. Dorms are large rooms with several beds, providing no privacy but cheap prices. At the top end, "suites" typically consist of a bedroom, lounge and perhaps two bathrooms. Four people can occupy a suite, and hotels will provide extra beds at low cost.

3. ROOMS
This quotes the total number of rooms in the hotel and any annexes.

4. A/C - AIR CONDITIONING
This typically adds 25-40% to the price of a room. In the cool season (November-February), A/C is not really necessary.

5. FAN
Except in the most basic guest houses, all non air conditioned rooms will have fans. They can be noisy and irritating, but are fairly essential in the hot and wet seasons.

6. EN SUITE BATHROOMS

The number of en suite bathrooms is quoted, followed by the number that have hot water (hw) or cold water (cw). Hot water is very desirable in the cool season (November-February) but is unlikely to be needed for the rest of the year.

7. COMFORT

☆☆☆☆☆	Luxury rooms with A/C, hot water, carpets, fridge, minibar, TV and video, telephone.
☆☆☆☆	Very comfortable rooms, but with one or more of the above absent.
☆☆☆	Rooms of average comfort, typically with en suite bathroom, table, chair and wardrobe.
☆☆	Rooms providing the minimum facilities needed for comfort with bed and fan, sometimes bathroom.
☆	Rooms with no facilities except a bed, or basic facilities but small or dirty.

8. DESIGN

This refers to the hotel building, its attractiveness and practicality.

☆☆☆☆☆	Beautifully designed.
☆☆☆☆	Attractive building, but not exceptionally so
☆☆☆	Reasonably pleasant and practical design, but lacking beauty or character.
☆☆	Functional but not pleasing to the eye.
☆	Ugly.

9. SITUATION

This refers to the situation of the hotel or guest house. Rural accommodations tend to score highly here, but city hotels with pleasant or convenient locations also gain merit.

☆☆☆☆☆	Exceptionally beautiful surroundings.
☆☆☆☆	Very pleasant and attractive surroundings.
☆☆☆	Unexceptional but acceptable surroundings.
☆☆	Poor location, lacking any attractive features.
☆	Ugly location.

How to Use this Book

10. **POSITION**
If within 500 metres of the town centre, described as "central", otherwise the position is described.

11. **QUIETNESS**
Determined by position and the level of soundproofing within rooms.

☆☆☆☆☆	Exceptionally quiet rural location.
☆☆☆☆	Quiet location, or well soundproofed rooms.
☆☆☆	Not noisy enough to be a problem for most people, but some background noise.
☆☆	Quite noisy, near a busy street or market, but only unacceptable to the sensitive.
☆	Very noisy, near a very busy street, market or factory, thin walls, unpleasant.

12. **RESTAURANT**
It is unusual to find poor food in Thailand - the standard is uniformly high, so most restaurants score ☆☆☆.
International hotels serve Thai and western food, Thai hotels and resorts tend to only serve Thai food. Guest houses serve a mixture of westernised Thai food and western food.

☆☆☆☆☆	Excellent food and service, extensive menu.
☆☆☆☆	Good food, but menu not extensive, ambience not exceptional.
☆☆☆	Good, basic food, limited menu.
☆☆	Below average food and service.
☆	Poor food and service.

13. **FACILITIES**
This refers to "extras" such as swimming pools, tennis courts, and golf courses, as well as facilities which might not be expected in a hotel or guest house in its price range.

14. **TOURS/TREKS**
Hotels catering to westerners usually have a range of local tours, commonly by air conditioned minibus, and a tour agency in the foyer. Guest houses specialise in treks - walking tours of several days to more or less remote areas. This is a major business, particularly in Chiang Mai, where guest houses depend on

selling treks for their profits. If staying at one of these establishments, there is some pressure to take the guest house trek.

OTHER PLACES TO STAY

TEMPLES
Any temple will provide accommodation, but of course facilities will be minimal. The visitor may be provided with sheets and blankets, and there are usually toilets and showers in the compound. Payment is expected, but must be offered in an envelope, since monks should not touch money directly. The donation is at the guests discretion, but 50 *baht* per person is a suitable figure.

HILL TRIBE VILLAGES
These are generally safe to stay in. Indicate with the usual "sleep" gesture to any adult that you would like to stay. You will then be taken to the headman, who will allocate a room or space, usually in his hut. Food will probably be offered, but it is safer, for health reasons, only to accept plain rice and boiled water. Expect to pay 30-50 *baht* per person per night.

SHORT TIME HOTELS
These are not described in this book, since their function is more for illicit sexual intimacy than for resting. They are identified by their romantic signs, often pink lights and a characteristic structure. The rooms are fronted by high walls making a forecourt and entered under a large tarpaulin for complete anonymity. It is possible to stay at these hotels, but be prepared to be pestered by staff who might misconstrue your reason for staying there!

PLACES OF INTEREST

Any town, village, geographic or cultural feature of interest or beauty is indicated by bold type. A tick after the name indicates its level of interest according to the following criteria:

✓✓✓ Not to be missed. A feature of exceptional beauty or interest.
✓✓ Of great interest or beauty, well worth seeing.
✓ Of slight interest, worth visiting for some.

Chapter One

Land and People

LANDSCAPE

FLAT VALLEYS filled to the brim with the lush, iridescent green of growing rice, surrounded by sharp peaked forested hills and mountains characterise the scenery of Northern Thailand.

The paddy fields of the lowlands are immensely fertile, fed with nutrients by the erosion of topsoil from the nearby hills, and producing two or three rice crops a year. A complex system of irrigation channels and low mud walls to trap the water in which the young rice grows produces a patchwork of vivid greens, broken only by the scattered villages of bamboo and teak and the extravagant colours and designs of Buddhist temples. In the fields teams of farm workers can be seen planting, weeding or harvesting the rice, assisted by the water buffaloes, giant but placid grey or pink beasts ubiquitous to South East Asia.

The hills which look down upon these fertile lowlands are a different world. They are naturally covered in dense tropical forest, with a huge number of species of trees. At low levels the trees are low and spindly, losing their leaves in the long dry season. At higher altitudes, where the rainfall is greater and the temperature lower, the size, density and lushness of the forest increases, culminating in cloud forest above 2000 metres, where the trees are covered in a thick flora of epiphytic mosses, ferns and creepers. It is at these higher altitudes that the dazzlingly beautiful and highly prized orchids can be found - perhaps the most familiar symbol of Northern Thailand.

Mountain streams rush down the steep slopes of the hills, punctuated frequently by waterfalls, many of great beauty. Around these falls, the permanently high humidity creates a hothouse profusion of dazzling flowers and foliage, and the pools below the torrents make delicious swimming holes. The streams run into giant rivers, placid in the dry season, but fast and powerful during the monsoons.

Where the mountains meet the plain, in suitable places huge dams have been built to create reservoirs, two of which stretch for over 100 kilometres up the valleys. A vital source of water in a land with a six month dry season, they also offer recreational facilities, with fishing, boating, swimming, floating restaurants and guest houses.

The predominant limestone rock leads to the formation of a myriad of caves and potholes, many still undiscovered and unexplored. Home to bats and cave swifts, they are sacred places to the Thais, who, for hundreds of years have decorated them with shrines and Buddha images. Many contain artifacts from earlier civilisations, still a puzzle to archaeologists.

The peoples of these hills scrape a precarious living by burning the forest to create temporary fields in which they grow a meagre crop of mountain rice and other vegetables. Many grow opium at high altitudes, both as a cash crop and to fuel their own addiction. The vast majority of these hill peoples are not Thai, but belong to a variety of different hill tribes, each with its own customs, language and costume.

CLIMATE

Northern Thailand has a tropical monsoon climate, but since it lies well north of the equator (between 17° and 20° north), it does experience marked seasonal temperature variations.

The "wet season" monsoon rains start in May or early June and continue until October. Temperatures in the lowlands are around 32°C in mid afternoon, falling to a minimum of about 23°C at night. It rains on most days, but rarely continuously. A typical day will dawn bright and sunny, clouds build up during the afternoon leading to heavy rain for an hour or two, frequently followed by a sunny evening. In August and September, typhoons sometimes occur (although rarely severe), with heavy rain, thunderstorms and high winds for three or four days.

In the "cool" season from November to February, humid tropical air from the Indian ocean gives way to cold, dry air originating in central Asia to the north. The sun is still high enough to send temperatures above 28°C during the afternoon, but following sunset the temperature drops rapidly, frequently to below 10°C, so that the early mornings are delightfully cool and misty. The sky is generally cloudless all day, and rain is very unlikely - perhaps one shower a month. From December, many of the trees lose their leaves as a protection against drought, and the lush greens of the countryside give way to sombre browns.

The "hot" season is mercifully short - from mid March to May. As the sun climbs higher in the sky, daytime temperatures approach 40°C degrees and the humidity gradually increases, making any exertion difficult.

During this season jungle is burned to prepare for next seasons planting, so the hills are very smoky and dusty. The start of the rains (usually a massive thunderstorm) brings great relief as the temperatures drop. Temperatures decrease and rainfall increases with altitude, so the wet season is significantly wetter and cooler in the hills. In the cool season, temperatures below freezing at night are not uncommon above altitudes of 1500 metres.

CLIMATE STATISTICS

CHIANG MAI

	Jan	Feb	Mar	Apr	May	Jun	Jul	Aug	Sep	Oct	Nov	Dec
Temperature °C(°F)												
Average daily max	29(84)	32(89)	34(94)	36(97)	34(94)	32(90)	31(88)	31(88)	31(88)	31(87)	30(86)	28(83)
Average daily min	13(56)	14(58)	17(63)	22(71)	23(72)	23(74)	23(74)	23(74)	23(73)	21(70)	19(66)	15(59)
Rainfall (mms)	0	10	8	36	122	112	213	193	249	94	31	13

CHIANG RAI

	Jan	Feb	Mar	Apr	May	Jun	Jul	Aug	Sep	Oct	Nov	Dec
Temperature °C(°F)												
Average daily max	27(81)	30(86)	33(91)	35(95)	33(91)	32(90)	31(88)	31(88)	31(88)	30(86)	29(84)	27(81)
Average daily min	12(53)	13(55)	15(59)	19(66)	22(72)	23(73)	23(73)	22(72)	22(72)	20(68)	17(63)	13(55)
Rainfall (mms)	19	9	28	72	224	229	292	436	260	130	35	23

MAE HONG SON

	Jan	Feb	Mar	Apr	May	Jun	Jul	Aug	Sep	Oct	Nov	Dec
Temperature °C(°F)												
Average daily max	30(86)	33(91)	36(97)	38(100)	35(95)	32(90)	31(88)	31(88)	31(88)	32(90)	31(88)	29(84)
Average daily min	14(57)	14(57)	17(63)	22(72)	24(75)	23(73)	23(73)	23(73)	23(73)	22(72)	19(66)	16(61)
Rainfall (mms)	13	2	3	46	171	182	211	261	226	103	24	8

TAK

	Jan	Feb	Mar	Apr	May	Jun	Jul	Aug	Sep	Oct	Nov	Dec
Temperature °C(°F)												
Average daily max	32(90)	35(95)	37(99)	38(100)	37(99)	33(91)	32(90)	32(90)	32(90)	31(88)	31(88)	30(86)
Average daily min	15(59)	19(66)	23(73)	26(79)	25(77)	25(77)	25(77)	25(77)	24(75)	23(73)	20(68)	16(61)
Rainfall (mms)	4	5	20	45	189	89	100	100	241	161	41	4

THE HISTORY OF NORTHERN THAILAND

Northern Thailand has been inhabited since prehistoric times. The remains of bronze age settlements have been found at several sites, including **Phayao** and **Soppong**. Two thousand years ago the *Lawa*, now a remote and little visited hill tribe, were the dominant culture. The first Thai related culture to colonise the area lived in Northern Burma and spilled into western Thailand, where they are still found today and known as the *Tai Yai* (high Thais). The province (*Changwat*) of **Mae Hong Son** still has a preponderance of these peoples.

The origins of the modern Thai peoples (who make up 80% of the population of Thailand) are obscure and the subject of much debate. Until recently, it was believed that the Thais originated in Southern Mongolia, and were pushed south east by the expansion outwards of the Chinese empire. Recently, evidence has come to light suggesting that a race known as the Austro Thais in South-East Asia were among the first peoples to develop agriculture and an advanced civilisation which spread first north into southern China, then recolonised their former territory in a southern migration several centuries later. Whichever theory is correct, there was, without a doubt, contact and eventually conflict between Thai and Chinese, which continued for many centuries.

The Thai civilisation was first threatened in the 9th century BC by the Tartars of central Asia, who over a period of 600 years split the Thais into three groups. One group migrated south west to colonise east Burma and west Thailand and became known as the *Shan* or *Tai Yai* mentioned above. Another group moved east to the gulf of Tonkin and the third, destined to be the modern inhabitants of Thailand, moved less far, to the southern part of what is now Szechuan in south west China. Here they established a number of city states, which although at the time independent, came more and more under the sway of the developing Chinese empire. During this period, Buddhism became accepted as the religion of the Thais, introduced by Sinhalese monks from Sri Lanka.

In the first century AD the Chinese attempts to absorb the Thais led to battles in which the Thais were overwhelmingly defeated, and over the next two centuries they moved steadily south towards their present home. In the 5th Century AD, internal dissention in China allowed the Thais still in China to establish an independent kingdom known as **Nan-Chao,** stretching from Tibet in the west to Szechuan in the north and controlling most of what is now Laos and Burma. China was forced to respect this new kingdom which withstood many invasion attempts, at times allied with the kingdoms of Tibet but eventually turning against it (with China as an ally!) when it became too powerful. In 863 AD the Thais seized the city of Tonkin (now Hanoi).

In the following centuries the Thais attempted to extend their control into the south of the Chinese empire, but eventually were conquered and made a Chinese province under Kublai Khan in 1253 AD. Many Thais still live in an area of Southern Yunnan known as "**Sipsong Panna**". The conflicts described above had caused a steady trickle of Thai people southwards and across the Mekong river into northern Thailand, where they settled particularly in the area now occupied by the cities of Chiang Rai, Chiang Mai and Sukhothai. Here, they would come into contact with two Indian based cultures. The Khmers, whose pineapple shaped *chedis* can be seen throughout central Thailand, were based in Cambodia, and had been extending east and northwards. The Mons, another culture with Indian roots, were established further west and north.

The first Thai king to control territory in northern Thailand had as his capital the town of **Chiang Saen**, established in 773 AD, on the banks of the Mekhong. Over the next two centuries, Chiang Saen was destroyed by an earthquake and seized for short periods by the Khmers and later the Vietnamese, who were driven out and, in turn, had their territory seized by Chiang Saen, which also at times controlled most of Laos and Cambodia. In succeeding centuries the royal families of Chiang Saen came to establish principalities in **Phayao** and Chiang Rai. South of Chiang Rai, the territory of Northern Thailand was held by a powerful tribe, the Mons, who controlled large areas of South East Asia. In the 13th century a Thai king, Mengrai, drove the Mons from their northern bastions, the empire known as **Haripunchai**, and extended his lands south to **Lampang** and the Harpunchai capital, **Lamphun**. He called his new, enlarged kingdom "**Lannathai**", meaning "land of a million ricefields", and brought prosperity and stability to the whole area. Many towns and temples were built, and arts and crafts were encouraged. Administration was organized around rice growing. Each person was allowed enough land to grow 5 *muen* (about 60 kilos) of rice. Nobles were given more land, a prince 1000 rice fields. Princes were given new lands on the edge of established territories and so acted as a bulwark against external attack.

Mengrai first established and fortified the city of Chiang Rai, in which he kept his palace until he died. The name "Chiang Rai" is believed to have initially been "Chiang Moi", footprint of the elephant, since according to legend an elephant led Mengrai to that spot on which the city was built. He then moved south establishing and defending new towns at **Fang, Kumkarn** and **Chiang Mai** in 1296 AD, the latter being in such a good situation that it later became the capital of the new kingdom. From Chiang Mai, Mengrai moved south in 1281 AD to take the city of Lamphun from the Mons by using *Lawa* hill tribe allies to spread dissention in the city, thus ensuring little resistance when Mengrai's army appeared. Fourteen years later, in an unsuccessful attempt to retake the city, the king of Lamphun led an army from Lampang to the emerging kingdom of Lannathai.

Sukhothai, which was to be the capital of a united Siam in later centuries, had up until the 13th century been controlled by the Khmer civilisation based in Cambodia. However, much of the population was Thai (the result of an earlier colonisation) and they eventually overthrew their Khmer masters. In 1287 AD King Mengrai of Lanna, King Ramakhamphaeng of Sukhothai and King Ngam-Muong of Phayao made an allegiance which led to the expulsion of all other claimants to control Northern Thailand, and laid the groundwork for the first Thai Kingdom of Siam.

At the height of his power, Mengrai controlled a large kingdom in North Thailand and received tributes from many other kingdoms in South East Asia. He is said to have been killed at the age of eighty by a lightning bolt whilst visiting his son in Chiang Mai, the site marked by a statue which can still be seen in the centre of the city.

Over the next centuries, the fortunes of Lannathai waxed and waned, with a long list of battles with neighbouring states, led by heroic kings and princes mounted on elephants. Military might, deceit and treachery determined the outcome of these confrontations, aided or abetted by supernatural talismans and spirits. Despite these squabbles, Lanna continued to enjoy prosperity, the wars of the nobility usually affecting the average inhabitant but little. Lanna enlarged, absorbing Phayao, Phrae and Nan, and resisting domination from the emerging state of the central plains - the *Ayutthaya* empire. However, in the 14th century the kingdom of **Luang Prabang** in Laos took territory from Lannathai along the Mekhong, including the city of Chiang Khong, and caused the official capital of Lannathai to be moved to Chiang Mai in 1345.

The 15th century was the golden age of Chiang Mai, when Lanna art and power reached its peak during the reign of King Tilokaraja. He was a great warlord and a devout Buddhist, able in 1455 AD to arrange the eighth world Bhuddist council in Chiang Mai. The fact that this was feasible attests to the power, wealth, safety and communications that Lanna enjoyed. It was not to last long, though. Squabbling between pretenders to the throne by a succession of kings and princes weakened the nobility.

In 1545 AD Chiang Mai suffered a devastating earthquake, and in 1558 AD Chiang Mai was taken by the Burmese empire of Pegu. Most of Lanna remained under Burmese control for over 200 years, although for much of the population the effects were barely noticeable except during the odd small scale rebellion, when the Burmese would sack a rebellious dukedom as a punishment. There was no direct colonisation, but annual tributes to Pegu had to be paid, and a Burmese prince sat on the throne in Chiang Mai. Once secure in Lanna, the Burmese nobility looked to extend their influence further, particularly towards the kingdom of Ayutthaya to the south. Finally, in 1767 AD, the Burmese King Syn Byu Shin took and sacked Ayutthaya, destroying most of the culture and heritage of this previously magnificent city.

Now secure in most of central South East Asia, the Burmese, together with an army recruited from Lanna, turned their attention eastwards, and mounted an attack on the empire of Luang Prabang (now Laos). The war drained Lanna of wealth and population, and pushed the people too far, leading to a series of determined rebellions. From the city of Tak, a general named Taksin achieved victories over the Burmese, and eventually became the first king of a new central Thai empire based at Thonburi (on the west bank of the Chao Phraya, opposite Bangkok). Further north, the chief of Lampang, Kawila, mounted a rebellion which led to the retaking of Chiang Mai, and the end of Burmese domination, in 1774 AD.

Taksin become the first king of a united Thailand, and appointed Kawila as governor of Chiang Mai. The city was in a state of awful disrepair, in fact it was a ghost town until the beginning of the 19th century. In 1781 AD Taksin was declared insane and executed. His successor, and former general, Phra Buddha Yod Fa, moved the capital of Thailand across the river from Thon Buri to its present position at Krung Thep (Bangkok) on the east bank, more easily defended from any more Burmese attacks from the west. Phra Buddha established the Rama dynasty who have ruled Thailand ever since (the present king, Bhumipol, is Rama IX). It was not until 1804 that the last toehold of the Burmese in Thailand, at Chiang Saen, was retaken.

In the 19th century Lanna became an unnoticed backwater of Thailand. It was ruled by a series of ineffectual governors, and the population declined in numbers and vigour. In the mid 19th century, European powers began to view Lanna with interest.

The French established an Indo Chinese empire in Vietnam to the east, and the British controlled India and Burma to the west. It was a delicate time, with both super powers eyeing Lanna and each other. It was largely thanks to the statesmanship of King Mongkut and his son Chulalongkorn that Lanna preserved its independence.

Territory was ceded to France to the east of the Mekhong river, and logging concessions given to the British. Much was made by the kings of Thailand of the importance of the neutral buffer zone between French and British dominions. There was a small skirmish with boats of the French navy over ownership of some tiny islands in the Mekhong river, and a rapid migration of Thais to the disputed area around Mae Hong Son which the British claimed because the population was more Burmese than Thai. King Chulalongkorn, belatedly realising how ineffectually Lanna had been governed, appointed a talented High Commission to administer the north, and encouraged missionaries who imported not only Christianity (which was largely rejected by the Thais) but modern education, health care and administration.

In the 1920's, a British governor was appointed by the King as Governor of Lampang. The railway reached Chiang Mai in 1927, which together with a comprehensive road building programme, drew Lanna into the mainstream of Thai life and prosperity.

CULTURE

Northern Thailand is distinct in many ways from the rest of the country. Traditionally called "Lanna" it has for most of its history been a separate kingdom.

Northern Thai is a very different language from the official Bangkok Thai heard elsewhere in the country and varies considerably within Northern Thailand. To complicate the picture further, Northern Thailand is now the home to several different peoples, each with their own culture and language. In the far north west, Shan or *Tai Yai* people predominate. The Shan are closely related to the Thais and extend over a range centred in northern Burma (where Shan state has long been fighting for independence).

In addition, the nine or ten hill tribes of Northern Thailand maintain separate cultures and languages, despite gradual integration. This ethnic and cultural diversity is one of the reasons this area is so fascinating for the visitor.

THE THAI CHARACTER

All visitors to Thailand find the people to be charming, polite, good natured and fun. Despite the ease with which foreigners and Thais appear to accept each other, the Thai thinks in a very different way from the westerner. However, since it is an important part of Thai social behaviour to reflect and agree with the views of others, these differences rarely appear. Thais have taken the "inscrutable oriental" to its ultimate level - they are so inscrutable that even their inscrutability lies hidden.

Westerners' minds tend to follow the rules of fact and logic. The Thai is far more intuitive. Ask a Thai monk "when was this temple built and by whom?", and he is likely to answer, "It doesn't matter, it is more important to feel its spirit". Whereas most westerners might mistrust feelings as being difficult to analyse and therefore unsafe, the Thai does not trust facts in a society where it is sometimes important and acceptable to hide the truth.

The extreme politeness of the Thais is very necessary in a society in which social harmony is paramount. To preserve this harmony it is frequently necessary to hide ones true feelings. The greatest compliment is to be described as *jai yen* (cool heart), which means the ability to always appear calm and in control, whatever the circumstances. Thais will never criticise an individual in their presence. As well as making that person "lose face", and so being socially unacceptable, it would also challenge the right to make ones own decisions. To Thais: "What I believe and do is right for me". This attitude explains the great apparent tolerance of Thais, but it is only apparent. Although the eccentric and deviant will never be made to feel uncomfortable, Thais will secretly gossip, scorn and deride the unconventional since Thai society is quite rigid. The topless western sunbather or joint smoking hippy will feel completely at ease with the genial Thais, unaware that the native population may well feel embarrassment and disgust, but will never let the oblivious foreigners know their mistakes. It is therefore important to read the section on etiquette carefully. It is so easy to unwittingly cause offence and never know.

Status, and its outward manifestations, are very important to Thais. They do not have a rigid caste or class structure, but every Thai knows exactly where they fit in a very complex mix of factors which determine their position. Age, family, occupation and wealth are some of the more obvious factors. All Thais respect their elders, and will use the term *pea* in front of the name of an older colleague or friend to mark this respect. Being a member of a wealthy or professional family brings respect, as do occupations such as monk (the most respected), doctor, teacher, headman etc. As Thailand has entered the "market economy", wealth has become more significant in the individual's position - and wealth is unashamedly flaunted. The more gold you can wear the better. Rich individuals will commonly be adorned with heavy pendants, bracelets and rings of pure 24 carat gold. Cars have become a very important status symbol. Despite the huge tax on imported vehicles, many Thais will make great sacrifices to buy a BMW or Mercedes.

Buddhism, which is a vital factor in the life of almost every Thai, teaches that life is suffering - so make the best of the good times as they may not last. Thais tend not to think too much about the future, but to enjoy to the full the present. They tend to buy on credit, looking not at the total price but how much they must pay for something now. "We cannot see tomorrow" is a very common Thai expression. They never miss an opportunity to have fun - *sanuk* - since it may be their last chance.

Thais do not have a concept of "sin" and "guilt" in the same way that Christians understand these terms. They do not believe in a supernatural being watching over their actions and judging them. The individual is free to behave well or badly, according to his own conscience - not according to the "will of god" which underlies western thought and culture

ETIQUETTE

Thai people are extremely polite and their behaviour is tightly controlled by etiquette, much of it based on their Buddhist religion. It is a non confrontational society, in which public dispute or criticism is to be avoided at all costs. To show anger or impatience or to raise your voice is a sign of weakness and lack of mental control. It is also counter productive, since the Thai who will smile embarrassedly at your outburst of anger or frustration is far less likely to be helpful than if you had kept better control of your emotions.

Revealing clothing, worn by either men or women, is a little disgusting to most Thais. Short shorts, low cut dresses and T-shirts and skimpy bathing suits come into this category. In temples, long trousers or skirts must be worn, and monks should on no account be touched in any way by women. Shoes should always be removed when entering temples and private houses. For this reason, most Thais wear slip-on shoes to avoid constantly tying and untying laces.

The head is the most sacred part of the body, so should not be touched. The feet are the least sacred, so when sitting they should not point at anyone - most Thais sit on the floor with their feet tucked under their bodies behind them. To point particularly with the foot, is extremely insulting.

When eating, it is considered very rude to blow your nose or to lick your fingers. The right hand must be used to pick up food eaten in the fingers.

Clothing from the lower parts of the body should never be left anywhere in a high position. This applies particularly to socks and underwear, but also to shorts and skirts. This is the case even when washing and drying clothes. Thais have two clothes lines - a high one for most clothes and a low one for underwear and socks.

Thais do not traditionally shake hands, the *wai* is the usual greeting. The hands are placed together as in prayer, and raised upwards towards the face, while the head is lowered in a slight bow. The height to which the hands should be raised depends on the status of the person you are *waiing*. In the case of monks, dignitaries and old people the hands are raised to the bridge of the nose, with equals only as far as the chest. Young people and inferiors are not *waid*, but nodded slightly to. You will be regarded as a little foolish should you *wai* to these.

Thais are famous for their smiles. Beware! The Thai smile can say many things, from "I love you" to "I am about to kill you!" Thais smile when they are happy, amused, embarrassed, uncertain, wrong, annoyed or furious. As westerners, we are not generally able to interpret the type of smile we are receiving - but be aware that it may not mean what you think it means. It is good to smile back, but do not take this too far. It is not unusual to see tourists grinning like Cheshire cats at everything and everyone. They may be taken to be simple minded.

SOCIAL LIFE

The centre of social life in Thailand is the family. In a country with no social welfare system, the family is most people's only source of help in times of need. Family ties are very strong and widely extended - taking in great aunts and uncles and second cousins. The family group to which allegiance is owed, then, may include several hundred people.

The role of women in Thailand is rather ambiguous. On the surface, women have lower status than men. The man is the head of the family and receives the greatest respect. In a typical family, the man is the bread-winner and the woman's job is to care for him and the children. In practice, business women are seen everywhere in positions of power and authority. In all families, the women control the finances and make the major decisions. Most men are content to do their jobs, hand over all responsibility to their wives and enjoy themselves.

Children are brought up within an extended family. There is not the exclusive parent/child bonding typical of the west. The average child is happy to be cared for by parents, grandparents, aunts or cousins, and parents do not hesitate to leave their children with relatives for long periods of time. To our eyes, Thai children are spoiled. They are rarely disciplined and allowed to do more or less as they please. In the long term this does not seem to have serious effects. Children are expected to become adult at an early age, and social pressure seems eventually to have the same effect as discipline. Old age is treated with great respect. It is the first responsibility of all Thais to care for their parents, even if this means great sacrifice. They consider our way of putting elderly relatives in homes as very cruel and inhuman. The oldest person in a family group is the leading member and belongs with the family until death. A baby sitter is never needed in a Thai family.

ENTERTAINMENT
The people of North Thailand are generally easy going, tolerant and fun. Since Buddhism teaches that life is suffering, the Thai attitude is to make the most of any good times going!

Singing and dancing are very popular, both traditional and modern. The exquisite traditional Thai dance is seen at many social functions, and traditional music, although rather bizarre to western ears, has a unique fascination. The Thai pop music industry is thriving, generally a catchy blend of west and east that produces many songs which would do well if exported to the west.

Many Thai restaurants, even in small towns, will have a live band, usually with a team of overdressed singers, where Thais eat, drink and generally make merry. At night these restaurants are advertised by a multitude of fairy lights.

Prostitution has always been common in Thailand. Thai men do not generally regard it as a social stigma to go to a prostitute. Tourism has changed the nature of the business in resorts, but even small towns will have at least one brothel. The tourist oriented "girl bars" are rather different in nature. The prostitutes who work here may be well educated and speak quite good English. Although they are to some extent outcasts in their own society, they can become quite wealthy, after a few years having enough savings to start a small legitimate business. They are expert at extracting money from tourists in a multitude of ways. Many westerners lose their hearts and their bank balances to a charming, beautiful and devious bar girl. For many the aim is to get a visa and ticket to the west, where they believe they can earn large amounts of money before coming back to Thailand.

The end point of this money may well be the family, who do not question where the money is coming from - Thais are very adept at not knowing what they do not want to know.

LANGUAGE

The Thai language is extremely difficult to master, but it is well worth learning a few basic phrases - not only for practical reasons, but for the effect it will have on any Thai listeners. Thais do not expect foreigners to speak their language at all, and any attempts, however clumsy, will be received with pleasure and will win respect.

Thai is one of the oldest languages of Asia - it may well pre-date Chinese, which it resembles, both being essentially mono-syllabic tonal languages.

Many of the sounds of the Thai language are very alien to us. The muscles of the mouth and tongue which form words develop differently in infancy, as the language is learned and used. It is very hard for westerners to produce many of the sounds of the Thai language. One example is what is called "the smiling U" - a U sound that can only be produced by turning up the corners of the mouth whilst emitting the sound. Similarly, Thais find it almost impossible to produce many of our sounds, for example our "th" sound, and pronounce our "r" or "l"' as something half way between the two.

It is the tones which give foreigners most trouble. Each syllable has five meanings, depending on the tone which is used - low, high, neutral, rising or falling. Since Western languages use tones to express emotion, it is hard to remember to use the correct tone and to prevent tones of emotion creeping in. For example, we use a rising tone to indicate a question. In Thai, we would have completely altered the meaning of the last word of the sentence if we did this.

It is best, then, to keep sentences as short as possible when using Thai. For the listener, four syllables with the wrong tones give a total of 600 possible sequences of possible words. It is usually easy for a Thai to work out what is being said from the context of the conversation, but not always.

The Thai language stresses the beginning of each syllable, the end either trailing off if it is a vowel, or cut short if a consonant. For this reason, Thais speaking English tend to ignore the end of English words - guest house is pronounced "gehhow", motor bike "moto-by".

Fortunately, in view of the problems outlined above, many Thais, and most young Thais, speak some English. It is taught for several years in secondary schools, and every town has schools of English for adults. To speak English is widely perceived as a way to 'get ahead', and many Thais will be very pleased to practice their English with western visitors.

For a basic word list see Appendix 1.

RELIGION

The Thais are a deeply religious people. For the Buddhist majority it underlies all activities and is the backbone of the Thai culture - a culture that has survived intact and independent for so long largely because of the principles of the Buddhist faith.

Ninety percent of the population are Theravada Buddhists. The Theravada school of Buddhism is based more purely on the teachings of Guatama Siddharta (Buddha) without the refinements added on by later monks. Buddhists believe that existence is suffering, suffering is caused by desire, so the elimination of desire leads to a state of perfect non suffering and non existence called *nibbana* (nirvana).

It is a non individualistic philosophy which preaches that the suppression and eventual extinction of the ego are the only way to be content. Almost all Thais believe in reincarnation, hopefully to a higher form of life, leading ultimately to the achievement of *nibbana*. To this end they "make merit" by doing good deeds. Ways to make merit include giving money to beggars, releasing caged birds and giving food to monks who do their early morning "alms round". Most males will do a spell (although generally only a few weeks) as novices in a temple. This brings merit to the family, and is expected of all boys once they reach the age of eighteen. Within the temple, they will be trained in Buddhist history and philosophy, the paths to enlightenment and the principles of meditation.

There are two sects of Buddhist monks in Thailand, the orange robed *Mahanikai* and the stricter, more academic red-brown robed *Thammayut* who can eat only one meal a day (before noon), for which they beg, and cannot touch money.

Monks are needed for every occasion. New houses or cars must be blessed to bring good luck. Nine monks are required for a marriage, and three days of chanting by a team of monks for a funeral.

Underlying Buddhism in Northern Thailand is Animism - a belief that all things, such as trees, stones and rivers, have living souls. "Spirit houses" outside all buildings in Thailand are made attractive to any possibly harmful spirit so that it will not "haunt" the humans living nearby. Buddhism has managed to mould itself onto Animism in Thailand, producing a strange blend of moral philosophy and superstition. Some of the Chinese and Shan of Northern Thailand are Muslim. There are several mosques in the cities, and the town of **Doi Mae Salong** (Santikiree) in the far north, settled by Chinese Muslims, has a Muslim majority.

Christianity, introduced recently by missionaries, has gained many converts in the hill tribes. Up to 50% of Karen claim to be Christians. Their legends are very similar to Christianity, and since the Karen may have originate in the Middle East, it is possible that the two religions were once connected. Most hill tribe people, though, are Animist, with some converts to Buddhism and Christianity. Many Yao people, who originated in Southern China, are Taoist, practising a primitive form of Taoism which was known in China 600 years ago.

TEMPLES

The intense colours and rich visual imagery of Buddhist temples (*wats*) are almost an assault to the eyes of the average cold climate visitor to Thailand. Gaudy, sometimes even vulgar, but always exciting, they will long remain in the memory as typifying Thailand - an intensely, but never intolerantly religious country.

There are so many temples - even a small village is likely to have a miniature version of the massive edifices of Bangkok's most prestigious religious monuments.

In Northern Thailand, a temple is much more than a place to worship. The *wat* is the centre of village life, serving as a school, orphanage, theatre, meeting hall, crematorium, youth club, playground - even sometimes a market, political centre or restaurant. Although one's behaviour must always be correct and polite in a temple, there is no feeling of remoteness or superiority in a Thai *wat* - it is a repository for all aspects of the life and spirit, as well as the spirituality of the community it serves.

Thais love to "make merit" with Buddha by donating religious objects to temples. These are always accepted, which means that temples are cluttered with religious bric-a-brac. The richer the populace, the more extensive and impressive the objects donated. Recently, a poor lady won six million *baht* in the national lottery. She spent all the money on the building of a new temple, so staying poor but making enough merit to assure her of a good incarnation at her death. Truly a long term investment!

Although *wats* are exclusively Buddhist, there are elements of pre-Buddhist, Hindu beliefs in most temples. Hindu gods such as Shiva may have their statues included, and Thais combine Buddhism with ancient Animist beliefs so that temples have become centres of local superstition as well as Buddhism. For many visitors, *wats* can become too much. Having seen a few, they merge in the mind's eye into an unfathomable riot of strange sculptures and bright colours.

Without some understanding of the design and function of the various parts, the brain can switch off and "no more temples" is the unfortunate response.

A *wat* is a complex of several buildings. There is no fixed pattern, but in general the largest and most central building is the *wiharn*. This building will have one or more Buddha statues at the far end (Buddhas should always face east), before a large open area for the general public. In this area people come to worship, and to receive instructions from the monks. The chief monk may have a special low dias of ornamented wood to the left of the altar area. The walls of the *wiharn* are usually decorated with murals depicting the life of Buddha. These vary from exquisite ancient depictions to ugly modern ones.

To one side of the *wiharn* there will usually be one or more *chedis*. These conical structures of brick, coated with plaster painted white or covered in brass or gold, are said to resemble piles of rice. When asked at his death how he should be remembered, Buddha replied "Make piles of rice to remember me by". *Chedis* contain the bones or other relics of religious leaders. The most prestigious (giving the temple the name of *Wat Prathat* or *Wat Mahathat*) contain relics of Buddha himself. Many Thais, on cremation, have their remains interred into the side of a *chedi*, identified by a small plaque set into the surface.

The *bot* is the building where monks are ordained. It may contain the most sacred Buddha sculpture, but is often closed when not in use, and the building may be quite small, tucked away in a corner. The area of consecrated ground is marked by eight black stones around the corners and axes of the *bot*.

Most temples also contain a library, usually a decorated wooden building raised on a podium, and a *sala* where novice monks or orphaned children are educated by ordained monks. It is customary to have a *bothi* tree within the temple grounds. It was under this thick trunked tree with heart shaped leaves that Buddha became "enlightened". To one side of the temple grounds, identified by the saffron robes hanging out of windows, are the monks' quarters. Monks administer, clean and look after the *wat*, as well as teaching and meditating in it.

All temples are covered in small, highly reflective mosaics of coloured glass. Their significance is to drive away evil spirits - if they approach too close they will see their reflection and be frightened away. There are other precautions to ward off bad spirits, including the monster figures often guarding doorways. Many temples are approached by long flights of steps, guarded at the base by pairs of fearsome serpent heads (*nagas*) whose long scaly back forms the walls on either side of the steps.

The *naga* is a serpent which can change shape at will. One guarded Buddha in the wilderness by growing seven heads to form an umbrella over Buddha's head, and promised to give his body for use by Buddha for all time. Candle holders near the altar within the *wat* are normally made in the form of a *naga*.

Singhas are very popular in Northern Thailand. These are stylised lion statues, and originate in Burmese folklore. They represent strength and power and are usually depicted with mouth half open, seated outside temple doors, or devouring a frightened victim. The *kala* is a monster that devours itself, representing the relentless passage of time. It is usually shown without its lower jaw, which it has already eaten. Originally a Hindu god, it is often seen above windows and doors.

Kinnari are beautiful women above the waist, but with the wings and legs of a bird. They are companions to the gods, and are Himalayan and Animist in concept. Ornate *kinnari* are popular in Chiang Mai temples.

The *Hongse* is a mythical swan-like creature, the mount of the god Brahma. It is often seen in Northern Thailand as a decoration for ornamental gates or standing on a tall pole in front of the *wiharn*.

All temples contain at least one, and usually many, Buddha images. They can be made from a wide range of materials, but are commonly brick based and covered in cement or plaster stucco. Smaller or more venerable statues will be made of moulded bronze, brass or gold. Most of these moulds come from a factory in **Phitsanulok** (see page 224). In front of the main image in every temple will be a range of offerings, including lotus blossoms covered in a tea cosy like hood of dried flowers, bronze or copper money trees and commonly a host of lesser Buddha statues, donated by worshippers to make merit.

The physical features of Buddha are largely determined by convention. These vary over time and from place to place. All Buddhas, though, have certain features in common. There is a lotus bud on the head to symbolise enlightenment, and very long earlobes which show he was of a royal family who wore such heavy earrings that the ears became lengthened. The fingers are, in most styles, of equal length, as are the toes.

Some statues of Buddha are very different. The Chinese favour an obese, pot bellied Buddha. One at *Doi Tung* (see page 144) has a large deep navel in which visitors are invited to toss coins. This Buddha is associated with happiness, wealth, food and plenty. A fine example towers over the food market at Chiang Rai. Another Chinese Buddha shows Buddha as a woman - in fact it is hermaphrodite. An emaciated statue refers to Buddha's experiment as an ascetic - when he decided that total self denial was unnecessary, and developed the idea of 'the middle path'.

Buddha may be pictured in a number of different poses. Most usually he is seated cross legged, which indicates meditation. If the right hand is raised, palm outwards, this indicates that Buddha is imploring peace. With left hand raised, palm up, he is teaching. If two fingers are held up, he is blessing. If both hands are down, then Buddha has achieved enlightenment.

The reclining Buddha, in which he is seen resting on a cushion with one arm holding his head, refers to the death of Buddha - the point at which he achieved nirvana.

The walking Buddha refers to walking meditation - regarded as very difficult by most monks. Standing with both hands raised, palms outwards, is a sign of power and refers to a legend in which Buddha stopped the sea from engulfing a village by adopting this pose.

All Buddha images are designed according to precise convention. The sculptor has no artistic freedom in which to work. The changes through time and place of the statues is a catalogue of cultural evolution, not artistic development.

FOOD AND DRINK

Thai food is delicious. Many would argue that it has the most exciting cuisine in the world. It is also unique, combining the best culinary aspects of those two great influences on everything Thai - China and India. Some Thai food, but by no means all, can be very, very hot and spicy. Most restaurants have menus in English as well as Thai. If you want to avoid hot food, say *"my pet"*. English translations of Thai food can be interesting - how about "Big crap in pot", "Prawn throb" or "Three Vikings in the soup"!

Of course, rice is the staple part of almost all dishes - so much so that the words for to eat, *"kin cow"*, translate literally as *"eat rice"*.

Northern Thai food is in general less spicy than that of the rest of the country. It has a greater Chinese influence, and, uniquely in Thailand, has a number of Laotian and Burmese or *Tai Yai* dishes, notably the irresistible and inexpensive *cow soy*.

Western food is available in most towns, and is quite popular as a status symbol amongst rich Thais. Apart from at a few expensive restaurants and hotels, it is not generally well prepared or cooked, and although still inexpensive by western standards, costs considerably more than the Thai equivalents. Unless you are an extremely conservative diner, or feel an occasional craving for the taste of home, it is best avoided.

EATING

Thais almost always eat communally with family or friends. Several dishes are ordered and put in the centre of the table (although at home, most Thais eat on mats sitting on the floor).

Each person eating receives a plate of rice, and takes a small spoonful from whichever dish is most appealing and eats this with a small spoonful of rice. It would be most rude to empty the contents of one dish onto one's plate! Chopsticks are used for certain dishes such as noodles, but otherwise a spoon and fork are used. Knives are not necessary, since items of food are always cut into small pieces before cooking. It is considered rude to lick the fingers whilst eating, or to blow the nose at the table. As a mark of respect to their staple food, Thais first eat a small spoonful of plain, unflavoured rice before adding meat, vegetables and sauces.

COOKING

Much cooked food is quick-fried in a large wok at high heat. This has the great advantage that little fat is absorbed by the food, and vegetables are crunchy and high in the vitamins which are often cooked out by other methods.

Noodle dishes are boiled quickly in water. A popular dish is the "steamboat" (*more fye*) which is a vessel filled with boiling water, kept at the boil by a charcoal heating chamber. The water contains herbs and spices which flavour the food as it is cooking. The liquid is poured out as soup and the food extracted with chopsticks and eaten with rice. Fish, prawns and squid are commonly eaten in this way. A variation of this from Japan - sukiyaki - is becoming popular, in which raw food is cooked by the diners themselves by immersing it in a charcoal fuelled vessel brought to the table. Barbecuing is very common - chicken, pork, sausages, bananas etc. are prepared on makeshift barbecues on many streets in most towns. Resist the aroma if you can!

RESTAURANTS

Thailand must have more restaurants per square metre than anywhere in the world. They range from a grass shack with one table and bench to the largest restaurant in the world. Most Thais eat out frequently - in fact they eat frequently, tucking into some obscure concoction at any time of the day or night.

Prices in a typical Thai restaurant are extremely low. It is still possible, even in Chiang Mai, to have a delicious and filling meal for under 10 *baht*.

Thai restaurants fall into three categories. Most common is the small, basic restaurant which serves the equivalent of our 'fast food' - but much better!

These tend to specialise. Commonest is the noodle stall - a range of different ingredients added to the basic noodles. A bowl of noodles is quickly and efficiently served with chopsticks and a spoon. These tend to be lunch time places and often close in the afternoon. Similar are those restaurants which have chickens, ducks and pork joints hanging in the window. These serve rice with meat and a variety of sauces, served separately in tiny dishes. A third type specialises in fried rice and noodle dishes, always served with a slice of lime.

Evening restaurants are rather different in nature. Here, the food is secondary to alcohol and entertainment. They are usually large, and lit up at night with coloured flashing lights. They always have live music, from a small orchestra to the more common rota of female singers. These places are for a prolonged night of *sanuk* (fun), which usually involves getting quite drunk on Thai whisky. This type of restaurant is often just outside the town, and is rarely visited by tourists, which is a shame as it is a very enjoyable experience and a fascinating glimpse into Thai life.

Tourist oriented restaurants, particularly those catering to the "back-packer", serve basic Thai and Chinese food moderated to the western palate. This is an interesting example of cultural culinary evolution. It tastes good, but has all those aspects of "real" Thai food, which might be too much for the westerner, taken out. Most guest houses serve this type of menu. Generally it is cheap, but not as cheap as its more genuine cousin, probably available within 100 metres!

TIPPING

Tipping is a new phenomenon in Thailand. It is still not expected, except in the large hotels, but it is becoming common to tip 10% for good food or service. Since waiters and waitresses are probably trying to live on less than 1000 *baht* per month, a small tip will be greatly appreciated.

CONDIMENTS

At most Thai restaurants you will be presented a range of different condiments. Most of these are to "spice up" your meal - so be careful! Prominent will be a red chili powder or sauce which should be used very sparingly. Many dishes are served with a tiny bowl of small sliced chilies in a pale brown fish sauce. Only the liquid should be added to your meal - the chilis are exceptionally hot.

A less hot suspension of larger pale green chilis in a clear vinegar are commonly included on the condiment stand. These are piquant, added to noodle dishes. Thais add a spoonful of sugar to many noodle dishes. The pale brown fish sauce (*nam pla*), usually in a bottle on the table, is used in place of salt, which is generally not available except in restaurants catering to westerners. White pepper is sometimes used, especially in soups.

PEPPERS

Red, green or brown - watch out for these in your dishes, since many are very hot and could wreck your enjoyment of your food if eaten. The antidote to excess spiciness is a mouthful of plain rice, not water which tends to extend the period of pain.

In general, the smaller the pepper, the more deadly. The common tiny red or green one is the worst. Its name is *prik key nu*, which translates as "mouse dropping", since this describes the shape. The larger thin red or green ones are spicy but not excessive. The dried brown ones, served particularly with meat and garlic dishes, have a wonderful flavour. The large capsicums, usually green, are served sliced, and not at all hot.

SOUP

These are rather a misnomer, since they are usually far more interesting and filling than the liquids we call soup in the west. A range of herbs and spices are added to give a delicious aroma and delicate flavours. Many of these herbs should not be eaten. Lemon grass, pale yellow sticks, are completely inedible but give a delightful delicate spicy aroma to many soups. Similarly, inedible chunks of ginger are also frequently used. Fennel, garlic, shallots, coriander leaves, galangal, kaffir lime leaves and, of course, peppers, are other common ingredients.

MAIN COURSES

Although most main courses are served with fluffy rice, the staple rice for northerners is sticky rice *cow neow*. This is eaten with the fingers, moulded into a ball which is dipped into various more or less fierce sauces.

These sauces are also used (sparingly!) with normal rice. Known as *nam prik*, they all consist of ground small chilis, shallots, garlic, coriander, fish sauce and meat. The mildest, called *nam prik ong* is made with ground pork, and is sometimes disparagingly referred to as Thai spaghetti sauce. At the other end of the scale, *nam prik ta deng* is made with the hottest red chilis. Thais believe that no westerner can eat this sauce. They may be right!

There are a range of different noodle dishes, which usually contain a blend of bean curd, boiled meat balls, sliced meat or liver and green vegetables. The local noodle dish, deservedly famous, is *cow soy* - a thick coconut milk curry poured over crispy golden noodles, served with chopped raw shallots, pickled vegetables and limes. The meat can be beef or chicken (not pork, as it is originally a muslim dish). Also very popular is *gen-gurry-guy* - a mild chicken curry, coconut based, with potatoes. A local speciality for the brave is *laab*. Cooked or commonly raw chopped liver, pork or chicken is mixed with chilies, mint and fennel, served usually on or with lettuce and cucumber. The slightly bitter taste comes from the animal's bile. It is fiercely hot, even making Thais wince. Thai salads are often also very hot, with a mixture of ground pork, prawns, squid, garlic, lemon, fish sauce, chilis and glass noodles (tiny, transparent, glutinous noodles). *Pak Thai* is a non spicy Thai staple. Large, flat noodles are fried with bean sprouts, egg, vegetables and usually a choice of meats.

Thai omelettes come in two varieties. The better, kay yak-sigh is a thin beaten fried egg envelope enclosing a delicious sauce of ground pork and finely chopped peppers. *Kigh tea-oh mussap* is made by frying a mixture of egg and pork, and is served with an orange chilli sauce. It can be rather greasy.

Fish (*pla*) is highly prized as a main course. Commonest is catfish (*pla dook*), barbecued on skewers with a tomato and chilli sauce. *La chon* is served in a bubbling sauce of vegetables and chilies, usually in a fish shaped steel plate kept hot with charcoals underneath.

Although very far from the sea, seafood is available at many restaurants at reasonable prices. Prawns *goong* are used in many dishes, but crab *pwo*, lobster, sea fish such as bream and tuna and green lipped mussels are highly prized. Squid is served everywhere - especially by street vendors, dried and barbecued, smelling of old socks but tasting great.

Chinese dishes are on most menus. These include the common staples which most tourists largely live on. Fried rice (*cow pat*), with one or more meats and usually eggs, is served with lime and spring onions. Not the most exciting of dishes, but tasty, cheap and nutritious. Sweet and sour *peo wan*, with vegetables and meat, is another favourite with visitors. Chinese steamed rice dumplings, with a filling of ground meat or mashed fruit, are worth trying.

DESSERTS

Thai desserts (*corn-wang*) are always very, very sweet. Choice is limited, the commonest being a sticky concoction with the consistency of glue *sank-ka-ya*, flavoured with coconut or banana *(goo-ay)*. Sweet shredded egg yolk (*for-we tong*) is usually served inside a small crispy sweet pancake. Fried bananas are popular (*goo-ay kek*).

FRUIT

Thailand has a huge range of fruits, both tropical and temperate, many exotic and delicious, which must be tasted. Apart from the fruits commonly available in the west - pineapples (*sapparot*), strawberries, mangoes (*mamuang*), coconuts (*maprow*), apples, lychees, oranges (*som*), watermelons (*teng-moo*) and papayas (*malaco*), the following are usually available.

Mangosteen. The size and shape of a tomato, mangosteens have a thick, bitter, purple skin. Within is a cluster of white flesh covered seeds, which are extracted and eaten. They have a wonderful fragrant sweet aroma and an even better taste, unlike any other fruit.
Rambutan. Juicy white fruit the size of a ping-pong ball inside a thin spiky red skin which is easily pinched open. Delicious.
Durian. Enormous green fruits the shape and size of an American football. Inside are large seeds surrounded by creamy yellow flesh. The smell is disgusting, but the taste ambrosian (for some).
Lamyai (longan). A regional speciality, the size of a large grape with a papery brown outer skin resembling lychees in appearance, but with a sweeter, more delicate flavour. Season May - June.

DRINKS

NON ALCOHOLIC
Only bottled or boiled water (*nam*) should be drunk. Bottled water is available everywhere, the most convenient size is the 1 litre bottle at about 5 baht. It is a tradition in the north for every home and temple to have an earthenware pot at the roadside with a lid which functions as a cup, for use by all who pass. Nice as this tradition is, this water is a potential health hazard, so should be avoided. Rural Thais and hill tribes usually have a pot of weak China tea permanently on the boil - this is safe and refreshing to drink.

Ice cubes (*Nam keng*) in the form of hollow thimbles are safe to use, but avoid crushed ice, which may have been made with tap water. Thai soft drinks are usually very sweet. Coke (*colah*), pepsi, fizzy orange (*fantah*), lemon, cherry lime and Seven Up are very common. There is an interesting soya milk drink called *lactosoy*. If your drink is served in a bottle, shops require its return, since it will be reused. Frequently soft drinks are served in a plastic bag tied at the corner and drunk through a straw. The price of a soft drink varies widely, from 5 *baht* in a village shop to 30 *baht* in an expensive bar.

Crushed fresh fruit drinks are mainly drunk by tourists. Banana, mango, papaya and watermelons are all delicious, costing 5-10 *baht* more.

Coffee is a fairly new drink to the Thais, but becoming very popular and available almost everywhere. It is almost always instant, served with synthetic whitener, and for some reason cups are usually half filled. Prices are 5-10 *baht* per cup. Traditionally tea is made with locally grown leaves, the large leaf fragments floating in the cup. It has a fragrant aroma, and a pleasant, if weak, taste. In most towns, western tea-bag tea is usually served, at a price of 5-10 *baht* per cup.

WHISKY

The local whisky, of which the most popular brand is called Maekhong, is very cheap and palatable. It is not particularly strong, but is usually drunk with soda or coke and ice. A litre bottle costs 90-110 *baht*, or a glass in a bar 20-30 *baht*.

Rice whisky (*lao*), transparent and deadly, is even cheaper, at about 20-30 *baht* per litre, but can only be drunk in quantity by the determined! Western spirits are widely available, at prices a little lower than the west. A glass of Scotch in most bars costs 30-50 *baht*, a bottle from a store 300-400 *baht*. Most shops and bars stock brandy, rum, bourbon, gin and vodka, and most other spirits can be found.

BEER

Thai beer is liked by some, hated by others. (It resembles British lager, but is rather stronger). Singha is the most popular brand, selling for 30-50 *baht* per bottle in bars, 20-25 in shops. Kloster is slightly more expensive, less strong and preferred by many. Amarit is less common, but is occasionally on draft. Foreign beers are not usually available, due to a high import tax, but a few bars stock Carlsberg, Budweiser and Tsing-Tao, amongst others.

WINES

Thai wine varies from undrinkable to mediocre. It is very sweet, and only available at a few restaurants. It is, however, very cheap, at about 25-40 *baht* per bottle. Imported wines are very expensive - from about 300 *baht* per bottle in a restaurant, 200 in a shop.

THE HILL TRIBES

One of the main tourist attractions of the north, the hill tribes of Northern Thailand have preserved their way of life with little change over thousands of years. Originating in different parts of South-East Asia and resisting persecution by other cultures, they have migrated into Thailand in a quest for freedom and security.

Although the hill tribes can be regarded as "primitive", in that they are pre-industrial, pre-literate societies, hill tribe communities are not groups of simple people living simple lives. Their customs, laws and beliefs are complex and very sophisticated, designed to harmonize relationships between individuals and to conserve their environment. It is only in recent years, with the effects of too rapid population growth and competition for land, that their ancient way of life has proved to be insufficient to cope with the stresses resulting from external forces.

In Northern Thailand there are several hill tribes living within a small geographical area. Each tribe has its own language, customs, religious and social organization. All the tribes are welcoming and hospitable to visitors, providing them with a unique opportunity to see and experience ways of life which have been forgotten in the west.

THE TRIBES

The Karen, (called *Kaliang* or *Yang* in Thai) are found throughout the west of the region. Their population is about 300,000 in Thailand, with over four million in Burma. They are concentrated mainly in Mae Hong Son province, and western areas of Chiang Mai, Chiang Rai and Phayao. There are four sub groups. The Pwo are the most secretive. All their villages are between Mae Sariang and Hot. Other groups include the Sgaw (the most numerous) and Dam (black). Originally Animist, over 30% of the Karen in Thailand have been converted to Christianity by western missionaries.

The Karen costume for women is very attractive and distinctive. Unmarried girls wear loose white or undyed V necked blouses, decorated with jobs tear seeds at the seams. Married women wear blouses and skirts in bold colours, predominantly red or blue. Men wear blue baggy trousers with red or blue shirts, a simplified version of the womens' blouses. Black Karen men wear black shirts with a red cummerbund or head scarf.

Karen houses are not usually large. Adult children must leave the home when married - there is no extended family. Houses are on stilts, made of bamboo or teak. Central steps lead to a porch, with a store room or kitchen to one side, a living area and bedroom on the other. Beneath the house is a working area, often with a foot operated rice pounder.

The Karen have strict laws against immorality. They are matrilineal societies, so that two married women cannot live in the same house. In some villages, the punishment for adultery is death. The village chief has great power over his community, and is regarded as the spiritual as well as the administrative leader.

HMONG

Called by the Thai *Meo* (a derogatory term since it means barbarian), the Hmong are found widely in Northern Thailand. There are two sub-groups, White and Blue. Around and to the west of Chiang Mai, most of the villages are Blue Hmong, in the east only White Hmong villages can be found. Their population in Thailand is about 70,000. They originate in western China, possibly Mongolia.

Blue Hmong women wear beautiful pleated skirts with parallel horizontal bands of red, blue and white, intricately embroidered. Jackets are of black satin, with wide orange and yellow embroidered cuffs and lapels. The hair is tied in a large bun. Men wear baggy black pants and jackets embroidered in a similar way to the women's, closing over the chest with a button at the left shoulder. White Hmong women wear black baggy trousers with a long wide blue cummerbund with a central pink area which hangs almost to the ground. Their jackets are simple, with blue cuffs. A brimless blue cap is worn by some groups. Hmong villages are usually at high altitudes, below the crest of a protecting hill. Houses have a dirt floor and a roof which extends almost to the ground. They live in extended families, with two or more bedrooms. There is a large guest platform. The headman has little power, since the Hmong are fiercely independent people who take orders from no one. Before marriage, promiscuity amongst the young is normal. Marriage is followed by a trial period before the bride price is paid. Hmong men are expected to do most of the work within the family. Men do the heaviest work, but in practice this means they do little, and expect to be supported by their wives. The Hmong grow much opium, and addiction rates in some villages are high, mainly among the males.

Hmong clothing is much in demand in Thailand, and the Hmong have proved in the last few years to be good business people. Hmong women will be seen at markets throughout Thailand selling their handicrafts. Although, like the other tribes, generally poor, some families have become quite wealthy.

Some build the more expensive and comfortable Thai style house, but in general the Hmong have retained their traditional way of life.

There have been few converts to Christianity or Buddhism amongst the Hmong. They are strict animists, whose shamans use dramatic methods to contact the spirits. Every house has an altar of a piece of paper covered in cock's feathers affixed with chicken blood.

AKHA

The poorest of the hill tribes, well known to tourists for their extraordinary costumes and exotic appearance. The Akha originate from Tibet, and have only recently entered Thailand, the first immigrants arriving in 1911. They are less open to change than other hill tribes, clinging to their old customs stubbornly.

The women's costume consists of broad horizontal striped leggings, a short black skirt with a white beaded sporran, a loose fitting black jacket with heavily embroidered cuffs and lapels. The headgear, which is never removed, is a conical wedge of white beads interspersed with silver coins and topped with plumes of red taffeta. The man's costume of plain black pants and a lightly embroidered loose jacket is much less impressive. The different subgroups of Akha have slightly different costumes and headgear.

The Akha live at high altitudes, in a position offering good views over the surrounding country. Their houses are on low stilts, with a large porch leading into a square living area with a stove, usually at the back. The roof is steeply pitched. They are deeply superstitious, their religion prescribing exactly how each action should be performed. Any deviation from the correct is believed to lead to disaster. All birth abnormalities, even twins, leads to the killing of the newborn by the elders of the tribe.

Every Akha village is entered through ceremonial gates, decorated with carvings of "human" life, to indicate to the spirit world that beyond here only humans can pass. Outside the gates are wooden sculptures of copulating couples, and the gates may be decorated with a wide variety of "human" artifacts - weapons, tools, and nowadays cars and airplanes. To touch these carvings, or to show any lack of respect, is punishable by fines or sacrifices. The gates are replaced every year, so every village has a series of gates, the older ones in a state of decomposition and disrepair.

Peculiar to the Akha, there is a giant swing in each village. Every year, in August, there is a "swinging festival", in which the headman, followed by the rest of the village, take turns in using the swing. The reasons for this practice are unknown.

Many Akha villages still grow opium, generally not of high quality. Opium addiction, especially amongst the older men, is a serious problem.

LISU

The Lisu are a fiercely independent people, who are in general adjusting well to the changes taking place in their society. They originate in Eastern Tibet, and the first settlers arrived in Thailand at the beginning of this century. They are only found in the west - particularly between Chiang Mai and Mae Hong Son, but also in western Chiang Rai, Chiang Mai and Phayao provinces.

The women wear brightly coloured costumes, consisting of a blue or green parti-coloured knee length tunic, split up the sides to the waist, with a wide black belt and blue or green pants. Long hair is tied at the back. Sleeves, shoulders and cuffs are heavily embroidered with narrow, horizontal bands of blue, red and yellow. At New Year festival, in mid January, dazzling displays of wealth are worn, including waistcoats and belts of intricately fashioned silver and hats with multi-coloured pom-poms and streamers. Men wear green, pink or yellow baggy pants and a blue jacket opening vertically.

The Lisu live at moderate to high altitudes. Their houses are built on the ground, with dirt floors and bamboo walls around a central ridge. They live as extended families, the number of bedrooms depending on the family size. Unmarried girls have a private bedroom after puberty. Every home has an altar at the back of the communal living area with a shelf holding vessels and incense sticks honouring their ancestors.

Although promiscuous, courtship and marriage are highly stylized, involving a high "bride price". There are twelve clans of Lisu, marriage should be between members of different clans. The Lisu believe strongly in the spirit world, and their shamans are used to divine the causes and cures of all problems and sickness.

Many Lisu villages are involved in the opium trade, and are reputed to grow the best opium. Addiction rates are declining, and the Lisu are responding well to alternative cash crop production, but the link between wealth and opium is still strong. A Lisu headman has little power over his community, the clan system generally over-riding his authority.

LAHU

The Lahu tribes originate in south west China, and have migrated into Thailand from Northern Burma. Most of their settlements are concentrated close to the Burmese border, in Chiang Rai, northern Chiang Mai and Mae Hong Son province. The Lahu language has become a "lingua franca", spoken throughout the other hill tribes, since, amongst the Lahu, hiring out labour to other hill tribes has become common.

There are four tribes within the Lahu - Black, Yellow, Red and She-leh. The Black Lahu are the most reserved, but wear the most distinctive costumes- women wear a black cloak with diagonal cream stripes. The top of the sleeve is decorated in bold colours of red and yellow, at the whim of the sempstress. Red Lahu women wear black trousers with white edging and vivid sleeves of broad red and blue stripes. Amongst the other Lahu tribes, traditional costume has been supplanted by the Thai shirt and sarong. Lahu men wear a plain black shirt and baggy black trousers.

Lahu villages are at high altitude. The Red Lahu are the only tribe to build a central Animist temple, surrounded by banners and streamers of white and yellow flags. Houses are built on high stilts with walls of bamboo or wooden planks, thatched with grass. A ladder leads to an open central living area, with a store room to one side and living quarters to the other. There is one large bedroom, partitioned off as necessary according to family size. The main room has a central fireplace.

A high proportion (about one third) of Lahu have been converted to Christianity, and many have abandoned their traditional way of life as a result. Animist Lahu believe in one spirit with overall control of all the others, and beneath him is a "village spirit" who protects the community. Lahu girls are rather predatory in search of a marriage partner, but divorce and adultery are common.

YAO

The Yao consider themselves rather aristocratic. They originate in southern China, and at one time had considerable power within the Chinese empire, to the extent that at one time a Yao princess was married to an emperor of China. They are the only hill tribe to have a written language, and a written religion based on medieval Chinese Taoism, although in recent years there have been many converts to Christianity and Buddhism.

Their villages are widely scattered throughout the north east, with concentrations around Nan, Phayao and Chiang Rai. They are a very peaceable and friendly people, who pride themselves on cleanliness and honour. The costume of the women is very distinctive, with a long black jacket with lapels of bright scarlet wool. Heavily embroidered loose trousers in intricate designs are worn, and a similarly embroidered black turban. The teeth are commonly capped with gold. The caps of babies are very beautiful, richly embroidered with red or pink pom-poms. On special occasions, women and children wear silver neck rings, with silver chains extending down the back decorated with silver ornaments. Men wear a loose jacket which buttons diagonally across the front, with embroidered pockets and edgings.

Yao villages are at high altitude, built usually of wooden planks on a dirt road. There is a guest platform of bamboo in the communal living area, and two or more bedrooms. Girls of marriageable age have a private bedroom in which they can entertain suitors.

Some Yao grow opium, although in general the incidence is declining. The Yao are integrating well into Thai life. Their exquisite embroidery is a very saleable commodity, and their willingness to adopt new crops gives hope for their future within Thailand.

PHI TONG LUANG (MLABRI)

Translated as "Spirits of the Yellow leaves", these truly primitive people live in a small remote area to the west of Nan. There are only 107 individuals still alive, and the nature of their society is changing rapidly.

Traditionally, the *Phi Tong Luang* are nomadic hunter gatherers. They build temporary shelters of leaves, moving on to another spot when these leaves turn yellow. They hunt with long spears, and build traps to catch birds and small mammals. Roots are dug up with sticks, and nuts, seeds and honey collected. They have little social organization, and speak a language which appears to be related to a mixture of local hill tribe languages. Their "costume" is a white or fawn cotton loin cloth for males, a white shift or skirt for females. They appear to have no organized religious beliefs, but bury their dead and move their shelters immediately.

Recently, they have begun to work for Hmong hill farmers. Reputedly they are hard and reliable workers. They are paid with food, but are now beginning to understand and use money. Disease rates are high, however, and it is probable that their society will disappear within a few years.

LAWA

The history of the Lawa people is long and poorly understood. It is certain that they have inhabited Thailand for a very long time - since before the Thais established their homeland here 800 years ago. They believe that they migrated from Cambodia, but some archaeologists think their origins lie in Micronesia, perhaps 2000 years ago.

With such a long history of cohabiting with the Thais (the legendary king Mengrai who unified Northern Thailand was probably half Lawa), there has been large scale integration, so that most Lawa villages are indistinguishable from Thai settlements. However, in an area of about 500 square kilometres between Hot, Mae Sariang and Mae Hong Son, they still live a largely traditional life, although even here the majority have adopted Buddhism and Thai style houses. Unmarried Lawa girls wear loose white blouses edged with pink. Around the neck distinctive strings of orange and yellow beads are worn. The tight skirt is in parallel bands of blue, black, yellow and pink. On marriage, these brightly coloured clothes are replaced with a long fawn dress, but the strings of beads are still worn. The hair is tied in a turban, and it is usual for women to smoke tobacco from a wooden pipe. Most Lawa speak Thai, but the Lawa language, related to that of the Wa tribe of Burma, is still spoken in many villages.

HILL TRIBE LIFE

COSTUMES AND HANDICRAFTS

The most obvious and remarkable characteristics of the hill tribes are their colourful, exquisitely crafted costumes and the beauty of their adornments. Their skills can also be seen in their tools, basketry, weapons and musical instruments.

Each tribe has a unique range of styles and colours particular to it. Great time, pride and imagination are exercised in the production of clothes and jewellery. They are an expression of status, pride and art. Most women still wear traditional costume at all times, but many men and children are adopting western shorts, jeans and T-shirts for everyday wear.

Most articles are produced within each family. Women spin cloth and make their clothes, whilst men make tools and weapons. Specialist blacksmiths and silversmiths have high status within the community, and may attract business from other villages many kilometres away.

Jewellery is commonly made from silver, most melted down from Indian and Burmese silver coins. Brass, copper and aluminium are also used. The jewellery amassed by a family are the outward display of their wealth, worn by the women at the New Year festival.

Clothing and handicrafts were not until the last ten years regarded as marketable products. With encouragement from the Thai government and the Kings Royal Project, co-operatives have been set up to manufacture and market their traditional goods, which are now big business in the markets of Thailand, and can be purchased at countless outlets throughout the world.

RELIGION

The hill tribes are predominantly Animists, although amongst the Karen, Yao and Akha there are Christian and Buddhist minorities. Animists believe that conscious spirits with powers over humans exist throughout their surroundings.

The hill tribes believe in these spirits most profoundly - they are as real as the physical, visible world. There are spirits in such things as rocks, trees and rivers, which have power to bring great good or harm. Ancestor spirits are cared for by their descendants, and all spirits must be propitiated carefully to prevent harm to the family or village. For this reason, every village will have a shaman, who can communicate with the spirits and ensure the correct actions at all times.

BIRTH AND MARRIAGE

Birth is the most dangerous time for all hill tribe people. Amongst women, complications in childbirth are the commonest cause of death, and infant mortality is very high. The average number of births per couple is six, partly to offset infant mortality. Children are insurance for their parents against sickness and death, so it is vital to have enough to ensure that some survive to adulthood.

Death rates have been falling over the last thirty years, with improvements in health care and education, so that the natural growth rate of hill tribe populations, even excluding immigration, is very rapid. Because of the dangers, pregnancy and childbirth are surrounded by taboo and ritual. The women usually give birth squatting on a bamboo or dirt floor, usually assisted by a female relative or specialised local midwife. The baby is not considered a human being for several days after its birth - the several souls within the body take this time to enter the new-born. The mother's behaviour before and during childbirth is carefully watched. To die giving birth is a "bad death", leading to a high risk of the dead mothers spirit returning to haunt the village.

Courtship varies from tribe to tribe. Most are promiscuous before marriage, except the Karen. Once a girl has become pregnant, it becomes necessary for her to find a husband. There is a high degree of etiquette in the finding of a mate. Lineages must be consulted and good omens looked for before permission can be given. Monogamy is usual, although amongst the Hmong a second wife is acceptable. The marriage ceremony is always a great celebration, very expensive for the bride or grooms family. It is usual for the bride and groom to come from different villages, so the celebration of one marriage frequently spawns others!

SICKNESS AND DEATH
Hill tribe people value health above all other attributes, as do we all, but the hold of the hill tribe person on his health is rather more tenuous than ours. Life expectancy is low, due to poor sanitation, polluted water, lack or ignorance of medical facilities, drug addiction and endemic disease. Health is never taken for granted, but must be worked at.

Sickness is regarded as the will of the spirit world, caused by some sin or insult to the gods. Death is a transition between this world and a parallel spirit world, which is opposite to ours. The death ceremony is essential to prevent the soul of the departed returning to take more souls to the underworld, and various strategies must be used to prevent this happening. The sick have various options. First, a shaman must be consulted to discover what action has insulted which spirit. The shaman will recommend and carry out the correct sacrifice. These actions will be followed by the use of local herbs - the commonest is opium, very effective as an analgesic and anti-diarrhoea drug, but there are many others, whose efficacy has been little researched. Finally, western medicine will be tried, but unfortunately, since this is often a last resort it is frequently too late to effect a cure.

AGRICULTURE AND ECONOMY
The hill tribes have a predominantly subsistence economy. Money is unnecessary, since everything needed is produced within the village. In recent years, this economy had begun to change, firstly with the cash crop opium, now being replaced with money from the sales of clothes, handicrafts and new cash crops such as coffee, lettuce, strawberries and other temperate fruits and vegetables.

The traditional agricultural base of the hill tribes is slash and burn farming. In February or March, an area of jungle is burned. The ashes from the trees provide fertiliser for the crop - rice, corn, chilies or other vegetables. Commonly two crops will be grown together, for example rice with corn. Crop rotation may be used, but after two or three seasons the cleared area must be abandoned for several years to recover its fertility. This system is sustainable with a low population density which allows jungle enough time to regain nutrients before it is used again, but with the increase in population the pressure is too great, fields are returned to prematurely, soils are being exhausted and the decreasing forest cover is leading to soil erosion and perhaps permanent climate change.

SEEING THE HILL TRIBES

The hill tribes are big business in Northern Thailand. In Chiang Mai there are over 200 agencies organising treks, which include spending a number of nights in a hill tribe village. Trekking agencies will also be found in Chiang Rai, Mae Hong Son, Pai, Mae Sariang and Nan. Most tours, by coach or mini-bus, include a visit to a hill tribe village. For the independent traveller, there are about 8000 hill tribe villages. With rapidly improving road links, a large number of unspoilt villages which do not receive trekking or tour groups are now accessible by jeep or motor bike. Many of these villages are described in this book.

TOURS

Every large hotel, and a multitude of tour companies, offer one or two day tours of Northern Thailand. There are only a few well travelled itineraries which the majority of companies use. The vehicles are restricted to metalled roads, so that only the few villages along this route can be visited. The result is inevitably that these villages receive a huge number of tourists daily. The village economy has switched from agriculture to tourism, and in every case the village street has become a collection of souvenir stalls, where tribespeople sell handicrafts.

Very often, these handicrafts do not originate in the village, and frequently not even from that tribe. With so much western contact, the villagers may well have lost their cultural integrity, in many cases only wearing traditional clothes because it is good for business. However, for those tourists who do not have the time, means or physical fitness to see the hill tribes in any other way, it is perhaps marginally better than nothing.

TREKKING

The trekking business began in Chiang Mai about 20 years ago. Its huge popularity has led to an enormous number of companies setting up business, and in certain areas the flood of trekking tourists has created pressures on the hill tribe peoples which is spoiling the experience for many.

At present, the most heavily trekked areas are the Mae Taeng valley, 40 kilometres north west of Chiang Mai, the Pai region and the hills between Chiang Rai and Doi Mae Salong. The least trekked hill tribe villages are west of Phayao, the Laos border country east and north of Nan, and the Mae Sariang-Mae Sot area. For the majority of tourists, a trek is a unique, wonderful and memorable experience. However, it can only be recommended for those with at least average physical fitness, and a tolerance of conditions generally squalid and uncomfortable. For most, the benefits of travelling through beautiful tropical countryside, the excitement of elephant riding and river rafting, the experience of living with peoples of such a different culture and way of life, far outweigh sweat, dirt and cockroaches.

A typical trek is of three to five days duration. There should be at least two guides, who may well be of hill tribe origin themselves. There is no need for the guides to speak hill tribe languages, since in all villages Thai is spoken and understood by a large number of villagers.

Every trek starts with a drive of a few hours in the back of a song-thaew (converted pick-up), followed by a walk of an hour or two to the first village. Each day, there will be three to five hours of walking, almost certainly much of it up and down steep hills, often under a burning sun. Some of the trek (usually about three hours) will be on elephant back, and some on a bamboo raft (exciting to the point of dangerous if the river is running fast!). Tourists stay together as a group, usually in the headman's hut, in hill tribe villages. The guide cooks communal meals, with food generally brought from outside, since the risk from eating hill tribe food is great, hepatitis and food poisoning being common. After dinner, there may be music, singing and dancing from or with the village community, who are generally pleased to see tourists. Early to bed, on a hard bamboo floor or platform, frequently without mattresses. Blankets are always provided, but usually not enough in the cool season, when night time temperatures frequently dip close to freezing.

When choosing a trek, there are several things to look for. A well organized trek should have three guides - a leader, back marker and link man (tourists have got lost for days through losing contact with the rest of the group). Ask about transport from base at the beginning and end of the trek, since sometimes the trip can end with a long, uncomfortable public bus ride.

Meet and talk to the guides, who should speak reasonable English. Ask what food will be eaten and what medical supplies are being taken. Get a copy of the route map to see where you are going and how much walking is involved per day. Bear in mind that *Shan* villages are not hill tribe, but a sub group of Thais, and the dominant group in most of the western areas of the region. In the cool season, ask how many blankets you will be given. If it is less than three, take your own as well, if you want to sleep. Look at the list of group members - it can be lonely being the only British member in a group of non English speaking French or German trekkers (or vice versa). The right clothing is essential. Ideally, wear strong boots with ankle protection, although in the dry season training shoes are adequate. Long trousers should be worn, to protect against thorns, and in the wet season, leeches (which should be removed by dousing in alcohol or touched with a burning cigarette or stick, never plucked off). All clothing should be thin and loose, and if prone to sunburn arms should be covered. At least two changes of clothing are needed, plus a towel and toiletries. A hat should be worn to protect the head. Insect repellant is essential, and a mosquito net is a good idea.

Antiseptic, antihistamine and anti diarrhoea medicine should be taken. Water and a water container are usually provided by the guides, as well as a small back pack.

INDEPENDENT TRAVEL

It is possible for the independent traveller to visit hill tribe villages and find accommodation. Many villagers will offer to provide accommodation to the visitor with the usual sleep gesture. Expect to pay 50 *baht* per person per night. For this, you may be offered dinner and breakfast. It is safe to accept plain rice and boiled water or tea, but better to politely decline anything else, for health reasons.

It is usual to stay in the headman's hut, often on a guest platform, but increasingly villages are building "guest houses" for the odd visitor. Most villages are safe to stay in, but if possible check with local guides, or the Hill Tribe Research Institute in Chiang Mai, who have a series of maps marking the position of suitable villages where people can stay. All villages described in this book are suitable for the visitor.

HILL TRIBE ETIQUETTE

Hill tribe people are soft spoken and gentle. Loud voices and behaviour are very out of place. Treat the people with respect and you will be respected too. Smiling is a universal expression of good intent, so smile and nod at villagers.

Most hill tribe houses contain a religious shrine. Do not touch or photograph this shrine, or sit underneath it. Some villagers like to be photographed, most do not. Point at your camera and nod if you want to take a photograph. Never insist if the answer is an obvious "no". Be particularly careful with pregnant women and babies - most tribes believe this might affect the soul of the foetus or new born. Taking "gifts" is dubious, since it may encourage begging, but writing materials and medicine are very welcome.

OPIUM

Obtained from the sap of the opium poppy, *Papaver Somniferum*, opium is an important cash crop of the Hmong, Yao, Lahu, Lisu and Akha hill tribes.

The drug has a fascination for many tourists. The common name for the region north of Chiang Mai, the "Golden Triangle", conjures up an exotic vision of drug warlords, mule trains, fields of pretty flowers and the intrigue of the opium den. In fact, the crop is a threat to all who are involved in its production or use. Amongst the Hmong, up to 30% of the male population are addicted. The typical addict will smoke twenty or thirty pipes a day. They cannot work efficiently or at all, life expectancy is reduced and families are pushed into malnutrition and misery. The production of opium has been illegal since 1959, but despite the attempts of the government to eliminate it, the drug is still produced in large amounts. However, in Thailand the size of the crop has been reduced by 80% in the last ten years, but Thailand is still an important conduit for opium from Burma and Laos, where production is still rising.

About 50% of opium is converted to the more dangerous, but even more profitable heroin. Six kilogrammes of opium can be converted into about one kilogramme of heroin. Small scale heroin "factories" are located in remote spots on or near the Burmese border, patrolled by armed guards and frequently mined. The advantages to the hill tribe of opium farming are that it has high value for small volume, it can be stored without spoilage, it is an easy crop to grow on land that would otherwise be infertile, the dealers come direct to the growers and there is no competition with lowland farmers.

Poppies and maize are usually grown in the same field. Maize is planted in April and harvested in August. In September and October the poppy seeds are sown amongst the maize stalks which protect the young seedlings. The crop must be weeded several times before harvesting in February or March. A few days after the petals have fallen, the outside of the flower pod is scored with a three bladed knife. The white sticky sap exudes from the pod and dries on its surface overnight. It oxidises to a brown gum which is scraped off with a broad bladed knife, formed into balls and wrapped in banana or mulberry leaves and buried until collection. Each pod can be tapped several times. The seeds from the most productive flowers are kept for planting next season.

Opium is the source of a wide variety of drugs given the general name of opiates. The most important include morphine, heroine and codeine. They are all powerful analgesics, but opium, heroin and morphine are all highly addictive and tolerance quickly develops so that larger and larger doses are needed. Depression of the higher centres of the brain causes feelings of euphoria in which fear, apprehension and inhibition are reduced, the ego is expanded and there is a general sense of well being. The user may experience a state in between sleep and wakefulness, with vivid, usually pleasant dreams. Other less enjoyable effects may include nausea, sweating, drowsiness, mental and physical impairment, poor concentration, apathy, reduced hunger and lowered sex drive. Some individuals feel depressed, anxious and fearful. The opiates also suppress the activity of the muscles of the intestine, leading to constipation or reduced diarrhoea. With high doses the respiratory centre of the brain is incapacitated, potentially causing respiratory failure and death.

The narcotic and sleep producing properties of opium have been known for thousands of years. The Sumerians in 5000 BC were the first to record its use. The Greeks used it extensively. Hippocrates noted its effects and the Roman physician Galen was enthusiastic about its therapeutic properties. The Arabs introduced it to Persia, China and India in the early middle ages. In Europe, Paracelsus discovered laudenum, tincture of opium. Later paragoric, camphor combined with laudenum, was used to control diarrhoea. For 200 years opium was regarded as a universal panacea. Until this century it was the only effective painkiller known to western medicine, when its addictive dangers were not appreciated.

In the latter part of the 18th century, Britain discovered a lucrative trade in opium. It was grown in British India and exported to China in exchange for gold and silver. This was used to buy tea and silks for import into Europe. The trade was controlled by the British East India Company but they did not carry the drug themselves as it was illegal in China. They used instead "country traders", licensed by the company to bring goods from India to China. These traders sold opium to smugglers along the coast and passed the proceeds on to the East India company. Opium addiction in China became so high that in the mid 19th century the Chinese government engaged in two "opium wars" with Britain to restrict its import. In 1860 China agreed to import the drug and impose a high tax on it. By 1917 voluntary restrictions on its production finally ended the trade on a large scale.

In the 19th century its use in Europe was widespread. Patent medicines contained high doses, to encourage clients to come back for more. Many prominent persons were unwittingly addicted, particularly writers and artists, who believed it increased their creative powers. In this century vigorous attempts to restrict its use, and particularly that of its more dangerous relative heroin, have been largely unsuccessful. Heroin addiction in Asia and the west is a chronic problem, particularly since its preferred method of intake by injection has helped to spread AIDS throughout the world.

The opium and heroin trade in Thailand is largely controlled by two "armies". The Shan State army was founded to establish an independent Shan state in Burma. The funds for its weapons and manpower are provided by the production of heroin from opium. The Shan army has attempted to extend its influence inside Thailand, meeting opposition from the Kuomintang (KMT).

Historically, the KMT controlled most heroin production in Thailand. They were the legitimate government in China before the communist revolution of 1949. Following this defeat, they fled in two directions. One group settled in Formosa, founding the state of Taiwan, still controlled by the KMT today. The other group, led by General Lee, settled in Northern Thailand and Burma. Their original intention was to retake China from Mao in a two pronged attack. This never took place, but the remnants of the army in Thailand developed the heroin trade. They were useful to the Thai government, and to the west, who were pleased to have a fiercely anti communist and well armed group patrolling the northern borders. They turned a blind eye to the heroin trade, which consequently expanded.

Many hill tribe boys were recruited into the Kuomintang and Shan armies, from which there was no escape. The armies were powerful enough to dictate prices and production levels to the villages, who either supported or were rightly afraid of them. In the last ten years, the danger of communist incursion into Thailand has largely disappeared, so the government has been able to concentrate on the elimination of the crop, which has met with considerable success. At the same time, it has been necessary to replace opium with other cash crops. Soft fruits, tea, coffee and temperate vegetables have been introduced into hill tribe farming patterns, and now contribute greatly to the economies of many villages.

NATURAL HISTORY

Northern Thailand is at the edge of three very different ecological regions. To the south, the tropical rain forests of Southern Thailand and the Malay peninsular. North west, the Himalayan region, to the north east the plains of central Asia. This creates a great natural diversity of species, both plant and animal. Sadly, due to human pressures, most large mammals can only be seen in National Parks, and even here most are scarce. Nevertheless there is a huge variety of plants and animal species to be seen. Most obvious are the insects. There are over 800 species of butterflies and moths in the Chiang Mai area, many of them the huge "birdwings", the size of small bats, which are common wherever there are flowers. Giant beetles, praying mantis and dragonflies are ubiquitous.

Reptiles are abundant. All buildings except the most expensive hotels have a population of geckos, both the small *chink-chok* and the larger *tokay*, whose strange, loud call can frequently be heard at night. Geckos are generally welcomed, since they keep the population of insects down (particularly the horribly common and unloved mosquitoes). On bushes and walls in the daytime, look for the pretty agamid lizards, whose males glow with red or blue heads, bobbing to each other in search of a mate. Snakes are common, particularly harmless brown water snakes, but there are also thirteen species of poisonous ones. There are stories of cobras wrapping themselves around pipes in toilets, but this is a rare event. The average inhabitant sees a poisonous snake once a year or less. They are shy, nocturnal creatures who if seen will be intent on a rapid escape.

The small mammal population is still quite large. Strangest is the pangolin, a small primitive, scaly creature with a long snout that eats ants. It is commonly seen hanging outside hill tribe huts as a protection to women in pregnancy. Ground and tree squirrels, porcupines, civets, mongooses, weasels, hog badgers, fruit bats, rats and mice are all common. Several species of primates are endemic. Gibbons, whose haunting cry can sometimes be heard in the jungle at night, are becoming rare, but several species of macaque monkey can still be found. Cutest is the slow loris - a ball of grey fur with huge eyes, which clambers laboriously through the trees.

All large mammals have become extremely rare. There are probably less than 400 tigers left, most in the deep jungle on the Burmese border. Leopards, including the black panther, once a threat, have almost disappeared, but smaller cats such as the marbled cat, jungle cat and Asian golden cat are still widely distributed. There are 200 wild water buffalo left in Thailand, and perhaps 1000 Asian elephants, in the jungle south of Mae Sariang. The tapir is probably extinct, as are the Sumatran and Indian rhinoceros. The commonest deer is the Sambur, but the three other species are still present in small numbers. Of the two bear species - the Himalayan and Sun, only the former can still be found in any quantity.

There are a huge number of bird species - 362 species on Doi Inthanon alone. From Europe and West Asia, jays, hoopoes and rollers are common. Hornbills and sunbirds, whose range is centred to the south, Chinese egrets and Siberian robins from the north, all co-habit in Northern Thailand.

The flora of Northern Thailand is equally diverse, with a huge variety of flowering plants and trees. Most plants blossom towards the end of the dry season in February, the time of Chiang Mai's Flower Festival. The natural vegetation of the lowlands has been completely replaced with farmland. The hills, to an altitude of about 1000 metres, are covered in dry, deciduous forest, of over 100 species of tree. Here, in January and February, the leaves change colour, resembling a temperate autumn, and by March they are almost bare. At this time of year, the risk of fire is extremely high. When the monsoons start, in May or June, a miraculous transformation takes place. Within a few days, grasses and shoots thrust upwards, and trees rapidly put out new leaves. Barking deer may wander downhill from their more usual haunt to feed on the new shoots. Termites march through the ground flora searching for dead wood. In the day time, most animals shelter from the heat, but at night ferret badgers emerge from their burrows to search for snails, lizards and birds eggs. Early in the morning, it is possible to see scarlet backed flower peckers, common tailorbirds, long tailed shrikes, bulbuls and barbets. In the heat of the day, buzzards circle overhead looking for ground squirrels and other small mammals.

At an altitude of around 1000 metres, the forest begins to change. The hot, dry forest gives way to evergreens, where the trees are taller, the canopy denser and the atmosphere in the forest is cool and shady. The soil changes from brick red laterite to a rich dark brown. This soil is more efficient at holding water and retains moisture longer, so there is no need for the trees to lose their leaves. The rainfall here is higher, about double that of the plains, and water drains slowly through the soil into the streams which provide the water supplies to the lowland towns and cities.

The trees here are similar to those of western Europe - pines, oaks and chestnuts. At the highest elevations, rhododendrons are found. Most of the wildlife is to be found in the treetops. Around dawn, you will see iridescent green pigeons, barbets and leafbirds, orange and black minivets and tiny flycatchers. Flying lizards and flying squirrels are quite common, as well as several other squirrel species. Slow loris are rarely seen but not uncommon. There are over 1000 species of orchid found in Thailand, most in the north. Large flowered, intricate and incredibly beautiful, they are one of the symbols of Thailand. They flower in the driest part of the year, when they have no leaves. Most are epiphytic - they grow attached to the trunks of jungle trees. Each species is specifically adapted to a narrow range of temperature and humidity, so is found only at particular positions and altitudes to which it is pre-adapted.

In 1961, 61% of the land surface of the north was forest. That figure is now around 40% and decreasing rapidly. The loss of this forest, caused by overfarming and logging, has potentially disastrous effects on Thailand's economy and climate, quite apart from the loss of irreplaceable plant and animal species.

Chapter Two

Practicalities

NORTHERN THAILAND, despite having been until recently part of a third world culture, is now an efficient, well organized region, with an excellent infrastructure for the visitor. Within and between all cities there are excellent health, police, communication and tourist facilities. English is widely spoken, particularly by young people who all study the language at school, and the natural helpfulness of the population makes any problem easily solved.

BANKS AND MONEY

The currency of Thailand is the *baht*, which is divided into 100 *satangs*. There are coins of copper 25 and 50 *satangs*, and silver coins of 1, 5 and 10 *baht*. Confusingly, the 1 and 5 *baht* silver coins come in different overlapping size, and older ones have their denomination written in Thai script. However, the 5 *baht* coin has a milled copper coloured edge, the 1 *baht* does not. The notes are easier, and increase in size with value, which is written in Thai and Arabic numerals. There is a brown 10 *baht*, green 20, blue 50, red 100 and purple 500.

A 1000 *baht* note is planned for the near future, and the 10 *baht* note is to be phased out. It is frequently difficult to get change for the 500 note.

The value of the *baht* is loosely linked to the US dollar, so is always around 25 *baht*/dollar. The rate with other currencies, then, varies with the dollar. Against the British pound, the rate between 1990 and 1991 varied from 40 to 50.

EXCHANGE FACILITIES
Money can be exchanged at any bank very easily, and all money changers are linked to a bank. Rates are fixed, and commissions are low, so there is no point in shopping around - although the rates given by hotels are always low.
Banks are open Mondays to Fridays, 8.30 am to 3.30 pm, but money changers are open until late in the evenings. Banks will be found in all towns, but money changers only in Chiang Mai, Chiang Rai, Sukhothai, Mae Sai and Phitsanulok. Travellers cheques and bank notes in most western currencies are acceptable at all banks, but travellers cheques have a considerably higher rate.

There are now no restrictions on the import or export of currency up to US $10,000. It is legal to open a bank account at any bank, as long as all the funds originate abroad. If you need money from home, it can be sent by telegraphic transfer, and should arrive within four days.

GETTING THERE

For almost all visitors, **Chiang Mai** is the jumping off point for any tour of the north. Geographically central, and a natural transport hub, it makes an ideal base, and is itself worth a stay of several days.

Most visitors reach Chiang Mai via Bangkok, although it is now possible to fly direct from Phuket or Surat Thani (near Ko Samui) in the south of Thailand on Wednesdays and Saturdays, and there are weekly flights from or to Hong Kong.

FROM BANGKOK

There are frequent services to Chiang Mai by plane, air conditioned coach or train. Bear in mind that crippling traffic congestion in Bangkok, particularly between 8.00-10.00 am and 4.30-8.30 pm lengthens travel time in the city enormously. Allow at least two hours to get to the airport or Northern Bus Terminal at these times.

AIR CONDITIONED COACH

This is the cheapest way of getting to Chiang Mai comfortably, with fares from Bangkok from about 180-250 *baht*. The more expensive fare (on the so-called "VIP" buses) does give you a seat on an extremely luxurious coach, with reclining seats with plenty of leg room, blankets, free drinks, toilet on board, stewardess and meal stops included, but the 10 hour trip is inevitably tedious.

Minibuses for the coaches call daily at most hotels in Bangkok, where tickets can be booked, but the minibus shuttle from hotel to hotel can last for hours. It is better to buy your ticket from a travel agent and get a taxi to the Northern Bus Terminal, from where all coaches to the North leave. Normally, a coach ticket can be purchased on the day of travel. Coaches leave between 6.30 and 8.30 pm on the 10 hour trip to Chiang Mai. They arrive at the Arcade coach station, Kaew Nawarat Road, telephone (053) 242644. This is three kilometres east of Chiang Mai, where *tuk-tuks* (three wheeled taxis) and *songthaews* (bus pick-ups) ply a continuous trade into Chiang Mai. There are also day coaches to Chiang Mai leaving at 6.30 to 8.30 am but they are not popular. Other coach services to the North go to Chiang Rai, Mae Hong Song via Mae Sariang and Nan via Sukhothai, Phitsanulok and Phrae.

There are occasional complaints of pick-pocketing on all coaches, so be careful. Never accept drinks from other passengers since these may be drugged.

TRAIN

There is an excellent train service to Chiang Mai, and most people find the trip more enjoyable and comfortable then the coach. There are three ticket classes. First class tickets cost 827 *baht* per person, providing a twin berth air conditioned cabin with en-suite bathroom. Second class air conditioned berths cost 535 *baht* for a lower berth or 485 *baht* for a slightly cramped upper berth. The temperature is maintained so low that sleep is difficult for many, and is only worthwhile for most in the hottest season. Second class seats are quite comfortable and recline well for sleeping, but a berth is generally worth the extra 100 *baht*. Second class berths with fan at 455 *baht* for an upper berth and 505 *baht* for a lower, are probably the best choice.

Along either side of the carriage are rows of wide comfortable single seats in facing pairs. At night, the chairs are converted into comfortable upper and lower berths. The more expensive lower berths have a large window with a screen, which ensures good ventilation. The upper berths are ventilated only by a small central fan, and the light which remains on throughout the night, is impossible to fully obscure with the curtain which is drawn across each bunk for privacy. Third class seats at 150 *baht* are cheap, but the seats are hard and the carriages frequently overcrowded.

Rapid trains with second and third class seats leave at 6.40, 20.25 and 22.00 hours and take 15 hours for the journey to Chiang Mai.

Express trains, also with second and third class, leave at 18.00 hours and take twelve hours. The special express, with first and second class seats, leaves at 19.40 and also takes 12 hours, but provides superior facilities. There is an extra charge of 50 *baht* for second class seats on the express train.

Trains leave from Hualampong station in Bangkok, where tickets must be booked (some travel agents will book tickets for clients). At weekends, and at the peak of the high season it may be necessary to book several days ahead to ensure a seat, and particularly a berth. Telephone 2230341, extension 4211 for same day bookings, extension 4200-4203 for advance bookings. There is a very well organized booking office at the railway station, to the far right of the building from the main entrance. There is also a very helpful central information desk. Same day bookings must be made at the ticket office. There are separate booths for each train, and each booth is clearly marked with the destination in English above the window.

PLANE

Thai Airways flights to Chiang Mai take 55 minutes. A meal is provided. Flights leave Bangkok from the domestic terminal of Don Muang Airport at 7.30, 9.50, 12.00, 15.45, 16.30, 19.00 and 20.45 daily.

Tickets can be bought from any travel agent, at the airport or at any Thai Airways Office. The price is 1645 *baht*. Chiang Mai airport is 3 kilometres south of the city. There are taxis at the airport for 100 *baht*, or a Thai Airways shuttle bus to the centre for 40 *baht*. There are also flights direct to Phitsanulok, Mae Sot and Mae Hong Song. Chiang Rai and Nan can be reached via Chiang Mai.

LOCAL TRANSPORT

Samlors: these are bicycle rickshaws, ideal for short distances if you are not in a hurry. Expect to pay about 5 *baht* for a short distance, 10 *baht* or more for distances of over a kilometre. All towns and cities (except Bangkok) have *samlors*.

Tuk-tuks are small, three wheeled taxis, fast and noisy, fitted with motor bike engines. They can seat two comfortably, four at a pinch. They are only found in Chiang Mai, Chiang Rai, Phitsanulok and Mae Hong Son. The drivers charge what they like, and bargaining is often necessary. In Chiang Mai, you should expect to pay 20 *baht* for a short trip, up to 40 for longer journeys.

Songthaews are the best value. They are covered pick-ups with two benches facing each other. They pick up and put down passengers like a bus, and have a flat rate of 5 *baht* for any distance, unless they are asked to go outside their normal route, when they will charge more. At busy times they may be very full, and one is never sure exactly where they are going. You must state your destination clearly to the driver when you flag him down.

Buses outside Bangkok are used more for long distance than local travel.

Taxis are uncommon in the north, but there are a few in Chiang Mai, mainly used to get to and from the airport, and from major hotels.

BUSINESS HOURS

Most department stores are open from 10.00 or 11.00 am to 7.00 or 8.00 pm. Smaller shops open at about 8.30 am to 5.00 pm, although many small shops stay open until late in the evenings. Many towns have night markets open until midnight or later.

Traditional Northern Thai dancing in the Night Bazaar, Chiang Mai

Monks with alms bowl, Chiang Mai

Metal engraving, Sankamphaeng, Chiang Mai

Wat Chamadevi, Lamphun

Cloth weaving, Chom Tong, Chiang Mai

Wat Doi Suthep, Chiang Mai

TELECOMMUNICATIONS

It is possible to telephone anywhere in the world from major cities. The main post offices are the best places for this, but many private offices advertise this service. The rate to Europe is about 60-80 *baht* per minute. It is not possible to make international calls from public phone booths, and most telephones can only be used for local calls. When making calls, write down the number on the form provided by the staff, and they will dial for you.

Public telephones are either red or blue. Red ones can only be used for local calls, blue ones for long distance anywhere in Thailand. Local calls cost 1 baht (you will need a small one *baht* coin). Pick up the phone first, drop the coin in the slot, dial the number and wait. A sequence of long tones indicates the number is ringing, a rapid number of short notes that the number is busy. Long distance phones accept only 5 or 10 *baht* coins.

Fax machines are becoming widely available in most towns, usually advertised with a large sign. International Faxes can be found, but only in major cities. Most large hotels now have Fax machines, useful for booking rooms.

POST

Post offices open at 8.30 am and close at 4.30 pm, Mondays to Fridays, and 8.30 am to 12.30 pm Saturdays.

The postal service is cheap and efficient. Letters and cards to Europe take four to seven days, to America six to ten days. This can be reduced by one or two days by paying a small "express"supplement. For very urgent material, ask for "EMS" - the delivery time for this is one or two days to Europe, two or three days to America. A standard letter sent "EMS" costs 250 *baht*.

Parcels take seven days to Europe air mail, five weeks by sea mail. Air-sea takes three or four weeks. Prices vary greatly according to destination, but by air mail to Britain is 200 *baht* per kilogram. Stamps can only be purchased from post offices, with the exception of stamps for post cards, which many hotels and some shops sell. It is better to go to the post office to send material. Red post boxes are widely available, but some are for local letters only, others for long distance. Since this is written in Thai on the box, it is safer not to use them. Hotels will accept post cards for posting.

ADMINISTRATION

POLICE

There is a strong police presence throughout Northern Thailand. Police boxes and check points are found near all towns and many villages, as well as in sensitive remote areas. Route plans for all tours and treks must be registered with the police. Since tourism is so important to the Thai economy, the police will always be very helpful to the visitor with a problem. A large branch of the police force - the tourist police - is responsible for the well being of visitors. However, they punish very severely anyone found carrying or selling drugs. The death penalty is frequently imposed for the smuggling or selling of heroin, although it has yet to be carried out on a westerner.

GOVERNMENT

Thailand is a constitutional monarchy. The royal family, although highly respected (it is the height of bad manners - and illegal - to criticise them), has no political power.

There is a two tier parliament, with, in theory, an elected lower house and an appointed upper one. The Thais have been toying with democracy for forty years, but in practice the military always have the upper hand. There have been sixteen coups and eleven constitutions since 1939, but none of these have more than rippled the calm surface of the Thai nation. The political leader is the Prime Minister, usually himself a military leader, or at least strongly supported by the armed forces.

LOCAL GOVERNMENT
Northern Thailand is divided into 10 *changwats* (states), named after the principal city - Chiang Mai, Chiang Rai, Mae Hong Son, Phayao, Nan, Phitsanulok, Sukhothai, Tak, Lamphun and Lampang. Each *Changwat* is divided into several *Amphurs* - the administrative district around each major town. The lowest level of administration is the *Ban*, or village. At the entrance to every settlement, its name will be displayed on a signpost, prefixed by *Ban* or *Amphur*.

THE ECONOMY

The economy of Thailand is booming. It had a growth rate in 1991 of over 10% - the most rapid in the world. In 1990 it became a "newly industrialised country", recognized by the United Nations, so has formally left the third world. It is one of a small group of Asian countries, dubbed the "tiger cubs", which are rapidly catching up with the economic giants of Japan, Hong Kong, Singapore and Taiwan.

Tourism is Thailand's biggest industry, contributing over 70 billion *baht* in 1989. Thailand is the worlds largest exporter of tapioca, second largest of rubber and sixth in coconuts. There is a large and growing seafood canning and exporting industry, and Thailand is the largest rice exporter in South East Asia. Manufactured goods exports are increasing rapidly, particularly clothes, wood products, furniture and textiles, and electrical goods manufacturers are investing heavily in Thailand. Gemstone cutting remains an important secondary industry.

CONSULATES

The only consulates in the north are the Indian, Japanese and USA consulates in Chiang Mai.
    India: 113 Bamrungrasd Rd. Tel: (053)243066
    Japan: 12/1 Boongreungrit Rd. Tel: (053)221451
    USA: 387 Wichayanon Rd Tel: (053)252629-31
N.B. The British Council at 198 Bumrungrasd Rd., Chiang Mai, does not provide any consular facilities. Contact the British Embassy in Bangkok: 1031 Wireless Road, Bangkok: Tel (2)253 0191.

VISAS

Tourists from the west can visit Thailand for up to 14 days without a visa. For stays up to 60 days, a tourist visa is needed. A non immigrant visa allows a stay of 90 days. All visas must be used within 90 days of issue. Extensions of up to two weeks for tourist visas or one month for non immigrant can be bought at the immigration office near Chiang Mai airport.

Transit visas are also available, but only if you hold a plane ticket flying out of Thailand to a destination other than the origin.

TIME

Thai time is seven hours ahead of GMT (London). Noon in Chiang Mai is 1 am in New York, 10 pm the previous day in Los Angeles, 1 pm in Perth and 5 am in London.
The Thai calendar is based on the years after the death of Buddha, so that the year 1992 is 2535. Both calendars are used.

WEIGHTS AND MEASURES

Thailand uses the metric system for distance (kilometres) and weight (kilogrammes). Land is measured in *rai*, one *rai* being 1600 square metres. The weight of gold and silver is measured in *baht*, one *baht* being about 15 grammes.

ELECTRICITY

Electric current is 220 volts AC, so British equipment will work without adaptors. Batteries of all sizes are widely available and very cheap.

PHOTOGRAPHY

Film is available widely in Northern Thailand, at prices slightly lower than the west. Look for the sell by date, however, and avoid buying from displays which have been exposed to the sun, since high temperatures can quickly damage colour balance.
    Slide film is less common, but still available in most large towns. Kodachrome slide film, however, is not available, nor can it be processed in Thailand. In most cities, computerised modern film processing equipment is available. Prices are from 3 *baht* per small print. Enlargements are particularly cheap compared to the west, and the quality is good.
    Avoid taking external photographs between 10.00 am and 3.00 pm. The light is usually too bright, and film cannot compensate for the very high contrast. A polaroid filter reduces this problem, but even then it is better to take photographs in the early morning or evening, when the light is wonderful for photography.

HEALTH

Thailand is, in general, a clean and health conscious country. The standard of medical care is good, and hospitals or health clinics can be found throughout the country. Most doctors speak good English, and although medical advice and treatment is not free, charges are modest. They vary according to the hospital and treatment, but the cost per day for a private room in a good hospital will be around 500 *baht*, excluding treatment.

Chemists supply a wide variety of western drugs, many not available without prescription in the west. Chinese druggists supply a huge range of alternative therapies - some very effective.

The chances of contracting a serious disease are low, but before visiting Thailand it is advisable to be immunised against **hepatitis A, typhoid, polio, cholera** and **tetanus. Rabies, dengue haemmorrhagic fever** and **Japanese B encephalitis** are rising in incidence - vaccines are available for all these. None are common, but occasional outbreaks, particularly in remote areas, have been reported. Hepatitis is a viral infection of the liver causing jaundice and general malaise which lasts for several weeks. **Hepatitis A** is rarely fatal. It is contracted from infected food or water and has a long incubation period. There is no vaccine, but a shot of serum gives temporary protection for several weeks. Compared to other Asian countries, the incidence is low, but protection is well worth having. There are many cases of the more dangerous **Hepatitis B** in Thailand, where it is a major killer. It is contracted through sexual contact or infected needles (particularly amongst heroin addicts). There is an effective vaccine but no cure.

Malaria has been eradicated from all urban areas and is rare except in some areas of remote mountain jungle close to the Burma border. It is spread by the bite of the Anopheles mosquito. The parasites invade liver cells causing episodes of high fever and liver pain. There are two forms in Thailand, benign and malignant, and without treatment the malignant form has a high mortality rate. Since the young forms of the mosquito need pools of still water, it is a wet season disease.

Unfortunately the parasite is now resistant to most prophylactic drugs, so the regular taking of anti malarial medication no longer guarantees protection. New drugs are constantly being developed, see your doctor for the currently most effective prophylactic.

If you should experience the early symptoms of malaria - high fever and shaking chills - see a doctor as soon as possible.

The best protection is to avoid being bitten. the malaria mosquito only feeds in the middle of the night, so the use of a mosquito net in suspect areas is effective. Slow burning mosquito coils are an alternative. If the smell of these is offensive buy an electrical version - small insecticide pads which are placed in a tiny heating element. They have the rather unfortunate name of "Ars mat".

Diarrhoea is a common problem for visitors, but is almost always mild and temporary. It is usually caused by a bacterium which is found in all individuals, but against which newcomers have no natural immunity to the endemic strain. If affected, take an anti diarrhoea drug such as Immodium and drink electrolyte solution to prevent dehydration. Chemists sell this in powder form as ORS (oral rehydration solution), or the rather tasty "Sponsor" - a yellow solution on sale everywhere. Only if there is fever or blood in the stools is diarrhoea likely to be something more serious. If these symptoms should persist, seek medical advice as soon as possible.

Cholera is rare, but outbreaks of typhoid are not, so vaccination is strongly recommended.

Rabies is not uncommon in Thailand. If bitten by any animal, seek medical advice at once.

The health risks from food and drink are not as great as in most comparable countries. Thais are very clean people and most food and drink is hygienically prepared, but it is wise to avoid crushed ice (cylinders of ice are prepared from sterilised water) and to check the cleanliness of the restaurant or food stall at which you eat. All raw food, and especially raw fish, should be avoided. Only bottled water should be drunk, since tap water is not intended for consumption and may well contain disease causing organisms. You should definitely not eat food offered in hill tribe villages, although plain rice is generally safe.

It is not wise to bathe in still water - lakes or slow flowing rivers - since there are a number of parasites which can be picked up through skin or mouth. The major risks to health for the tourists who put themselves at risk are venereal diseases. Rates of gonorrhoea and syphilis are high, but AIDS is now the biggest problem. The tourist oriented sex industry in Thailand is big business, although prostitution is illegal. Rates of AIDS are terrifying. In the north, according to recent statistics, between 40 and 60% of prostitutes carry the AIDS virus. It is obviously verging on the suicidal not to protect yourself against this risk.

Snakebite is a risk to health which is grossly exaggerated by many tourists. Thailand does have a high number of poisonous snakes, but the chances of being bitten are very low. Snakes are not aggressive to humans, and will only bite if cornered or trodden on. In Thailand they are usually nocturnal, rarely seen during the day except following heavy rains when they may be flooded out of their homes. If walking at night, it is sensible to check where you are putting your feet and if there is undergrowth, sweeping ahead with a stick. If you are unlucky enough to be bitten, tie a tornique (for example rolled up clothing) above the bite tightly enough to stop venom entering the rest of the body, releasing every 10 minutes to allow blood to enter the limb, reduce movement and get to a doctor as soon as possible. Antivenin is only used in severe cases, but all health centres will have a supply against the most dangerous venoms. The death rate from even the most poisonous snakes is not high, nor as sudden as commonly believed.

The four most dangerous snakes found in Thailand are the Indian cobra, king cobra, banded krait and green tree viper. The Indian cobra is up to 2 metres long, pale brown to black in colour, and before striking extends a "cowl" around its head. Similar but much larger is the king cobra. The banded krait is 1.5 - 2 metres in length, with black and gold thick vertical stripes. The green tree viper is bright green in colour with a brown tip to its tail, 1 - 2 metres long with a flat triangular head.

The other main animal health risk, apart from rabid mammals, is the scorpion. Although rarely fatal, its sting is extremely painful. It is found under logs or stones, but sometimes finds the inside of shoes a pleasant place to rest, so check before putting them on!

A common irritation to tourists arises from the high sweating rate at tropical temperatures and humidities. **Prickly heat** is the least serious problem, but fungal infections, particularly of the groin, are frequent. Frequent showers, and the use of a medicated talc, will probably prevent these conditions.

SANITATION

The mysteries of the traditional Thai shower and toilet are a cause of embarrassment and confusion to many visitors. Modern hotels and guest houses are usually equipped with western style facilities, but most visitors at some time will have to come to grips with ablutjng Thai style.

The basic Thai toilet has a ceramic bowl on the floor with foot plates either side. There is commonly no flushing system, but next to the bowl is a large urn or tank of water with a ladle floating on the top. Excretion is in the squatting position. Many westerners find this uncomfortable, but in fact this position is far more natural and better for the body than the western way (think of this as the blood supply to your feet ceases and you struggle desperately to stand up afterwards!).

Now to the delicate question of how to cleanse your nether regions. Thais do not use toilet paper, but clean themselves with the left hand using water ladled from the water supply, washing the hands afterwards. As they put it "If you accidentally put your hand on some dog excreta, do you wipe it off with tissue or wash your hands ?". They have a point. However, it is perfectly acceptable to take a supply of toilet paper with you and use the conventional western cleaning technique, but do not expect paper to be provided. Normally, Thais take off their lower garments and wrap themselves in a towel before going to the toilet.

The shower works in a similar way. If there is no shower head, water from the urn or tank is ladled over the body. Never wash your hair or clean your teeth in the main supply, since this is supposed to last all day and should never be polluted. Tourists who jump into the urn and wash themselves in it become very unpopular.

DRIVING IN THAILAND

The road system of Thailand is surprisingly good. All major roads are well surfaced and signposted, and link all main towns. The network is being constantly extended and improved - although some of the worst driving is to be experienced on roads undergoing improvement.

Signs and road markings are based on those of the USA, and are easily understood. Signposts to even the smallest towns are usually in Thai and English. Minor roads in Thailand, however, which often provide the most beautiful and interesting sights, are generally unsurfaced and many may be impassable without 4 wheel drive during the long wet season.

Petrol stations are well distributed, but in rural areas are commonly a small wooden shack with hand operated petrol drums on view. It is important to be able to ask for the correct fuel at these, since the drums are not marked and the attendant may well not understand English. Petrol is called *"benzeen"*, diesel fuel is *"dee-zen"* or *"so-lah"*. High octane fuel is called *"super"*.

Driving in Thailand is on the left, and the rules of the road are ostensibly the same as the west. Roundabouts are unusual, busy intersections are generally controlled by traffic lights or police. In general the speed of traffic is low, even on motorways vehicles rarely cruise above 100 kilometres per hour. It is now compulsory for drivers to have a valid international driving licence, or a legally translated copy of their native driving licence. Without one, you risk being fined up to 500 *baht* if stopped by the police. If hiring a vehicle, you should have held a full driving licence for at least one year.

It is most important to ensure that you have good insurance cover whilst driving in Thailand. Third party cover is particularly important, since damage to other vehicles, or more important injury to persons, can be very expensive. Westerners are likely to be blamed for any accident, and face a hefty fine.

The accident rate in Thailand is high. It is therefore most important to be extremely vigilant at all times. Compared to western driving, Thai driving is unpredictable and at times completely incomprehensible. Try to maintain a big gap between your vehicle and the vehicle in front. Be prepared to brake if a following vehicle overtakes in the face of oncoming traffic. Vehicles frequently stop or pull over with little or no warning. A particular problem is the large number of mopeds and motor bikes, frequently overloaded and, most unnervingly, often without lights at night. Traffic commonly drives onto a road without the driver stopping or looking at the junction, or driving along the hard shoulder in either direction waiting for a gap in the traffic. It is quite unnerving to see a vehicle coming towards you on your side of the road - even if it is on the hard shoulder. At traffic lights, it is general practice to go as soon as the opposing lights have turned red. This is a frequent cause of accidents. On bends, particularly on mountain roads, oncoming vehicles often cut the corner to minimize braking. It is therefore a good policy to use the horn before entering any blind bend. Extreme corner cutting on right hand bends is also common practice, and another cause of accidents.

In general, small vehicles are expected to give way to larger ones. This is particluarly important to remember with long distance coaches and trucks, which drive with an apparent total disregard for smaller oncoming vehicles. It is a good policy when seeing a coach or truck coming towards you to slow down and drive as far to the left as possible.

A convoy of large vehicles may be accompanied by police cars at front and rear. Oncoming vehicles should immediately slow down and pull over to the left. In the event of an accident or breakdown, police advice is that if possible drivers and passengers should stay with the vehicle until a police car arrives. If this is unlikely, flag down a passing vehicle and ask the driver to report the accident at the next police station, when a police car will be despatched to you. Only as a last resort should you leave your vehicle. If someone is injured, then passing vehicles should be asked to convey the injured to the nearest medical help, but the police should be informed as soon as possible.

VEHICLE RENTAL

A growing part of the travel scene in the north, and deservedly so. With the recent improvements in communication and tourist infrastructure, the visitor has little to fear and much to gain by hiring a vehicle.

CAR RENTAL
Jeeps are the most popular form of car rented for touring Northern Thailand. They are the perfect vehicle for this terrain, able to cope with the pothole rich roads away from big towns, fun to drive and giving the user a real sense of adventure.

There are two types generally available - the open, army type jeep and the more expensive and luxurious air conditioned Suzuki jeeps.

Open jeeps may have their origins deep in the past. Old chassis are modernised in Thailand with parts from a wide range of other cars, so your jeep may be a mongrel of many different makes under the bonnet. Despite this, they are generally well built and reliable.

Four wheel drive is very desirable and almost essential for many areas in the wet season (May-October). Diesel engines are cheaper to run and less prone to faults than petrol, but are slower, noisier and smellier.

Jeeps should not be driven at over 90 kilometres per hour. Their handling is very different from normal saloons, so drive slowly and carefully at all times. Be careful when driving with the top down - it is very easy to suffer sunburn without realising it until too late! In the dry season, dust is a problem, especially on dirt roads. The dust is fine enough to penetrate clothes and users will be completely encrusted within a few hours.

The price for an open jeep will be between 500-900 *baht* per day, depending on season, including comprehensive insurance (check the policy closely). You may be able to get a price reduction for an extended rental of over three days. The Suzuki jeep available at most agencies is a good compromise between comfort and off road driving capabilities. The air conditioning system allows dust to be kept out of the car, as well as providing a pleasant temperature - particularly appreciated when sitting in traffic jams. It has an excellent four wheel drive system, quite good visibility and is easy to drive. However, it cannot be driven like a saloon, as it has a high centre of gravity and can be rolled over if corners are taken too fast. Prices per day, including insurance, vary between 800-1200 *baht*

MOTOR BIKE RENTAL

There are many agencies in Chiang Mai and other tourist centres renting motor bikes. Two types of bike are available. Small 100cc mopeds are the cheapest, fine for around the city and on good roads with no steep hills, but not really adequate for the hill country. Rates for these vary with supply and demand. In the high season, (November to March) you should expect to pay 120-140 *baht* per day. At other times, and with hard bargaining, it may be possible to rent a bike for as little as 80 *baht* per day.

MTX 120cc trail bikes are available from most agencies. If you have some skill and experience on motor bikes, they are well suited to touring the whole region. They vary in price between 120-200 *baht* per day depending again on supply and demand.

Generally, the hirer is responsible for repairs and damage to these bikes, so check the condition of the bike carefully before you rent it, and make sure your insurance covers you for any eventuality. Bearing in mind the high accident rate in Thailand, anyone who drives without a helmet is taking a great risk, since most motor bike deaths are caused by head injuries.

Chapter Three

Chiang Mai

Central Chiang Mai

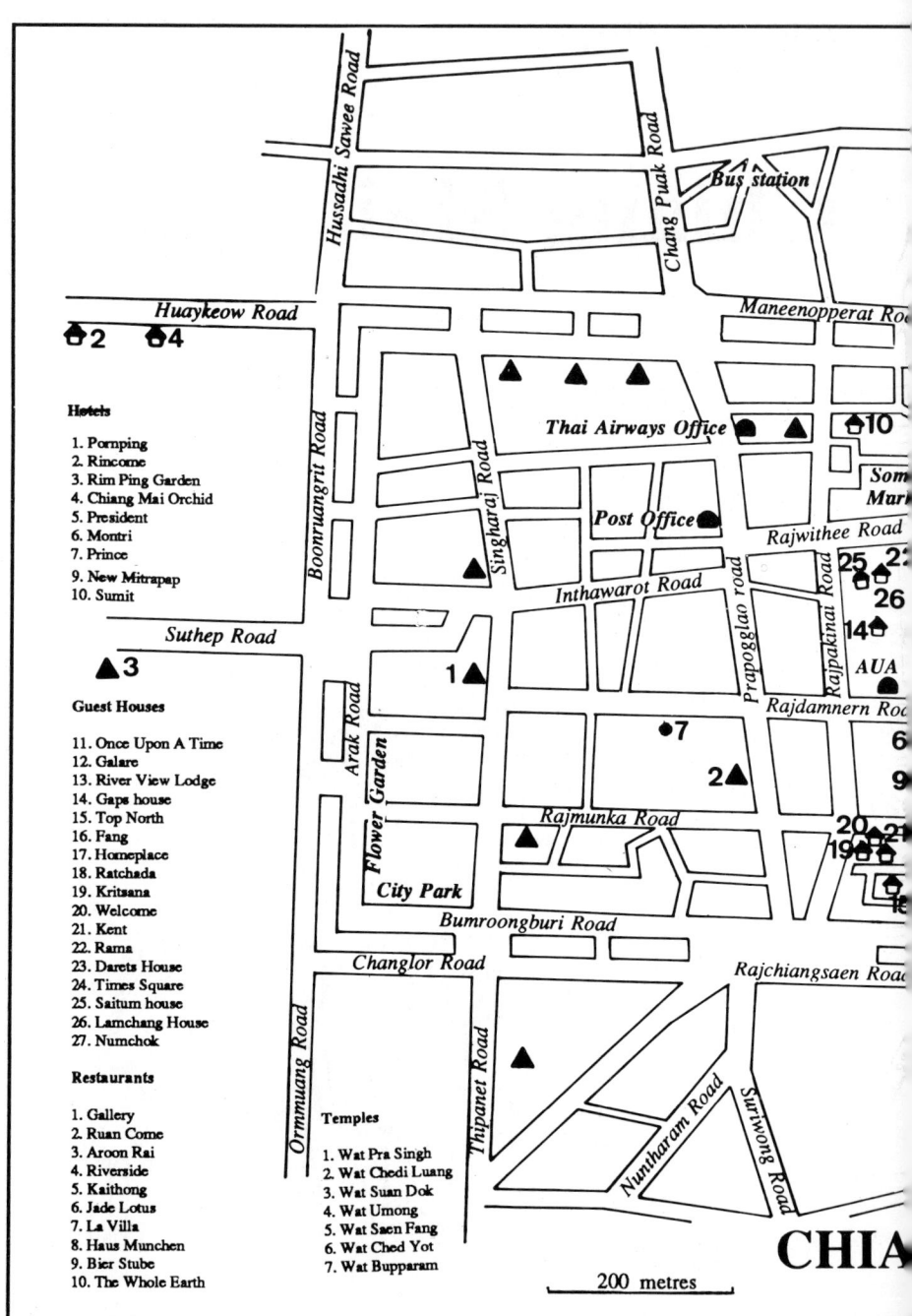

Touring Northern Thailand

Central Chiang Mai

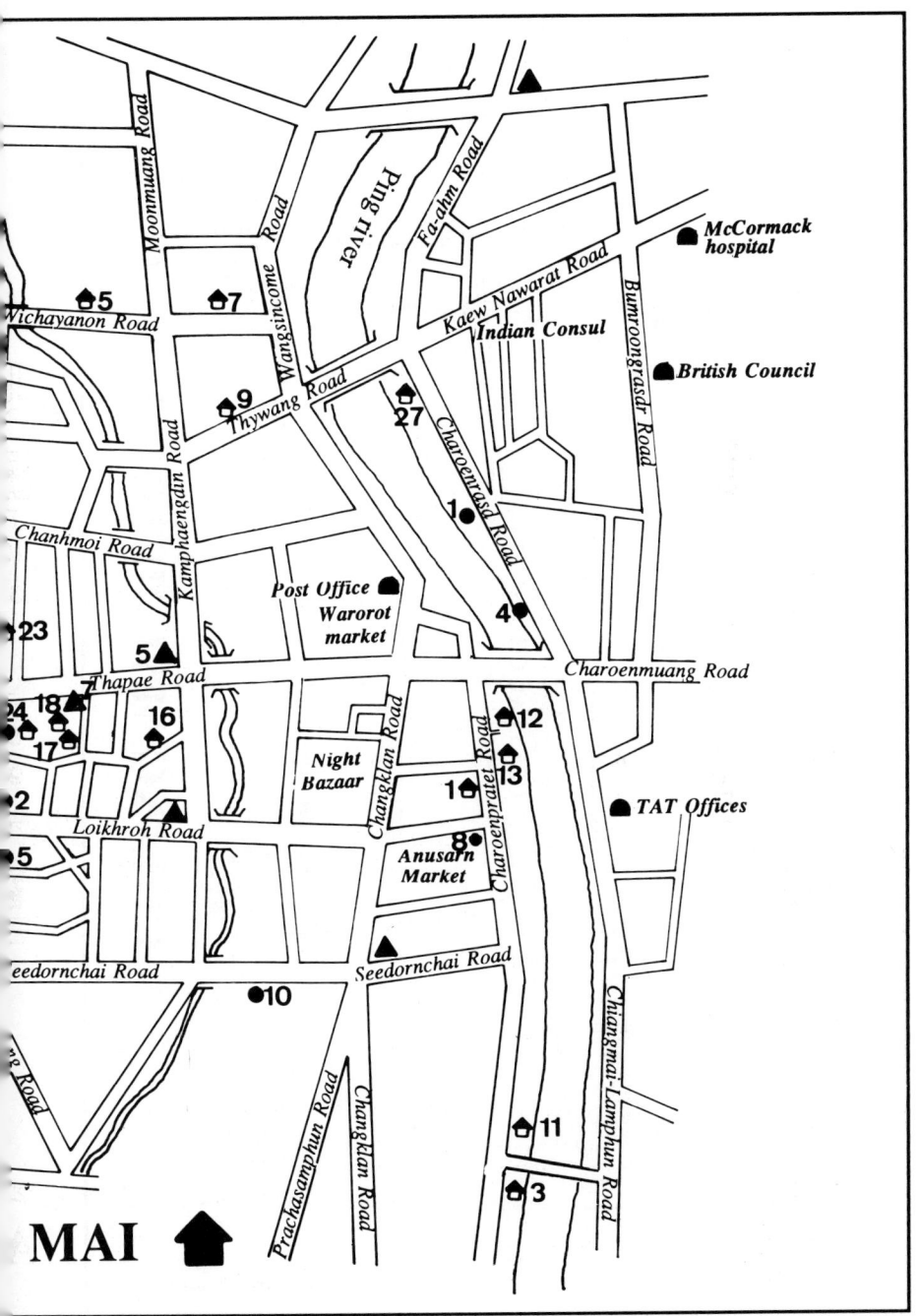

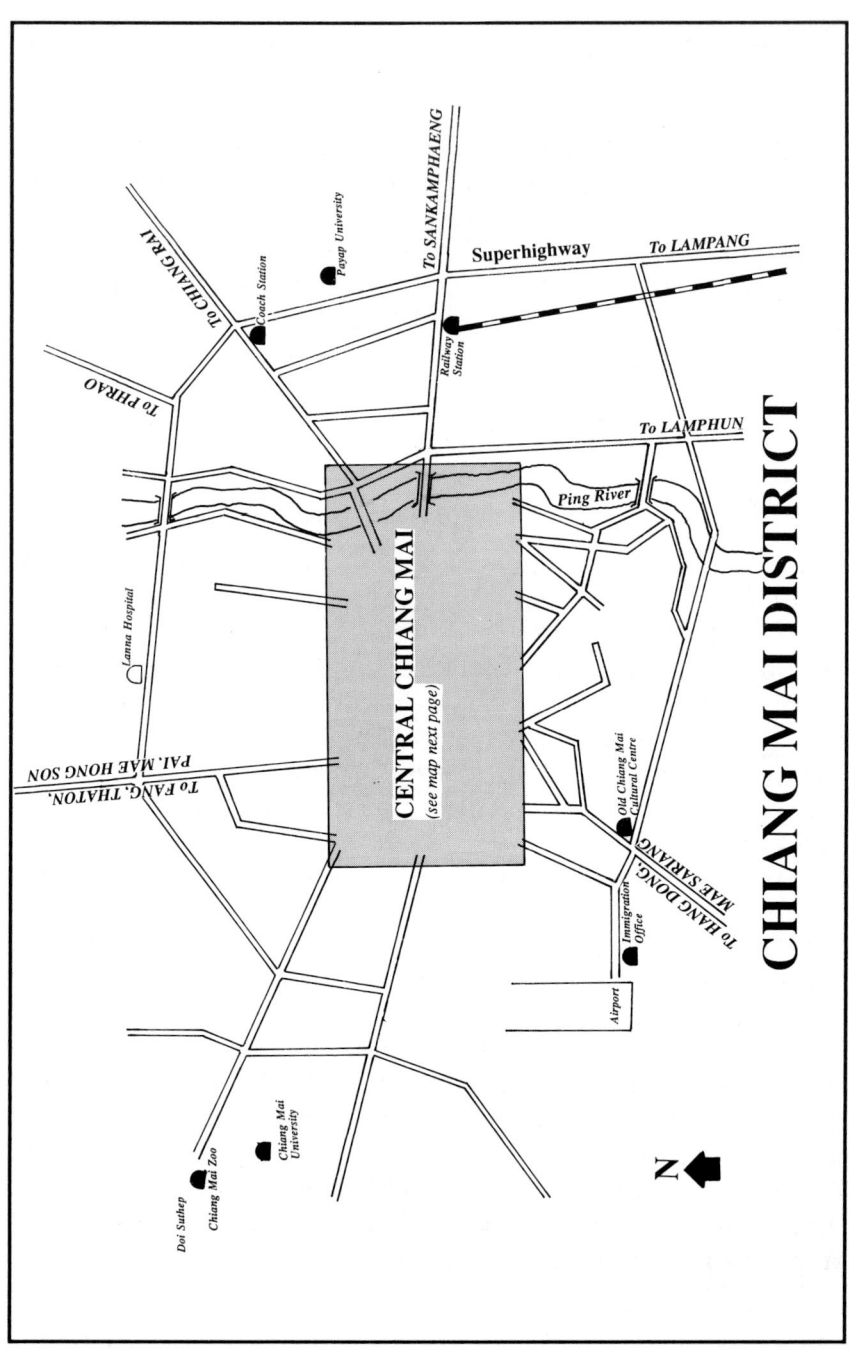

INTRODUCTION

EVERYONE LIKES CHIANG MAI. Tourists - both Thai and international - flock here in their millions. The ambition of many Bangkok natives is to move here to escape the heat, overcrowding and pollution of the capital. Chiang Mai seems able to combine the relaxed, slow motion world of the Thai village with the facilities and sights of a big city - and it is big, Thailand's second biggest, with a population estimated at over one million. Its popularity has led to rapid growth, with plans afoot to build a new town five kilometres to the east of its present site.

For the tourist, Chiang Mai has a great deal to offer. It has a huge range of excellent accommodations, restaurants, bars, nightclubs, temples, museums, gardens and probably the best shopping in the country.

In a land of smiling and beautiful people, the inhabitants of Chiang Mai are even friendlier and more beautiful. It is said by other Thais that the girls of Chiang Mai are lazy - they are so beautiful they do not have to work.

Tourism has become Chiang Mai's biggest industry, but there is here a great diversity of other business. Chiang Mai produces silverware, silk, paper, leather goods, statuary, lacquerware, clothes, implements and art. It is a market and service centre for a huge area of the north. The city is in a very fertile, wide valley, so is a major centre for the sale and production of agricultural products. It is an educational centre, with two major universities, two international schools and a Hill Tribe Research Centre as well as many colleges. Chiang Mai's three hundred temples give the city an important religious and architectural heritage.

Chiang Mai is very busy but never rushed. Its people go about their business with grace and good humour, always prepared to enjoy to the full what free moments can be spared.

For the tourist, Chiang Mai, apart from the charms of the city itself, makes an important base for exploring the rest of the north. Within twenty kilometres of the city centre are high mountains covered in dense forest, rushing streams and waterfalls, elephant camps, orchid farms and unspoilt hill tribe villages. Within seventy kilometres are the two highest mountains in Thailand with altitudes over 2200 metres. Burma, Laos, Chiang Rai and the Maekhong and Maekok rivers are within 250 kilometres to the north.

HISTORY

Chiang Mai was founded by the illustrious King Mengrai - that hero of north Thai history who moulded the Lanna nation from the disparate groups of Thai, Mon and Lawa people who inhabited the area previously. Mengrai started his conquest probably in Chiang Saen, establishing Chiang Rai as his first capital, but moving it to Chiang Mai in 1296 AD, following his defeat of the Haripunchai empire based at Lamphun. The site had been occupied before, by a tribe of the Lawa, who seem to have been absorbed rather than conquered by the Thais (some historians suggest that Mengrai himself was half Lawa). Although Mengrai had his main palace at Chiang Rai, according to legend he was killed by lightning whilst visiting Chiang Mai.

The original city was entirely within a moat and high walls, which have been reconstructed since and still surround the centre of town. The royal palace was on the site now occupied by Yupparat High School, but was demolished 80 years ago.

Continuous wars with the Burmese from the 15th to the 18th century, during most of which time Chiang Mai was under Burmese suzerainty, saw the population fall, and the city was even abandoned for some years. With the defeat of the Burmese in 1780 AD, the city bloomed again, and expanded beyond its moated walls. In the early 19th century new walls were added in a semi circle to the south west of the old city. These walls, now overgrown with vegetation, can still be seen on the south side of Kamphaengdin Road. This outer town became, and still is, the busiest area, containing most of the markets and shops. Chiang Mai at the turn of the century was a busy international trading centre, regularly receiving caravans from Yunnan in South West China, the Shan states of Burma and Luang Prabang in Laos. At this time 8000 elephants were used as beasts of burden in and around the city. Links with Bangkok were difficult, involving a journey of up to 66 days, until the railway was completed in 1927. Until the 1860s, westerners were unknown in the region. Then, in 1867, a team of American Presbyterians established a mission in Chiang Mai. Although not successful in gaining converts to Christianity, they did open schools and hospitals and improved the life of the population. Realizing this, the central government, under the enlightened King Mongkut, (of " The King and I" fame), encouraged missions throughout the north. In Chiang Mai, missionaries were responsible for the founding of Payap university, McCormick Hospital and the Mckean Leprosy Hospital, all of which are in existence today. In the early years of this century, British logging companies established themselves in Chiang Mai. Some old colonial buildings are still standing, notably the British Council off Nawarat Road.

The British had plans to add Northern Thailand to their Burmese territories, but were put off by Thai shrewdness and a fear of having a common border with French Indo-China to the east. In 1927 the King of Siam (the former name of Thailand) visited Chiang Mai. This was the first visit of a Bangkok based king, indicating the new found importance of the north. From this date, Chiang Mai became completely integrated into the mainstream of the Thai nation, and is now one of the most prosperous cities in Thailand.

GEOGRAPHY

Chiang Mai, at an altitude of 300 metres, is situated on the banks of the Ping river, which rises on the Burma border 200 kilometres north, and flows into the Chao Phraya at Nakhon Sawan 300 kilometres south. Although almost surrounded by mountain ranges, there is no feeling of being in a mountain town. Chiang Mai itself and the surrounding valley is very level, but to the west of the city is the mountain and National Park of Doi Pui, with a good metalled road almost to the summit only 20 kilometres distant. It frowns over the city causing cloud and occasional rain, even in the dry season. Continuing west, almost unbroken mountain ranges extend to the Burmese border. Chiang Mai itself is at the edge of a flat valley 15 kilometres wide, with more high mountains to the east through which the road to Chiang Rai passes. North, the Ping valley gradually narrows, the main road to Fang and Thaton crossing hills north of Chiang Dao before entering the Maekok river valley. Seventy kilometres south, the Ping river has been dammed to produce the 100 kilometre long Bhumipol reservoir.

LAY OUT

The centre of Chiang Mai is on the west bank of the Ping river, but the city has spread several kilometres to the east, particularly around the railway station, so that the busiest part of town is on and around the Nawarat bridge, one of five bridges crossing the river in the city.

The old walled city has sides 1.5 kilometres long, facing exactly north, south, east and west. Within the walls are a number of important temples, schools, government offices, a large and pretty park in the south west corner, a food market and "flower garden" where plants and animals are sold. Most activity focuses on the four gates into the old city.

Busiest is Thapae Gate, the west gate. This is at the top of the main shopping street of the city, Thapae Road, which leads up from Nawarat bridge. The road is lined with supermarkets, travel agents, restaurants, specialised shops, food stalls and street vendors. At the bottom of the road, on the north side near the river, is a busy night and day market in a maze of tiny alleys. To the south, 200 metres west of the river on Changklan Road is the "Night Bazaar", mainly under cover, surrounded by several large hotels. This is the main shopping area for tourists, selling every possible type of souvenir. This opens at 6.00 pm and closes at 11.00 pm. It is the busiest part of Chiang Mai in the evenings. There are several small, pleasant and peaceful *sois* off Thapae Road in which a number of good guest houses are situated. Around Thapae Gate is a large pedestrian square under the city walls where open air festivals, concerts and meetings are held. Near and to the west of the square is a concentration of guest houses, shops, bars and restaurants - really the "tourist quarter" of the city. Moon Muang Road and its several *sois* are almost entirely devoted to tourism.

The northern gate is Chang Puak (white elephant). Another busy intersection, Chang Puak Road leads north from here, to the bus station for services to Fang, Hot and Lamphun. Of little interest to visitors, Chang Puak specialises in electrical goods and furniture.

Suan Dok Gate (beautiful garden) is on the east wall. Just outside, along Sutep Road, is the large Suan Dok hospital, with medical and nursing schools. Further along on the south side is Wat Suan Dok, one of the most important and splendid of Chiang Mai's temples. To the south of the Gate, inside the moat, is the flower garden, selling plants and livestock. There are a number of restaurants continuing along the inside of the moat towards the southern gates. Suan Prung Gate leads to the park, and further east Chiang Mai Gate has a large food market inside the moat.

Huay Kaeo Road, leading from the north west corner of the moat, leads to Doi Sutep and Doi Pui National Park. There are several luxury hotels, Chiang Mai University, the Zoo and Botanic Gardens along this road.

TRANSPORT

PLANE

There are at least nine arrivals a day from Bangkok, and four a week from Phuket. Chiang Mai is the hub of the Thai Airways network for Northern Thailand, with direct flights to;

Bangkok:	07.45, 9.20, 12.10, 14.05, 17.35, 18.35, 20.45 (daily)
Chiang Rai:	13.15 (Monday, Wednesday, Sunday)
	14.35 (daily except Friday and Sunday)
Mae Hong Son:	10.40 and 16.55 (daily)
Mae Sot:	14.45 (Monday, Tuesday, Thursday, Saturday)
Nan:	15.35 (Wednesday, Friday, Sunday)
Phitsanulok:	13.55 (Monday, Tuesday, Thursday, Saturday)
	15.35 (Wednesday, Friday, Sunday)
	18.30 (Thursday, Saturday)
Tak:	13.55 (Monday, Tuesday, Thursday, Saturday)

For those continuing on to the beaches of the south, there are flights to:

Phuket: 11.35 (Monday, Wednesday, Friday, Sunday)
Surat Thani (for Ko Samui): 12.45 (Monday, Thursday)

TRAIN

Trains for Bangkok leave at 06.30, 15.30, 17.15, 19.30, 20.45. They stop in the north at Lamphun, Khun Tan National Park, Lampang, Denchai and Phitsanulok. Second class seats and particularly sleepers should be booked at least three days in advance at the railway station, Charoenmuang Road.

COACH

The coach station is between Kaew Nawarat Road and the Superhighway. There are frequent and extensive services to all towns in the north, Bangkok and Pattaya. There are many private companies, with constantly changing schedules and prices. The most comfortable coaches are called "VIP".

THINGS TO SEE

TEMPLES

As the capital of the Lanna Empire, at one time Chiang Mai was the religious centre of a vast area extending into Laos, Burma and Southern China. Its temple designs were distinct and much copied and admired throughout the north. With the conquest of the city by the Burmese, many features were added on or changed, and in the 1930's, on the integration of Chiang Mai into Bangkok centred Thailand, many temples were modernised to reflect the capital's tastes and features. Since at this time western taste had become fashionable, and western artists used as designers, some temple art may remind visitors of European "art deco". There are 36 temples within the walls of the old city, and another 85 inside the city limits. Very few, however, have survived intact, and temple purists may be disappointed with the "improvements", which many find garish and lacking in character.

 Wat Phra Sing ✓✓✓ Near the junction of Ratchadamnoen and Singhawat Roads, this temple was founded in 1345 AD to receive the remains of the Lanna King Kham Fu. There is a large but unexceptional *wiharn* built in 1925 AD, and behind this is an older *wiharn* built in 1806 AD. This very beautiful building - known as the Lae Kham chapel - houses the famous Buddha Phra Sing - an early bronze brought from Chiang Rai by King Saen Muang Ma, and the subject of many tales and legends.

 The walls of the *wiharn* are a series of lovely murals, depicting Buddhist tales including *Sawannahonse*, the golden bird monster. The style is primitive, and depicts revealing glimpses of ordinary Chiang Mai life from 100 years ago, when the murals were completed. In front of the wiharn are *nagas* and *singhas* in pure Lanna style. The library, constructed in 1920, is a beautifully proportioned building atop a white podium decorated with stucco *devas*. It houses delicate Sa or mulberry leaf papers on which holy men recorded folklore and the teachings of Buddha.

 Wat Chedi Luang ✓✓✓ On Phra Pokkloa Road, was built in 1401 AD, but destroyed by an earthquake in 1545 AD and never restored. The *chedi* was at one time 86 metres high. Its ruins are decorated with beautiful figures flanking the steps. Within the compound is a tall gum tree - it is said that if this dies, Chiang Mai will fall. At its base is an obelisk marking the spot where King Mengrai was supposedly struck by lightning.

Wat Suan Dok ✓✓✓ To the west side of Sutep Road, one kilometre north of Suan Dok Gate. Originally a flower garden for the Lanna royal family, built in 1383 AD, the temple contains tombs of the royal families of Chiang Mai behind the vast 1930's built *wiharn*. The main feature is a large white Sri Lankan style *chedi* built at the end of the 14th century. The temple complex is spacious and well tended. It is a good spot to watch the sunset over Doi Pui. Near the main entrance on Sutep Road is a school of Thai massage, where the best traditional massages can be enjoyed for 180 *baht*.

Wat Umong ✓✓ Reached by turning west near the top of Sutep Road. The temple is 1.5 kilometres along a narrow lane, surrounded by forest. The trees at the entrance to the temple are decorated with sayings in English and Thai. Built in the 13th century by King Mengrai as a peaceful meditation centre for his monks, most of the above ground structures have been lost, leaving underground tunnels to the monks cells, some containing traces of the earliest known examples of Lanna art from the 15th century. The *chedi* above the cells is a recent construction, but lying among the trees can be found fragments of old sculptures and statues. The modern monastery is very active - and has several western Buddhist monks who give sermons in English.

Wat Saen Fang ✓✓ On Kamphaengdin Road, near Thapae Road. A very ornate and pretty temple with much Burmese influence, it was built about 100 years ago. The high chedi is decorated with singhas, golden parasols and old guns, and is approached by a *naga* path. Opposite, **Wat Bupparam ✓** has a tiny old wooden chedi containing three large Buddha images.

Wat Ched Yot ✓ Is alongside the Superhighway near the National Museum. It was built by King Tilokaraja in 1455 AD. It houses a unique *chedi*, with a design based on the Indian temple of Bodgaya, where Buddha received enlightenment. The *chedi* is composed of seven *chedis* on a rectangular base, the largest containing the ashes of King Tilokaraja. It is decorated with statues of seventy deities which have a delicate charm reflecting the peak of Lanna art.

CHIANG MAI ZOO ✓✓

At the end of Huay Kaeo Road, at the foot of the steep road ascending Doi Sutep and Doi Pui. A good zoo, with generally well housed animals. Most local mammals and birds of interest, as well as fauna from many other parts of the world, are kept here. There is a particularly good collection of South East Asian gibbons, some now very rare. Also a breeding pair of pygmy hippos. The gardens are pretty and well tended. Entrance 20 *baht*.

HILL TRIBE RESEARCH CENTRE ✓✓

At the far end of Huay Kaeo Road, 200 metres before the zoo, on the campus of Chiang Mai University. Open weekdays, 9.00 - 4.30.
 Essential visiting for anyone with an interest in the hill tribes. The nine hill tribes of Northern Thailand have been extensively researched, particularly by American anthropologists in connection with the Vietnam war. The research centre, funded by the west, contains an excellent museum of hill tribe life, and much up to date information. The library next door is an excellent reference centre, and sells maps of recommended routes to hill tribe villages.

CHIANG MAI NATIONAL MUSEUM ✓✓

On the Superhighway, close to **Wat Jed Yot**. An extensive collection of northern arts and crafts, including the face of the largest Buddha image cast in Thailand. Many terracottas from Haripunchai (Lamphun), and a good display of hill tribe artifacts.

THINGS TO DO

TREKS AND TOURS

Chiang Mai is the perfect base from which to tour Northern Thailand. There are many agencies running tours and treks to all parts of the north. For details of hill tribe treks and tours, see page 51-54.

RIVER CRUISES ✓✓
From the Riverside Restaurant, just north of Nawarat bridge, there is a boat trip along the Ping river every evening. The ticket price includes dinner.

ELEPHANT RIDES ✓✓✓
Elephant trips into the jungle are not to be missed - although after one hour it does become a little uncomfortable. The elephants are ridden and trained by mahouts, almost always Karen hill tribesmen. The mahout sits on the elephants

neck, and passengers on a two seat howdah behind. There are two elephant camps close to Chiang Mai, both in the Mae Sa valley 20 kilometres north of town.

Mae Sa Elephant camp is in a beautiful jungle clearing by the Mae Sa river. There is a show every morning at 9.30 am, after which rides of various durations are available. Pyongyang elephant camp is another 10 kilometres up the valley. The terrain here is a little more rugged, so the rides rather more adventurous. There are waterfalls and hill tribe villages to visit on elephant back.

Both camps charge about 600 *baht* per hour for an elephant.

ORCHID, SNAKE AND BUTTERFLY FARMS AND WATERFALLS ✓✓✓
Are all found in the Mae Sa valley. Without private transport, a tuk tuk can be hired for 250 *baht* per day. Buses and *songthaews* go the nearby town of Mae Rim from Chiang Puak bus station, from Mae Rim get another songthaew to the valley.

SHOPPING ✓✓✓
Chiang Mai is a wonderful shopping centre. The main centre for souvenirs and goods of interest to tourists is the Night Bazaar, on Changklan Road. There is an enclosed area on three floors, and on the streets outside is an informal jumble of stalls. Next to the night bazaar is a large square in which Thai music, dancing and displays are held on most nights. The area is always busy at night, and browsing through the enormous variety of goods on display, from childrens toys to priceless antiques, is always enjoyable. The best bargains are in clothes, leather goods, cassettes, watches, lacquerware, wooden carvings and games, luggage and hill tribe handicrafts. In one corner, skilled artists paint umbrellas, T-shirts and portraits. At the rear, hill tribes people sell traditional jewellery, clothing, bags, carvings and curios. The area is littered with food stalls selling fried bananas, doughnuts, *satay*, barbecues, meats and fried rice. On the edge of the bazaar are many small bars and restaurants with cheap prices.

The day market - Talaat Warorot - is to the north of Thapae Road, near the river. The goods here are a little more prosaic, but the prices for items such as clothing are lower than the Night Bazaar. At night, the main street parallel to the river is a vegetable and flower market, open till about 4.00 am, although after 2.00 am, many of the stallholders will be sleeping on their produce.

PLACES TO EAT

Chiang Mai has a huge number of restaurants - from 7 *baht* delicacies at one of the thousands of food hawkers to a gourmet extravaganza at many a restaurant or hotel. Apart from Thai, there are foods for every taste and nationality - Indian, Chinese, Mexican, Japanese, French, Italian, American, British, German, at prices from ludicrously cheap to cheap!

THAI
Once Upon A Time, 385/2 Charoenpratet. Exquisite Thai food in a traditional Lanna-style teak building on the banks of the Ping river. Beautiful decor and service. (Expensive)
Gallery, Charoenrasad Road. On the east bank of the Ping river, 300 metres north of Nawarat bridge. Superb Thai food, decor, ambience and service. There is an art galley at the entrance, selling high quality works by local artists. (Expensive)
Galae, 2 kilometres north of town, at the top of Sutep Road. By a lake, with tables under the trees. All the food is good, but specialises in barbecues. (Medium)
Riverfront, 43/3 Changklan Road. By the Ping river, 1.5 kilometres south of the town centre. Lovely antique filled wooden Lanna house, good food and atmosphere. (Medium-expensive)
Ruan Come, Corner of Kotchasarn and Loikhro Roads. Good, traditional Thai food in covered, open air restaurant with excellent traditional Thai singers. (Medium)
Aroon Rai, 45 Kotchasarn Road. Famous locally, specialising in traditional Chiang Mai food. Pick your selection from the display - which usually includes deep fried grasshoppers and ants. Not plush, but good, authentic food.(Cheap)
Klua Kun Pen, Intharawot Road, 100 metres east of Suan Dok Gate. Large selection of Thai food, served buffet style, in a pleasant, clean, Lanna style wooden restaurant. (Cheap)
Riverside. On the Ping river, 200 metres north of Nawarat bridge. The food is not exceptional, but the menu is vast and the position and ambience excellent. The best live music in Chiang Mai. Very popular. (Medium)
Kaithong, 67 Kotchasarn Road. A bit of a tourist trap, specialising in "jungle"

food. The menu includes python, cobra, crocodile and tortoise - and that's just the reptiles! (Expensive)
Baan Suan, 51/3 Chiang Mai-Sankampaeng Road. Specialising in Northern Thai food. Lovely garden setting. (Expensive)
JJs A very popular airconditioned restaurant in the Montri Hotel close to Thapae Gate. Excellent service and atmosphere, good choice of Thai and western food. The best coffee in Chiang Mai. (Cheap)
Anusarn Market. East of the Night Bazaar, between Loikhro and Sridonchai Roads. A complex of outdoor restaurants, many specialising in seafood. Very busy and exciting, browse for the restaurant that appeals to you (they are all good). At the bottom end of the market, on Charoenpratet Road, is a "flying vegetable" restaurant. Here, the chef will throw a pan of frying morning glory plants across the road to the diner, who stands on a high platform and tries to catch his dinner in mid-air. (Cheap-medium)
Sompet Market. 200 metres north of the Night Bazaar, many small, very basic restaurants serving a variety of Thai, Laotian and Chinese foods. (Cheap).

KHANTOKE THAI
Khantoke dinners are a traditional form of Thai hospitality. Several local dishes are served on a low table around which diners sit on cushions. A show of local singing, dancing and acrobatics accompanies the food.
Old Chiang Mai Cultural Centre, 183/3 Wualai Road. Several large teak houses have been converted and restored into a museum/restaurant serving khantoke dinners nightly. Cost 200 *baht*.
Lanna Khantoke, 183/5 Charoenpratet Road. Part of the Diamond Hotel, in a small theatre. Cost 200 *baht*.

CHINESE
Jade Lotus, 41 Moon Muang Road. Superb Cantonese food in a very beautiful air-conditioned restaurant. (Expensive)

ITALIAN
La Villa, 145 Ratchadamnoen Road. Pasta and pizza in a wood fired oven, nice atmosphere. (Medium)
Mr Chan and Miss Pauline, 2/4-6 Prachasamphan. Nice atmosphere, good service, pleasant decor, good pizzas and pasta. (Expensive)

GERMAN
Haus Munchen, Charoenpratet Soi 6, opposite Diamond Hotel. Open air restaurant in a lovely garden. German and Thai food. (Medium)
Bier Stube, 33/6A Moonmuang Road. German and Thai food. Popular with expats, pleasant service and atmosphere. Good breakfasts. (Medium)

JAPANESE
Sansui, 3/3 Mu 1, Chiang Mai-Sankampaeng Road. Japanese design and authentic Japanese food. (Expensive)

FRENCH
Le Jardin. Rooftop restaurant in the centre of town serving French and Thai food. Interesting setting, friendly service. (Medium)
Cafe de Paris, 14-16 Kotchasarn Road. Specialising in steaks with good French sauces. (Expensive)

INDIAN
The Whole Earth, 88 Sridonchai Road. Delicate, delicious Indian, Pakistani and Thai food. The restaurant is in a very beautiful Lanna house surrounded by a pretty tropical garden. (Medium).

MEXICAN
Taco Bell. No relation to the restaurant chain, a small restaurant with good Mexican meals and snacks. (Cheap).

KOREAN
Korean Restaurant, 193/3 Changklan Road. Specialising in steaks with hot and spicy Korean sauces. (Medium).

NIGHTLIFE

Nothing like the steamy, aggressive and frenetic nightlife of Bangkok, Chiang Mai nevertheless abounds with bars, nightclubs and discos to suit everyone's taste. Prices are generally low, and facilities vary from a bamboo shack with a few stools on the street to sumptuous establishments with laser shows and satin covered arm chairs.

Entertainment

BARS

Many bars in Chian Mai employ "hostesses", who will sit with any unattached males to encourage them to drink and to buy them drinks. Most are looking for a western 'boyfriend', many for a potential western husband, usually for economic reasons. They can be regarded as little better than prostitutes, or as part of an informal dating agency. Most of these bars are concentrated around the western tourist area just to the west of Thapae Gate. The atmosphere in these bars is pleasant, and couples should not feel intimidated by the girls.

HOSTESS BARS
Paradise, 26/1 Ratchamanka Soi 2. A nicely designed and decorated bar with very friendly staff and service. Music videos in the evenings.
Black Cat, 25 Moon Muang Road. With a pretty garden, serving barbecued snacks in the evenings. Video movies from 13.00. Comfortable and very relaxed.
Big Bar Beer. A popular nightspot, simply furnished with bamboo walls and furniture and many hostesses. Cheap drinks.
Spotlight. A dark, cavernous bar with very loud music videos and slightly aggressive hostesses.

NON HOSTESS BARS
Hard Rock Cafe, 6 Kotchasarn Road, Soi 1. No relation to the chain. Good, mainly 70's rock music, pleasant staff, good burgers. Popular with ex-pats.
The Pub, Huay Kaew Road. For nostalgia seeking Brits, authentic British pub decor and atmosphere in a lovely tropical garden.
Marble Bar, 100/3 Huay Kaew Road. Popular with rich Thais, lovely decor and excellent live Thai music - but expensive drinks.
Domino Bar, Moonmuang Road, opposite Thapae Gate. British snacks, excellent live folk and rock music.
Bar Beer Centre. West side of Thapae Gate, along a small soi. A complex of 25 small bars, Thai boxing displays every evening at 8.00 pm, entry 20 *baht*.

GAY BARS
Homosexuality is far more accepted in Thailand than in the west. Chiang Mai has a number of gay bars, most having transvestite cabaret or male go-go dancers.
Coffee Boy, 248 Toonghotel Road, Tel: (053)244458. Beautiful Lanna decor, very luxurious. Shows weekends 11.00 pm

Butterfly Room, 126 Loikhro Road. Tel: (053)279315 Newly refurbished.
Macho Bar, Nantaram Road, Soi 1. Friendly bar with excellant go go dancers.

DISCOTHEQUES
Discos are very popular and fashionable in Thailand. They are usually expensively equipped with light shows, etc. Drinks tend be pricey, but nevertheless most will be very busy after 11.00 pm, especially at weekends. Thai pop music, excellent for dancing, is interspersed with western pop. **Bubbles**, in the **Pornping Hotel**, Charoenpratet Soi 2, the **Plaza disco** in the Plaza Hotel at 92, Sridonchai Road and **The Wall** in the Chiang Inn Hotel, next to the Night Bazaar, are the most prestigious.

MASSAGE

Traditional Thai massage is an ancient art which calms the mind and soothes the body. It is however, rather vigorous in application, and can be uncomfortable at the time. The flexibility of the western body is usually less than that of the more sinuous Thais, and masseurs tend to push our joints rather further than they have ever been pushed before. However, for most the benefits outweigh the pain! There are several establishments offering a massage service. The price varies between 150-200 *baht*. Many tuk-tuk drivers act as touts for the bigger parlours, and will receive a hefty commission for delivering you, which pushes up the price to the customer.

Many so called massage parlours are in fact selling sex - make sure the word "authentic" or "ancient" is included in the text, if you do not require "sensual" massage - which is much more expensive!
Rinkaew Complex. Expert masseurs, with Thai herbal and Finnish sauna, lounge, restaurant and night club.
Suan-Dok. Outside Wat Suan Dok along Sutep Road. Basic facilities but perhaps the best massage in Chiang Mai. One month massage training courses also offered.

BOOKSHOPS

DK Books, half way down Thapae Road, has the largest selection of English language books and maps, but **Suriwong Book Centre**, 54/1 Sridonchai Road comes a close second. Near Thapae Gate, on Thapae Road and Kotchasarn Road are two small English language bookshops selling maps, newspapers and guide books. The *Library Service* on 21/1 Ratchamanka, near Thapae Gate, has a large collection of second-hand books for sale, and some new titles. Snacks and drinks are served at the pleasant "browsing tables". The management here is expert in touring the north, and are always happy to give advice. Ask for David.

POST OFFICES

The main post office is at Charoenmuang Road, 200 metres north of the railway station. On the second floor is an efficient international telephone office. Other post offices are at Praisanee Road, Prapogglia Road, Chotana Road and Chiang Mai airport.

TOURIST AUTHORITY OF THAILAND

The main TAT office for Northern Thailand is near the Rimping supermarket on the Chiang Mai - Lamphun road, just south of the Nawarat bridge on the east bank of the river. They provide lists of accommodation, and are an important source of help and advice.

HOSPITALS AND CLINICS

Lanna Hospital, on the Superhighway, is the most expensive. Tel: (053)211037-41. The other major hospitals are **McCormick Hospital**, Kaew Nawarat Road. Tel: (053)241107, **Suan Dok Hospital** on Sutep Road (often crowded). Tel: (053)221122 and **Huay Kaeo Polyclinic**, Huay Kaeo Road. Tel: (053)223060. There are many clinics scattered around Chiang Mai, identified by a green cross outside.

ACCOMMODATION

There are over 200 hotels and guest houses in Chiang Mai. The range of prices and levels of comfort are enormous, from a 30 *baht* dormitory bed to a 14,000 *baht* luxury hotel suite. However much you pay, you will get good value for money.

The selection of accommodation given below offer some features which stand out in some way - very beautiful or interesting location, good value for money, good atmosphere and high standards. The omission of any guest house or hotel from this list does not indicate any negative inference.

RESORTS

Chiang Mai Lakeside Ville ❂❂❂❂
Lovely traditional Thai chalets built on and around a small natural lake. Rooms comfortable but not luxurious. Attractive design and peaceful location.
Address: 308 Moo 1, Nong Phung, Soi 8, Sarapee, Chiang Mai. **Tel**: (Bangkok Office) (01)5100258
Price: 800-1000 **Rooms**: 20 **Fan**: 20 **Bathroom**: 20(hw) **Comfort**: ☆☆☆ **Design**: ☆☆☆☆☆
Location: ☆☆☆☆ **Position**: 7 kilometres south of Chiang Mai 500 metres west of Lamphun Road
Quietness: ☆☆☆☆☆ **Restaurant**: ☆☆☆

Riverfront ❂❂❂❂
A large and ornate teak Lanna Thai house converted to popular guest house and restaurant on the banks of the Ping river.
Address: 43/3 Muang, Tambon Pardad, Changkarm Road, Chiang Mai 50000 **Tel**: (053)275125
Price: 250-600 **Rooms**: 21 **A/C**: 2 **Fan**: 19 **Bathroom**: 7(hw), 14(cw) **Comfort**: ☆☆☆ to ☆☆☆☆
Design: ☆☆☆☆☆ **Location**: ☆☆☆☆ **Position**: 1.5 kilometres south of city centre on Ping river
Quietness: ☆☆☆ **Restaurant**: ☆☆☆☆

HOTELS

Pornping ❂❂❂❂❂
International standard luxury hotel, beautifully furnished rooms and with all facilities, good central location.
Address: 46-48 Charoenpratet, Chiang Mai 50000 **Tel**: (053)270099.
Price: 1200-9000 **Rooms**: 324 **A/C**: 324 **Bathroom**: 324(hw) **Comfort**: ☆☆☆☆☆
Design: ☆☆☆☆ **Location**: ☆☆☆ **Position**: Central **Quietness**: ☆☆☆☆ **Restaurant**: ☆☆☆☆
Facilities: pool, TV, VDO, bar, fridge, disco, nightclub **Tours/treks**: Range of tours

Yao mother and daughter, Mae Chan, Chiang Rai

Akha ladies, Doi Tung, Chiang Rai

Geyser, Fang National Park, Fang, Chiang Mai

Statue gilding, Chiang Rai

The stream separating Thailand from Burma, Mae Sai, Chiang Rai

Rincome ●●●●●
Luxury hotel with beautifully designed interiors.
Address: Huay Kaew Road, Chiang Mai 50000 **Tel:** (053)221044, 221130 **Fax:** (053)221915
Price: 1900-7000 **Rooms:** 150 **A/C:** 150 **Bathroom:** 150(hw) **Comfort:** ☆☆☆☆☆
Design: ☆☆☆☆ **Location:** ☆☆☆☆ **Position:** 2kilometyres north of town centre
Quietness: ☆☆☆☆ **Restaurant:**☆☆☆☆ **Facilities:** pools, TV, VDO, bar
Tours/Treks: wide range of tours

Rim Ping Garden ●●●●●
Elegant large and luxurious rooms in an exclusive small hotel surrounded by a tropical garden and pretty swimming pool on banks of Ping river.
Address: 411 Charoenpratet, Chiang Mai 50000 **Tel:** (053)281060 **Fax:** (053)281059
Price: 1452-1694 **Rooms:** 20 **A/C:** 20 **Bathroom:** 20(hw) **Comfort:** ☆☆☆☆☆ **Design:** ☆☆☆☆☆
Location: ☆☆☆☆ **Position:** 1 kilometre south of city centre **Quietness:** ☆☆☆☆
Restaurant: ☆☆☆☆ **Facilities:** pool, TV, video, bar, fridge

Chiang Mai Orchid ●●●●●
Elegant luxury hotel close to Doi Pui National Park.
Address: 100-102 Huay Kaew Road, Chiang Mai, 50000 **Tel:** (053)222099
Price: 1700-14000 **Rooms:** 267 **A/C:** 267 **Bathroom:** 267(hw) **Comfort:** ☆☆☆☆☆
Design: ☆☆☆☆ **Location:** ☆☆☆☆ **Position:** 2 kilometres north of city centre
Facilities: pools, TV, video, bar, fridge, nightclub, disco. **Tours/Treks:** Range of tours

President ●●●●
Formerly a luxury hotel, now offering 5 star facilities at a comparatively cheap price.
Address: 226 Vitchayonom Road, Chiang Mai 50000 **Tel:** (053)251020 **Price:** 700-3000
Rooms: 120 **A/C:** 120 **Bathroom:** 120(hw) **Comfort:** ☆☆☆☆ **Design:** ☆☆☆
Location: ☆☆☆☆ **Position:** central **Quietness:** ☆☆☆ **Restaurant:** ☆☆☆
Facilities: pool, fridge, bar, TV, video. **Treks/Tours:** Range of Tours

Montri ●●●●
Very central, recently refurbished hotel with comfortable, well furnished rooms and a lively atmosphere.
Address: Thapae Gate, Chiang Mai 50000 **Tel:** (053)211069, 211070. **Fax:** (053)217416
Price: 320-470 **Rooms:** 80 **A/C:** 55 **Fan:** 25 **Bathroom:** 80(hw) **Comfort:** ☆☆☆ to ☆☆☆☆
Design: ☆☆☆☆ **Location:** ☆☆☆☆ **Position:** central **Quietness:** ☆☆☆ **Restaurant:** ☆☆☆☆
Facilities: TV, video **Tours/treks:** wide range

Prince ●●●●
Pleasant, comfortable well appointed rooms in a popular, well organized hotel, just below luxury level.
Address: 3 Tai Wang Road, Chiang Mai 50000.
Price: 600-1800 **Rooms:** 46 **A/C:** 35 **Fan:** 11 **Bathroom:** 46(hw) **Comfort:** ☆☆☆ to ☆☆☆☆
Design: ☆☆☆ **Location:** ☆☆☆ **Position:** central **Quietness:** ☆☆☆ **Restaurant:** ☆☆☆
Facilities: small pool, minibar, TV, video

New Mitrapap ✪✪✪
Very comfortable and spotlessly clean rooms in a utilitarian well organized hotel catering mainly for Thai guests. Good value.
Address: 94-98 Rachawong, Chiang Mai 50000 **Tel:** (053)235205-6 **Fax:** (053)251260
Price: 250-550 **Rooms:** 90 **A/C:** 57 **Fan:** 33 **Bathroom:** 57(hw) **Comfort:** ☆☆☆ to ☆☆☆☆ **Design:** ☆☆☆ **Location:** ☆☆☆ **Position:** central **Quietness:** ☆☆☆ **Restaurant:** ☆☆☆
Facilities: TV, bar (A/C rooms)

Sumit ✪✪
Large Thai hotel, going to seed a little but good value.
Address: 198 Rajpikinai Road **Tel:** (053)211033
Price: 200-350 **Rooms:** 80 **A/C:** 18 **Fan:** 62 **Bathroom:** 80(hw) **Comfort:** 200-350 **Design:** ☆☆ **Location:** ☆☆☆ **Position:** central **Quietness:** ☆☆☆

GUEST HOUSES

High Price Range (over 400 baht)

Once Upon A Time ✪✪✪✪✪
Idyllically romantic rooms with all modern facilities but traditional design and furnishings in very lovely teak houses on banks of Ping river.
Address: 385/2 Charoenpratet **Tel:** (053)274932
Price: 483-2036 **Rooms:** 10 **A/C:** 10 **Bathroom:** 10(hw) **Comfort:** ☆☆☆☆☆ **Design:** ☆☆☆☆☆ **Location:** ☆☆☆☆ **Position:** 1 kilometre south of town centre **Quietness:** ☆☆☆ **Restaurant:** ☆☆☆☆ **Facilities:** minibar, flowers, fruit, perfume provided daily

Galare ✪✪✪✪
Lovely Thai style guest house on east bank of Ping river. Very comfortable but slightly small rooms.
Address: 7 Charoenpratet, Chiang Mai 50000 **Tel:** (053)273885.
Price: 444-555 **Rooms:** 35 **A/C:** 22 **Fan:** 13 **Bathroom:** 35(hw) **Comfort:** ☆☆☆ to ☆☆☆☆ **Design:** ☆☆☆☆ **Location:** ☆☆☆☆ **Position:** central **Quietness:** ☆☆☆ **Restaurant:** ☆☆☆
Tours/Treks: range of tours

River View Lodge ✪✪✪✪
Pretty luxury guest house in beautiful gardens on banks of Ping river near town centre.
Address: 25 Charoenpratet Soi 2 **Tel:** (053)271109 **Fax:** (053)279019
Price: 1000-1500 (inc. bkfst) **Rooms:** 36 **A/C:** 36 **Bathroom:** 36(hw) **Comfort:** ☆☆☆☆ **Design:** ☆☆☆☆ **Location:** ☆☆☆☆ **Position:** central **Quietness:** ☆☆☆☆ **Restaurant:** ☆☆☆ **Facilities:** TV, fridge, minibar **Tours/treks:** range of tours.

GUEST HOUSES

Mid Price Range (100-400 Baht)

Gaps House ●●●●
Very beautiful teak bungalows in an antique strewn garden. Large and well furnished rooms with good facilities in lovely setting.
Address: 3 Rajadamnern Soi 4, Chiang Mai 50000 **Tel** and **Fax:** (053)278140
Price: 300-525 (inc bkfst) **Rooms:** 18 **A/C:** 18 **Bathroom:** 18(hw) **Comfort:** ☆☆☆☆
Design: ☆☆☆☆☆ **Location:** ☆☆☆☆ **Position:** central **Quietness:** ☆☆☆ **Restaurant:** snacks
Tours/treks: wide range

Top North ●●●●
Large, well managed, comfortable guest house, best rooms in new wing. Pretty swimming pool.
Address: 15 Moonmuang Soi 2, Chiang Mai 50000 **Tel:** (053)213900
Price: 250-400 **Rooms:** 44 **A/C:** 26 **Fan:** 18 **Bathroom:** 44(hw) **Comfort:** ☆☆☆ to ☆☆☆☆
Design: ☆☆☆☆ **Location:** ☆☆☆ **Position:** central **Quietness:** ☆☆☆ **Restaurant:** ☆☆☆
Tours/treks: wide range, well organized

Fang ●●●●
Very nicely designed and furnished new guest house in quiet but central Soi near Thapae Road.
Address: 46-48 Kampaengdin Road Soi 1, Chiang Mai 50000 **Tel:** (053)282940,272505,272500
Price: 150-250 **Rooms:** 28 **A/C:** 12 **Fan:** 16 **Bathroom:** 28(hw) **Comfort:** ☆☆☆ to ☆☆☆☆
Design: ☆☆☆☆ **Location:** ☆☆☆☆ **Position:** central **Quietness:** ☆☆☆☆
Restaurant: ☆☆☆ **Tours/treks:** range of treks

Homeplace ●●●
Pleasant, comfortable, well furnished rooms in a small, quiet but central soi.
Address: 9 Soi 6, Thapae Rd, Chiang Mai 50000 **Tel:** (053)273493-4
Price: 200-400 **Rooms:** 26 **A/C:** 10 **Fan:** 36 **Bathroom:** 26(hw) **Comfort:** ☆☆☆ to ☆☆☆☆
Design: ☆☆☆☆ **Location:** ☆☆☆ **Position:** central **Quietness:** ☆☆☆ **Restaurant:** snacks
Tours/treks: range of treks.

Ratchada ●●●
Modern guest house with large, clean and comfortable rooms and a pleasant atmosphere.
Address: 55 Thapae Road Soi 3, Chiang Mai 50000 **Tel:** (053)275588
Price: 180-220 **Rooms:** 21 **Fan:** 21 **Bathroom:** 21(hw) **Comfort:** ☆☆☆ **Design:** ☆☆☆☆
Location: ☆☆☆☆ **Position:** central **Quietness:** ☆☆☆☆ **Restaurant:** snacks
Tours/treks: range of treks

Kritsana ●●●
Beside a pretty temple garden at quiet end of busy soi. Pleasant situation, clean and comfortable rooms.
Address: 50\1 Moonmuang Soi 2, Chiang Mai 50000 **Tel:** (053)217762
Price: 120-150 **Rooms:** 12 **Fan:** 12 **Bathroom:** 12, 8(cw) 4(hw) **Comfort:** ☆☆☆ **Design:** ☆☆☆
Location: ☆☆☆☆ **Position:** central **Quietness:** ☆☆☆☆ **Restaurant:** snacks

Welcome ❀❀❀
Fairly clean and comfortable rooms in guest house with pleasant atmosphere.
Address: 48/4 Moonmuang Soi 2, Chiang Mai 50000 **Tel:** (053)278447
Price: 100-150 **Rooms:** 20 **Fan:** 20 **Bathroom:** 15(cw), 5(hw) **Comfort:** ☆☆ **Design:** ☆☆☆
Location: ☆☆☆ **Position:** central **Quietness:** ☆☆☆ **Restaurant:** snacks
Tours/treks: range of treks

Kent ❀❀❀
Modern, clean, tiled rooms in a shady and secluded but central guest house.
Address: 5 Soi 1 Ratchamanka Road, Chiang Mai 50000 **Tel:** (053)278578
Price: 100 **Rooms:** 16 **Fan:** 16 **Bathroom:** 16(cw) **Comfort:** ☆☆ **Design:** ☆☆☆☆
Location: ☆☆☆☆ **Position:** central **Quietness:** ☆☆☆ **Restaurant:** snacks
Tours/treks: range of treks.

Rama ❀❀❀
Clean, large rooms looking over garden and teak houses.
Address: Moonmuang Soi 5 **Tel:** (053)216454
Price: 110 **Rooms:** 17 **Fan:** 17 **Bathroom:** 17(cw)(hw outside) **Comfort:** ☆☆☆ **Design:** ☆☆☆
Location: ☆☆☆ **Position:** central **Quietness:** ☆☆☆ **Restaurant:** ☆☆
Tours/treks: range of treks

GUEST HOUSES

Low Price Range (under 100 baht)

Darets House ❀❀❀
Very popular guest house with large restaurant and excellent trekking.
Address: Chaiyapoom Road, near Thapae Gate, Chiang Mai 50000.
Price: 70-110 **Rooms:** 18 **Fan:** 18 **Bathroom:** 18(hw) **Comfort:** ☆☆☆ **Design:** ☆☆☆
Location: ☆☆☆☆ **Position:** central **Quietness:** ☆☆ **Restaurant:** ☆☆☆☆
Tours/treks: well organized treks

Times Square ❀❀❀
Popular guest house in small central soi. Most rooms basic, but A/C, large and comfortable. Good atmosphere.
Address: 2/10 Soi 6, Thapae Road, Chiang Mai 50000 **Tel:** (053)282448
Price: 70-280 **Rooms:** 15 **A/C:** 4 **Fan:** 11 **Bathroom:** 4(hw)(hw outside) **Comfort:** ☆☆ to ☆☆☆☆
Design: ☆☆☆ **Location:** ☆☆☆ **Position:** central **Quietness:** ☆☆☆
Restaurant: ☆☆☆(rooftop) **Tours/treks:** range of treks

Ban Pai ❀❀❀
Lovely clean and well kept pretty teak house in delightful tropical garden.
Address: 8/2 Thapae road Soi 4, Chiang Mai 5000 **Tel:** (053)279714
Price: 80-100 **Rooms:** 13 **Fan:** 13 **Bathroom:** 0(hw outside) **Comfort:** ☆☆ **Design:** ☆☆☆☆
Location: ☆☆☆☆ **Position:** central **Quietness:** ☆☆☆

Saitum House ✿✿✿
Pleasant rooms in small teak bungalows within a pretty garden, central but secluded and quite comfortable.
Address: 21 Moonmuang Road, Chiang Mai 50000 **Tel:** (053)278575
Price: 80-90 **Rooms:** 16 **Fan:** 16 **Bathroom:** 16(cw) **Comfort:** ☆☆ **Design:** ☆☆☆☆
Location: ☆☆☆☆ **Position:** central **Tours/treks:** range of treks

Lamchang House ✿✿✿
Large and pretty traditional style teak house in shady garden. Basic facilities but attractive and atmospheric.
Address: 24 Moonmuang Soi 7 **Tel:** (053)210586
Price: 80-90 **Rooms:** 8 **Fan:** 8 **Bathroom:** 0 (cw outside) **Comfort:** ☆ to ☆☆ **Design:** ☆☆☆☆
Location: ☆☆☆☆ **Position:** central **Quietness:** ☆☆☆ **Restaurant:** snacks

Numchok ✿✿
Lovely old colonial house in shady gardens. Rather neglected and basic rooms, but spacious and interesting accommodation.
Address: 193 Charoenraj road, Chiang Mai 50000 **Tel:** (053)241414
Price: 60-80 **Rooms:** 15 **Fan:** 15 **Bathroom:** 7(cw) (hw outside) **Comfort:** ☆ to ☆☆
Design: ☆☆☆☆ **Location:** ☆☆☆☆ **Position:** central **Quietness:** ☆☆☆☆ **Restaurant:** ☆☆

AROUND CHIANG MAI

Within a few kilometres and two hours driving of Chiang Mai, many of the most beautiful sights and enjoyable experiences of the north can easily be reached. These are all detailed in the following pages.

Surprisingly close to the city is the mountain and National Park of **Doi Pui** ✓✓✓. The hills reach to the western outskirts of the city, the good road climbing steeply upwards, passing close to a lovely waterfall, the **Matrathorn** ✓✓, to the magnificent temple of **Doi Sutep** ✓✓✓, visible from the city centre, but 1300 metres up. Four kilometres further leads to **Phuping palace** ✓✓, with its exquisite gardens open to the public at weekends, occasional home to the Thai royal family. Further on leads to some hill tribe villages and lovely mountain

Chiang Mai Area

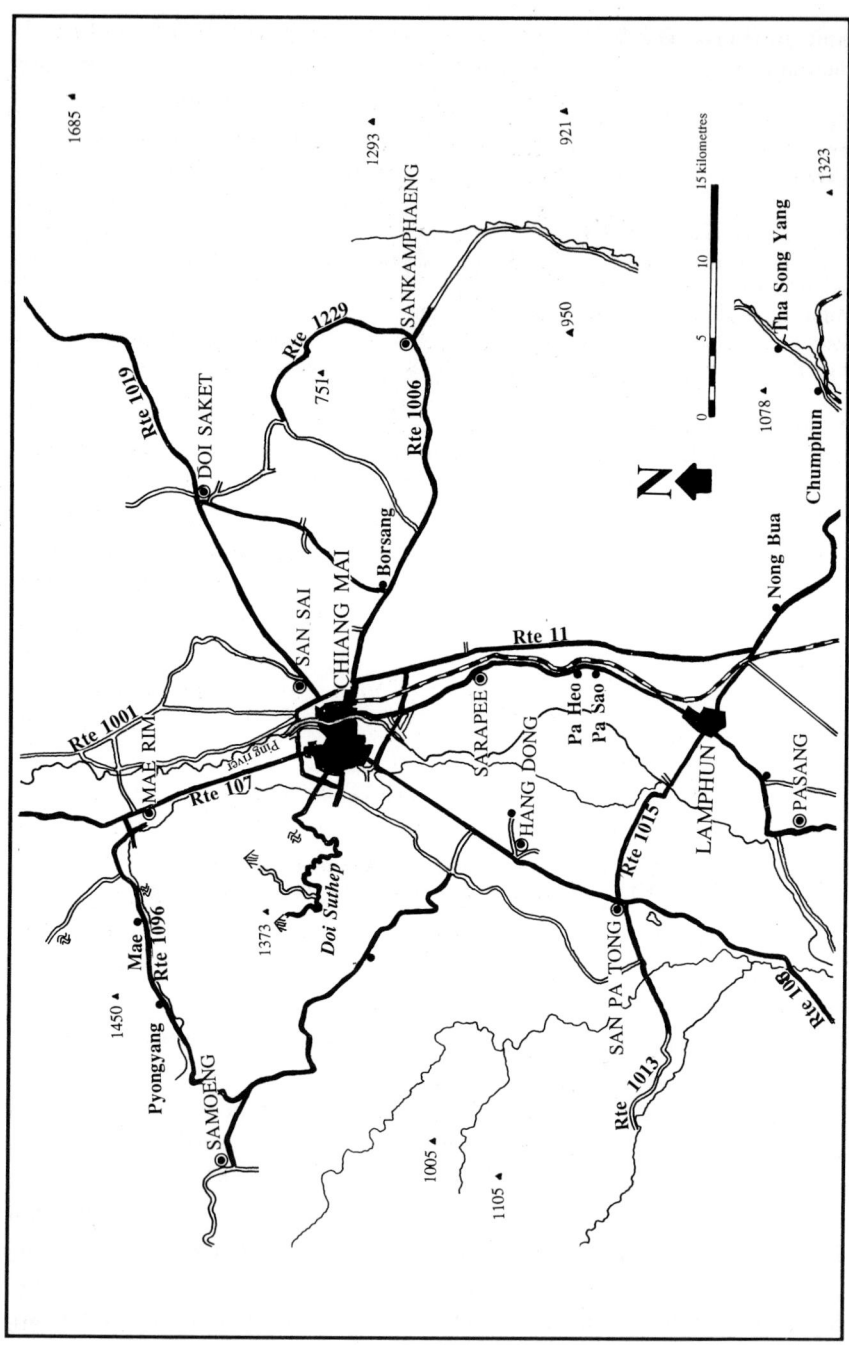

Around Chiang Mai

and jungle scenery. By rented vehicle, the trip can be completed comfortably in three hours.

For the shopper, and those interested in local arts and crafts, the villages of **Borsang** ✓✓ and **Sankampaeng** ✓✓ are only a few kilometres to the east of town. Here, factories specialising in such industries as silk spinning, lacquerware, silver engraving, umbrella making and china production are concentrated. Woodcarving is the speciality of **Hang Dong** ✓, 11 kilometres south of Chiang Mai. Slightly further afield, but still only 25 kilometres north of Chiang Mai, is the **Mae Sa valley** ✓✓✓. Here, amidst very beautiful hill scenery, elephants can be ridden and orchids and butterfly farms visited amongst some lovely trails leading to waterfalls and hill tribe villages. Continuing on this road, a circuit around the west of Chiang Mai is possible. After the tourist attractions of the valley itself, the road winds up and down hill to the sleepy, pretty mountain town of **Samoeng** ✓✓ and back to Chiang Mai through some remote and unspoilt countryside. At least four hours is needed for the valley itself, but one full day is needed to complete the circuit, and two days allows the visitor to spend a night at one of the lovely resorts in the valley. 25 kilometres south of Chiang Mai is the ancient city of **Lamphun** ✓✓. 1200 years ago the capital of an empire that predates Thailand, with a legendary queen, the temple architecture is magnificent and very different from anywhere else in the country. Lamphun is just 30 minutes drive from Chiang Mai, and makes an excellent half day trip.

Eighty kilometres south of Chiang Mai is the National park of Doi Inthanon. This is the area around the highest mountain in Thailand, which abounds in delightful waterfalls, mountain jungle scenery, caves and hill tribes. For those with an interest in walking and wildlife - particularly birds, this area is very special. Nearby is the town of **Chom Thong** ✓✓, with perhaps the prettiest old temple in the north. This trip is an easy day, although it is possible to stay in bungalows in the park.

SANKAMPHAENG

It is quite difficult not to go Sankampaeng if you are staying in Chiang Mai. Within minutes of arrival, *tuk-tuk* drivers will be flashing before your eyes lavish brochures showing the wonders to be seen on the road to this small town a few kilometres east of the city - and they will take you there very cheaply. The road to Sankamphaeng is lined for the first 12 kilometres with small workshops and showrooms where local artisans demonstrate their skills, producing goods which go straight into the showroom next door. The town is also famous for its beautiful girls, although in a country of beautiful girls it seems unfair to pick out one small town.

The driver who is so keen to take you there is not solely concerned for your enjoyment. He receives a fat commission from every showroom he takes you to, whether or not you buy anything. Although "direct from the factory", prices are not low. The objects you see being made are better bought in the night bazaar in Chiang Mai or in the small town of Borsang seven kilometres along Sankamphaeng Road. If you can resist buying, though, your visit will be fascinating and inexpensive. There are factories producing silk, lacquerware, silverware, umbrellas and leather goods.

The silk factories are perhaps the most interesting. Behind the showrooms are displays showing silkworm moths (rather dull looking creatures) mating and egg laying, the caterpillars busily eating mulberry leaves and making cocoons which are then boiled and the silk unravelled and spun into thread and dyed. The looms on which the thread is woven are in permanent action producing a constant wooden clatter.

The main source of silver for the silverware factories is coins from the British Raj. Visitors can watch the silver being beaten and embossed by hand, and the intricate skill of forming the silver into tiny links to make chains for pendants and bracelets.

The umbrella factories produce beautiful paper umbrellas and parasols of all sizes. The process starts with the manufacture of the paper and continues through to the finished product, hand painted in rich colours. After all the factories, the road continues through the town of Sankamphaeng, where a right fork leads to a quiet country lane leading to Lamphun, 25 kilometres south. The left fork leads to Sankamphaeng hot springs, complete with small geysers in a pretty park, via an interesting cave. Continuing past the springs leads to the temple of Doi Saket and the main road back to Chiang Mai.

CHIANG MAI - SANKAMPHAENG - DOI SAKET - CHIANG MAI
(60 kilometeres- 80 minutes) Map page 102

Kilometres

0   The road begins at the Nawarat river bridge in Chiang Mai. Continue east along this busy road.
2   Railway Station on the right.
4   Superhighway junction. Continue straight ahead.
5-13   A number of factories - silk, umbrella, silverware etc line the road. Each factory offers similar displays.
13   North turn along Rte 1014 to **Doi Saket** (14 kilometres). The large village of **Borsang** ✔✔contains, at the road junction, the largest umbrella factory, the destination of many coaches and *tuk-tuks*. Further along Rte 1014 are many small shops selling locally produced handicrafts. Prices here (with bargaining) are generally lower than at the factories.
23   The small town of **Sankamphaeng** ✔with yet more handicraft shops. At the road fork in the centre of town turn left.

NB KILOMETRE POSTS NOW NUMBERED FROM SANKAMPHAENG

3   **Wat Don Moon** ✔An interesting example of modern ultra-garish temple design.
8   In the village of Ban Mai:
    Sankhamphaeng Resort ●●●● Comfortable rooms in pleasant landscaped gardens.
    Address: 108 Moo 10 Ban Mai Long Bo Deng, Samkamphaeng, Chiang Mai 50000
    Tel: (01)5100510
    Price: 400-1500 **Rooms:** 13 **Fan:** 13 **Bathroom:** 13(hw) **Comfort:** ☆☆☆
    Design: ☆☆☆☆ **Location:** ☆☆☆☆ **Position:** 8 kilometres north of Sankamphaeng
    Quietness: ☆☆☆☆☆ **Restaurant:** ☆☆☆
10   Right turn signposted Roon Aroong Hot Spring, 2 kilometres after the village of Ban Mai.

NB KILOMETRE POSTS NOW NUMBERED FROM THIS TURNING

3   **Tam Muang On caves** ✔✔✔Turn left in small village of Moo Song to dirt road with small signpost. The cave is 1 km along this track. There is a long winding serpent (*naga*) staircase leading up to the cave which is a near vertical shaft descended by very steep concrete steps. The cave is lit by a small generator. In the large cavern at the base are two Buddha statues - the larger one reclining. They are surrounded by stalactites and stalagmites creating an eerie scene.
5   **Sankamphaeng hot springs** ✔✔ Geothermal water emerging from springs and geysers in a large park. For 200 *baht* baths can be taken in the sulphur rich water which is reputedly excellent as a cure for skin diseases. Entry 10 *baht*. The site is managed by the government. Another 200 metres along the road is **Roong Aroon hot springs** ✔✔. Privately owned and somewhat better cared for, but with the same facilities. There is a resort within the grounds of the park.
    Roong Aroon Resort ●●●●● Luxurious bungalows with en suite mineral baths in lovely gardens.

Address: Sankamphaeng, Chiang Mai 50000 Tel: (053)248475
Price: 900-1100 Rooms: 36 A/C: 36 Bathroom: 36(hw) Comfort: ☆☆☆☆☆
Design: ☆☆☆☆☆ Location: ☆☆☆☆☆ Position: 10 kilometres west of
Sankamphaeng Quietness: ☆☆☆☆☆ Restaurant: ☆☆☆☆ Facilities: thermal baths in rooms, massage

13 Doi Saket ✓✓ A rather circuitous route through two small villages and fertile farmland with few signposts. For details of Wat Doi Saket and the route back to Chiang Mai see page 125.

DOI SUTEP AND DOI PUI

Doi Pui is the mountain that overlooks Chiang Mai to the west. At an altitude of 1385 metres, with its steep slopes rising suddenly from the western suburbs of the city, it dominates and broods over Chiang Mai. Even at the height of the dry season its peak is likely to be swathed in cloud that extends eastwards, even on occasions giving the city a brief and welcome shower. Much of the mountain is a National Park, where building and farming are strictly banned, so that within four kilometres of the centre of Chiang Mai undisturbed jungle and cool, clean air can always be enjoyed. There is a good but very steep and winding metalled road extending almost to the summit, with waterfalls, temples, palaces and hill tribe villages to be seen en route.

CHIANG MAI - DOI PUI - CHIANG MAI (46 kilometres - 80 minutes) Map page 102

Kilometres

0   Travel along Huay Kaeo Road, passing Chiang Mai Orchid Hotel, the university and zoo. 200 metres after the zoo is a large shrine on the right. This was built to commemorate the monk Phra Kubra Srivijaya who organized the construction of the road. At its base are a number of food stalls, souvenir sellers and pick ups (*songthaews*) which ascend and descend the mountain at frequent intervals. The road suddenly rises in a series of hairpin bends after the shrine, and the jungle begins - rather scrubby at first but becoming rapidly thicker and more luxuriant as the altitude increases.

6   Matrathorn waterfall ✓✓✓ Well signposted, 2 kilometres along a dirt road to the north. The road ends in a car park in the forest. Just below the car park is a very lovely waterfall, with a drop of 30 metres. There is a path to the side of the waterfall which leads along the stream for 300 metres upstream to a pool suitable for paddling beneath it, fed by a second waterfall whose plunge creates a natural shower. Although so close to the city, these falls are little visited by locals, and are a perfect place to relax for an hour or so.

15 Wat Phra That Doi Sutep ✓✓✓ This lovely temple looking out over the city and east

to the mountains beyond is one of the most visited sights in Chiang Mai. Avoid going there on Sundays or during public holidays - it's just too crowded to enjoy. The large car park is just below the temple. Beyond the car park are a number of souvenir shops. There is a small funicular railway beside the car park (5 *baht*) which avoids climbing the 200 step *naga* staircase.

Legend has it that in the 14th century relics of Buddha were given to King Geu Na in Chiang Mai. Some he placed in Wat Suan Dok, but the others he placed on a white elephant which was freed to travel at will. Where it stopped would be the site of a new temple. The elephant promptly charged up the mountain, arrived at the spot where the temple was later built, trumpeted three times and sat down. The relics were interred in a central *chedi* which was later encased in a thick layer of gold from the treasury of King Chao Kawila. It is today an exceptionally beautiful *chedi* flanked by 4 splendid multi tiered umbrellas. The temple is one to which monks must make pilgrimages every year in early January to atone for their sins. They must walk barefoot, perhaps over 100 kilometres, to Doi Sutep, camp and pray there overnight, then walk back to their home temples

19   **Phuping Kings Palace** ✓✓ Only open Friday-Sunday and public holidays when the king is not in residence. The palace itself is closed to the public, but the manicured English- style parks and gardens are very beautiful.

21   North turn along dirt road to a white **Hmong village** ✓✓✓ (7 kilometres). Although close to Chiang Mai, this village is still traditional and culturally remote. high on the slopes of Doi Pui, it is a strange sight to see elderly women in full costume spinning cloth almost within sight of a modern city far below. It is possible to continue along this road which eventually leads to another Hmong village before descending into the Mae Sa valley at Ban Thai. Between these villages the track passes a number of experimental highland crop growing stations interspersed with lovely mountain jungle and pine forest, but the road is very poor and it is easy to get lost.

23   Blue Hmong village of **Doi Pui** ✓ Really a travesty of a hill tribe village, which has become a giant open air tourist supermarket for real and supposed hill tribe products. The village receives so many tourists that it has lost its own culture and found nothing but tourists to replace it with. The village has an opium museum containing a few dirty old tools and opium pipes. There is also an opium garden in which a few poppies are grown (flowering December-March).

MAE SA VALLEY

This round trip though the Mae Sa valley to Samoeng, returning via a lonely mountain road back to Chiang Mai is an excellent one day trip, allowing the visitor ample opportunity to see some lovely mountain scenery combined with elephant riding, orchid, butterfly and snake farms, beautiful landscaped gardens and a number of Hmong hill tribe villages. There is so much to see and do that it could well be worth while taking two days over the trip and staying in one of the tranquil mountain resorts en route.

CHIANG MAI-MAE SA-SAMOENG-CHIANG MAI
(86 kilometres - 3 hours) Map page 102

Kilometres

0-18   After the horrors of the 4 kilometre journey along Chiang Puak road from the centre of town, the fast dual carriageway to Mae Rim is a relief, passing through flat rice fields and suburban villages.
4   Lanna 18 hole golf course on west of road.
5   Chiang Mai city hall to west of road.
16   **Mae Rim.** Small busy market town
18   Turn west onto Rte 1096, signposted Samoeng (35 kilometres)

NB DISTANCES NOW ALONG ROUTE 1096

1.6   Turn south 200 metres to **Sainamphung Orchid and butterfly farm** ✓✓, entrance 5 baht. Large collection of butterflies and orchids attractively displayed. Gold plated orchids made (demonstration 11.00-13.00) and culturing techniques illustrated. Good open air restaurant beside large aviary. 1 kilometre further along this road is:
   Mae Rim Lagoon ✪✪✪✪ A new luxury hotel on the shores of a small lake.
   Address: 65/1 Moo 6 Mae Rim, Chiang Mai 50000 Tel: (2)828428
   Price: 1600-4000 **Rooms:** 30 **A/C:** 30 **Bathroom:** 30(hw) **Comfort:** ☆☆☆☆☆
   Design: ☆☆☆☆ **Location:** ☆☆☆☆ **Quietness:** ☆☆☆☆☆ **Restaurant:** ☆☆☆☆
   Facilities: boating, music, lounge
3   **Mae Sa Snake Farm** ✓✓ Large display of local snakes, poorly housed. Impressively dangerous display of snake taunting and venom collecting. Entrance 60 *baht*.
4   North of road 400 metres:
   Mae Sa Valley resort and golf course ✪✪✪ Nice bungalows near very pretty 9 hole golf course.
   Address: Kilometre 4, Mae Rim-Samoeng road, Mae Rim, Chiang Mai.
   Price: 600 **Rooms:** 20 **Fan:** 20 **Bathroom:** 20(hw) **Comfort:** ☆☆ **Design:** ☆☆☆
   Location: ☆☆☆☆ **Quietness:** ☆☆☆☆☆ **Facilities:** golf course, 50 *baht*/round, club hire 100 *baht*.
4.5   **Mae Sa House Private Collection** ✓ Display of antiques and curios from 3000 BC to the present day in large teak museum surrounded by orchid gardens. Entrance 30 *baht*.
4.8   **Mae sa Valley Butterfly Farm** ✓ Small collection of butterflies and moths in enclosed garden. Entrance 5 *baht*.
5   Dirt road to north leading to **Tard Mork waterfall** ✓✓ (7 kilometres). Small waterfall in jungle valley. Picnic tables and benches scattered along the path.
6   **Mae Sa waterfalls** ✓✓✓ 500 metres along road to south. Series of cascades and small waterfalls in lush mountain jungle. 3 kilometre path follows river upstream, with picnic spots along the way. Very crowded on Sundays and holidays. Several inexpensive restaurants built over the river by the car park.
7   **Ton Tong** restaurant and gardens. Beautiful restaurant in delightful tropical gardens. Excellent Thai food at moderate prices. 3 bungalows for rent, 600 *baht*.
9.5   **Rintr Garden Resort** ✪✪✪ Bungalows in a small park by the river.
   Address: Ban Mai Mai, Mae Rim, Chiang Mai
   Price: 450-600 **Rooms:** 21 **Bathroom:** 21(hw) **Comfort:** ☆☆ **Location:** ☆☆☆☆
   Design: ☆☆☆☆ **Quietness:** ☆☆☆☆ **Restaurant:** ☆☆☆

Mae Sa Valley

10	**Mae Sa Elephant Camp** ✓✓✓ On south of road. Very large and popular elephant camp in lovely setting. Elephant show 9.30-11.00, short ride 40 *baht*, Longer trips 600 *baht*/elephant/hour. Entrance 40 *baht*.
13	**Mae Sa Valley resort** ●●●●● Well appointed bungalows and restaurant in near perfect setting amidst large park of tropical flowers and trees. **Address:** 86 Moo 2, Mae Rim-Samoeng Road, Bong Yaeng, Chiang Mai **Tel:** (053)297980 **Price:**600 **Rooms:**44 **Bathroom:**44(hw) **Comfort:** ☆☆☆☆ **Design:** ☆☆☆☆ **Location:** ☆☆☆☆☆ **Quietness:** ☆☆☆☆☆ **Restaurant:** ☆☆☆☆ **Facilities:** Elephant rides **Tours:** half day 400 *baht* (including elephant).
17	**Pyongyang.** Large village with small restaurant, temple with large Buddha statue.
17.5	North turn by Buddha statue, 1 kilometre to; **Erewan Resort** ●●●●●. Charming cottages in an extensive park built around a lake backed by mountains. **Address:** 149/10 Changklan Road, Chiang Mai (053)252120 **Price:** 800-1600 (tent 300) **Rooms:**11 **Fan:**11 **Bathroom** 11(hw) **Design:** ☆☆☆☆☆ **Location:** ☆☆☆☆☆ **Quietness:**☆☆☆☆☆ **Restaurant:** ☆☆☆☆ **Facilities:** fishing, swimming, wind surfing, cabaret.
18.5	Turn south down new road 1 kilometre to: **Kangsadal Resort** ●●● Chalets and log cabins perched on steep hillsides at high altitude near waterfall. **Address:** Kilometre 18 Mae Rin-Samoeng Road, Chiang Mai **Tel:** (053)252853 **Price:** 400-600 **Rooms:** 12 **Bathroom:** 12(hw) **Comfort:** ☆ to ☆☆☆ **Design:** ☆☆☆ **Location:** ☆☆☆☆☆ **Quietness:** ☆☆☆☆☆ **Restaurant:** ☆☆☆. 2 kilometres further down this road, **Pyongyang Elephant Camp** ✓✓. Elephants 600 *baht*/hour. Interesting rides through mountain terrain to waterfalls and hill tribe villages.
23.3	Dirt road to north, 3 kilometres to **Hmong village** ✓✓ Very pretty location, but the villagers are very tourist conscious.
23-30	Very beautiful views of mountain ranges to the west stretching to the far horizons.
26.4	Dirt road south, very steep, to unspoilt **Hmong village** ✓✓.
30	Junction with Samoeng-Hangdong road, turn right to **Samoeng** ✓✓ (5 kilometres), a pretty and typical small Thai mountain town, with hospital and school. Small restaurant on right at entrance to town looks tatty, but serves great local food at very low prices.

DISTANCES NOW MEASURED FROM SAMOENG

0-10	Steep climb out of the Samoeng valley. Countryside of unbroken, uninhabited mountain jungle.
12.4	**Mae Kanin.** Large village of lovely old teak houses.
20.6	**Mae Ha.** Large village with temple, petrol station and restaurants.
22-32	As altitude decreases, jungle gives way to farm land and a succession of small villages. Several estates and resorts under construction for wealthy Thais.
41	Junction with Rte 108, a fast dual carriageway leading back to Chiang Mai (10 kilometres).

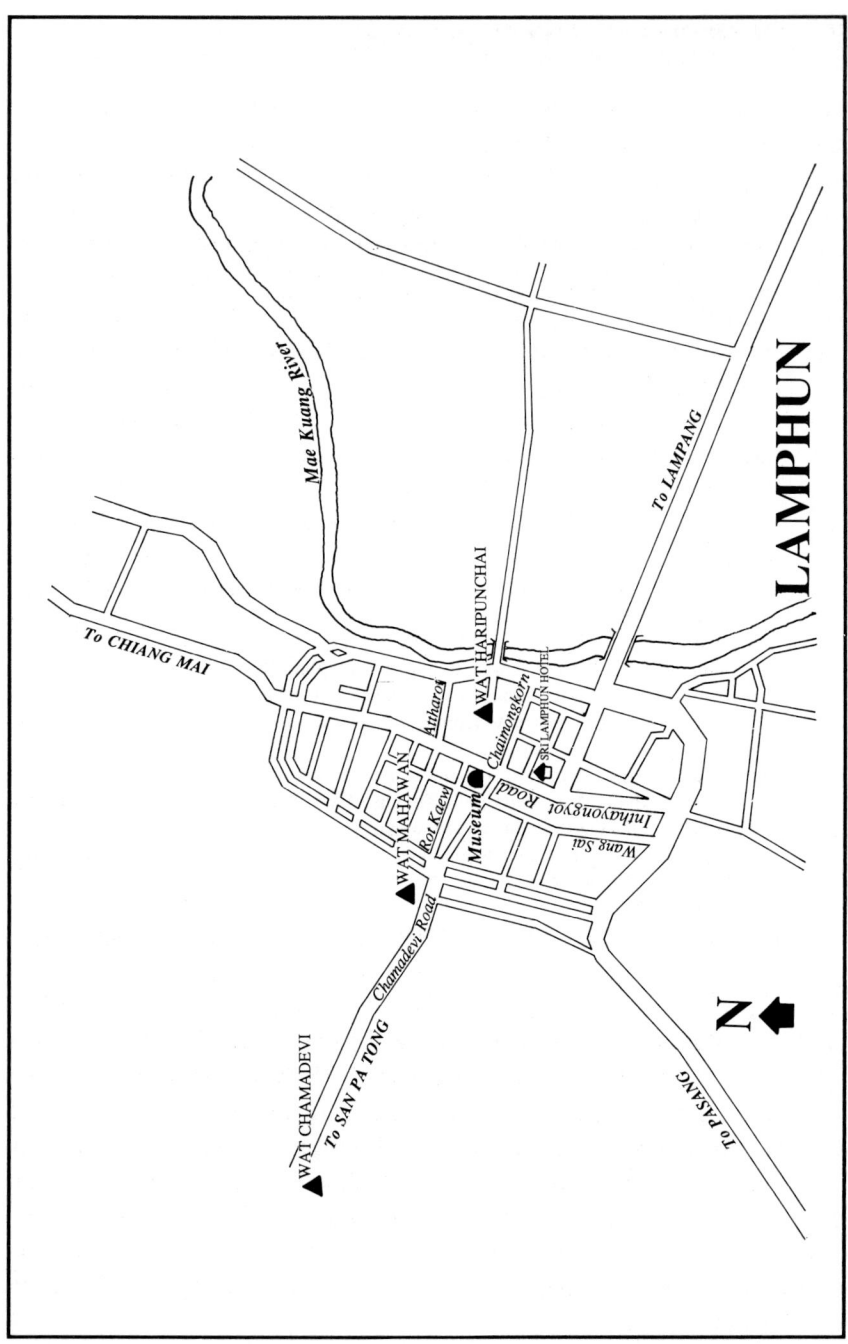

LAMPHUN AND PASANG

A small town 26 kilometres south of Chiang Mai with an illustrious history. Lamphun is a typical large Thai town, almost untouched by tourism despite its proximity to Chiang Mai, and provides the visitor with a more realistic picture of Thai life than its tourist oriented big brother up the road. Lamphun is a much older city than Chiang Mai. It was at one time the capital of the Kingdom of Haripunchai, which maintained its independence for several hundred years until eventually succumbing in the 13th century to the might of King Mengrai, the founder of the united Northern Thai realm of Lanna. The first monarch of Lamphun was the legendary Queen Chamadevi, who ruled in the early 8th century AD, and whose modern statue can be seen near the moat. It is said that the women of Lamphun are strong willed and proud as a result of her influence.

Haripunchai was a Mon kingdom, owing allegiance to the larger empire of Dveravati. The Mon civilisation had Thaton in eastern Burma as its progenitor, and was strongly influenced by Indian culture from across the Bay of Bengal. This culture was absorbed and defeated both by Khmers from the east and Thais from the north, but Lamphun stood as its last bastion in Thailand. Remains of this proud past are visible in several places in Lamphun.

TEMPLES

Wat Prathat Haripunchai ✓✓✓ A large and very important temple complex, elements of which have been widely copied throughout Thailand. It was founded in 897 AD, built to house a lock of Buddhas hair (it is said Buddha himself visited Lamphun). Nothing of the original temple remains except some fragments in the museum. The temple was renovated in the 12th century AD, then again in the 14th after the town's incorporation into Lanna. This renovation was carried out by a Sri Lankan monk, and the design of the main *chedi* has been copied widely - notably at Doi Sutep in Chiang Mai. The temple is in the centre of Lamphun, although the main entrance faces not the main road but the river. At the entrance, guarded by two Singha lions, is a large *bot* housing a reclining Buddha. The main *wiharn* was rebuilt in 1925 and contains a splendid 15th century Chiang Saen style bronze Buddha. To the left of the *wiharn* is a 200 year old Lanna/Burmese style library, and behind this the very impressive *chedi* flanked by golden parasols. To the right is a huge gong, said to be the largest in the world. The ancient looking *chedi* behind the *wiharn* is a copy of a Dveravati *chedi* built in 1418 AD.

Wat Ku Kut (Wat Chamadevi) ✓✓✓ The grounds of this temple house one of the oldest *chedis* in Thailand. Reputed to have been built by Queen Chamadevi in the 8th century AD, it is a stepped foursided pyramid with standing Buddhas in niches. Close to it is a smaller but no less fine *chedi* from the same period. They are the only remaining monuments from the Mon civilisation in Thailand.

National Museum ✓✓ Close to Wat Phrathat Haripunchai in the centre of town, a small but well designed museum with commentaries alongside the exhibits in English. The collection ranges from 40,000 year old axe heads to present day artifacts. A wide range of Buddha statues are on display, showing the designs of the different schools of sculpture, from the rather coarse, frizzy haired Haripunchai Buddha to the elegant, graceful features of the Phayao school.

WHERE TO STAY

Sri Lamphun ✿
An old style hotel, basic but fairly clean.
Address: 512/2 Inthayongot Road, Lamphun 51000 **Tel:**(053)511176
Price: 60-120 **Rooms:** 22 **Fan:** 22 **Bathroom:** 22(cw) **Comfort:** ☆☆ **Design:** ☆
Location: ☆☆ **Quietness:** ☆

EATING

There are two small restaurants in the centre of Lamphun serving basic Thai-Chinese food.

GETTING THERE.

Pick-ups (*songthaew*) travel from Chiang Mai to Lamphun and back every 5 minutes from the east side of the Nawarat Bridge. The fare is 10 *baht*. Buses leave from Chiang Puak bus station for the same trip.

CHIANG MAI - LAMPHUN - PASANG (50 kilometres - 45 minutes) Map page 102

Kilometres

From Chiang Mai, cross the Nawarat bridge, on the east side turn south at the traffic lights. Continue on this road for 4 kilometres to the superhighway junction. Lamphun is signposted here along route 11. The road is lined with tall, beautiful Tong khee-lek trees for 15 kilometres.

DISTANCES ON KILOMETRE POSTS FROM LAMPANG

174	**Khong Sai.** This small village does a flourishing trade in the manufacture of colourful, multi tiered coffins and other funeral furniture.
172	West turn to **Chiang Mai Lakeside Ville** ✓✓✓ - for details see page 96.
171	**Sarapee** ✓ A small town with a busy market. The local industry is basket making and bamboo furniture manufacture. Several shops selling these goods at very low prices line the road.
165	**Pa Heo.** A large village on a stream. Just before the bridge on the left is a small restaurant specialising in goat dishes.
163	**Pa Sao.** Noted for the finest Lamyai fruit (*longan*) in Thailand. Trees bearing these lychee like fruits can be seen around the village. The harvest is collected in August, followed by a festival in nearby Lamphun.
159	The city of Lamphun (see above) Continue through Lamphun on Rte 106
150	To east of road, a large, Haripunchai style *chedi*.
143	**Pasang** ✓ noted for the quality of its cotton weaving. Pasang has a reputation for the most beautiful women in Thailand. Possibly they have moved.
136	**Wat Phra Phutthabat Taak Phaa** ✓✓ To the east of the main road, approached by a straight, 1 kilometre road. An important place of pilgrimage, and a very impressive sight. The temple complex was built to venerate Northern Thailand's most illustrious monk - Luang Pu Phromaa. The *wiharn* contains a wax effigy of him. Behind the grounds is a steep staircase with a path leading to an ornate *chedi* at the top. A large number of monks study here, under a disciple of Luang. The temple is named after a reputed footprint of Buddha, in a small building in the centre of the temple complex.

DOI INTHANON

A National Park around the highest mountain in Thailand, with an altitude of 2565 metres, only 70 kilometres south of Chiang Mai by good road. The area has much of beauty and interest, including three of the loveliest waterfalls in Thailand - one (Mae Ya) also the highest. There are many unspoilt hill tribe villages, an exceptionally rich and diverse wildlife and dramatic mountain scenery.

The mountain is named after the last king of Chiang Mai who died at the turn of the century. He had a great love for this mountain, so much so that his remains rest in a shrine at the summit. The climate varies greatly with altitude. At the summit, a temperature of -8°C has been recorded, and it is always 10°C cooler than the plains below. Rainfall is high, frequent showers occurring even in the dry season, and land above 2000 metres is semi-permanently covered in mist, creating true cloud forest. This helps the myriad of plants such as ferns, mosses and orchids which cling to the trunks of the tall trees. The coolness encourages temperate plants to grow - including three species of rhododendron. The area is particularly rich in birds - 362 species have been recorded, including two species found nowhere else.

GETTING THERE

PUBLIC TRANSPORT
From Chiang Puak bus station, buses leave for Chom Thong every 40 minutes. From the town, rent a *songthaew* to take you to the summit and back for 150 baht.

PRIVATE TRANSPORT
Much preferable, a jeep (600 *baht*) or an MTX motorbike(150 *baht*) hired for the day from Chiang Mai. The smaller engined mopeds cannot ascend the steep inclines. Allow one hour to get to the park, plus 45 minutes to the summit.

WHERE TO STAY

Around the National Park Headquarters there are several houses for rent, from a four person cottage for 500 *baht* to a large house sleeping 20-30 people for 3000 *baht*. Hot water is provided, and meals can be ordered from the headquarters. There is a campsite charging 5 *baht* per person, or a two person tent can be rented for 50 *baht*. there is a small, basic restaurant on the east side of the main road.

Accommodation can only be booked at the park headquarters. Booking in advance is possible by writing to: The Superintendent, Doi Inthanon National Park, Chom Thong, Chiang Mai 51061.

CHIANG MAI - DOI INTHANON - CHIANG MAI (216 kilometres - 5 hours)Map page 171

Kilometres

0-59   See page 179.
59   Turn west onto Rte 1008 1 kilometre before Chom Thong, signposted Doi Inthanon.

Doi Inthanon

NB. DISTANCES ALONG ROUTE 1008

1	South turn to **Mae Ya** waterfalls (see page 179).
7	West turn to **Mae Klang Falls ✓✓**(1 kilometre). A very popular spot for Thais on any sunny day, but especially Sundays and holidays, when it is overcrowded. The wide falls and rapids spill over a granite exposure to pools in the woods below, great for swimming and picnicking. There are several food stalls and cafes. A trail climbs to the falls (5 *baht*) and beyond to the visitors centre.
8	Checkpoint at entrance to National Park, entry 20 *baht* per vehicle.
9	**Brichinda Cave ✓✓** An impressive limestone cave with a gigantic entrance chamber and tower, and a second large chamber with a skylight opening to the surface. The cave is a one hour walk from the road, ask for a guide at the visitors centre.
9	**Visitors centre ✓✓**. Detailed maps, descriptions and displays of the National Park. Cabins can be booked here, and guides hired.
20	**Vachirathin Falls ✓✓✓** Signposted on the east (right) side of the road, reached by a steep path (700 metres). The waters tumble down a large granite escarpment, creating a veil of mist and rainbows in the sun. There is a small restaurant near the path.
21	500 metres along a dirt track east of the road, the small Karen village of **Sop Had ✓✓** a friendly and unspoilt Karen village.
23	Dirt road north, opposite 23 kilometre post. 2 kilometres to an idyllic Karen village, **Nong Lum ✓✓✓**, traditional and friendly, with a lovely mountain setting. This road continues for 13 kilometres before rejoining the main road at the Hmong village of **Khun Klang ✓** at kilometre 30. At Khun Klang there is a dirt road to the twin falls of **Siriphun ✓✓** Generally passable with 4wd, it offers lovely mountain scenery, hill tribe farmland and another Karen village.
30	**Park Headquarters**. With camp ground and guest houses nearby. Guides for trail walking, information and meals can be provided.
38	West (left) turn to **Mae Chaam ✓** (18 kilometres). A well surfaced but narrow road, very steep and winding in places, descending rapidly with sudden climate and vegetation changes as altitude decreases. Mae Chaam is a pretty little town with a small guest house: **Mae Chaam Guest House ●●●** 500 metres north of town surrounded by rice paddies, pleasant wooden huts. **Address**: Mae Chaam, Chiang Mai **Price**: 70-100 **Rooms**: 8 **Bathroom**: 0(hw outside) **Comfort**: ☆ **Design**: ☆☆☆ **Location**: ☆☆☆☆ **Position**: 500 metres north of town **Quietness**: ☆☆☆☆ **Restaurant**: ☆☆☆
41	**Napamaytanidol Chedi ✓✓** Built in 1989 to celebrate the 60th birthday of King Bhumiphol, this magnificent chedi has a large modern Buddha statue. It is built on a high spur overlooking the valleys and mountain ranges to the north and west.
41	Starting 300 metres above the *chedi*, a trail leading through magnificent mountain jungle for 3 kilometres, including sections on a precipitous mountain ridge. Allow 2 hours for the walk.
48	400 metres before the summit car park, a path to the north of the road leading to a fascinating area of bog and forest. The one kilometre path ends at a strange shrine to a monk killed in a helicopter crash. Parts of the wreckage are included in the shrine
48	**Summit ✓✓✓** Marred by a large radar station, there is a car park with fine views if clear, and to the right the shrine of King Inthanon in thick forest commonly swathed in mist. At this altitude a jacket is needed even in the hot season.

Chapter Four

The Golden Triangle and The Far North

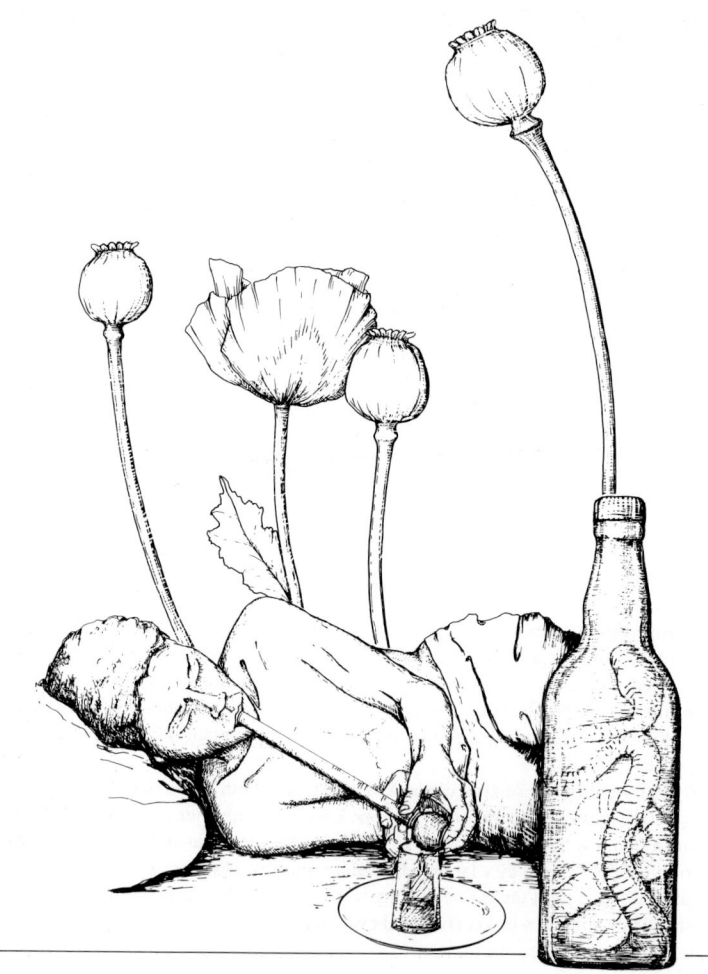

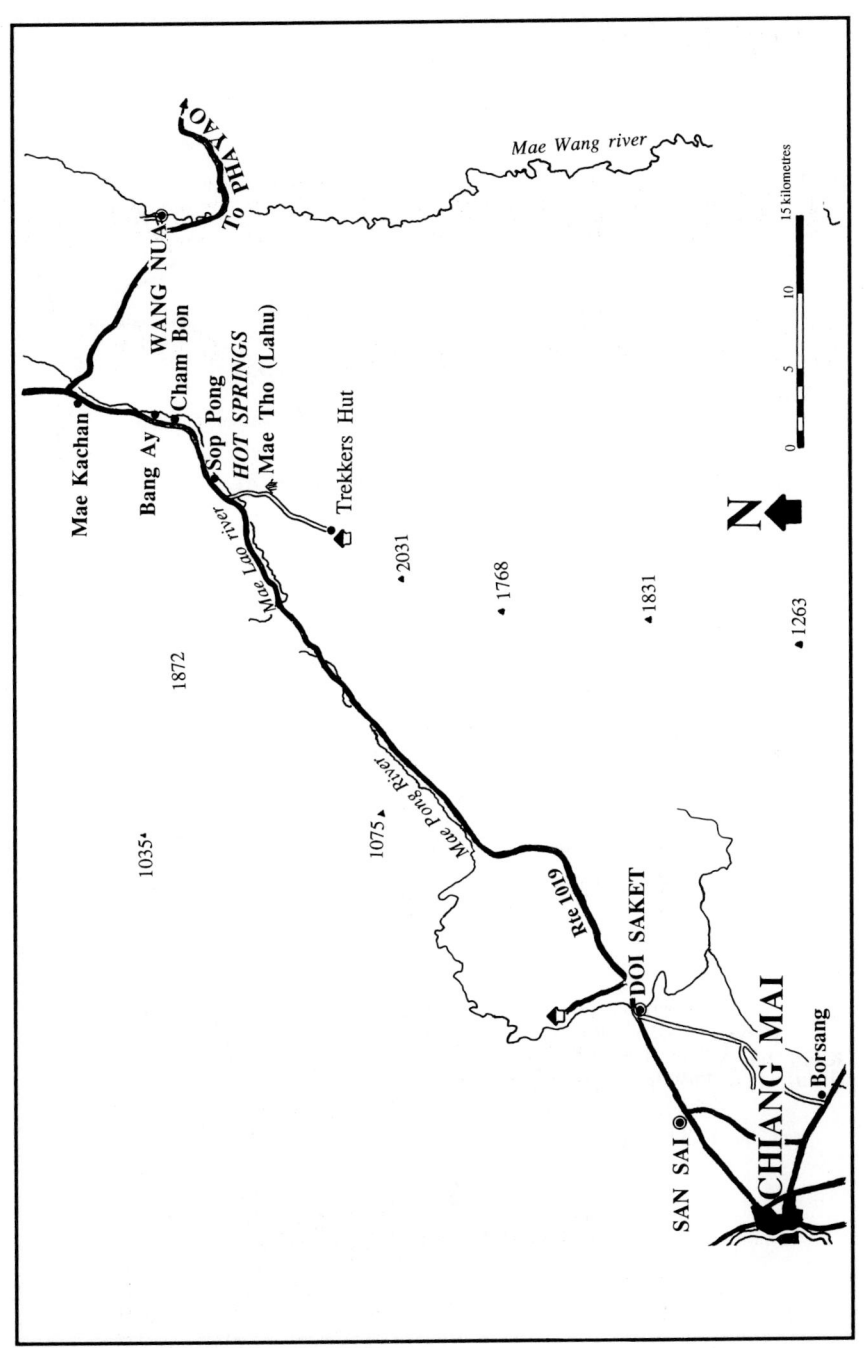

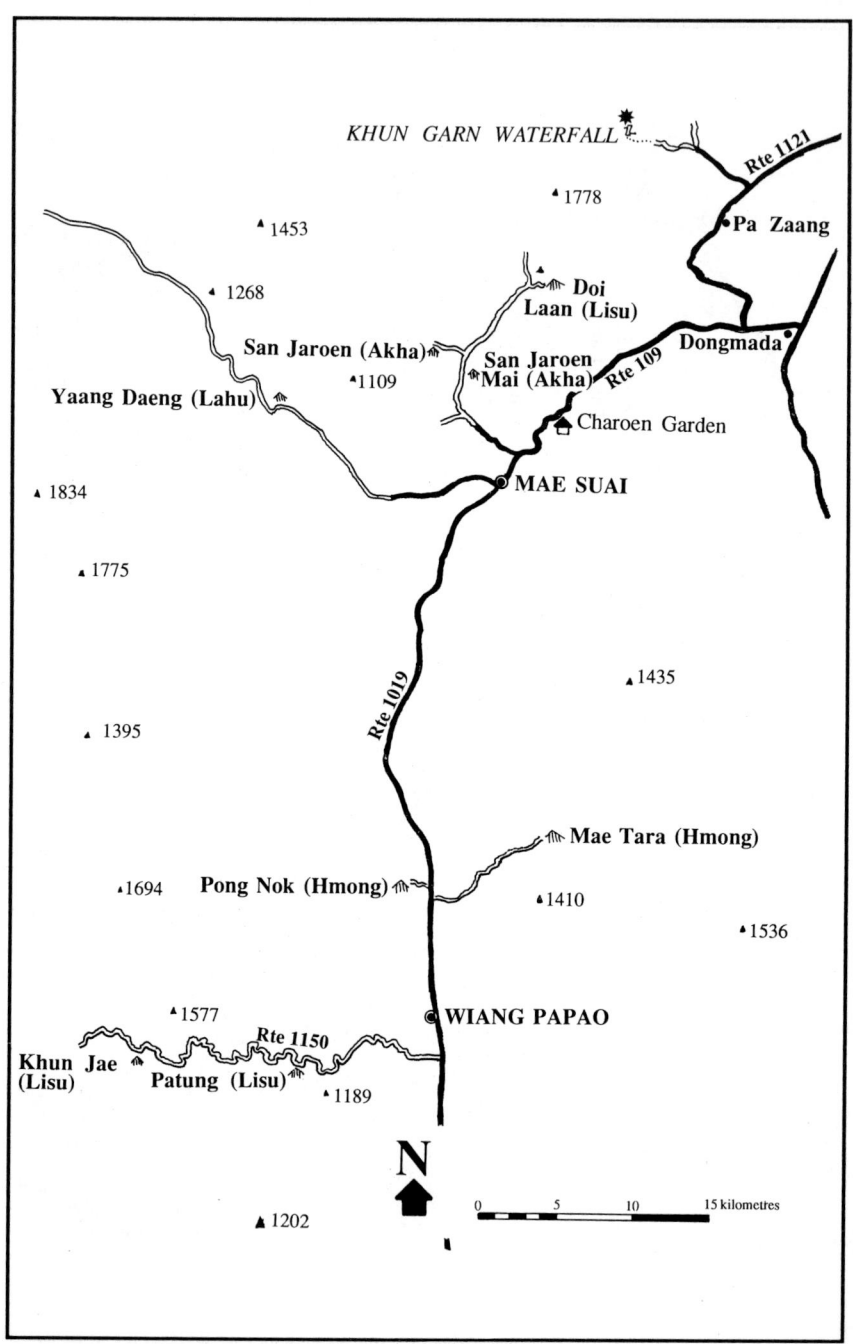

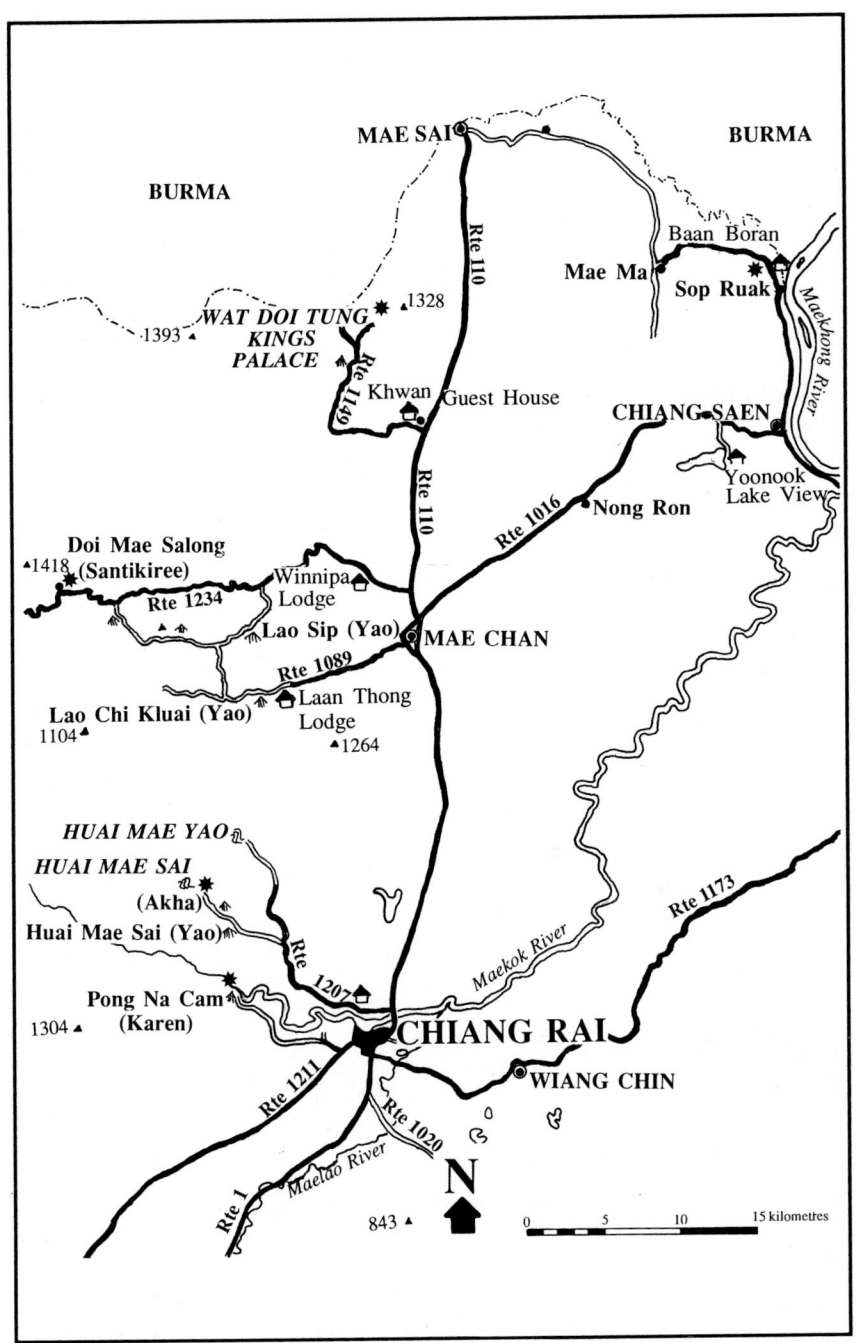

Doi Mae Salong - Chiang Dao

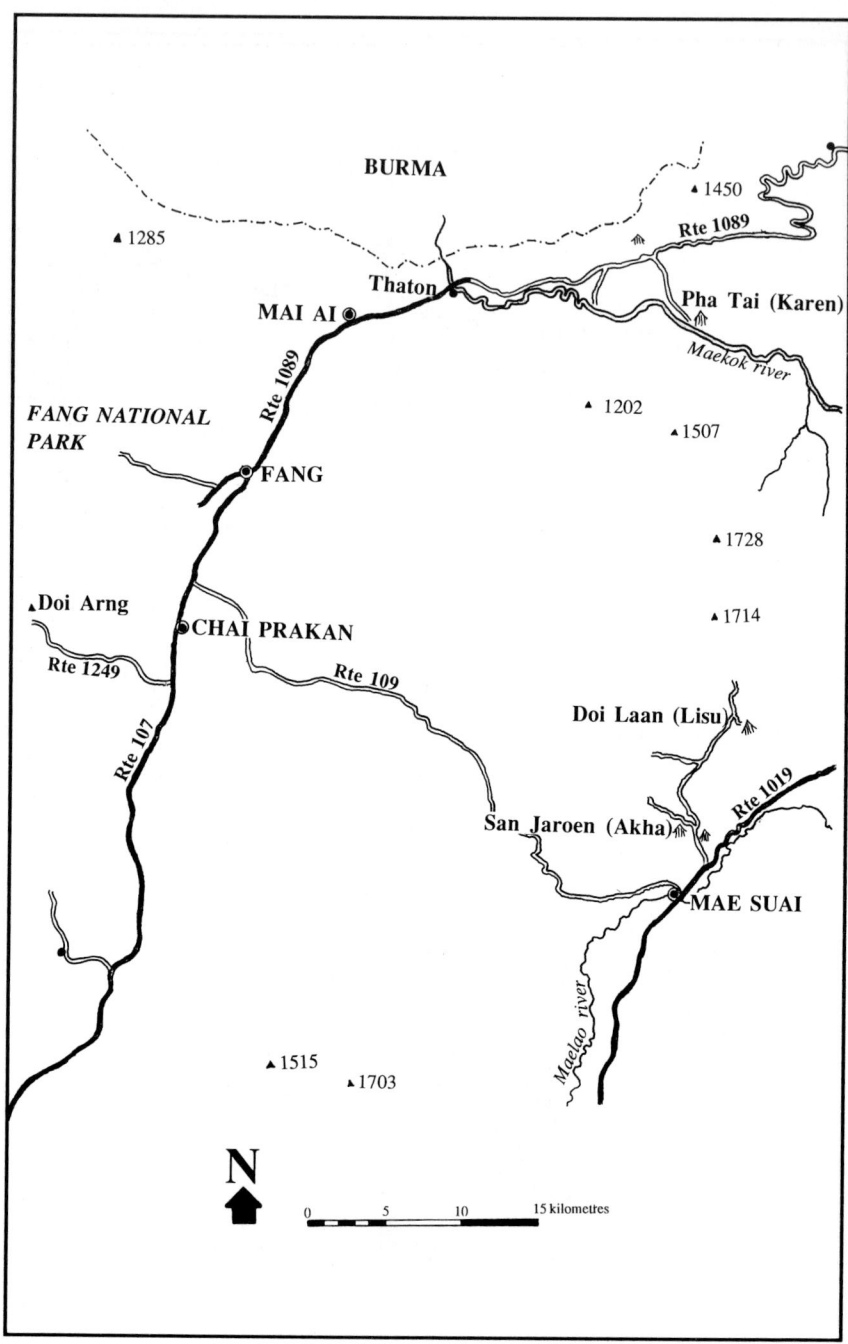

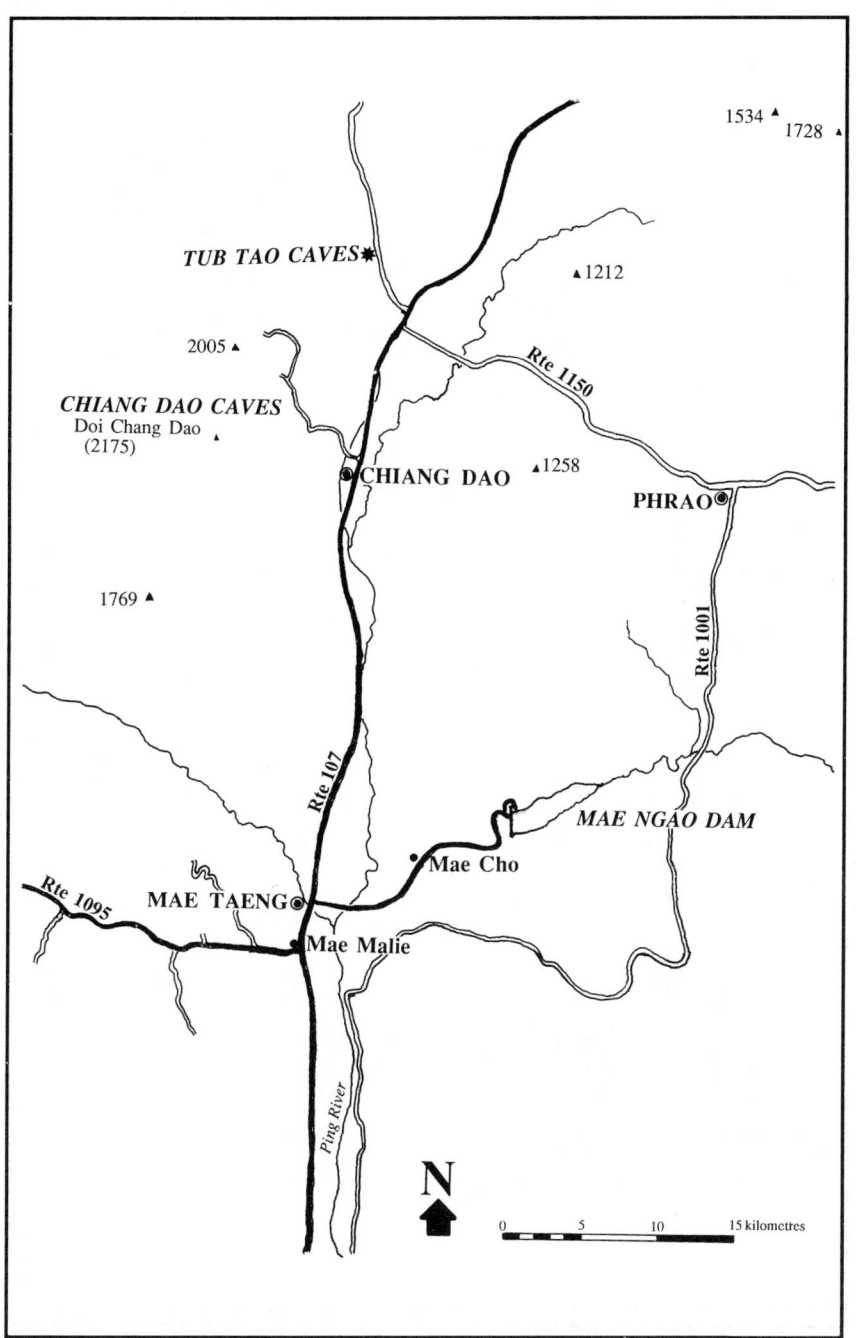

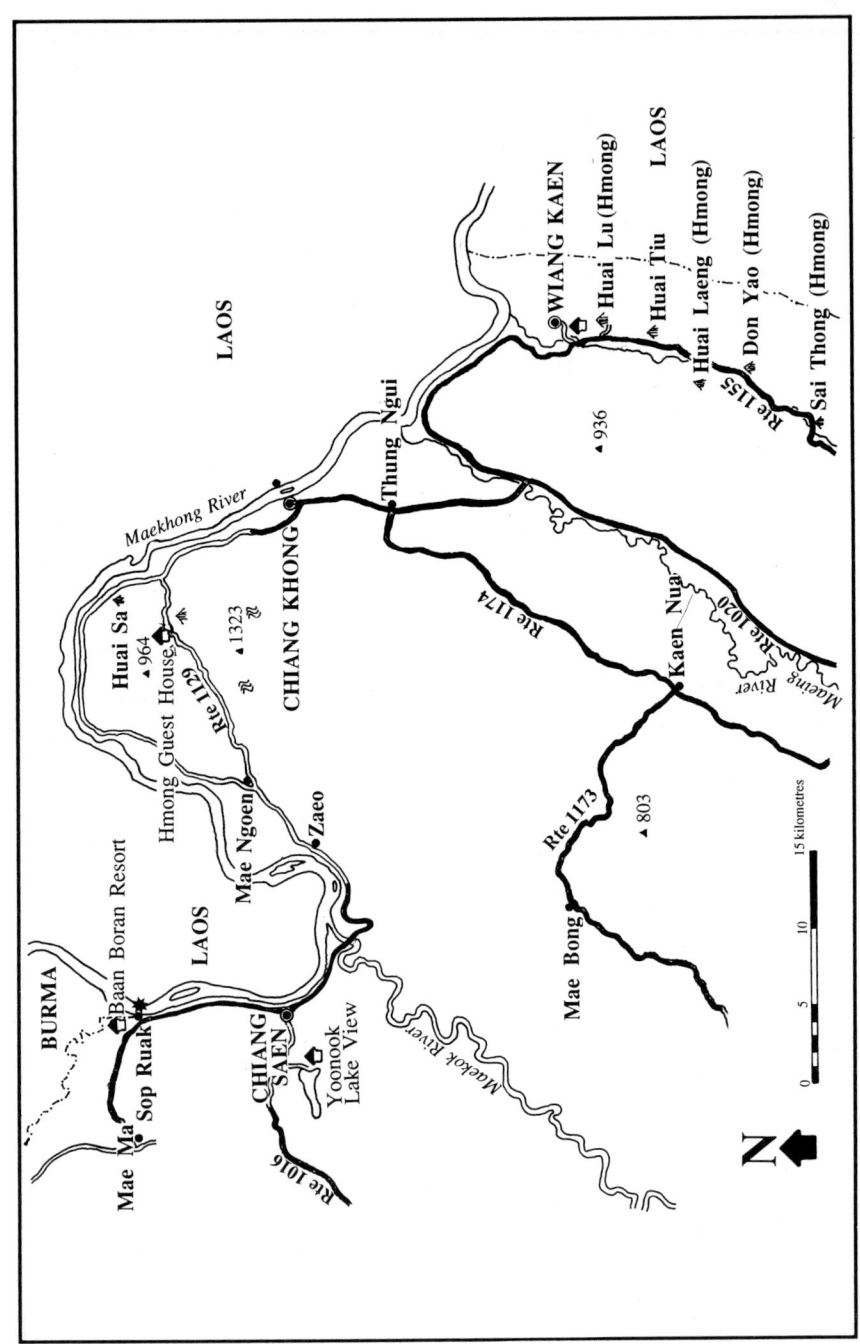

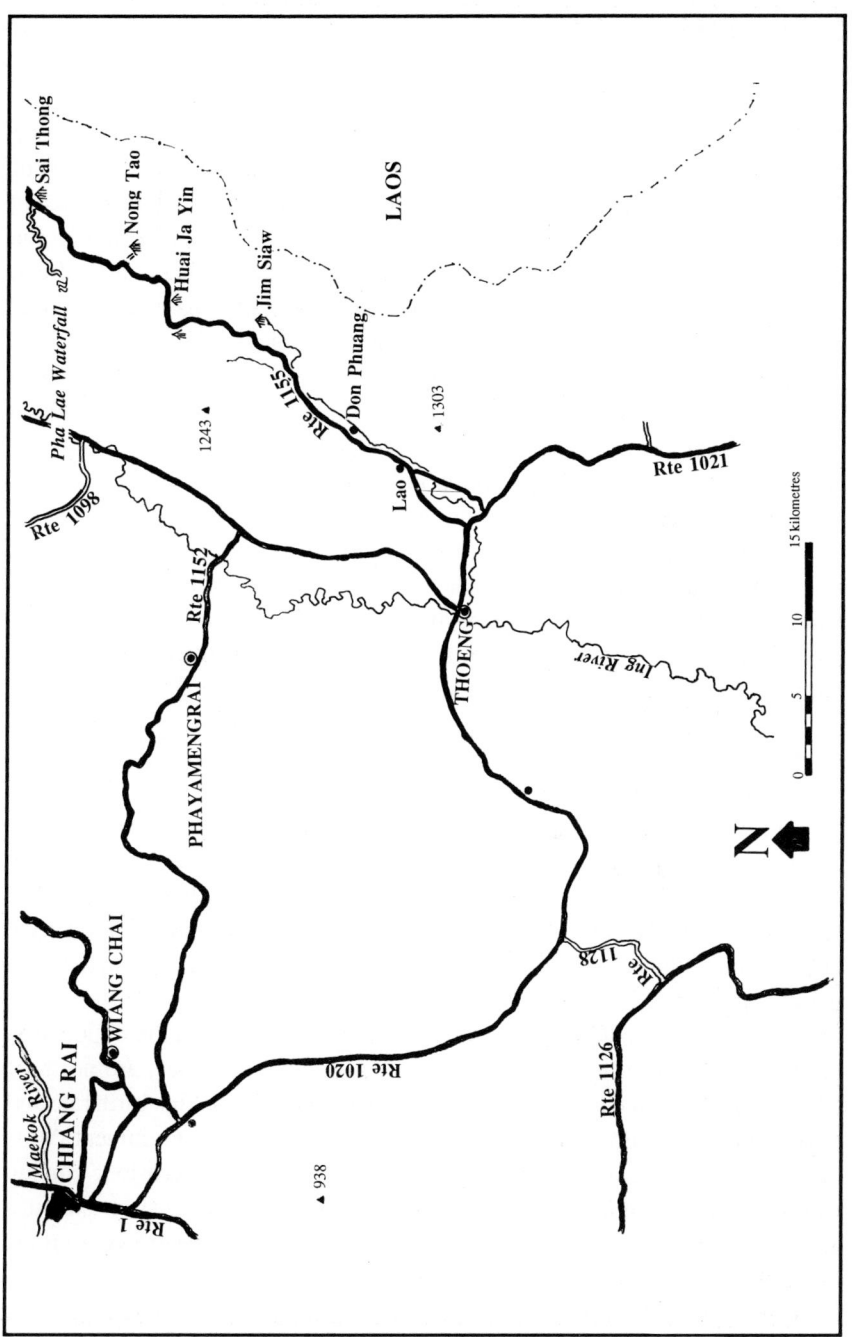

INTRODUCTION

THE CRADLE OF THAI CIVILISATION in Thailand, the massive Maekhong river, the meeting place of Thailand, Burma and Laos, the historic cities of Chiang Saen, Chiang Rai and Fang. Hill tribes, mountains, plains, ancient temples, caves and waterfalls - the far north has a deserved fascination for the visitor who seeks the exotic. Mass tourism in the last decade has had its effect, but it is still easy to deviate from the well travelled tourist path and discover some of the most beautiful and mystical places in Thailand.

The term "the Golden Triangle" historically refers to a large area of northern Thailand, eastern Burma and western Laos - a vaguely triangular area - in which the opium poppy is grown extensively and illegally. Opium is the raw source of heroin, morphine and codeine, and is in fact a purplish brown substance, so "golden" refers to the wealth its production generates. In the centre of the Golden Triangle area is the village of Sop Ruak, where the borders of Thailand, Burma and Laos meet on the Maekhong river. An arch has been built here to which all tourists make pilgrimages, through which all three countries can be seen. Geographically the far north is a fertile plain interrupted by high hills, bordered by steep sided mountains to the west and the Maekhong river to the east, beyond which is Laos. A large tributary of the Maekhong, the Maekok river, runs straight across the north from west to east. There are only three bridges across the Maekok, at Thaton close to the Burmese border, Chiang Rai centrally and close to Chiang Saen in the east. Chiang Rai, by far the largest city in the region, is thus a natural gateway. At the apex of Thailand, its most northerly point, is the town of Mae Sai, on a small stream separating Thailand from Burma. A real frontier town this, with much coming and going over the bridge joining the two countries, and many goods, genuine and fake, to tempt the visitor.

This area has the highest density of hill tribe settlement in the region, and most Akha villages in Thailand, the most exotic of the tribes, are north of Chiang Rai. Hill tribe populations are growing rapidly, with high birth rate and continued immigration, having serious effects for the local environment. Most of the natural forest cover has already gone, and serious erosion, climate warming and loss of fertility are already being felt as a result of slash and burn agriculture. In the wet season the hills are a livid green with the growing crops, but in the dry season the brown hills look bare and barren.

Tourists have been visiting the area for several years, so some English is spoken by most inhabitants and the range and standard of accommodation is excellent. The major roads are in good condition, and the new road from Thaton to Doi Mae Salong is one of the most dramatic in Thailand. Apart from these, though, be prepared for potholes, dust or mud.

CHIANG MAI-CHIANG RAI (188 kilometres - 3.5 hours) Map pages 117-118

Kilometres

Leave Chiang Mai on Rte 1019 via Doi Saket. Carry straight on at the superhighway lights, following signs to Chiang Rai. The road is well surfaced and in good condition.

0-14	Fast straight road passing through flat paddy fields and several small villages.
16	**Wat Doi Saket** ✓✓ Atop a steep hill approached by a serpent staircase of 298 steps giving fine views of Chiang Mai and the plains and mountains to the west. New *wiharn* and *chedi*, sumptuously decorated. Several small chapels and a monastery school. Displays of seven Buddhas, one for each day of the week. Grotto of pools and seated spirits enclosed by serpents tail. Sculpture of Buddha receiving gifts from animals.
18	Hydro-electric power station reservoir to west of road. East turn here 7 kilometres to; **Wang Tarn Resort** ❂❂❂❂ A large park of beautifully laid out gardens. Very well furnished chalets and a large swimming pool.
	Address: 35/1 Loung Nua, Doi Saket, Chiang Mai
	Price: 600-1000 Rooms: 62 A/C: 44 Fan: 18 Bathroom: 62(hw)
	Comfort: ☆☆ to ☆☆☆☆ Location: ☆☆☆☆ Position: 7 kilometres west of Doi Saket
	Quietness: ☆☆☆☆☆ Restaurant: ☆☆☆☆ Facilities: pool, tennis
19	Separation of mountain and plain.
20-40	Several new estates and resorts under construction in this lovely mountain valley. As elevation increases, the jungle becomes lusher and more beautiful.
21	Shrine to fertility goddess on west side. All the superstitious toot their horns as they pass.
40	Christianised Karen village to west of road.
43	**Keeree Orchid farm** ✓ with displays. Many prize winning hybrids have been produced here.
52	Several shrines marking road deaths.
53	Pass marked by border between Chiang Mai and Chiang Rai province, with police office and check point.
53-62	Road descends steeply after the pass. The valley gradually widens northwards giving lovely views of 2000 metre+ mountains to the west.
63	On east side of road, turning to "**Trekkers Hut**"(7 kilometres). Interesting friendly Black Lahu village ✓ after 3 kilometres.
	Trekkers Hut ❂❂❂ Large, basically equipped mud walled huts in a lovely garden looking over fields and jungle to nearby mountains. Cool and very pleasant.
	Address: 130/1 Moo 8, Bang Mung Noi, T. Chedi Mai, Wiang Papao, Chiang Mai.
	Price: 80 Rooms: 10 Bathroom: 7(cw) Comfort: ☆☆ Design: ☆☆☆☆
	Location: ☆☆☆☆☆ Quietness: ☆☆☆☆☆ Restaurant: ☆☆☆
	Facilities: fascinating local treks, 3 or 4 days.

The Far North

65	**Ban Sop Pong Hot Springs** ✓ Two hot sulphurous springs by the river. Thais delight in boiling eggs in the hot water. Several souvenir stalls, mainly uninteresting but good cheap orchids. Excellent Thai restaurant on west side of road with tables built over a lily pond.
69-71	**Cham Bon Bang**. Major centre for the production of grass brooms, basketware and bamboo products, sold cheaply at the roadside.
76-80	**Mae Ka Jahn**. Market town with several small Thai restaurants.
80	Turn east to **Phayao** on lovely new mountain road (see page 245) via **Wang Nua**.
84	Meechai Population Control Centre ✓ to east of road. Mr. Meechai is famous in Thailand for popularising the condom. Soft drinks in garden, display of contraceptives. Honey and ceramics for sale.
91	Dirt road (4wd) to pretty town of **Phroa** ✓ (30 kilometres). Spectacular mountain road (under improvement), many Lisu villages.
95	**Wang Pa Pao**. Large town and regional centre, busy markets. **Wiang Pa Pao Hotel** ●● Typical Thai country town hotel. **Address:** Paholyothin Road, Wiang Pa Pao, Chiang Rai **Price:** 80 **Rooms:** 22 **Bathroom:** 22(cw) **Comfort:** ☆☆ **Location:** ☆ **Design:** ☆ **Quietness:** ☆☆
102	**White Hmong village** ✓ 1 kilometre to west of road (signposted "cultural centre"). Many stalls selling embroidery to tourists.
131	**Mai Suai** ✓ Small town and administrative centre. Small, primitive but excellent restaurant by the bridge. Many Lisu, Akha, Yao, Karen and Lahu villages to north in mountains. Pick-ups go from the centre of Mai Suai to many of these villages.
131	Intersection of Rte 109 with Rte 1019. Turn east for Chiang Rai, west this route is under improvement, linking with Fang (80 kilometres west). Incomplete sections of this road are very poor.

NB DISTANCES NOW ON ROUTE 1019

25	East turn to dirt road (first kilometre paved) leading to several hill tribe villages. Four kilometres to large Akha village of **Saen Jaroen** ✓✓ to west of road. The largest Akha village in Thailand, still fairly traditional but well integrated into Thai society. The road forks just before the village- the west fork leads to the village, then deteriorates, leading to Karen and Lahu villages. The east turn leads to a large Lisu village - **Doi Laan** ✓✓ at an altitude of 1300 metres. Beautiful mountain scenery, but the road a little hairy in places, 4 wd needed in the wet season.
21	**Charoen Gardens** ●●●● to east of road. Rose growing nursery, resort and elephant camp by the side of a pretty river. Very comfortable and pleasant. **Price:** 450-600 (dorm 100) **Rooms:** 10 plus dorm **Bathroom:** 10(hw) **Comfort:** ☆☆☆☆ **Design:** ☆☆☆☆ **Location:** ☆☆☆☆ **Quietness:** ☆☆☆☆ **Restaurant:** ☆☆☆ **Facilities:** elephant rides in high season
20	Rest area and picnic spot with food and drink stalls by the river.
4	North turn Rte 1211 to Chiang Rai (31 kilometres). A prettier, less busy and more interesting route, no slower than the main road.

NB DISTANCES NOW ALONG ROUTE 1211 FROM CHIANG RAI

15	North turn along surfaced road (Rte 1208), 12 kilometres to **Khun Gorn Waterfall** ✓✓✓. The road winds up a mountain stream passing a number of exquisite teak Thai villages. The last three kilometres are unsurfaced, but easy. From

1	the car park at the end of the road take the well marked footpath through perefect evergreen jungle scenery to the waterfall. The path is steep in places, but is an easy 20 minute 1.5 kilometre walk. The falls have a vertical plunge of 30 metres into a deep rocky pool West turn to **Pong Na Cam Elephant Camp** ✓✓✓ Details page 143.
0	**Chiang Rai** ✓✓✓ Large town on the Maekok river. A major tourist centre. Details page 132.

CHIANG RAI - THATON (110 kilometres - 3 hours)

From Chiang Rai town centre drive east 1 kilometre to reach route 1 - a very busy 4 lane road. Turn north here and drive over the Maekok river bridge, where Route 1 becomes Route 101.

NB DISTANCES NOW MEASURED ON ROUTE 1,01 KILOMETRES FROM BANGKOK

Kilometres

831	West turn along newly surfaced road (Rte 1207) 100 metres after Maekok bridge. The road leads for 20 kilometres to several hill tribe villages, elephant camp, guest houses. Details page 143.
832	**Handicrafts Centre** ✓ An enormous open plan store run by the Thai Tourist Authority. An interesting and comprehensive collection of ceramics, wood carvings, tools, musical instruments and clothing, for sale at reasonable prices.
833	**YMCA** ✪✪✪ Good, inexpensive hotel (details page 138)
835	West turn 8 kilometres along part metalled road to **Pong Pha Bat Waterfall**. A small and unimpressive waterfall amongst pretty scenery.
835-855	A fast straight road north. This area is famed for its pineapples - a different variety from the commoner, larger southern ones, but noted for their sweetness and delicacy of taste. The road is lined with stalls selling both the fruit and the most delicious pineapple juice at low prices.
855	The main road by-passes the town of **Mae Chan**, which has several cheap restaurants and a market.
856	West turn to **Mae Chan** on Rte 1089. Follow this road through the town. After Mae Chan, the road follows the course of the Mae Chan river through some lovely rural countryside. At kilometre 9 is a small hot spring, and at kilometre 13 is one of the loveliest guest houses in the north: **Laan Thong Lodge** ✪✪✪✪ Pretty traditional huts in a tranquil, beautiful location by the Mae Chan river. **Address:** Ban Phaki, Mae Chan, Chiang Rai **Price:** 70-180 **Rooms:** 13 **Fan:** 4 **Bathroom:** 4(cw/hw) **Comfort:** ☆ to ☆☆☆ **Design:** ☆☆☆☆☆ **Location:** ☆☆☆☆☆ **Position:** 13 kilometres west of Mae Chan **Quietness:** ☆☆☆☆☆ **Restaurant:** ☆☆☆☆ **Facilities:** fishing, tubing on river, swimming **Tours/treks:** local. In the area are a number of unspoilt Yao, Lisu and Akha villages.
860	Turn west on Rte 1130 opposite large petrol station (the last for 40 kilometres). This road is metalled but very steep and winding in places, with tremendous views of the mountains on and beyond the Burma border.

NB DISTANCES NOW FROM BEGINNING OF ROUTE 1130

4	To south of road, **Winnipa Lodge ❂❂**. Nice but expensive huts (cheap ones very small and basic) in lovely lychee orchard with good views of mountains. Address: 237 Pasang, Mae Chan, Chiang Rai Price: 200-400 **Rooms**: 10 **Fan**: 5 **Bathroom**: 5(hw) **Comfort**: ☆ to ☆☆☆ **Design**: ☆☆☆☆ **Location**: ☆☆☆☆ **Position**: 3kilometres west of Mae Chan **Quietness**: ☆☆☆☆☆ **Restaurant**: ☆☆☆
11	**Hilltribe Centre**. A small shop and display on north side of road. A dirt track leads north from here to a number of very remote and poor hill tribe villages (mainly Akha). This road enters a small spur of Thai territory extending into Burma that is lawless and generally unsafe for the tourist.
15	South turn to the Yao village of **Lao Sib** ✔✔ (4 kilometres). A good dirt road, but 4wd maybe needed in the wet season. A delightful village in a lovely location 900 metres up. the villagers are not tourist oriented, but extremely friendly and welcoming. After the village, the road deteriorates badly, leading to the Akha village of **Ar Lae** (6 kilometres) which is very wary of visitors.
16	The road climbs sharply out of the valley, with very tight bends and steep gradients for the next 50 kilometres.
17	On south side of road, the Yao village of **Pa Dua** ✔. One of the most visited of hill tribe villages, usually with a number of tour buses parked outside. The path through the village is lined with stalls selling hill tribe souvenirs. There is a small cafe and toilets for tourists. Despite its commercialisation, the villagers are friendly and the atmosphere is fun.
23	On north side of road, the Akha village of **Sam Laek** ✔✔. Another very commercialised village. The Akha people here are very traditional, and seem rather bemused by the large number of tourists. There are many stalls lining the path, selling a range of goods, many originating from Burma. The path north can be travelled by motor bike or 4wd jeep for 13 kilometres to the village of **Thoed Thai**, former base of opium warlord Khun Sa. This road is often closed by police or army, and is not safe.
36	Mountaintop town of **Doi Mae Salong** ✔✔✔ At an altitude of 1100 metres with views of wild hill country in all directions, this town is fascinating. A Chinese town, home to the Kuomintang, its name has been changed recently to **Santikiree** (hill of peace). Details of town and accommodations page 158.

AFTER DOI MAE SALONG DISTANCES FROM JUNCTION 12 KILOMETRES EAST OF THATON

The road from Doi Mae Salong west to Thaton (48 kilometres) is due for completion in 1992. Any unsurfaced sections can be difficult in the wet season, when 4wd is essential. It is a very dramatic road, much of it running along high mountain ridges, through jungle and bush. Hill tribe slash and burn fields edge the road in places, and small, primitive villages can be glimpsed clinging to ridge tops.

22	**Lon Jai**. A Chinese Kuomintang village to the east of a police check point. The police here frequently stop and search vehicles.
17	**Kaew Satai**. A large, partly Christian Akha village to the south of the road. Another police check point on the road just before the turn off.

...ping the ditches cleared in the dry season. In the background are the mountains of Doi Tung. Mae Chaam Valley

Lake fishing, Chiang Dao, Chiang Mai

The Golden Triangle. The east bank of the Maekhong river is Laos, the west bank to the north is Burma

Land and People

7	Lahu and Kuomintang village of **Huai Muang Ngam**.
0	Junction with dirt road leading east to Maekok river and several Lisu and Karen villages. Turn west here for **Thaton**. This road has a stony base, giving a very uncomfortable ride for the 12 kilometres to Thaton.

DISTANCES NOW FROM JUNCTION

1	Small, very pretty Lisu village of **Thaat ✓**, just visible to north of road.
12	**Thaton ✓✓✓** Small town on the Maekok river, with houses and boats clustered round the bridge. The Burmese border is only 2 kms upstream. Thaton is very scenic, capped with a hilltop temple and enormous white Buddha. The river upstream winds into steep hills, downstream it widens out and is thick with long tail boats and rafts. There are several good places to stay, and Thaton is a jumping off point for 2 or 3 day raft trips downstream to Chiang Rai. Thaton details page 161.

THATON - CHIANG MAI (175 kilometres - 3 hours) Map page 120-121

ROUTE 1089 LEADS SOUTH TO FANG. DISTANCES FROM FANG

16	**Mai Ai**. A small town famous as a past base for opium warlord Khun Sa. West turn here opposite the school. A poor dirt and gravel road climbs steeply into the mountains, with wonderful views of the Maekok valley. This road is frequently closed by the police for security reasons.
0	**Fang ✓**. A large and ancient town, founded by King Mengrai in the 13th century. There are no remains of its past, but Fang is an important industrial centre since it produces oil and, recently, geothermal power. Not a pretty town, but the National Park is well worth visiting. There are some good value accommodations in town. Details page 163.

KILOMETRE POSTS SOUTH OF FANG GIVE DISTANCES FROM CHIANG MAI

149	West turn to **Fang National Park** 33 (10 kilometres). Turn west opposite the market in the centre of town signposted in English, reached by a new metalled road. The car park is close to a large geothermal power station. The landscaped gardens are a patchwork of hot springs and steaming marshes. One very impressive geyser erupts every 30-40 minutes. There are trails leading through the park to hill tribe villages - Karen, Lahu and Akha. Maps of the park can be obtained from a small information centre.
142	East turn to **Mae Suai** on Rte 109 (65 kilometres). This road is under construction, but at present the many unfinished sections are very poor, impossible in the wet season. There are several Lahu villages on the first twenty kilometres of road, and the mountain scenery is pretty, but this route is not recommended.
138	West turn to **Doi Arng ✓** A newly metalled road (some sections incomplete), very steep and spectacular, leading 26 kilometres into the mountains on the Burmese border. Doi Arng is a mountain and experimental plant breeding station, researching the production of temperate fruit and vegetables in the cool, high altitude climate.
119	To the east of the road, 1 kilometre to **Forestland Resort ❂❂❂** Delightful location around pretty lake in jungle, lovely rooms, but rather neglected and run down. Address: 7/512 Ban Don Yeng, Fang, Chiang Mai Price: 550 Rooms: 7 Bathroom: 7(hw) Design: ☆☆☆☆ Location: ☆☆☆☆ Position: 25 kilometres south of Fang Restaurant: ☆☆☆(often closed) Facilities: boats for rent, fishing

The Far North

118 West turn 3 kilometres along good gravel road to a large Thai village under a cliff. At the base of the cliff is a large and beautiful temple complex with two covered staircases leading to **Tub-Tao caves** ✓✓✓. The left hand cave is the more interesting. It contains a very large seated Buddha and an equally impressive reclining Buddha surrounded by primitive statues of disciples. The cave is actually a large cavern lit by a small hole in the roof, entered through a wooden door guarded by bizarre demon figures festooned with cobwebs and vines. The walls of the cavern are decorated with various carvings, including a stalagmite which has been carved into a group of elephants. The overall effect of the cave is a rather fanciful "Indiana Jones" film set. The right hand cave has a large bat colony and three small and uninteresting Buddha statues. The history of the caves is unknown, but the statues appear to be very ancient, probably built by Shan or Chinese people.

South of kilometre 118 the road climbs steeply into a range of hills, and winds through these for 25 kilometres. To the west there are a string of spectacularly precipitous limestone peaks and pillars of rock, similar to those of Phang-Na bay in the south. In these hills are a number of hill tribe villages, but the area is not completely safe away from the road.

100 To the east of the road, the luxury resort of:
Chiang Dao Hills ●●●● Lovely bungalows set in gorgeous grounds.
Address: 28 Moo 6, Ping Kong, Chiang Mai **Tel:** (053)236995, 232434
Price: 600-1200 **Rooms:** 38 **Fan:** 38 **Bathroom:** 18(hw) **Comfort:** ☆☆☆☆
Design: ☆☆☆☆☆ **Location:** ☆☆ **Position:** 100 kilometres north of Chiang Mai
Quietness: ☆☆☆☆☆ **Restaurant:** ☆☆☆☆

99 West turn along dirt and gravel road through spectacular mountain scenery to **Lisu village** ✓✓(7 kilometres). A poor road (4wd may be needed in the wet season). This little visited village is in a wonderful location surrounded by near vertical rock pillars. The adults are a little reserved but the children are a delight. 4 kilometres along this road is a Christianised and non traditional Lahu village.

96 To east of road, Hmong village of **Huay Luk** ✓. A traditional Blue Hmong village at low altitude. Very accessible, so visited by many tourists, with several handicraft stalls in the main street.

95 To east of road is a lovely lake backed by distant mountains with a small bamboo cafe. Behind the lake is a Kings Royal Project where temperate and sub tropical fruit and vegetables are grown by hill tribe peoples.

83 To the east, Rte 1105 to **Phrao** (31 kilometres). An attractive mountain road, now almost completed with a good surface, to the small, isolated and beautiful town of Phrao. It is possible to continue through Phrao along Rte 1250 to the Chiang Mai-Chiang Rai road (Rte 1009 - 53 kilometres). This road is one of exceptional beauty, climbing high into the mountains and passing several remote Lisu villages. Some stretches of this road are difficult in the wet season, when 4wd may be needed.

75 West turn 5 kilometres metalled road to the Thai village of **Muang Ngai**. The road continues from here to the Burma border, but it is generally closed for security reasons, and is definitely not safe.

71 West turn 5 kilometres to **Chiang Dao caves** ✓✓✓. A famous tourist spot, the caves are extensive, running underneath **Doi Chiang Dao**, at 2180 metres, Thailand's second highest mountain. Within the caves are several Buddhist statues of various sizes. The caves are lit for the first 400 metres, but a guide with lantern is compulsory (100 *baht*), and necessary if you want to continue further. There are many high caverns with good stalactites and stalagmites, and several caverns with large bat colonies. The caves are reached by two covered staircases, and at the entrance is a large pool fed by an

70	underground river inhabited by giant carp. The road continues past the caves and up to Doi Chang Dao, and the Karen village of **Muang Khong** ✓(10 kilometres) and the Lisu village of **Ma La Mai** ✓, but is very dusty or muddy (4wd essential). **Chiang Dao** ✓✓ A town of two storey teak buildings, very traditional in design, brooded over by the massive bulk of Doi Chiang Dao to the west. The town was founded 200 years ago as a place of exile for people suspected of witchcraft or of being possessed by evil spirits. There are two or three passable restaurants, and one hotel: **Piong Chiang Dao** ● Interesting traditional design, but rather dirty and uncomfortable rooms. Address: Chiang Dao, Chiang Mai Price: 60-140 Rooms: 12 Fan: 12 Bathroom: 3(cw) Comfort: ☆ to ☆☆ Design: ☆☆☆ Location: ☆☆ Position: central Quietness: ☆☆ Restaurant: ☆☆
54	**Chiang Dao Elephant Camp** ✓✓(1 kilometre). In a lovely wooded valley, this camp is a popular tourist destination. There are displays of elephants at work from 9.30 - 11 am after which short rides (40 *baht*) or two hour elephant treks (600 *baht*) can be taken.
48	On east of road: **Apple Guest house** ●● 3 new bamboo huts in farmland. Address: Kilometre 48, Rte 107, Mae Tang, Chiang Mai Price: 80 Rooms: 3 Fan: 3 Bathroom: 3(cw) Comfort: ☆☆ Design: ☆☆☆ Location: ☆☆☆ Position: 10 kilometres north of Mae Tang Quietness: ☆☆☆ Restaurant: ☆☆☆
42	West turn along good gravel road to **Mae Tang river** and **Mae Taman Rafting and Elephant Camp** ✓✓ (15 kilometres). This road leads across the valley to the river, (6 kilometres), then north along the river to the camp. The wide valley north of here is a major trekking area, many treks ending with a raft trip downstream to this camp. In a pretty location, the camp offers a combination 3 hour trip with rafting, elephant and bullock cart ride (400 *baht*). There is also a guest house in a lovely riverside location. Address: 535 Moo 1 Rim Tai, Chiang Mai Tel: (053)297060 Price: 300 (dorm 100) Rooms: 3 Bathroom: 0 (cw outside) Comfort:☆ Design: ☆☆☆☆ Location: ☆☆☆☆☆ Position: next to elephant camp Quietness: ☆☆☆☆☆ Restaurant: ☆☆☆ Tours/treks: rafting, elephants The dirt road continues through the camp, reaching a small Hmong village after 8 kilometres, but is barely passable. The area north west of the camp contains many Lisu, Karen and Hmong hill tribe villages in the Mae Tang valley, only reachable on foot.
41	East turn along metalled road to **Mae Gnao Reservoir** ✓✓(15 kilometres). The road passes north below the huge dam and ends at a large car park on the edge of the water. The reservoir extends 35 kms up the valley, edged by high jungle covered hills. There are two restaurants by the car park, and boats can be rented for the half hour trip to: **Manohra Guest House** ●●●● Floating bamboo huts on the reservoir surrounded by jungle. Transport only by boat. Address: (Bookings and transport) Overlander Bar, Moon Muang Road, Chiang Mai Price: 200 Rooms: 16 Fan: 16 Bathroom:16(cw) Comfort: ☆☆☆ Design: ☆☆☆☆ Location: ☆☆☆☆☆ Quietness: ☆☆☆☆☆ Facilities: swimming, boating, fishing.
35	**Mae Malie**. Small town with a large market and two small restaurants. West turn here to Pai, Mae Hong Son.
16	**Mae Rim**. Busy market town. For details Mae Rim-Chiang Mai, see page 173.

TOWNS OF THE FAR NORTH

CHIANG RAI

NORTH THAILAND'S SECOND CITY, and a major tourist centre, Chiang Rai is, for most visitors, rather a disappointment. It has a longer history than that of Chiang Mai, and a more apparently exciting and romantic geographical position, but its development in recent years, rapid and random, has made little of the city's potential. It is, though, an excellent base for exploring the uppermost part of Northern Thailand, certainly the most culturally diverse part of the country. Chiang Rai has an excellent choice of accommodations in all price ranges, and a number of beautiful and interesting temples to offset the city's overall modern concrete drabness.

Chiang Rai is only 60 kilometres from the northernmost point in Thailand. It is built on the south bank of the Maekok river, roughly half way along its course between Burma and Laos. It is the only crossing point of the river between these two boundaries, so is a natural conduit for goods passing north or south. West and south of the city are ranges of hills and mountains, sadly not visible from within Chiang Rai. To the north and east is a very fertile plain specialising in the growing of pineapples and rice. The hills within 60 kilometres of the city are almost completely denuded of their natural jungle cover. This area has had a rapid influx of hill tribe peoples this century, whose slash and burn agricultural systems, as well as logging, are largely responsible for this deforestation. Increasingly, these tribes are being persuaded to grow stable crops such as fruit and coffee. It is to be hoped that these valiant efforts, by the King and government, will be in time to save this beautiful area before it becomes a desert.

The city has been called the "gateway to the Golden Triangle". This term has little meaning in reality. First used by Americans in the Vietnam war, in its original sense it meant the whole of Northern Burma and Thailand, where the bulk of Asia's heroin originated. It became a useful term for tourist promotion, where it refers both generally to the part of Northern Thailand north of the Maekok river, and to the spot on the banks of the Maekhong where the boundaries of Thailand, Burma and Laos meet. (see page 155). The city's dependence on opium and heroin has greatly declined over the last 20 years, and those tourists who come looking for drug warlords, mystery and intrigue will be sadly disappointed.

Chiang Rai

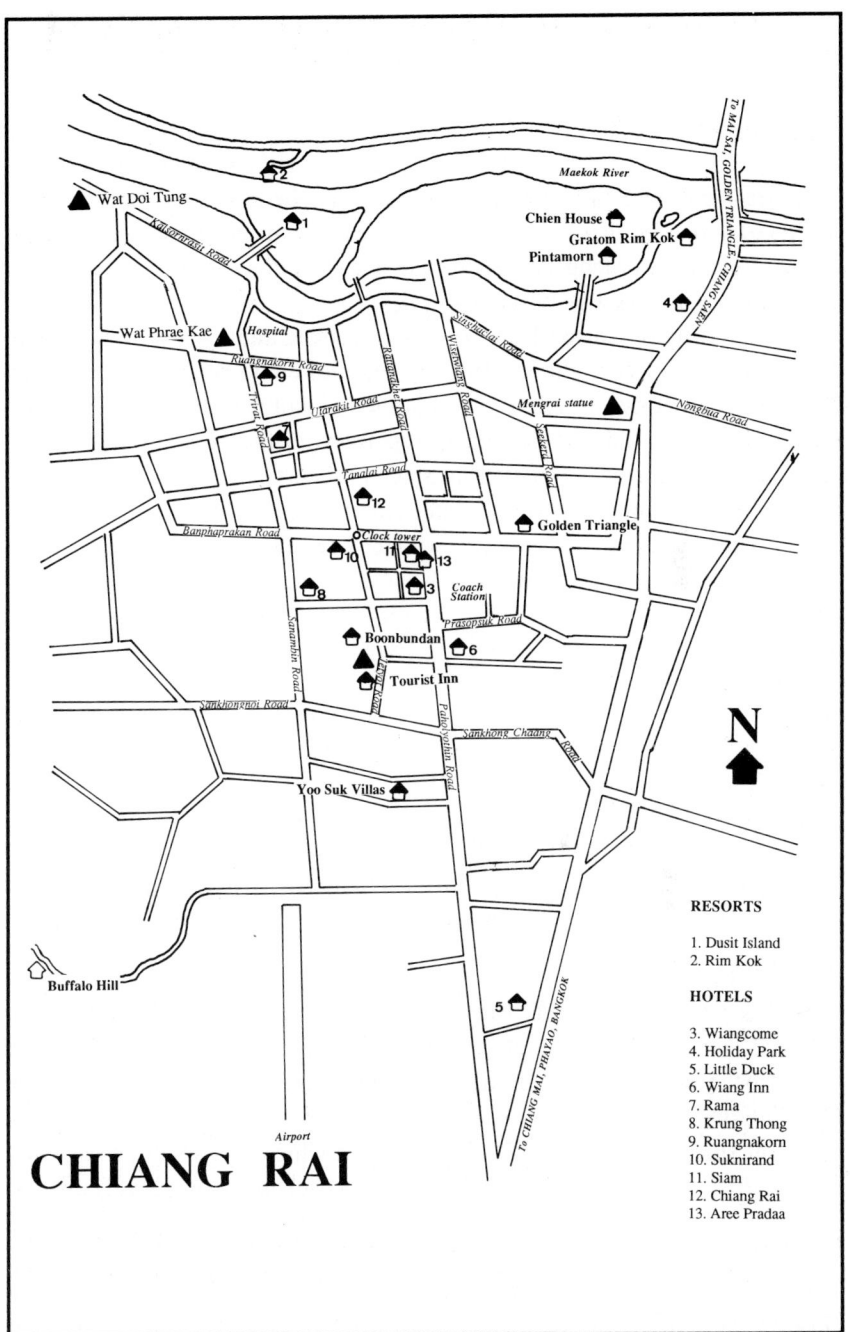

RESORTS

1. Dusit Island
2. Rim Kok

HOTELS

3. Wiangcome
4. Holiday Park
5. Little Duck
6. Wiang Inn
7. Rama
8. Krung Thong
9. Ruangnakorn
10. Suknirand
11. Siam
12. Chiang Rai
13. Aree Pradaa

Chiang Rai was built by the heroic King Mengrai in 1267 AD, founder of the Lanna dynasty, 29 years before Chiang Mai. He had first established his power base in Chiang Saen before expanding his kingdom outwards, first to Chiang Rai, but eventually as far as Lampang 200 kilometres south, and to Luang Prabang in Laos. The name of the city is believed to be based on the Thai for "Mengrai's elephant" ✓, since legend has it that the position of the city was decided by one of these. Very little of the ancient city remains, although recently a statue to Mengrai was erected, and the old walls of the city rebuilt with a totally unattractive new brick wall.

The majority of Chiang Rai is concrete block. Building is so rapid that in 1990 the price of concrete trebled, and supplies could not be ferried in fast enough. Some of the suburbs are still attractive, but the Thai obsession with tearing down the old and tasteful to replace with the new and tasteless is particularly noticeable in Chiang Rai. Since 1990 three enormous luxury hotels have been built catering to the package tourist. One is in the middle of the Maekok river - quite a shock to those who have rafted gently downstream from Thaton along the quaint and ageless waterway.

THINGS TO SEE

MAEKOK RIVER ✓✓✓
This is best seen from the bridge (Rte 1), or more pleasantly from the restaurant or coffee shop of the Chiang Rai Dusit Island Resort. Trips along the river can be taken from the boat station, near the resort on Trirat Road.

WAT PHRAE KAE ✓✓✓
This was where the famous Emerald Buddha, now in Wat Phra Kaeo in Bangkok, was first discovered in 1436 AD. According to legend, lightning damaged the old *chedi*, exposing a plaster statue. Later this cracked to reveal the Emerald Buddha inside. The present temple was built in 1890, and has a beautiful stucco and gold *chedi* at the base of which is a small passageway leading to a delightful painted reclining Buddha backed by some lovely murals.

WAT DOI TUNG ✓
This fairly modern temple complex (built 1945) is on a small hill west of town close to the river. It is very gaudy, with brightly coloured *wiharn*, *bot* and

mondops, and gives lovely views over the river and town. It is supposedly the spot from which King Mengrai chose the location for his new town.

MENGRAI STATUE AND WALLS ✓
The statue of Mengrai, close to the main Chiang Mai road, is surrounded by hundreds of wood and metal elephant statues. The reconstructed walls, a 250 metre line of bricks, are uninspiring.

RESTAURANTS

The Chinese restaurant just outside the **Dusit Island** resort, looking out over the river, serves exceptionally delicious Chinese food. Beautifully situated and decorated, it is expensive but very special.
The Holiday Hotel Restaurant on the west side of the main road leading north from Chiang Rai just before the bridge, is a new hotel/restaurant/shopping complex of great style. The restaurant is designed like a railway carriage. It is spotlessly clean and well organized with good furniture and fittings. The food is classic Northern Thai, not expensive and excellent.
The **Nakhon Pathom** on Ratanaket Road opposite the Thai Airways office serves cheap, clean and good Thai food, but closes at 6.00 pm.
Around the clock tower are a number of good, mainly cheap Thai restaurants. The **Lee O Sha** (with a large prawn painted over the door) is excellent but expensive. The **Haw Naliga** is cheaper but not as good. The **Phetburi**, with streaming basins of Thai food at the entrance, is good and very cheap. Good food and decor at the **T-Hut** on Paholyothin Road 300 metres east of the Wiang Inn. This is a restaurant for upper income Thais, and has nice decor, soft lights and classic Thai music. The food is exquisite, but portions are small.
There are a number of restaurants serving western food. **La Cantina**, in the western bar area just north of the Wiangcome complex, specialises in Italian food - an enthusiastic owner cooks really good pizzas and pasta dishes, and claims to have the best wine cellar north of Bangkok.
The other restaurants in the area are average - although **Frenchies Bar** has good steaks. On Paholyothin Road, opposite and 100 metres east of the Wiang Inn, is the **Bier Stube**. Good western breakfasts and a range of mainly German dishes compliment the basic Thai/western food. A popular place to hang out and meet friends.

NIGHTLIFE

There is one small bar area around the **Wiangcome Hotel**. At the back of the hotel are a number of massage parlours and nightclubs. 100 metres north of this square is a small *soi* catering mainly to western tourists. There are several small and friendly bars, some with video lounges. **Cheers** and **Easy** bars are good fun. There is also a go-go bar called **Rudis**.

TOURS AND TREKS

Most of the guest houses offer local tours and/or treks. There are several specialists in local tours on Rattanakat Road near the Wiangcome hotel, who also rent jeeps and motor bikes. Alexander at the Bier Stube specialises in treks to very remote areas.

TRANSPORT

PLANE

The airport is 2 kilometres south of the city, at the end of Sanambin Road.

Chiang Mai-Chiang Rai:	09.15, 13.15, 14.25 (daily)
Chiang Rai-Chiang Mai:	10.35, 11,15, 14.25, 15.05 (daily)
Bangkok-Chiang Rai:	09.20 (Fridays), 12.40, 16.40 (daily)
Chiang Rai-Bangkok:	13.25 (Fridays), 12.40, 16.40 (daily)

BUS/COACH

The bus station in on Prasopsuk road near the Wiang Inn, with good services throughout the north.

Aircom to Bangkok: (10.5 hours, 250 *baht*) 7.00, 8.00, 20.00 (daily)
Aircom to Chiang Mai: (3 hours, 70 *baht*) 10 buses daily
To Mai Sai: (1.5 hours, 15 *baht*): Every 15 minutes from 06.00-18.00.
To Chiang saen: (1.5 hours, 15 *baht*): Every 20 minutes from 06.00-19.00.
There are also frequent services to Phayao, Lampang and Nan.

LOCAL

Tuk-tuks are a recent arrival in Chiang Rai, with most trips costing 10-20 *baht*. There are many bicycle rickshaws (*samlors*) who charge about half. Local buses cost 3 *baht*. Pick ups (*songthaews*) will go anywhere within 20 kilometres of the city.

ACCOMMODATION

RESORTS

Dusit Island Resort ●●●●●
On an island in the Maekok river, an enormous concrete palace with a wonderful setting and beautiful internal design.
Address: 1129 Kraisorasit Road **Tel:** (053)715777 **Fax:** 715801.
Price: 2200-4000 **Rooms:** 271 **A/C:** 271 **Bathroom:** 271(hw) **Comfort:** ☆☆☆☆☆
Design: ☆☆☆☆ **Location:** ☆☆☆☆☆ **Quietness:** ☆☆☆☆☆ **Restaurant:** ☆☆☆☆☆
Facilities: pool, tennis, courts **Tours:** wide range

Rim Kok Resort ●●●●●
Very large resort with all luxury facilities on the north bank of the Maekok, beautiful internal design but rather bunker like externally.
Address: 6 Moo 4 Chiang Rai-Thaton **Tel:** (053)716445.
Price: 1400-4000 **Rooms:** 256 **A/C:** 256 **Bathroom:** 256(hw) **Comfort:** ☆☆☆☆☆
Design: ☆☆☆☆ **Location:** ☆☆☆☆☆ **Quietness:** ☆☆☆☆☆ **Restaurant:** ☆☆☆☆
Facilities: pool **Tours/treks:** wide range

HOTELS

Wiangcome ●●●●
Slightly fading but still luxurious hotel with large, beautifully furnished rooms.
Address: 869/90 Pemawabhata Road, Chiang Rai **Tel:** (053)711811 **Fax:** 712973
Price: 900-3500 **Rooms:** 221 **A/C:** 221 **Bathroom:** 221(hw) **Comfort:** ☆☆☆☆☆ **Design:** ☆☆☆
Location: ☆☆☆ **Position:** central **Quietness:** ☆☆☆ **Restaurant:** ☆☆☆ **Facilities:** pool
Tours/treks: wide range

Holiday Park Hotel ●●●●
New, well designed hotel with very well furnished but slightly small rooms.
Address: 216 Paholyothin Road **Tel:** (053)712443
Price: 600-800 **Rooms:** 48 **A/C:** 48 **Bathroom:** 48(hw) **Comfort:** ☆☆☆☆ **Design:** ☆☆☆☆
Location: ☆☆ **Position:** central **Quietness:** ☆☆☆ **Restaurant:** ☆☆☆
Facilities: pool

Little Duck ●●●●
Massive new hotel, beautiful internally but in a poor location.
Address: 99 Superhighway, Rob Wiang. **Tel:** 715620-38 **Fax:** 715639
Price range: 1452 **Rooms:** 330 **A/C:** 330 **Bathroom:** 330(hw) **Comfort:** ☆☆☆☆☆
Design: ☆☆☆ **Location:** ☆☆ **Position:** 3 kilometres west of town centre **Quietness:** ☆☆☆☆
Restaurant: ☆☆☆☆ **Facilities:** pool **Tours/treks:** wide range

Wiang Inn ✿✿✿✿
Luxury but ugly hotel in town centre.
Address: 893 Paholyothin Road, Chiang Rai **Tel:** (053)711533
Price: 1331 **Rooms:** 258 **A/C:** 258 **Bathroom:** 258(hw) **Comfort:** ☆☆☆☆☆ **Design:** ☆☆☆
Location: ☆☆☆ **Position:** central **Quietness:** ☆☆☆ **Restaurant:** ☆☆☆☆ **Facilities:** pool
Tours/treks: wide range.

Rama ✿✿✿
Typically anonymous not quite luxury International style hotel.
Address: 331/4 Trirat Road
Price: 360-500 **Comfort:** ☆☆☆☆ **Design:** ☆☆☆ **Location:** ☆☆☆ **Position:** central
Quietness: ☆☆☆ **Restaurant:** ☆☆☆

YMCA ✿✿✿
New brick hotel, very good value for standard of accommodation but poor location.
Address: 70 Phaholyothin Road, Chiang Rai **Tel:** (053)713785-6 **Fax:** 714336
Price: 220-400 (dorm 70) **Rooms:** 50 **A/C:** 28 **Fan:** 22 **Bathroom:** 50(hw)
Comfort: ☆☆ to ☆☆☆☆☆ **Design:** ☆☆ **Location:** ☆ **Position:** On Chiang Mai-Mae Sai Road 4 kilometres north of Maekok. **Quietness:** ☆☆ **Restaurant:** ☆☆☆ **Facilities:** paddling pool

Krung Tong ✿✿✿
Large characterless modern Thai hotel, but well furnished, clean and comfortable - good value.
Address: 412 Sanambin Road **Tel:** (9053)711033
Price: 160-280 **Rooms:** 110 **A/C:** 12 **Fan:** 98 **Bathroom:** 110(hw) **Comfort:** ☆☆☆ to ☆☆☆☆☆
Design: ☆☆ **Location:** ☆☆ **Position:** central **Quietness:** ☆☆☆

Ruangnakorn ✿✿
Fairly modern Thai hotel with comfortable but utilitarian rooms. Morning market outside starts at 4.30 am!
Address: 25 Ruangnakorn Road **Tel:** (053)711566
Price: 180-570 **Rooms:** 61 **A/C:** 28 **Fan:** 33 **Bathroom:** 61(55hw) **Comfort:** ☆☆☆ to ☆☆☆☆☆
Position: central **Quietness:** ☆ **Restaurant:** ☆☆☆

Suknirand ✿✿
Large Thai hotel near clock tower. Comfortable rooms but prison like design and atmosphere.
Address: 421/1 Banphaprakan Road **Tel:** (053)711055
Price: 300-450 **Rooms:** 105 **A/C:** 41 **Fan:** 75 **Bathroom:** 105(hw) **Comfort:** ☆☆☆ to ☆☆☆☆☆
Design: ☆☆ **Location:** ☆☆ **Position:** central **Quietness:** ☆☆ **Restaurant:** ☆☆

Siam ✿✿
Basic facilities, fairly clean but characterless Thai hotel.
Address: 531/6-8 Banphaprakerm Road **Tel:** (053)711077
Price: 150-210 **Rooms:** 52 **Fan:** 52 **Bathroom:** 52(cw) **Comfort:** ☆☆ **Design:** ☆☆
Location: ☆☆ **Position:** central **Quietness:** ☆ **Restaurant:** ☆☆☆

Chiang Rai ✹✹
Cement Thai-style hotel, hospital like and tatty but adequate.
Address: 519 Suksatit Road, Chiang Rai **Tel:** (053)771126
Price: 120 **Rooms:** 68 **Fan:** 68 **Bathroom:** 68(hw) **Comfort:** ☆☆☆ **Design:** ☆ **Location:** ☆
Position: central **Quietness:** ☆

Aree Pradaa ✹
Basic rooms on busy, noisy main street.
Address: 541 Paholyothin Road, Chiang Rai
Price: 80-120 **Rooms:** 12 **Fan:** 12 **Bathroom:** 0(cw outside) **Comfort:** ☆ **Design:** ☆
Location: ☆☆ **Position:** central **Quietness:** ☆

GUEST HOUSES

Buffalo Hill ✹✹✹✹
Beautiful cabins in pretty, shady gardens in rural location near airport.
Address: 481 Doi Khao Road, Chiang Rai **Tel:** (053)714420
Price: 220-300 **Rooms:** 28 **Fan:** 28 **Bathroom:** 28(hw) **Comfort:** ☆☆☆☆ **Design:** ☆☆☆☆☆
Location: ☆☆☆☆ **Position:** 2 kilometres south of Chiang Rai **Quietness:** ☆☆☆
Restaurant: ☆☆☆

Golden Triangle ✹✹✹✹
Very well designed and furnished rooms in well tended tropical gardens.
Address: 590 Paholyothin Road, Chiang Rai **Tel:** (053)711339
Price: 600-900 **Rooms:** 41 **A/C:** 41 **Bathroom:** 41(hw) **Comfort:** ☆☆☆☆☆ **Design:** ☆☆☆☆☆
Location: ☆☆☆☆ **Position:** central **Quietness:** ☆☆ **Restaurant:** ☆☆☆☆
Tours/treks: very wide range

Gratom Rim Kok ✹✹✹✹
Rooms and cabins of various standards in a lovely garden on the banks of the Maekok river.
Address: 339 Soi Hamnuan Paholyothin Road
Price: 150-450 **Rooms:** 20 **A/C:** 5 **Fan:** 15 **Bathroom:** 20(hw) **Comfort:** ☆☆ to ☆☆☆☆
Design: ☆☆☆☆ **Location:** ☆☆☆☆☆ **Position:** 2 kilometres east of Chiang Rai
Quietness: ☆☆☆☆ **Restaurant:** ☆☆☆

Pintamorn ✹✹✹
Inexpensive, well furnished rooms, excellent service and atmosphere.
Address: 199/13 Muri Singhaklan Road **Tel:** (053)714161
Price: 60-150 **Rooms:** 20 **A/C:** 2 **Fan:** 18 **Bathroom:** 20(hw) **Comfort:** ☆☆☆☆ **Design:** ☆☆☆
Location: ☆☆☆ **Position:** 1 kilometre north of town centre **Quietness:** ☆☆ **Restaurant:** ☆☆☆☆
Treks/tours: range of treks

Boonbundan ❂❂❂
Range of room standards, some excellent, in pretty garden in quiet lane, let down by poor service.
Address: 1005/13 Jedyod Road Tel: (053)712914
Price: 100-140 Rooms: 50 A/C: 12 Fan: 38 Bathroom: 12(hw)38(cw) Comfort: ☆☆ to ☆☆☆☆
Design: ☆☆☆☆ Location: ☆☆☆ Position: central Quietness: ☆☆☆☆ Tours/treks: wide range

Yoo Suk Villas ❂❂❂
Luxuriously equipped new concrete cabins, although rooms a little small, in central but quiet *soi*.
Address: 952/13 Ruamjilthawaj Road
Price: 395 A/C: 20(hw) Comfort: ☆☆☆☆ Design: ☆☆☆☆ Location: ☆☆☆ Position: ☆☆☆
Quietness: ☆☆☆ Restaurant: ☆☆☆ Facilities: TV, fridge

Tourist Inn ❂❂❂
Large teak house in quiet soi with new, clean, comfortable rooms, good atmosphere.
Address: 1004/6 Jedyod Road Tel: (053)714682
Price: 160 Rooms: 6 Fan: 6 Bathroom: 6(hw) Comfort: ☆☆☆☆ Design: ☆☆☆
Location: ☆☆☆ Position: central Quietness: ☆☆☆ Restaurant: snacks

Chien House ❂❂❂
Row of large, clean, comfortable rooms around swimming pool.
Address: 172 Sriboonruang Road Tel: (053)713388
Price: 100-150 Rooms: 12 Fan: 12 Bathroom: 12(5hw 7cw) Comfort: ☆☆☆ Design: ☆☆☆
Location: ☆☆ Position: 1 kilometre north of town centre Quietness: ☆☆☆ Facilities: pool

Chat House ❂❂❂
Pleasant inexpensive rooms around pretty teak house in wooded area near boat station. Good service and atmosphere.
Address: Sangkaew Road Tel: (053)711481
Price: 100 (dorm 30) Rooms: 20 Fan: 20 Bathroom: 6(cw)(hw outside) Comfort: ☆ to ☆☆☆
Design: ☆☆☆☆ Location: ☆☆☆ Position: central Quietness: ☆☆☆ Restaurant: ☆☆☆
Tours/treks: range of treks

Head ❂❂❂
Lanna style bamboo huts around large teak house in rural garden.
Address: 279 Soi 2, Ratchayota Road, Chiang Rai
Price: 40-100 Rooms: 13 Fan: 13 Bathroom: 6(cw) Comfort: ☆☆ Design: ☆☆☆
Location: 1 kilometre west of town Quietness: ☆☆☆ Restaurant: ☆☆☆.

Koh Loy River House ❂❂❂
Six joined chalets and rooms in main house surrounded by pretty garden on branch of river.
Address: 485 Tanom Road, Chiang Rai Tel: (053)715084
Price: 120-200 Rooms: 18 Fan: 18 Bathroom: 12(cw)(hw outside) Comfort: ☆☆☆
Design: ☆☆☆ Location: ☆☆☆ Position: 1 kilometre north of town
Quietness: ☆☆☆ Restaurant: ☆☆☆ Tours/Treks: day trips

Wisid ✪✪✪
Emphasis on treks, reasonable accommodation at reasonable prices.
Address: 21/4 Ratchayota Road
Price: 100-120 **Rooms:** 17 **Fan:** 17 **Bathroom:** 4(hw)13(cw)(hw outside) **Comfort:** ☆☆ to ☆☆☆
Design: ☆☆☆ **Location:** ☆☆ **Position:** 1.5 kilometres west of town **Quietness:** ☆☆
Restaurant: ☆☆☆ **Facilities:** motor bike rental, free bicycles **Treks:** extensive range, expert guides.

Mae Hong Son ✪✪✪
Few facilities but great character and atmosphere.
Address: 126 Singhaklan Road, Chiang Rai
Price: 45-100 **Rooms:** 5 **Fan:** 5 **Bathroom:** 1(hw)(hw outside) **Comfort:** ☆ to ☆☆☆ **Design:** ☆☆☆
Location: ☆☆ **Position:** 1 kilometre north of town **Quietness:** ☆☆☆ **Restaurant:** bkfst only
Facilities: motor bike and jeep rental **Tours/treks:** wide range.

Poppy Inn ✪✪✪
Large, clean, comfortable rooms but rather characterless.
Address: 216/1-8 Tanalai Road, Chiang Rai **Tel:** (053)712499
Price: 280-380 **Rooms:** 28 **A/C:** 19 **Fan:** 9 **Bathroom:** 28(hw) **Comfort:** ☆☆☆ to ☆☆☆☆
Design: ☆☆☆ **Location:** ☆☆ **Position:** central **Quietness:** ☆☆☆ **Facilities:** coffee shop

Jira House ✪✪✪
Four fairly new Thai houses in large garden, reasonably clean and pleasant.
Address: 74/1 Sanphaned Rd Chiang Rai
Price: 100 **Rooms:** 13 **Fan:** 13 **Bathroom:** 0(hw outside) **Comfort:** ☆☆ **Design:** ☆☆☆
Location: ☆☆☆☆ **Position:** central **Quietness:** ☆☆☆ **Restaurant:** snacks only

Nang Inn ✪✪✪ ?
Under construction. 30 good value rooms in concrete block, prices about 100-150, hw in all rooms.
Address: 248 Singhaklan Road, Chiang Rai

Srikerd House ✪✪
Primitive rickety rooms, but very cheap and cheerful.
Address: 717/1 Srikerd Road, Chiang Rai
Price: 40-80 **Rooms:** 6 **Fan:** 6 **Bathroom:** 3(hw) **Comfort:** ☆ to ☆☆ **Design:** ☆☆ **Location:** ☆☆
Position: central **Quietness:** ☆☆☆
Treks: motor bike treks, tours to see Phi Tong Luang (see page 47).

Fruit ✪✪
Small, very flimsy huts on banks of pretty stream.
Address: 91/2 Kohloy Road, Chiang Rai
Price: 50-80 **Rooms:** 8 **Fan:** 8 **Bathroom:** 5(cw) **Comfort:** ☆ to ☆☆ **Design:** ☆☆☆
Location: ☆☆☆☆ **Position:** 1.5 kilometres north of town. **Quietness:** ☆☆☆ **Restaurant:** snacks

Porn ✪✪
Clean rooms with few facilities in large teak house.
Address: 503 Ratanaket Rd, Chiang Rai
Price: 100 **Rooms:** 8 **Fan:** 8 **Bathroom:** 0(hw outside) **Comfort:** ☆☆ **Design:** ☆☆☆
Location: ☆☆ **Position:** central **Quietness:** ☆☆☆ **Restaurant:** bkfst only

White House ✿✿
Basic accommodation but good atmosphere.
Address: 789 Paholyothin Rd, Chiang Rai
Price: 80-180 **Rooms:** 13 **Fan:** 13 **Bathroom:** 13(cw)(hw outside) **Comfort:** ☆☆ **Design:** ☆☆☆
Location: ☆☆ **Position:** 200 metres south of Maekok bridge **Quietness:** ☆☆ **Restaurant:** ☆☆☆
Facilities: jeep/motor bike rental **Tours/treks:** wide range of expert treks

Pin Kaew ✿✿
Basic huts close to airport runway.
Address: 195/1 Sanambin Road, Chiang Rai
Price: 60-80 **Rooms:** 9 **Fan:** 9 **Bathroom:** 9(cw) **Comfort:** ☆☆ **Design:** ☆☆☆ **Location:** ☆
Position: 2 kilometres south of town **Quietness:** ☆ **Restaurant:** bkfst only
Facilities: jeep/motor bike rental **Treks/tours:** wide range

Bowling ✿✿
Small, flimsy, poorly furnished rooms in quiet *soi*.
Address: 399 Singhakhai Road, Chiang Rai **Tel:** (053)71704
Price: 50-100 **Rooms:** 8 **Fan:** 4 **Bathroom:** 4(cw)(hw outside) **Comfort:** ☆ to ☆☆ **Design:** ☆☆
Location: ☆☆☆ **Position:** central **Quietness:** ☆☆☆☆

Joke ✿✿
Concrete huts in small garden. Adequate but expensive.
Address: 795 Paholyothin Road, Chiang Rai
Price: 200-300 **Comfort:** ☆☆ to ☆☆☆ **Design:** ☆☆ **Location:** ☆☆
Position: 100 metres south of Maekok bridge **Quietness:** ☆☆ **Restaurant:** ☆☆☆.

Lek House ✿✿
Friendly atmosphere, basic but clean rooms.
Address: 95 Rajyothin Road. Chiang Rai **Tel:** (053)713337
Price: 50-120 **Rooms:** 12 **Fan:** 12 **Bathroom:** 7(cw)(hw outside) **Comfort:** ☆ to ☆☆ **Design:** ☆☆
Location: ☆☆ **Position:** central **Quietness:** ☆☆ **Restaurant:** ☆☆☆
Tours/treks: wide range, good value

Star Inn ✿✿
Clean, well furnished rooms but unattractive and unfriendly.
Address: 594/2 Paholyothin Road, Chiang Rai
Price: 160-200 Rooms: 16 **Fan:** 16 **Bathroom:** 16 (8 hw) **Comfort;** ☆☆☆ **Design:** ☆
Location: ☆☆☆ **Position:** central **Quietness:** ☆☆ **Restaurant:** snacks

OP House ✿✿
New Thai house on edge of town, clean but spartan and small rooms.
Address: 93/10 Rajyotha Rd, Chiang Rai.
Price: 80-100 **Rooms:** 4 **Fan:** 4 **Bathroom:** 0(hw outside) **Comfort:** ☆☆ **Design:** ☆☆☆
Location: ☆☆ **Position:** 1 kilometre west of town **Quietness:** ☆☆☆

Tip House ✪✪
Clean but sterile rooms in block behind bar area.
Address: 1017 Jedyod Rd, Chiang Rai
Price: 150 Rooms: 5 Fan: 5 Bathroom: 5(hw) Comfort: ☆☆☆ Design: ☆ Location: ☆☆
Position: central   Quietness: ☆☆

AROUND CHIANG RAI

Chiang Rai is a very good base and jumping off point for the northernmost areas of Thailand, including Mae Sai on the Burma border, the Golden Triangle where Thailand, Burma and Laos meet, the towns of Chiang Saen and Chiang Khong on the Maekhong river, boat trips on the Maekhong and Maekok and the hill tribes and mountains to the north west. The following trips can be completed in one day or less from Chiang Rai, or combined over two or three days.

MAEKOK RIVER TRIPS ✓✓✓
The boat station in Chiang Rai is at the western end of Singhaklai Road(see map). From here there is a daily long tailed boat service to Thaton, leaving at 10.30 am, arriving at Thaton at 3.30pm. The boat stops at a number of interesting hill tribe villages along the river. Boats can also be hired privately here, for about 600 *baht* per hour, seating up to eight people.

PONG NA CAM ELEPHANT CAMP ✓✓✓
In a Karen village on the south bank of the Maekok river, eleven kilometres east of Chiang Rai. One of the nicest elephant camps, on a knoll 100 metres above the landing stage. There are trips of various lengths - for 400 *baht* per elephant/ hour. One trip visits a waterfall and remote Karen village. At the camp is a pleasant cafe looking out over the river. It is possible to drive out to the camp on a good gravel road, but far more pleasant to arrive by boat, hired from Chiang Rai. The trip to the camp takes about 30 minutes. There are regular boats back to town.

CHIANG RAI - HUAI MAE SAI - CHIANG RAI (42 kilometres - 90 minutes) Map page 119

This is the name of a village and waterfall, 15 kilometres north west of Chiang Rai. En route there is a good elephant camp, Yao, Akha, Karen and Lahu villages.

The Far North

Leave Chiang Rai and cross over the Maekok river bridge. 200 metres north of the bridge turn west on Rte 1207, which has been newly metalled.

DISTANCES ALONG ROUTE 1207

Kilometres

2	South turn to the luxury **RimKok** resort (see page 137)
3	South turn to **Bank and Boons Guest House** ❶❶on the west of the road. Continue down this road to the river, spanned by a rickety bamboo bridge strong enough for motor bikes (just!)
7	South turn along poor dirt road to Karen village and river.
11	South turn along poor dirt road to **Yao village** ✓✓ (2 kilometres). This is a much visited village, with many stalls and small cafe, but pleasant and friendly. There are many handicraft stalls. On the road 500 metres east of the village is a small elephant camp, with trips to Huai Mai Sai waterfall and a Lahu village (300 *baht*/elephant/hour). A kilometre further is a pleasant Akha village, and at the end of the road the waterfall behind a small restaurant, Karen village, souvenir shop and elephant stop.
14	Karen village of **Huai Khom** ✓with lovely new bamboo bungalows in a wonderful setting. **Mountain View Bungalows** ❶❶❶ Address: 35/10 Mae Yao, Chiang Rai. Price:80-200 Rooms:14 Bathroom:14(cw)(hw outside) **Comfort:**☆☆ **Design:**☆☆☆☆ **Location:**☆☆☆☆☆ **Quietness:**☆☆☆☆☆ **Restaurant:**☆☆☆ Facilities: mountain bike hire *30baht*/day Treks:local
14-17	The road winds uphill past two Lahu villages, ending with a 2 kilometre walk to the waterfall of **Huai Mai Yao** ✓

CHIANG RAI - DOI TUNG - MAI SAI (92 kilometres - 2 hours) Map page 119

Mae Sai is the most northerly town in Thailand. It has a busy border crossing with Burma and several markets and gem shops selling gems reputedly from Burma. En route, a fascinating detour to the mountain top temple of Doi Tung✓✓✓ A supremely spectacular drive on a new, wide metalled road to a lovely temple in a breathtaking situation.

KILOMETRE POST DISTANCES FROM BANGKOK ON ROUTE 1

Kilometres

830-56	Fast straight road to Mae Chan (details page 127)
867	**Mae Cam Mai.** Cattle market, Mondays and Thursdays, 5.00-10.00 am
870	West turn Rte 1148 to **Doi Tung** ✓✓✓ (17 kilometres). The entrance to this new road is decorated with an arch featuring a huge painting of the King's mother. There is a royal palace at the mountain top, her favourite home, and this area has benefited greatly from

Chiang Rai - Mai Sai

royal patronage. It is said there is nothing the King's mother (now in her nineties) likes to do more than to roam these hills. The road climbs precipitously into the mountains, but since its rebuilding is always safe.

DISTANCES NOW ALONG ROUTE 1148

2   To the north of the road,
Khwan Guest House ✿✿
Simple but reasonably comfortable A-frame huts in a quiet field.
Address: Ban Huai Khrae, Mae Chan, Chiang Rai
Price:60-200 **Rooms:**15 **Fan:**15 **Bathroom:**8(cw)(cw outside) **Comfort:**☆☆
Design:☆☆☆ **Location:**☆☆☆☆ **Quietness:**☆☆☆☆☆ **Restaurant:**snacks

10   To west of road, Akha village of **Pa Klua ✓✓✓**. Very cosmetic village, the main street paved with new cobbles, Akha women in very beautiful, dramatic costumes. Hard sell of Akha handicrafts, but a stunning location perched on the edge of a mountain looking straight down to the plains far below. Very steep road (300 metres) to the village.

11   Turn south to **Doi Tung Kings Palace ✓✓**. Beautiful modern teak building looking out over Burma. Closed to visitors, but visitors centre and car park nearby.

12   Lahu village of **Bala** to north of road. In this area all the hill tribes are subsidised by the King's project, growing experimental temperate fruit and vegetables.

13   Turn to Doi Tung temple. Ahead, new road under construction skirting the Burma border.

15   Small temple, several food stalls outside.

17   To west of road, in woods strewn with boulders, strange collection of offerings - statues and sculptures of a bizarre array of gods, animals and demons, from 1000 years ago (a wicked looking stone Buddha head) to today (plastic, wood and stone Hindu deities, hobgoblins - even a giant pig!) The centrepiece is a large reclining Buddha surrounded by disciples. This is a sacred place, where Buddhists go to ask a favour of the gods. The statues are a "thank you" for a wish granted. To the side of this collection is a grove filled with old spirit houses, which failed to bring good luck to their owners.

17   The road ends at the temple of **Doi Tung ✓✓✓**. This important temple is built at the top of a vertical cliff. Looking east, it is possible on clear days to see the mountains of Laos, with Burma to the north and west. The open *wiharn* has an impressive collection of bronze Buddhas. On the cliff edge is a bronze fat Buddha, whose navel it is customary to throw coins in for luck. The temple is a place of atonement pilgrimage for all monks north of the Maekok. Return the 17 kilometres to the main road, continue north.

DISTANCES NOW ALONG ROUTE 1

877   West turn in Kuomintang village of **Tham** 1 kilometre to **Tham Pla ✓** and **Tham Ku Kaeo ✓✓** A temple complex at the base of a jungle covered cliff. Wild monkeys living in the cliff jungle come down to the temple grounds to taunt the village dogs and beg for food in the mornings. 100 metres to the north is a massive *chedi* in an unusual style, resembling ancient Mon *chedis*. There is a small shrine in a cavern at the base of the cliff. In the south of the complex is **Tham Pla**, the fish cave - a misnomer since it is a pool at the base of the cliff filled with large carp. The main temple, Chinese in design with an interesting hermaphrodite white Chinese Buddha, backs directly onto the cliff face.

884   Strawberry market to east of road. Delicious strawberries for 20 *baht* per kilo, strawberry juice 30 *baht* a litre. Produced by local hill tribes as an alternative to opium, it is a real

The Far North

884 pleasure to encourage this enterprise.
West turn 2 kilometres along a good gravel road into almost vertical peaks to **Tham Luang** ✓ (Royal cave). A cave system 7 kilometres long, extending westwards to cross the Burma border underground. Good stalactites and stalagmites. To one side of the car park is a large attractive Buddha in a high cavern. Guides and lanterns can be hired to explore the cave (100 *baht*)

890 **Mae Sai** ✓✓✓Frontier town not to be missed. Details page 149.

GOLDEN TRIANGLE - CHIANG SAEN (43 kilometres - 1 hour) Map page 122

NO KILOMETRE POSTS ALONG THIS ROAD - USE ODOMETER READINGS

Leave Mae Sai on east turn opposite market signposted "Golden Triangle". Although metalled, the road is in poor condition with deep potholes. The road passes through flat countryside of paddy fields and small villages.

Kilometres

22 Mae Ma. Large Thai village. Turn east here (signposted "Golden Triangle")
24 Turn north at T junction.
31 Wang Lao. Small village with handicrafts centre.
33 To east of road, luxury resort of
Baan Boran ●●●●●
Exquisitely furnished rooms in Lanna style on a hill overlooking the Maekhong river.
Address: Baan Boran, Sop Ruak, Chiang Rai.
Price:2400-5000 Rooms:110 A/C:110 Bathroom:110(hw) Comfort:☆☆☆☆☆
Design:☆☆☆☆☆ Location:☆☆☆☆☆ Position:1 kilometre north of Sop Ruak
Quietness:☆☆☆☆☆ Restaurant:☆☆☆☆☆ Facilities: Pool, jacuzzi, massage
Tours/treks:wide range of tours.
34 **Sop Ruak** ✓✓✓The "Golden Triangle" village. At this point the borders of Laos, Burma and Thailand meet. The Maekhong to the east separates Thailand and Burma from Laos, and the tiny stream of the Ruak river separates Burma from Thailand. An arch has been built at a central point, through which all three countries can be seen. Almost all visitors have their photographs taken standing in this arch. For a better view, turn east up a narrow road by the Phukam guest house to the small temple of **Wat Phra That Pu Khao** ✓✓✓ (300 metres).
The village is little more than a line of quite attractive souvenir shops and some restaurants overlooking the river, which is 1 km wide at this point. (Details of accommodation in Sop Ruak page 156).
34-43 Good metalled road running south along the banks of the Maekhong with views of the Maekhong to the eas
43 **Chiang Saen** ✓✓✓On the banks of the Maekhong river, possibly the oldest town in Thailand and the origin of the Lanna empire. Sacked and rebuilt several times, the town and area are littered with ancient *chedis* in various stages of disrepair. Details page 153.

Chiang Saen - Chiang Khong

CHIANG SAEN - CHIANG RAI (57 kilometres - 40 minutes) Map page 122

Good fast road (Rte 1016) to Mae Chan passing through lush farmland and prosperous villages.

KILOMETRE POSTS SHOW DISTANCES FROM MAE CHAN

Kilometres.

27 South turn 1 km to **Chiang Saen Lake** ✓ A sizeable lake surrounded by marshland noted for the variety of bird species to be seen here. On east side of lake:
Yoonook Lakeside villas ❍●●●
Large, comfortable bungalows by Chiang Saen lake.
Address:109 Unok, Chiang Saen, Chiang Rai.
Price:500 Rooms:5 A/C:5 Bathroom:5(hw) Comfort:☆☆☆☆ Design:☆☆☆☆
Location:☆☆☆☆ Quietness:☆☆☆☆☆ Restaurant:☆☆☆

0 **Mae Chan.** Turn south here onto Rte 110 for Chiang Rai (26 kilometres) A very fast, straight road. Details page 127.

CHIANG SAEN - CHIANG KHONG (53 kilometres 1.5 hours) Map page 122

A road at present under construction. Some sections good, some very poor. 4wd may be needed in the wet season. The main road follows the Maekhong river south, then cuts across a line of hills before rejoining the river north of Chiang Khong.

KILOMETRE POSTS SHOW DISTANCES FROM CHIANG KHONG, BUT MANY MISSING

Leave Chiang Saen on Rte 1129 heading south along the river.

Kilometres

49 To west of road **Wat Phra That Jom Jan** ✓ and at the top of the hill **Wat Borom Thaat** ✓✓. Magnificent views of the Maekhong and western Laos, with Chiang Saen and the Golden Triangle visible to the north.
48 To east of road, **Wat Phra That Song Phi Nong** ✓ with an ancient 20 metre seated Buddha.
45 Bridge over the Maekok just before its confluence with the Maekhong.
27 East turn (signposted Suan Dok 6 kilometres) for a very scenic but 10 kilometre longer journey to Chiang Khong, via a dirt and gravel road running along the west bank of the Maekhong, which is particularly beautiful along this stretch, especially in the dry season when curious rocky outcrops in the river are visible. 4wd needed in wet season.
16 As the road reaches the top of the pass, the white Hmong village of **Khue Garn** ✓✓✓. A large and traditional village on a steep hill. The path through the village to the north leads to the top of the hill, with fine views of the river and Laos. A small Lahu village is just above Khue Garn. 100 metres north of the road:

The Far North

	Hmong Guest House ✓✓✓ Unique accommodation facing one of the few patches of untouched primary jungle, where pythons and tigers are still occasionally seen. Address: Khue Garn, Chiang Saen, Chiang Rai Price:100 (dorm 50) Rooms:3 Bathroom:0 (cw outside) Comfort:☆ Design:☆☆☆☆ Location:☆☆☆☆☆ Quietness:☆☆☆ Restaurant:☆☆☆
11-16	Steep hill down to the Maekhong river.
0-11	The road, newly surfaced, follows the course of the river south to **Chiang Khong** ✓✓✓, a small riverside town facing Laos. Details page 157.

CHIANG KHONG - CHIANG RAI (167 kilometres - 3 hours) Map page 122-123

There are three possible routes south from Chiang Khong to Chiang Rai. The slowest and most mountainous is via **Wiang Chai**. Turn off Rte 1020 7 kilometres south of Chiang Khong onto Rte 1174. After 25 kilometres turn west onto Rte 1098, a difficult mountain road, unsurfaced in places. At kilometre 47 on this road turn south onto Rte 1173, after 41 kilometres turn north onto Rte 1020 6 kilometres south of Chiang Rai.
A much quicker but less interesting route is to keep on Rte 1020 all the way from Chiang Khong to Chiang Rai. Very pleasant but unspectacular scenery of river valleys and distant hills until Thoen, then a dull 53 kilometre drive across the plain to Chiang Rai.
The best route, detailed below, passes down a valley parallel to, but west of, Rte 1020. To the east is the line of hills marking the Laos border. The scenery is excellent, the road is well surfaced (although a little narrow in places) and passes through, or very near, many untouched hill tribe villages which rarely see tourists.

DISTANCES ON KILOMETRE POSTS FROM THOEN

Kilometres

136	East turn 300 metres along dirt road to **Haad Khrai** ✓. Famed throughout Thailand for its fishing. The Maekhong in this area has a population of giant catfish, weighing over 100 kilos. The season is only from mid April to mid May, however.
124	At village of **Thajaroen** turn north onto Rte 1155

KILOMETRE POSTS NOW MARKED WITH DISTANCES FROM START OF ROUTE 1155

83	Road skirts the Maekhong again in a particularly scenic bend in its course. Boats can be hired here (400 *baht* for up to 6 people) to cruise to the Laos border 15 kilometres downstream.
67	North turn 1 kilometre to the very old fashioned and traditional town of **Wiang Kaen** ✓. On the main road just south of this turn off: **Kit Kung** ●●● Small guest house with some new rooms in remote village in lovely countryside. Address: Ban Lai Lgoa Wiang Kaen,Chiang Rai Price:100 Rooms:13 Fan:13 Bathroom:5(cw) Comfort:☆☆ Design:☆☆☆ Location:☆☆☆☆☆ Quietness:☆☆☆☆☆ Restaurant:☆☆☆
66	Turn east 1 kilometre to Black Hmong village of **Huai Lu** ✓✓. Black Hmong are only found near the Laos border. This village is typical of many in the area - very traditional and shy, but fascinating.
66-24	The road climbs into low mountains with views of higher mountains to the east in Laos.

Touring Northern Thailand

	There are several villages, mainly Hmong, but also Yao and Akha, on and near the road on both sides.
51	East turn metalled road to **Pha Tang** (8 kilometres). This road is restricted for security reasons, so should not be used.
48	West turn to the beautiful waterfall of **Nam Tok Phalae** ✔✔(9 kilometres). A vertical drop of 20 metres into a large pool. The road to the falls is difficult and confusing. Guides can be hired in the nearby Hmong village of **Sai Thong** on the main road.
0	Junction with Rte 1021 6 kilometre east of Thoen. Turn west here, signposted Thoen, Chiang Rai. Rte 1021 is a very good, modern well surfaced and fast road.

KILOMETRE POSTS NOW SHOW DISTANCES FROM CHIANG RAI

68	**Thoeng.** A strangely modern small Thai town with a very wide main street flanked by concrete buildings and billboards, looking more like California than Thailand. One guest house: **Srivieng ●●** Basic rooms in new clean teak house. **Address:** 391 Moo 1 Thoeng, Chiang Rai **Price:**50-150 (dorm 20) **Rooms:**9 **A/C:**1 **Fan:**8 **Bathroom:**3(cw)(cw outside) **Comfort:**☆ to ☆☆☆ **Design:**☆☆☆ **Location:**☆☆ **Position:**300 metres north of main junction on main street, west side. **Quietness:**☆☆
68-0	The road passes through flat cultivated land with nothing of interest to see before Chiang Rai.

MAE SAI (Map page 164)

A busy town with a real frontier feel to it, Mae Sai is the northernmost town in Thailand, on the banks of a small stream that separates Thailand from Burma. Opposite is the small Burmese town of Tha Kee Lek, and linking the two countries is a large concrete bridge over the stream around which the life of both towns revolves. Burmese and Thai are free to cross the border between 6.00 am and 6.00 pm, and there is a constant traffic ferrying goods to and fro between the two countries. At present foreigners cannot cross, but there are plans to open this border in 1992, when it may be possible to stay in newly built tourist hotels in Burma.

Mae Sai is not a pretty town. It is dominated by the wide main road leading to the customs post and bridge. On either side are concrete storehouses and shops in various stages of disrepair. Ten metres before the bridge is a road leading west which hugs this stream, giving good views into Burma and ending where the hills come down to the river one kilometre upstream. A turning west

300 metres before the border is a surfaced road leading up a steep hill to the temple of **Wat Phra That Doi Wao** ✓✓. A long *naga* staircase of 207 steps leads to the small temple - pretty but most interesting for the views of the border towns and the Burmese countryside. There is a path at the base of the steps which encircles the temple and gives even better views in places.

Mae Sai is obviously a market centre for imported Burmese goods, but secondarily thrives on tourism. Be very careful in purchases made here. There are hundreds of stalls and shops selling "gems" purporting to come from Burma. Despite the lengthy "proofs" which the vendors show you of the authenticity of the stones, almost all are either fakes or poor quality stones. This applies equally to the "antiques", most of which come not from Burma but from the antiques "factories" near Chiang Mai. However, browsing through the piles of goods on display is enjoyable, and there are many very attractive souvenirs to purchase. It is interesting to look at the people of Mae Sai - a mix of mongoloid Thais, and Caucasian, Indian looking Burmese. This border is as much anthropological as political. This point is where, racially, east meets west. Memories of the British empire, too. Most of the Burmese, identified by their "skirts" *(longyis)*, as well as their more western features, speak good English and doggedly try to sell coins and other memorabilia, much dating from the British colonisation of Burma. A recent sales pitch is for Thai mothers to dress up their children in glamorised versions of hill tribe costumes. For 10 *baht* these charmingly dressed children will pose for photographs.

RESTAURANTS

The Riverside restaurant under the bridge (turn west at the bridge) is in a lovely position built over the stream and looking into Burma. Good Thai and Chinese food, helpful English speaking staff.

There are some cheap food stalls near the morning market, and all the guest houses serve adequate Thai/western food at cheap prices.

NIGHTLIFE

The Mae Sai Plaza by the river to the east of the bridge has some bars. Otherwise the Frontier Saloon 500 metres south of the bridge on the west of the road is interesting - not least for the "cowboy" waiters who wear lipstick and eye shadow.

Mae Sai

TOURS AND TREKS

Chad Guest House, signposted to the west of the main road 300 metres south of the bridge. The manager here is expert in the local area, has a collection of accurate local maps, and organises reliable treks and tours. Incidentally, the breakfast here is very good.

WHERE TO STAY

HOTELS

Thai Tung ✪✪✪
Comfortable well furnished rooms in modern hotel.
Address:6 Paholyothin Road, Mae Sai, Chiang Rai
Price:500 Rooms:47 A/C:47 Bathroom:47(hw) Comfort:☆☆☆☆ Design:☆☆☆
Location:☆☆ Position:central Quietness:☆☆

Mae Sai ✪✪✪✪
Good value fairly clean and well furnished rooms in 60s built hotel
Address:125/5 Pahloyothin Road, Mae Sai, Chiang Rai
Price:180-280 Rooms:50 A/C:6 Fan:44 Bathroom:10(hw)40(cw) Comfort:☆☆ to ☆☆☆☆
Design:☆☆☆ Location:☆☆ Position:central Quietness:☆☆☆

Top North ✪✪
Mid sized rather faceless hotel.
Address: 306 Phaholyothin Rd, Mae Sai, Chiang Rai
Price range:250-450 Rooms:36 A/C:20 Fan:16 Bathroom:25(hw) Comfort:☆☆ to ☆☆☆☆
Design:☆ Location:☆☆ Position:central Quietness:☆ Restaurant:☆☆

GUEST HOUSES

Mae Sai ✪✪✪✪
Delightful location on river, pretty group of bungalows, well organized with good service.
Address: 688 Wiangpangkan Mae Sai, Chiang Rai Tel: (053)732021.
Price:40-100 Rooms:25 Bathroom:6(cw)(hw outside) Comfort:☆☆☆ Design:☆☆☆☆
Location:☆☆☆☆☆ Position: 1 kilometre west of town. Quietness:☆☆☆☆ Restaurant:☆☆☆
NB No parking near guest house. There have been several robberies along this dark lane into town.

Northern ✪✪✪
In pleasant gardens on river, range of fairly clean but some rather small bamboo and wood huts in different styles.
Address: 402 Thumphajam Rd, Mae Sai, Chiang Rai.
Price:80-150 **Rooms:**45 **Fan:**25 **Bathroom:**27(hw)(hw outside) **Comfort:**☆ to ☆☆☆ **Design:**☆☆☆ **Location:**☆☆☆☆ **Position:**central **Quietness:**☆☆☆ **Restaurant:**☆☆☆
Facilities: motor bike rental. **Tours/treks:**wide range.

Chad ✪✪✪
Basic facilities but pleasant huts and garden and good service.
Address: 52/1 Soi Wiangpan, Mae Sai, Chiang Rai **Tel:** (053)732054
Price:60-120 **Rooms:**10 **Fan:**4 **Bathroom:**2(cw)(hw outside) **Comfort:**☆ to ☆☆ **Design:**☆☆☆
Location:☆☆☆☆ **Position:** 700 metres south of bridge **Quietness:**☆☆☆ **Restaurant:**☆☆☆
Tours/treks:wide range of expert treks/tours.

Mai Sai Plaza ✪✪✪
An amazing vertical wooden structure creating a rabbit warren of rooms and huts built into a cliff facing Burma across the river. Will it collapse?
Address:383/6 Sairon Jay Road, Mae Sai, Chiang Rai
Price:40-120 **Rooms:**53 **Fan:**53 **Bathroom:**24(cw)(hw outside) **Comfort;**☆ to ☆☆☆
Design:☆☆☆☆ **Location:**☆☆☆☆ **Position:**central **Quietness:**☆☆ **Restaurant:**☆☆☆
Facilities:motor bike rental **Tours/treks:**wide range.

Niran ✪✪
Barren but fairly comfortable rooms in neglected *soi*.
Price:180 **Rooms:**8 **Fan:**8 **Bathroom:**8(hw) **Comfort:**☆☆☆ **Design:**☆ **Location:**☆☆
Position:central **Quietness:**☆☆

PN ✪✪
Neglected set of bamboo huts in quiet garden, 3 nice new rooms.
Address: Paholyothin Road, Mai Sai, Chiang Rai
Price:80-180 **Rooms:**9 **Fan:**9 **Bethroom:**3(hw)(hw outside) **Comfort:**☆ to ☆☆☆ **Design:**☆☆☆
Location:☆☆☆ **Position:** 1 kilometre south of bridge **Quietness:**☆☆☆ **Restaurant:**snacks.

CHIANG SAEN (Map page 164)

Picturesquely sited on the bank of the Maekhong river, which is over one kilometre wide at this point, the city of Chiang Saen was of great importance in the early history of Thailand - as the great number of ancient ruins in the modern town indicate.

Modern Chiang Saen is a quiet, sleepy town, surrounded by a fairly intact city wall dating back to the 14th century. The monuments scattered haphazardly throughout the town, and the slow pace of life, make Chiang Saen a very pleasant and interesting place to stay for a day or two.

Many historians consider Chiang Saen the first part of what is now Thailand to be settled by the Thais - possibly as early as the 8th century AD. For some time Thai tribes had been moving south from their original home in Southern China, as the power of the Chinese empire expanded. Skimpy evidence from Chinese references suggest that in the 9th century the empire of Chiang Saen extended as far east as the Red river delta in modern Vietnam.

It seems likely that the growing power of Chiang Saen was destroyed by the stronger empire of Luang Prabang in Laos. No remains of this early history remain. Probably the site was abandoned in the 11th century AD. The city was rebuilt as part of the Lanna empire 200 years later. In 1558 AD the Burmese took control, and it remained in Burmese hands until 1804 AD, when it was sacked by King Rama I, the population first being deported to Lampang. Seventy years later their descendants returned to rebuild the town, under a prince of Lamphun.

THINGS TO DO

Maekhong River Trip ✓✓✓ Below the Sala Thai restaurant is a long tailed boat stop, from which trips can be taken up or downstream. The trips upstream to the Golden Triangle take 30 minutes. The six seater boats speed close to the Laos border on the east bank, then circle the Burmese and Laos borders to the north of the Golden Triangle before landing. The one way trip costs 350 *baht* per boat, and is much the best way to see the Golden Triangle.

The two hour trip downstream to Chiang Khong navigates a spectacular stretch of the river, particularly in the dry season when rock formations can be seen rising out of the river. The landscape on either side is wild and beautiful. This trip costs 2000 *baht* for up to six people.

THINGS TO SEE

City Walls ✓✓ The main road east to Chiang Rai passes through these 14th century walls one kilometre west of the river. Three to five metres high and built of small laterite bricks, they are surrounded by trees and make an attractive sight. In places the remains of the moat remain. A small road leads north alongside the walls to the ruins of **Wat Pa Sak** ✓✓, with the oldest *chedi* in the town, a beautiful ornate structure of a style reminiscent of Haripunchai, believed to date from 1295 AD. The ruins are well tended, and charge an entrance fee of 20 *baht*. Around the ruins is a large grove of giant teak trees. Continuing along this road leads to **Wat Phra That Chom Kitti** ✓✓ atop a small hill with good views of the Maekhong river and the town. Within the temple area is a 25 metre high *chedi* on a rectangular base with Buddha statues on the 4 sides. Within the city walls on the left of the main street leading down to the river is **Wat Chedi Luang** ✓✓, famed for its 58 metre high *chedi* built in 1331 AD. The remains of the adjoining *bot* have been covered with a new roof and houses a giant, brightly coloured seated Buddha.

Two hundred metres past Wat Chedi Luang towards the river is the **Museum** ✓✓, with a wide range of historical objects including large bronze Chiang Saen Buddhas. It is open 8.30 - 12.00, 1.00 - 4.30, closed Monday and Tuesday.

RESTAURANTS

The **Sala** restaurant is perched above the Maekok river looking towards Laos on the opposite bank. As well as a lovely position, the food is excellent and inexpensive. There are a few food stalls in the market 200 metres south of the Sala Thai. All the guest houses serve adequate food.

PLACES TO STAY

Gins ✪✪✪
Lovely new house with spotless 6 bed dorms and pretty bungalows in lychee orchard.
Address:446 Vieng, Chiang Saen, Chiang Rai.
Price:80-300 (dorm 50) Rooms:20 Fan:20 Bathroom:7(hw)(hw outside)
Comfort:☆ to ☆☆☆ Design:☆☆☆☆ Location:☆☆☆☆ Position: 1 kilometre north of town
Quietness:☆☆☆☆ Restaurant:☆☆☆ Tours/treks:wide range.

Chiang Saen ✪✪✪
Nicely furnished rooms for price in small cemented yard.
Price: 30-100 **Rooms:** 12 **Fan:** 12 **Bathroom:** 8(cw)(hw outside) **Comfort:** ☆ to ☆☆☆
Design: ☆☆☆ **Location:** ☆☆ **Position:** central **Quietness:** ☆☆☆

Siam ✪✪✪
Good sized, basic but inexpensive rooms in small garden.
Address: 294 Rimkok, Chiang Saen, Chiang Rai
Price: 40-80 **Rooms:** 8 **Fan:** 8 **Bathroom:** 4(cw)(cw outside) **Comfort:** ☆☆ to ☆☆
Design: ☆☆☆ **Location:** ☆☆☆ **Position:** central **Quietness:** ☆☆☆ **Restaurant:** ☆☆☆

Lanna ✪✪
Faded, jaded but cheap rooms in pleasant large garden.
Address: Rimkok, Chiang Saen, Chiang Rai
Price: 40-100 **Rooms:** 10 **Fan:** 10 **Bathroom:** 10(hw) **Comfort:** ☆☆ **Design:** ☆☆
Location: ☆☆☆☆ **Position:** central **Quietness:** ☆☆☆

GOLDEN TRIANGLE

The creation of tourist developers rather than a place with any real history or significance, the "Golden Triangle" is the point at which the borders of Thailand, Laos and Burma meet. Laos is on the east bank of the Maekhong River, Burma and Thailand on the west, separated from each other by a diminutive stream, the Mae Nam Ruak. A concrete arch has been built recently on the banks of the Maekhong, decorated with a map of the area, through which the three countries can be seen. Almost all tourists feel the need to be photographed standing in this arch. For 200 metres either side of the arch is a welter of souvenir stalls, restaurants and guest houses, creating the village of Sop Ruak.

Recently the two luxury hotels have been built. During 1992 it will be possible to cross the border here into Burma, where a new casino is being built (gambling is illegal in Thailand).

The best view of the Golden Triangle and surrounding countryside is to be had at the temple of Wat Pra That Pu Khao. Take the path leading uphill by the side of the "Poppy Museum" (not worth seeing). A 500 metre walk or drive leads to the temple, from which a panorama of three countries can be seen.

THINGS TO SEE

The souvenir stalls sell a good range of local arts, crafts and clothing. Although catering to the bus loads of tourists the prices are quite good (with bargaining).

BOAT TRIPS

There are several boat stops on the river. For 100 *baht*, a boat can be hired for the 15 minute tour of the riverbanks of Burma, Laos and Thailand, at high speed. For 300 *baht* this trip can be continued downstream to Chiang Saen.

RESTAURANTS

There are four restaurants on the river, all serving reasonably good westernised food.

PLACES TO STAY

RESORTS

Golden Triangle Resort ●●●●●
Lovely luxury hotel looking over the Maekhong.
Address: 222 Golden Triangle, Chiang Rai **Tel:**(053)714031 **Fax:** 714805
Price:1700-4500 **Rooms:**73 A/C:73 **Bathroom:**73(hw) **Comfort:**☆☆☆☆☆ **Design:**☆☆☆☆☆
Location:☆☆☆☆☆ **Position:**central **Quietness:**☆☆☆☆☆ **Restaurant:**☆☆☆☆ **Facilities:**pool
Tours/treks: wide range including boat tours.

GUEST HOUSES

Northern Villas ●●●●
Pretty, large, well furnished huts on the banks of the Maekhong.
Address: 127 Ban Sop Ruak, Chiang Rai.
Price:600 **Rooms:**19 **Fan:**19 **Bathroom:**19(hw) **Comfort:**☆☆☆☆ **Design:**☆☆☆☆
Location:☆☆☆☆ **Position:**1 kilometre south of Sop Ruak **Quietness:**☆☆☆☆
Restaurant:☆☆☆

Phu Cum ●●
Small, neglected bungalows in scruffy compound.
Price:80-120 **Rooms:**15 **Fan:**15 **Bathroom:**0(cw outdoors) **Comfort:**☆ **Design:**☆☆
Location:☆☆☆ **Position:**central **Quietness:**☆☆

Central ●●
Small, expensive rooms in new bamboo house
Price:150-300 **Rooms:**6 **Bathroom:**2(cw)(hw outdoors) **Comfort:**☆ to ☆☆ **Design:**☆☆☆
Location:☆☆☆**Position:**central **Quietness:**☆☆ **Restaurant:**☆☆☆

CHIANG KHONG

A small and sleepy town on a pretty stretch of the Maekhong opposite the Laos town of Huay Sai. Its only claim to fame is the giant 100 kilo catfish caught here in May.

THINGS TO DO

VISITING LAOS

The Anne tour company in Chiang Khong, in conjunction with the Laos government, is now organising trips to Laos from the Chiang Khong border checkpoint. Trips start at the small Laos town of **Huay Sai** on the opposite bank of the Maekhong. The one day tour, costing 535 *baht* inclusive, visits a number of Laotian villages, shopping at a municipal market, a temple and a sapphire mining village. A seven day tour costing 7000 *baht* visits the ancient city of Luang Prabang. The Laos government is building a new road to link Huay Sai, through Luang Prabang to the Chinese border, making tours to China possible in the future.

It is at present essential to obtain a Laos visa, only issued in Bangkok. Some travel agents in Chiang Mai and Nong Khai will obtain visas for between 1500 and 3000 *baht*.

RESTAURANTS

Country Roads opposite Ban Ti Mi La guest house serves reasonable Thai/western food. There is a basic and very cheap restaurant next to the Thai Farmers Bank in the town centre.

PLACES TO STAY

RESORTS

Plabuk ✹✹✹
Large, well equipped but utilitarian rooms in cement block facing the Maekhong.
Address: 122/1 Wieng, Chiang Khong, Chiang Rai
Price:400 Rooms:15 A/C:15 Bathroom:15(hw) Comfort:☆☆☆☆ Design:☆☆☆
Location:☆☆☆ Position: 700 metres south of town. Quietness:☆☆☆☆☆ Restaurant:☆☆☆

HOTELS

Chiang Khong ✿✿
Large clean rooms in new cement block.
Address: Sai Klang Road, Chiang Khong, Chiang Rai
Price:150 **Rooms:**20 **Fan:**20 **Bathroom:**20(cw) **Comfort:**☆☆ **Design:**☆☆ **Location:**☆☆
Position: 700 metres north of town **Quietness:**☆☆☆ **Restaurant:**☆☆☆

GUEST HOUSES

Wiangkaeo ✿✿✿
Lovely, spotlessly clean rooms in new traditional teak house with terrace on river.
Address: Soi 3, Sai King Road, Chiang Khong, Chiang Rai.
Price:2000 **Rooms:**4 **Fan:**4 **Bathroom:**0(hw outside) **Comfort:**☆☆ **Design:**☆☆☆☆
Location:☆☆☆☆ **Position:**central **Quietness:**☆☆☆☆☆

Ban Ta Mi La ✿✿✿
Wooden thatched huts in pleasant garden on banks of Maekhong.
Address:8/1-8/4 Sai Klang Road, Chiang Khong, Chiang Rai
Price:100 **Rooms:**4 **Fan:**4 **Bathroom:**0(hw outside) **Comfort:**☆☆ **Design:**☆☆☆
Location:☆☆☆☆ **Position:**central **Quietness:**☆☆☆☆ **Tours/treks:** boat tours of Maekhong.

DOI MAE SALONG (SANTIKIREE)
(Map page 164)

Perched on a mountain ridge with peaks and valleys visible in all directions, surrounded by faces, voices and houses which are certainly not Thai, the visitor can be forgiven for thinking that he has accidentally wandered across two borders and is in a Chinese mountain village.

Doi Mae Salong was founded in 1949 by refugees from the communist take over of China. The previous nationalist government - the Kuomintang - was forced to flee to escape persecution. One group settled in Formosa - now called Taiwan, which is still ruled by the Kuomintang(KMT). The other fared less well, settling in north Burma and Thailand with the avowed intent of retaking China for the nationalists. The money for this venture was to come from opium and heroin production. Many of the KMT became wealthy as drug barons, but no counter revolution ever took place. The KMT have been superseded as drug producers by the Shan State Army under Khun Sa, and most of their membership have settled down as upland farmers and merchants. There are many KMT villages in Northern Thailand, but Doi Mae Salong is the only community of any size. The population are 95% Chinese from Yunnan. Most now speak Thai, but only as a second language. They live in the long, low plastered houses typical of south west China, with a central door surrounded by written imprecations to ward off evil spirits. Most are Muslim, and there is a large modern mosque looking down over the town from the hilltop above.

The Thai government has attempted, with some success, to integrate these people into Thailand proper. All children are taught in Thai, and a loudspeaker system broadcasts local news and music in Thai in the early mornings. There is a strong army presence in the area, and around the town Thai army rangers are seen patrolling heavily armed. Tea and coffee plantations, with assistance from the government, surround the town, and local tea and herbs can be bought at any of the many stalls and shops concentrated at the west end of town. Most goods on display, though, come from China. Strange bottles of spirits containing whole giant centipedes, green vipers or ginseng roots can be bought, which purport to do wonders for your sex life. Tiny vials of balms or tinctures to cure everything from arthritis to heart disease, gourds, weighing scales, jade, teapots, daggers, opium pipes - a huge variety of fascinating items, providing some of the most interesting shop browsing in Thailand.

Doi Mae Salong is surrounded by hill tribe villages - mostly Akha, many desperately poor, recent emigrants from Burma. At 6.00 am the central market is filled with Akha women, all wearing their exotic costumes producing an extravagantly colourful picture.

At an altitude of 1200 metres, Doi Mae Salong is always cool, with temperatures below zero Centigrade not uncommon in January and December at night. Heating is not generally used, so be prepared to wrap up well at this time of year.

RESTAURANTS
There are two excellent, if somewhat expensive, Chinese restaurants in the town, one at Doi Mae Salong Resort and the other at Mae Salong Villa. Other than this, there are a number of noodle stalls selling very good Chinese specialities.

PLACES TO STAY

RESORTS

Kun Nai Phol ❋❋❋❋
Lovely wooden huts, well furnished and comfortable, overlooking the town.
Address: Santikiree, Chiang Rai **Tel:**(053)712485 **Fax:** 712485
Price:700 (150 dorm) **Rooms:**22 **Fan:**22 **Bathroom:**22(hw) **Comfort:**☆☆☆
Design:☆☆☆☆ **Location:**☆☆☆☆☆ **Position:**1 kilometre west of town **Quietness:**☆☆☆☆☆
Restaurant:☆☆☆

Doi Mae Salong ❋❋❋❋
Good but slightly faded resort in large pretty park above Doi Mae Salong.
Address: Santikiree, Chiang Rai **Tel:**(053)713400
Price:500-1000 **Rooms:**47 **Fan:**47 **Bathroom:**47(hw) **Comfort:**☆☆ to ☆☆☆☆ **Design:**☆☆☆
Location:☆☆☆☆ **Position:**central **Quietness:**☆☆☆☆ **Restaurant:**☆☆☆☆

GUEST HOUSES

Mae Salong Villa ❋❋❋❋
Large, comfortable well furnished rooms on hilltop overlooking Burmese mountains.
Address: Santikiree, Chiang Rai **Tel:**(053)713444 **Fax:**716339
Price:500-700 **Rooms:**44 **Fan:** 44 **Bathroom:**44(hw) **Comfort:**☆☆☆☆ **Design:**☆☆☆☆
Location:☆☆☆☆ **Position:** 700 metres east of town **Quietness:**☆☆ **Restaurant:**☆☆☆☆

Shinsane ❋❋
Primitive facilities but cheap, full of character and friendly.
Address: Santikiree, Chiang Rai
Price:50 **Rooms:**20 **Bathroom:**0(hw outside) **Comfort:**☆ **Design:**☆☆☆ **Location:**☆☆☆☆
Position:central **Quietness:**☆☆☆ **Restaurant:**☆☆☆

Mae Salong ❋❋
Rather dismal but adequate rooms in small Chinese house **Price:**150-300 **Rooms:**9 **Fan:**9
Bathroom:7(cw)(hw outside) **Comfort:**☆ to ☆☆ **Design:**☆☆ **Location:**☆☆☆ **Position:**central
Quietness:☆☆☆ **Restaurant:**☆☆☆

Chinese whisky cure-alls, Doi Mae Salong, Chiang Rai

Ancient statue, Doi Tung

The Maekok river at Thaton, Chiang Mai

Engraved temple doors, Wat Mae Yen, Pai

Wat Klang, Pai

THATON (Map page 164)

Tucked up against the Burmese border on both banks of the Maekok river, Thaton is a little town whose life centres around the river. There is a lovely temple on the hill 100 metres to the west of the road on the south side of the river - Wat Thaton with a large community of monks. In the temple compound is a giant white Buddha which looks east over the town, visible from several kilometres away. There are lovely views of the river and surrounding countryside from the temple. On the south side of the river near the bridge is a pier from which a long tail boat ferry leaves at 12.30 for Chiang Rai. The trip takes 3.5 hours and costs 200 *baht*. There are several stops at Thai and hill tribe villages en route. Eight seater boats can be hired for trips at any time before 3.00 pm, at a price of up to 2000 *baht*.

RAFT TRIPS TO CHIANG RAI

The bamboo rafts are constructed in Thaton and have a primitive cabin and sleeping area for 6-8 people. The toilet is simply a section of cabin which extends overboard. The trip takes 3 days and costs about 2000 *baht* inclusive. It is arguably one of the finest river trips in Thailand, with lovely scenery en route and some rapids which, although not dangerous, are fun.

RESTAURANTS

The **Maekok River Lodge** on the north bank of the river has an excellent, beautifully designed restaurant on the river. Apple restaurant on the south bank is passable. All the guest houses serve reasonable Thai/western food.

PLACES TO STAY

RESORTS

Maekok River Lodge ✪✪✪✪
Very pretty, comfortable rooms in beautiful buildings in superb location on river.
Address:(booking) 9/5 Plabpling Huay Kaew Road, Chiang Mai **Tel:**(053)215366 **Fax:**315336
Price:825 **Rooms:**28 **Fan:**28 **Bathroom:**28(hw) **Comfort:**☆☆☆☆ **Design:**☆☆☆☆☆
Location:☆☆☆☆☆ Position: on north bank of river, 250 metres west of bridge.
Quietness:☆☆☆☆☆ **Restaurant:**☆☆☆☆
Tour/treks:"Track of the Tiger" expert tours and treks.

Thaton Cottage ❶❶❶❶
Very comfortable large chalets with terrace in lovely tropical garden on river.
Price:400 Rooms:11 Fan:11 Bathroom:11(hw) Comfort:☆☆☆☆ Design:☆☆☆☆
Location:☆☆☆☆ Position: 700 metres east of town on south bank of river. Quietness:☆☆☆☆☆
Restaurant:☆☆☆

Thips Travellers Lodge ❶❶❶
Basic rooms in lovely house surrounded by beautiful tropical garden on river.
Price:80-150 Rooms:20 Fan:20 Bathroom:13 (3hw)(hw outside) Comfort:☆to☆☆☆
Design:☆☆☆☆ Location:☆☆☆☆☆ Position:central Quietness:☆☆☆☆ Restaurant:☆☆☆
Tours/treks: Raft trips to Chiang Rai. NB Annexe rooms on main street not so attractive.

Thips Travellers Lodge ❶❶❶❶
New bamboo huts in lovely location 4 kilometres north of Thaton on Doi Mae Salong road.

Chankasem ❶❶❶
Rooms varying from scruffy to very good in poor location
Price:80-300 Rooms:21 A/C:6 Fan:15 Bathroom:15((9.hw,6cw)(hw outside)
Comfort:☆☆ to ☆☆☆☆ Design:☆☆ Location:☆☆☆ Position:central Quietness:☆☆☆
Restaurant:☆☆☆ Tours/treks: Raft trips

Thaton House ❶❶❶
New bamboo rooms in pleasant garden north of river.
Price:80 Rooms:11 Fan:11 Bathroom:11(cw) Comfort:☆☆ Design:☆☆☆ Location:☆☆☆
Position: 100 metres west of bridge, north bank of river. Quietness:☆☆☆☆ Restaurant:☆☆☆
Tours/treks:wide range

Apple ❶❶
Small, primitive bamboo rooms behind restaurant.
Price:50 Rooms:5 Fan:5 Bathroom:0(cw outside) Comfort:☆ Design:☆☆ Location:☆☆☆
Position:central Quietness::☆☆☆ Restaurant:☆☆☆

FANG

An unprepossessing town backed by the mountains of the Burmese border to the west, Fang was one of the original cities founded by King Mengrai in the late 13th century AD. The Burmese destroyed the old city in the early 19th century, but it was rebuilt 80 years later. It was an important trading centre, but since the 1960s has developed a small scale oil extraction and refining business. In the last few years a geothermal power station has been built seven kilometres to the west, using superheated water within the rocks underlying the area.

Until 10 years ago Fang had more than its share of drug runners. Khun Sa, the leader of the Shan State Army, who now controls most heroin production in South East Asia, had a mansion here.

There are still several fine old teak buildings in Fang, although they are rapidly being replaced.

RESTAURANTS

The **Ku Charoen Chai** opposite the market serves good Thai food, and is a pleasant place to watch the Thai and hill tribe market users - there are several Karen and Lahu villages in the area.

WHERE TO STAY

RESORTS

Forestland ✪✪✪
Delightful location around pretty lake in jungle. Lovely rooms, but rather neglected and run down.
Address: 7/512 Ban Don Yeng, Fang, Chiang Mai.
Price: 550 (dorm 120) **Rooms:** 7 **Fan:** 7 **Bathroom:** 7(hw) **Comfort:** ☆☆☆ **Design:** ☆☆☆
Location: ☆☆☆☆☆ **Position:** 25 kilometres south of Fang 1 kilometre east of Rte 107
Quietness: ☆☆☆☆☆ **Restaurant:** ☆☆(often closed) **Facilities:** boats for rent, fishing.

HOTELS

Chok Thani ✪✪✪✪
Large modern hotel with good sized, well furnished rooms. Excellent value, but erratic service.
Address: 425 Chotana Road, Fang, Chiang Mai **Tel:** (053)451252
Price: 165-300 **Rooms:** 40 **A/C:** 19 **Fan:** 21 **Bathroom:** 40(hw) **Comfort:** ☆☆☆ to ☆☆☆☆
Design: ☆☆☆ **Location:** ☆☆ **Position:** 1 kilometre south of Fang centre **Quietness:** ☆☆☆
Restaurant: ☆☆☆ **Facilities:** coffee shop, massage.

Tip ✪
Rather run down old teak hotel. Cheap rooms squalid, more expensive not so bad.
Address: Srichukit Road, Fang, Chiang Mai.
Price: 50-120 **Rooms:** 22 **Fan:** 15 **Bathroom:** 4(hw)18(cw) **Comfort:** ☆ to ☆☆ **Design:** ☆
Location: ☆ **Position:** central **Quietness:** ☆☆ **Restaurant:** ☆☆

The Far North

GUEST HOUSES

Ueng Khum ✪✪✪
Comfortable inexpensive cement bungalows, clean and spacious, in large compound.
Address: 227 Thapae Road Soi 3, Fang, Chiang Mai **Tel:** (053)451268
Price: 100-150 **Rooms:** 16 **Fan:** 16 **Bathroom:** 16(hw) **Comfort:** ☆☆ **Design:** ☆☆☆
Location: ☆☆ **Position:** central **Quietness:** ☆☆

Dew ✪
Scruffy rooms in ranch style wooden building.
Address: 210 Thapae Road Soi 3, Fang, Chiang Mai.
Price: 60 **Rooms:** 10 **Fan:** 10 **Bathroom:** 0(cw outside) **Comfort:** ☆ **Design:** ☆☆
Location: ☆☆ **Position:** central **Quietness:** ☆☆☆

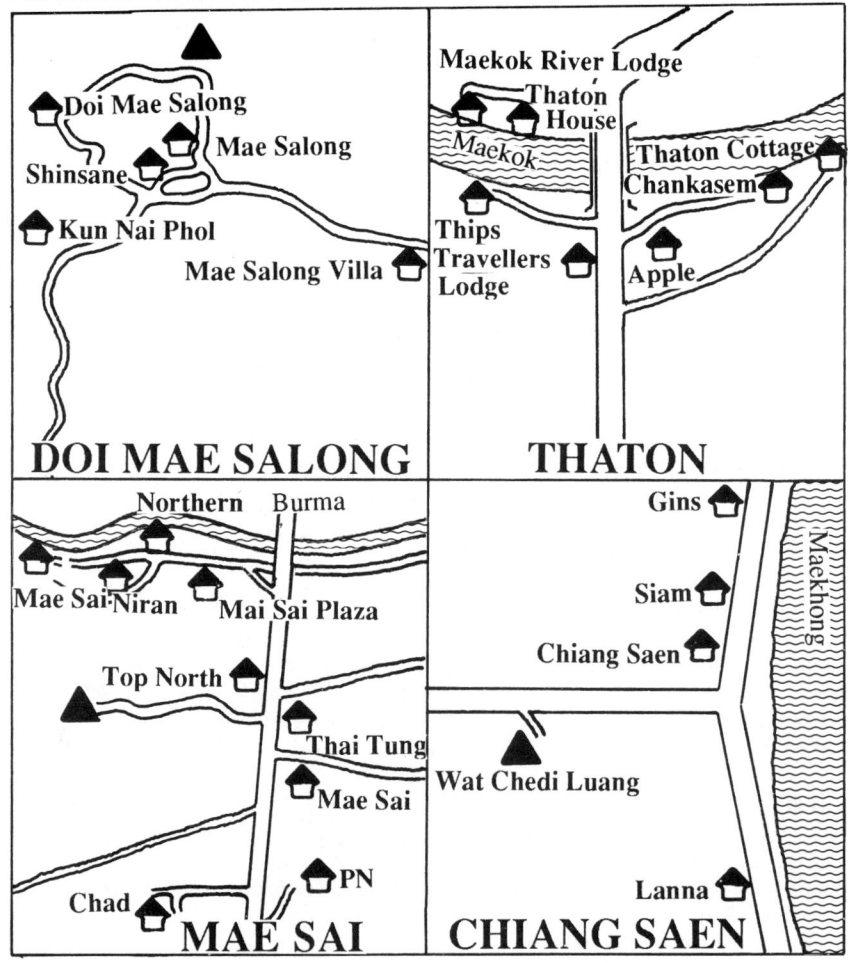

Chapter Five

The West

Chiang Mai - Huay Nan Dam

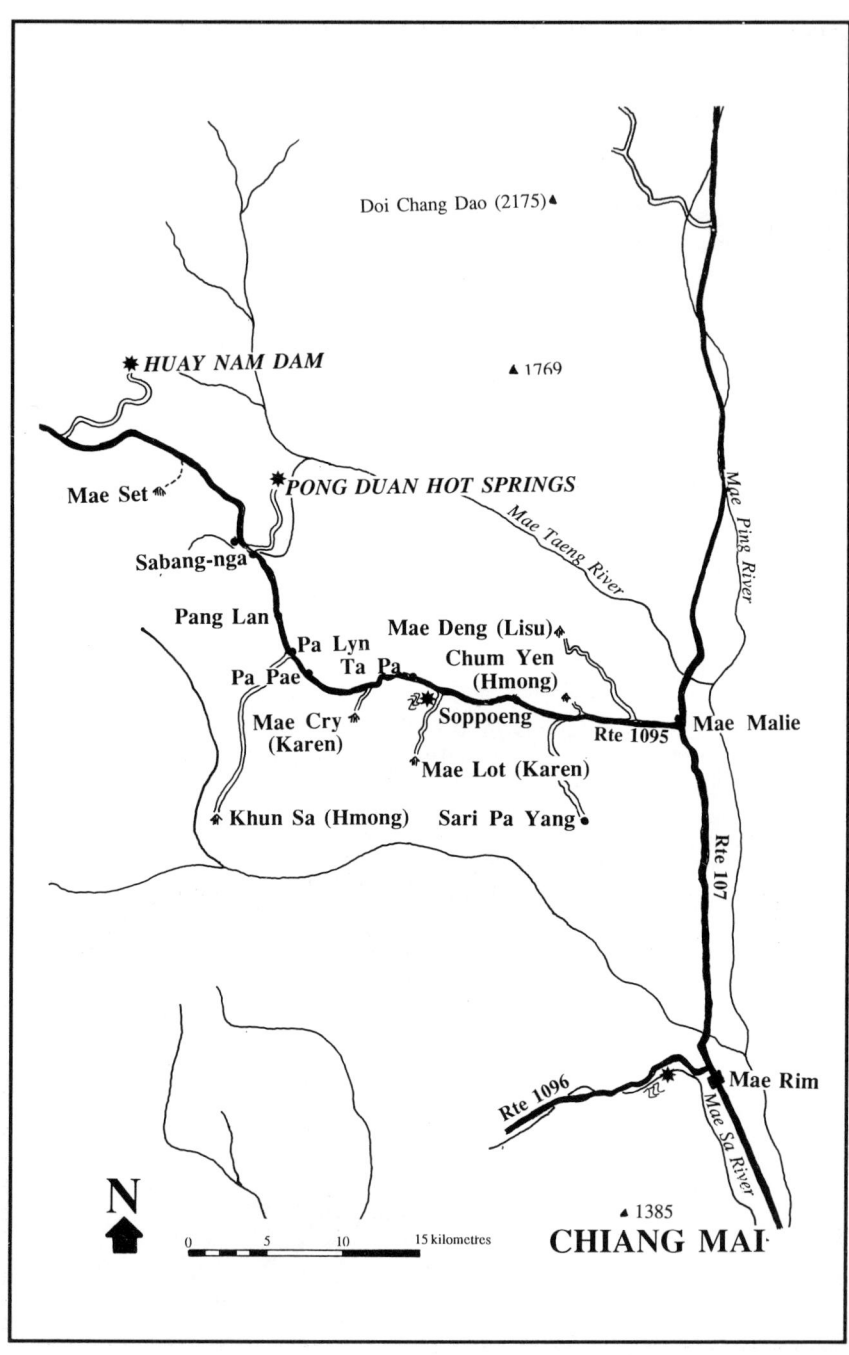

Huay Nan Dam - Pai - Sappong

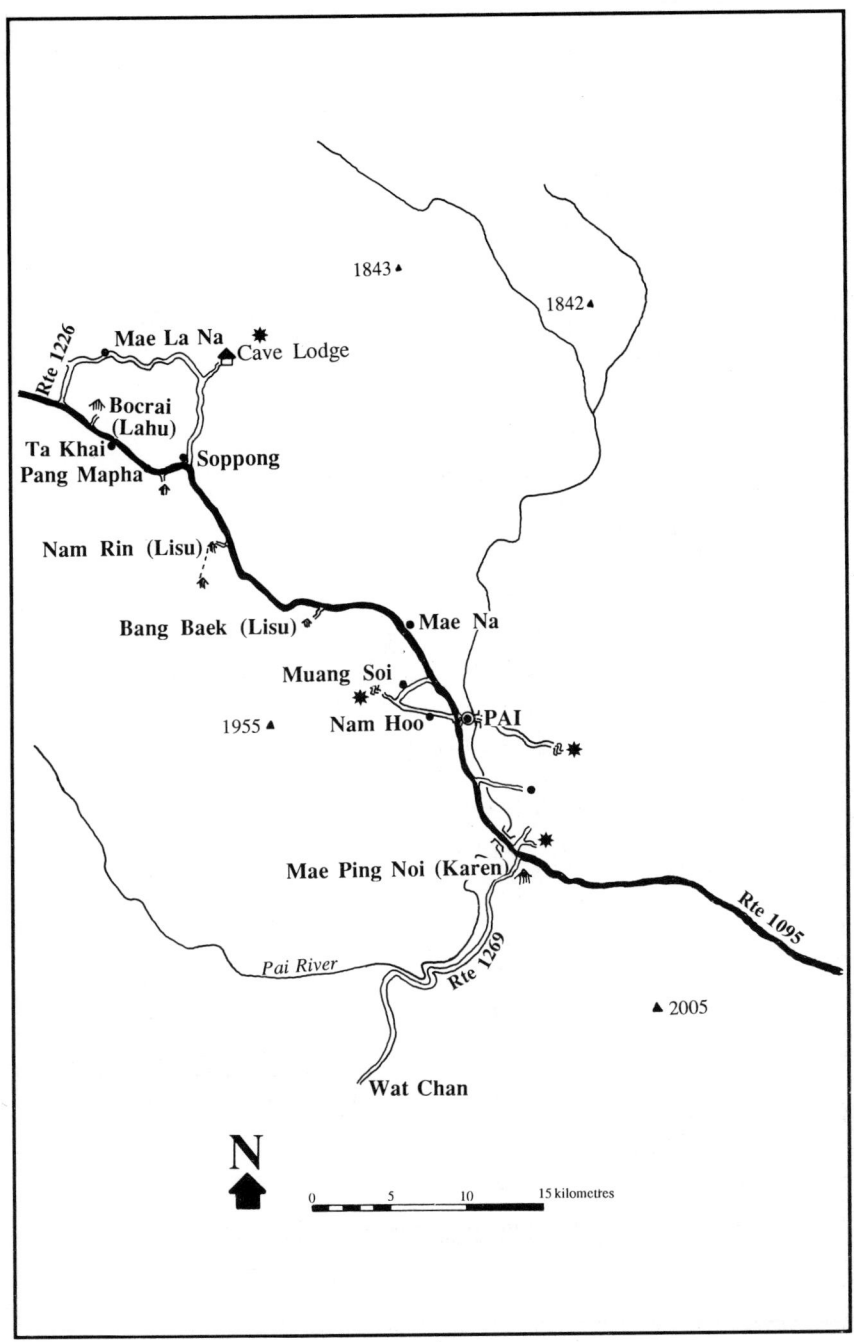

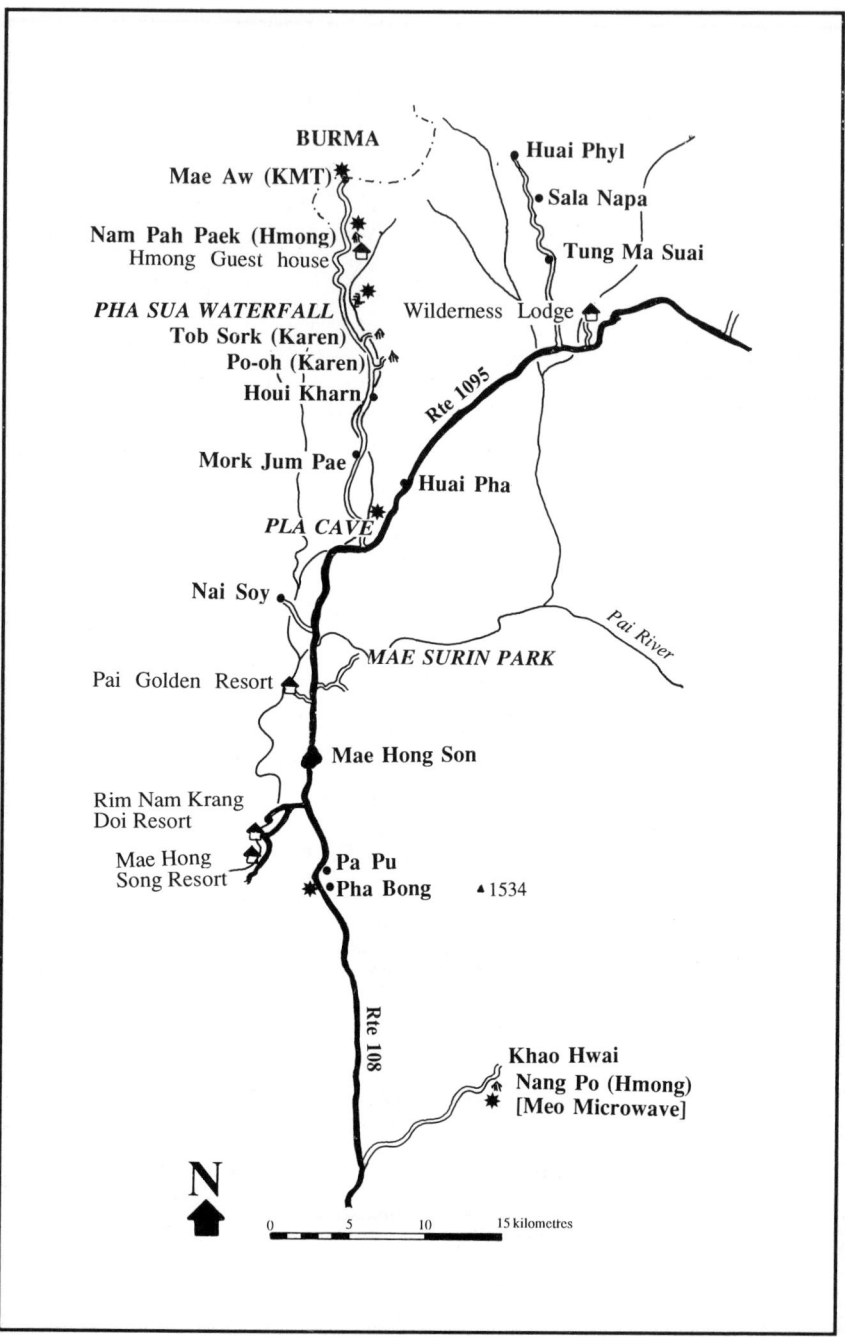

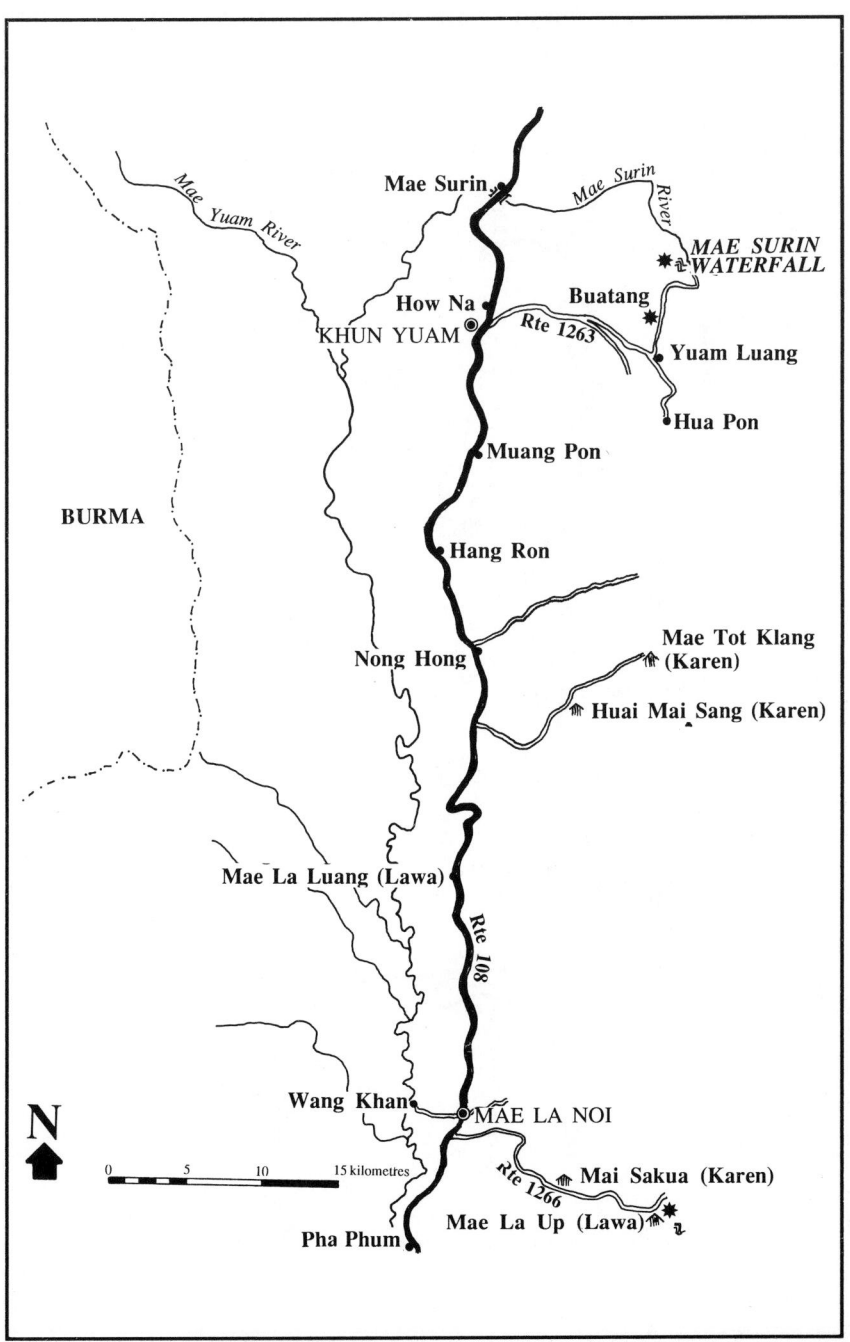

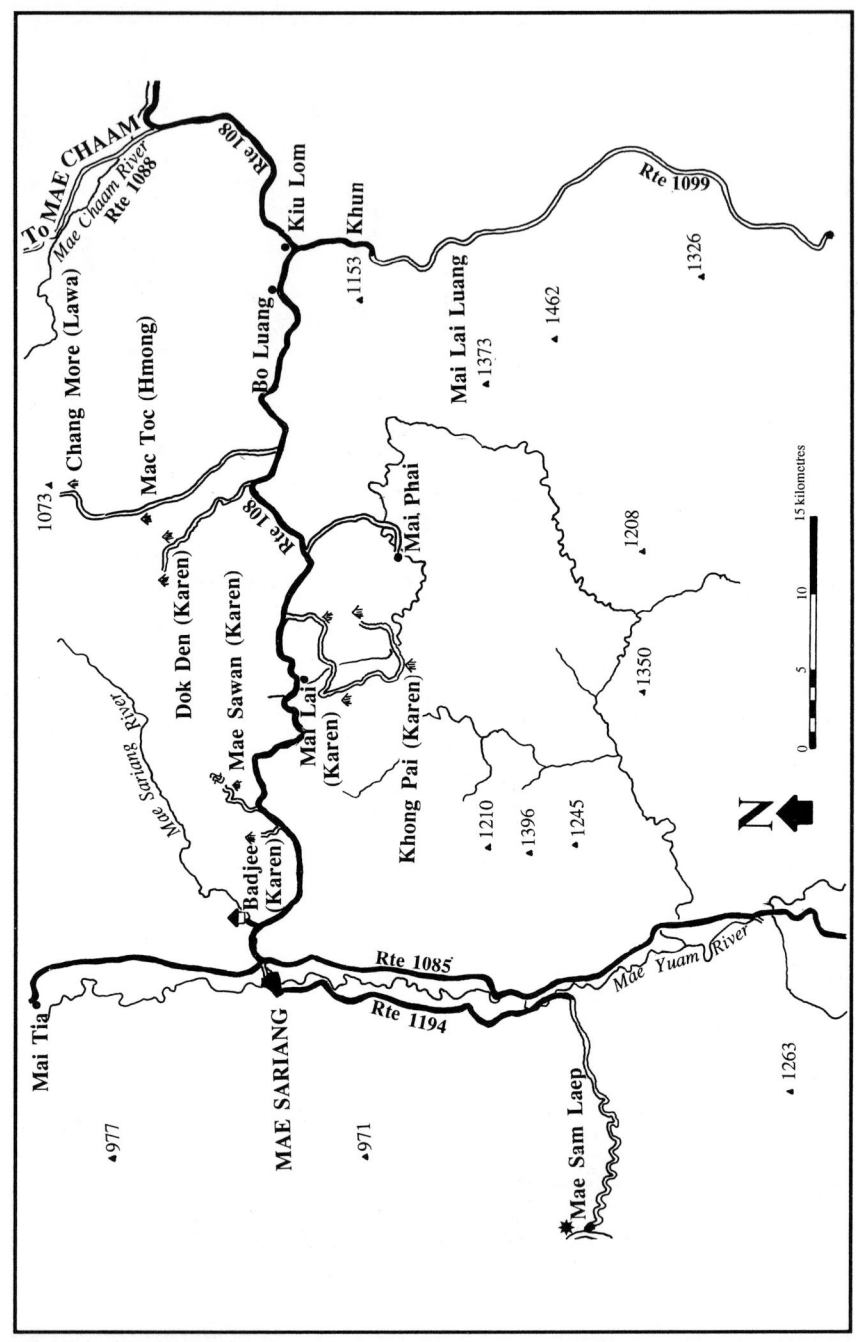

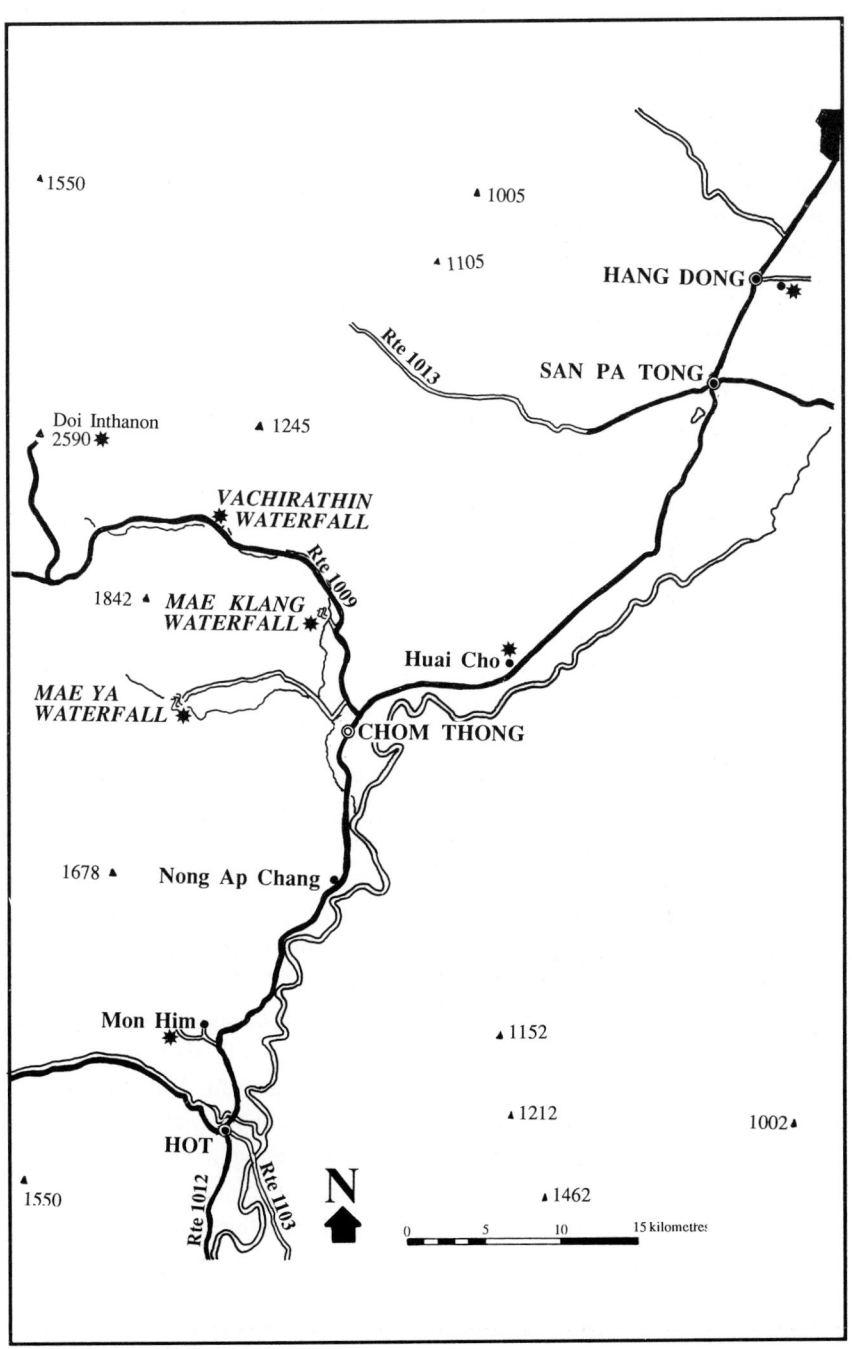

INTRODUCTION

MOUNTAIN RANGES, lush steep sided green valleys, rushing streams and waterfalls, cool plateaux, vast unexplored cave systems, tall jungles, sleepy villages surrounded by small patchworks of orchards and rice paddies, cosmopolitan towns in which colourful hill tribes, Shan, Burmese and even some ethnic Thais peacefully coexist. This is the west, a fascinating area to see, experience and explore.

With the completion of the road from Chiang Mai to Mae Hong Son via Pai in 1991, the west has only recently become easily accessible. For this reason most towns and villages are still unsophisticated and autonomous. The average inhabitant considers Bangkok as being as foreign and exotic as Paris or New York. In fact, the majority of the population have closer ties with Burma than with Thailand. Most are Shan or "Tai Yai", who emigrated from the Thais' ancestral home in China over 1000 years ago, and have developed a separate culture from their Thai cousins. Since most of the Shan population live in Shan state in Burma, they have absorbed many aspects of Burmese culture. Some are Muslim, and the Shan design of Buddhist temple is very different from the Thai. There is a very high hill tribe population in the area. The Karen have been steadily migrating from Burma over the last 200 years, and more recently Lahu, Lisu and Hmong tribes have moved in from Burma or south from China. The only town of any size is Mae Hong Son. With good air links to Chiang Mai and Bangkok, it is much the most sophisticated town in the region, and the only one to develop itself as a tourist resort. Many consider it the prettiest town in Thailand. Mae Sariang and Pai, although small towns, are beginning to develop their tourist potential, so far without any noticeable harmful effects, and are extremely relaxed and pleasant towns.

The best way to enjoy this area to the full is by jeep or motor bike. The main road is now good enough to take any traffic, but almost all other roads are dirt based, and many are impassable during the wet season. Without private transport, most locations in this book are reachable by bus or pick up truck from the nearest town, but this method can be time consuming and unreliable. You are never far from the Burma border. Exciting this may be, with drug warlords, police and troops guarding against smuggling and narcotics, but it is not always safe. If intending to visit areas west of the main road, check with local travel agents as to the current situation.

The route can be driven in two days. Mae Hong Son is about a four hour straight through drive from Chiang Mai. From Mae Hong Son to Chiang Mai via Mae Sariang to complete the circuit is about a seven hour drive. Four days, however, is a more realistic time for the trip.

In the high season (November-March) it is advisable to book rooms ahead, since the best hotels and guest houses are frequently full.

CHIANG MAI - MAE HONG SON (280 kilometres - 5 hours) Maps page 166-168

Kilometres

0-35	Leave Chiang Mai by Chiang Puak Gate. At super highway junction go straight ahead on roads signposted Rte 107, to Fang. Wide dual carriageway to **Mae Rim** (16 kilometres), then good wide road to **Mae Malie** (32 kilometres). The road passes through the fertile Ping river valley of rice paddies and orchards with a number of pleasant villages.
35	Turn west off Rte 107 at Mae Malie, onto Rte 1095. signposted Pai and Mae Hong Son.
0	Start of Rte1095 in Mae Malie. Small but very busy town with flourishing market. A shopping centre for surrounding villages, including many Lisu, Hmong and Karen.
2	North turn 1 kilometre to: **Goon Tee Tong Roses Resort** ❂❂❂ Pretty, well furnished one and two bedroom bungalows in a large and lovely rose garden. **Address:** 137/1 Wak Mua, Mae Tang, Chiang Mai. **Price:**500 **Rooms:**14 **Fan:**14 **Bathroom:**9(hw) **Comfort:**☆☆☆☆ **Design:**☆☆☆☆ **Location:**☆☆☆☆ **Quietness:**☆☆☆☆☆ **Restaurant:**☆☆☆
3	North turn along bumpy, all weather dirt road to: **Hilly Hut** ❂❂❂❂ Interesting and well equipped bungalows and tree houses in landscaped gardens with small zoo and swimming pool. **Address:**Pa Mae Deng, Mae Malie, Chiang Mai. **Price:**200-700 **Rooms:**15 A/C:1 **Fan:**14 **Bathroom:**15(hw) **Comfort:**☆☆ to ☆☆☆☆ **Design:**☆☆☆☆ **Location:**☆☆☆☆☆ **Quietness:**☆☆☆☆☆ **Restaurant:**☆ ☆☆ **Facilities:** pool, zoo. This road leads to the large, traditional and friendly Lisu village of **Joe-Kher** ✓✓ (7 kilometres)
7	North turn along dirt road to **Hmong village** ✓ with many souvenir and handicraft stalls
5-25	Gently undulating countryside of lychee orchards, farmland and forest. Slow climb in altitude.
23	South turn 2 kilometres to the very pretty waterfall of **Morkfar** ✓✓✓. There is a small car park by the stream, cross the stream and walk 500 metres upstream to the falls, which have a large pool at their foot.
33	**Pa Lyn**. West turn on dirt road (4wd) to Hmong village of **Khun Sa** (15 kilometres).
42	East turn to **Pa Duang Hot Springs** ✓(8 kilometres). Poor road (4wd).
52	Forest protection unit on west side of road. Path behind cottage to Lisu village of **Mae Set** ✓✓(15 minutes steep uphill walk). Lovely jungle scenery, pretty village.
59	In small mountain village of **Mae Set:**

The West

	Air Hill Trekkers Hut ●● New teak guest house on main road. Price:60 Rooms:12 Bathroom:0(cw outside) Comfort:☆ Design:☆☆☆☆ Location:☆☆☆☆ Quietness:☆☆☆☆ Restaurant:☆☆☆
60-64	Steep climb out of valley with many hairpin bends (use horn). Good views of mountains and jungle.
64	Enter Mae Hong Son province. Kilometre posts missing for 100 kilometres.
66	East turn beside small cafe down dirt road to **Huay Nam Dam** ✓✓(6 kilometres), a plant breeding research station with beautiful flower gardens (best January-March). Good views to Doi Chiang Dao, Thailand's second highest mountain, across the Mae Tang valley. Lisu village (10 kms).
66-80	Mountain road along high ridge (1300 metres) giving wonderful views of mountain ranges in all directions.
70-80	Long, steep descent from mountains to Pai river. Lonely, narrow road with no habitation, surrounded by tall jungle.
81	South turn on Rte 1265 which follows the Pai river west through several Thai villages before turning into the mountains. One kilometre along this road is a Karen village.
82	Turn north up wide dirt road to **Pong Rone Hot Springs** ✓ After 2 kms turn west (right) to hot springs (1 kilometre). Pretty location in wooded valley, but sulphurous springs themselves not very impressive. The hot water runs into concrete tubs in which bathers immerse themselves.
83	Long ancient wooden bridge, brought from Chiang Rai where it crossed the Ping river.
96	**Pai** ✓✓✓ A small, predominantly Shan, pleasant sleepy town (details page 180). Turn right at the petrol station to get to the town centre.
103	West turn along dirt road to Shan village of **Mor Peng** (4 kilometres). One kilometre past the village is: **Pai Mountain Lodge ●●●**, remote wooden cabins high in the mountains above the Pai valley Address: 84 Mor Peng, Mae Na Tang, Pai, Mae Hong Son. Price:150-300 (dorm 50) Rooms:9 Bathroom:9(3hw)(hw outside) Comfort:☆☆ Design:☆☆☆☆ Location:☆☆☆☆☆ Quietness:☆☆☆☆☆ Restaurant:☆☆☆. 1.5 kilometres after the Lodge is a Lahu village, then 1 kilometre after this **Mor Peng Waterfall** ✓✓ a small but pretty waterfall. At the end of the road is a small car park, 3 minute walk along the path to the falls.
109-138	Lovely mountain road, beautiful scenery and great views. This road is newly surfaced with some small stretches incomplete. Be careful on the many hairpin bends.
112	**Pan Baek** ✓✓ 1 kilometre to west on dirt road. Pretty, friendly and traditional Lisu village. On arrival you will be rapidly surrounded by small children, followed closely by old ladies with handicrafts for sale.
132	Lisu village of **Nam Rin** on west side of road. Path through mountains to Karen village (5 kilometre west).
140	**Soppong** ✓✓ A large, mainly Lisu village/town, entered by a small road to the north of the main road. There are 4 guest houses in and around Soppong, and the amazing Lot caves ✓✓✓(7 kilometres north) should not be missed. (Soppong details page 185)
141	100 metres past **Jungle House** (see page 187), south turn up poor dirt road to large and very pretty **Lisu village** ✓✓. Ask at Jungle House for details of walks in the area.
148	North turn up dirt road to **Red Lahu village** ✓✓ in dramatic location backed by cliffs and mountains.
150	North turn on good dirt road to **Mae La Na**, a small Shan town in a remote and very beautiful valley sheltered by massive limestone cliffs. Just before the village, next to the school:

	Mae La Na Guest House ●●● Very basic accommodation in a beautiful setting. Great atmosphere, very friendly. **Address:** Mae La Na, Mae Hong Son **Price:** 70 (dorm 30) **Comfort:**☆ **Design:**☆☆☆☆ **Location:**☆☆☆☆☆ **Quietness:**☆☆☆☆ **Restaurant:**☆☆☆
165	Turn north on dirt road 200 metres west of Lahu village of **Nam Khong** 50 metres past new cement bridge, 1 km to: **Wilderness Lodge** ●●●●. Aptly named, an exquisite "long house" design in clearing hacked out of the jungle beside a river. Remote and romantic. **Price:** 70 (dorm 35) **Bathroom:** 0(cw outside) **Comfort:**☆ **Design:**☆☆☆☆☆ **Location:**☆☆☆☆☆ **Quietness:**☆☆☆☆☆ **Restaurant:**☆☆☆ **Facilities:** Exploring a vast cave system, swimming and inner tubing in the river.
180	**Huai Pha** ✓✓ Large Shan villages with a lovely Shan temple on west of road.

NB DISTANCES ON KILOMETRE POSTS NOW FROM MAE HONG SON

17	On the west side of road is the much visited **Pla (fish) cave** ✓. It is not really a cave, but a hole in the rocks giving a view of the stream running underneath, which is crammed with giant (since overfed by tourists) carp. There is a shrine in the rock face above the pool, and the fish are considered holy. Not a hugely impressive sight, but the gardens are lovely.
16	North turn up good dirt road to **Pha Sua waterfalls** ✓✓(18 kilometres), the Hmong village of **Na Pha Pak** ✓✓(28 kilometres) and the Chinese Kuomintang village of **Mae Aw** ✓✓(36 kilometres) (details page 191) The Hmong village has a unique guest house **The Hill** ●●, run by Hmong people within the village. Primitive conditions but fascinating location. **Price:** 50 **Rooms:** 5 **Bathroom:** 0(cw outside) **Comfort:**☆ **Design:**☆☆☆ **Location:**☆☆☆☆☆ **Quietness:**☆☆☆☆☆ **Restaurant:**☆☆
14-10	After 100 kilometres of mountain road, a gradual descent into the Mae Hong Son valley, crossing the Pai river.
8	East turn to **Mae Surin waterfall park headquarters**. A pretty spot on the Pai river, although the waterfall is 60 kilometres south of here!
7	West turn 1 kilometre to **Golden Pai Resort** ✓✓✓(details page 193)
0	**Mae Hong Son** ✓✓✓Still a very pretty town, despite the tourist boom that has rocketed it into the 20th century in the last five years.

MAE HONG SON - MAE SARIANG (164 kilometres - 3 hours) Map page 175-177

From Mae Hong Son, take Rte 108 to Mae Sariang and Hot.

NB KILOMETRE POSTS MEASURE DISTANCES FROM HOT

262	Two kilometres south of Mae Hong Son, west turn to a number of resorts and hotels, Karen elephant camp, silk factory and boat station on the Pai river for trips to the long neck Karen village and Burma border.
255	**Pha Bong Hot Springs** ✓✓.To west of road. A large spring which has produced a lake of near boiling, pale blue water, amazingly colonised by algae and bacteria which thrive in these hostile conditions. There are nicely designed stone showering cubicles around the lake in which one can "take the waters".

The West

253   The road narrows as it climbs steeply out of the valley into the mountains. Turn east for good new road to **Pha Bong Dam** ✓
CAUTION: THIS MAIN ROAD IS VERY NARROW WITH SHARP BENDS. BEWARE OF ONCOMING LARGE VEHICLES AND KEEP WELL IN TO THE LEFT.

251   Scenic area to east of road gives good views of **Doi Hai Chaia** (altitude 1752 metres) and **Pha Bong Dam** ✓.

235   Steep surfaced road 10 kilometres to **Khao Hwai Hang Po** ✓✓(commonly known as **Meo microwave**), a large Hmong village at high altitude.

227   East turn 1 km to small Karen village of **Mae Dja** ✓

212   Small town of **Mae Surin** surrounded by tall palms in a lush valley. The road dips into the valley, then climbs steeply out.

210-200   High plateau of scattered pine and low teak forestry and occasional cultivation.

200   East turn onto good wide dirt road (Rte 1263) which climbs high into the mountains, passing close to three waterfalls: **Mae Yuam Luang** ✓(15 kilometres), **Mae Ankhoe** ✓(25 kilometres) and the magnificent **Mae Surin** ✓✓✓(37 kilometres). After 26 kilometres, **Buatang** ✓✓✓ - three mountains covered in sunflowers, a huge blaze of colour in October and November.

199   **Khun Yuam.** A small town on the plateau with a large market, some pleasant small restaurants and some nice places to stay the night

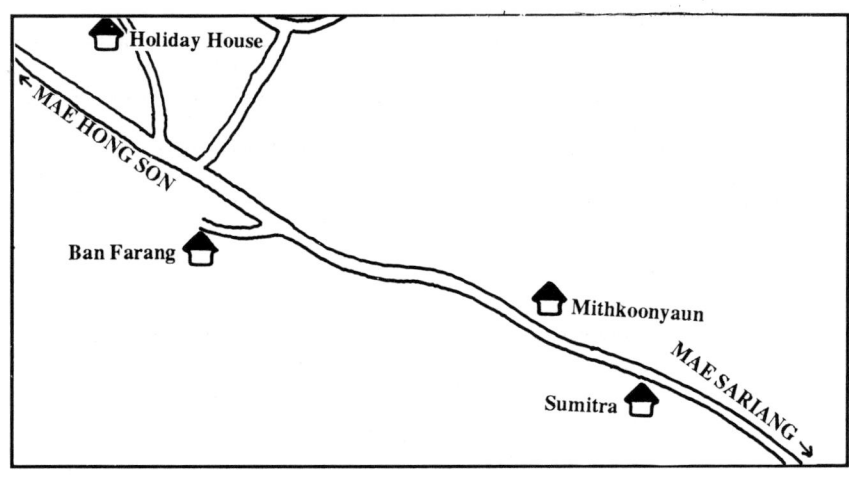

HOTELS

Mithkoonyaun Hotel ●●● A lovely old teak hotel with clean and well kept rooms.
Price: 40-100   **Rooms:** 17 **Fan:** 11   **Bathroom:** 4(cw) **Comfort:**☆☆ to ☆☆☆
Design:☆☆☆☆ **Location:**☆☆ **Position:** central, by bus stop, east side of road.
Quietness:☆☆

Sumitra ●● Ugly but adequate rooms in adequate but ugly concrete hotel.
Address: Sumitra Hotel, Khun Huam, Mae Hong Son.
Price: 80-250   **Rooms:** 21   **A/C:** 2   **Fan:** 19   **Bathroom:** 10(cw) **Comfort:**☆☆ to ☆☆☆
Design:☆ **Location:**☆☆ **Position:** central, opposite bus stop. **Quietness:**☆☆.

GUEST HOUSES

Ban Farang ✪✪✪ An exquisite red painted three storey Thai teak house with spotlessly clean rooms.
Address: Khun Yuam, Mae Hong Son.
Price range:30 Rooms:2(6 bed dorms) Fan:2 Bathroom:0(cw outside) Comfort:☆☆ Design:☆☆☆☆ Location:☆☆☆ Position:side road 500 metres north of town centre.
Quietness:☆☆☆ Restaurant:☆☆☆

Holiday House ✪✪✪ New, big and pretty log cabins in large garden on hill top.
Address: Khun Yuam, Mae Hong Son
Price:100 Rooms:3 Fan:3 Bathroom:3(cw) Comfort:☆☆☆ Design:☆☆☆☆ Location:☆☆☆☆ Position:1 kilometre on Rte 1263 to east of town
Quietness:☆☆☆☆☆

176	In town of **Nong Heng**, dirt road 15 kilometres east to hot springs.
167	Dirt road to east to three Karen villages, 7 kilometres **Huai Mai Sang**, 11 kilometres **Mae Tot Die**, 12 kilometres **Mae Tot Klang**.
153	West turn to the large Lawa village of **Mae La Luang** ✓(500 metres) not traditional, only oldest having retained their costumes, but a centre for Lawa handicrafts.
146	East turn to small Karen village.
133	**Mae La Noi** ✓Small town of teak houses on the Mae La Noi river with two Shan temples. East turn 100 metres north of river signposted waterfall and caves. This road is closed after 5 kilometres for logging operations upstream.
132	East turn onto Rte 1266, 200 metres south of the river. An all weather wide dirt road switchbacking over the mountains with spectacular scenery. 12 kilometres Thai village of **Huai Mak Khanum**, 14 kilometres Karen village of **Mae Sakua** ✓✓, in very pretty location. 25 kilometres very lovely hill top Lawa village **La Up** ✓✓✓. From here it is possible to walk or take an elephant to **Ban Tai waterfall** ✓✓(4 kilometres). Elephants can be hired form the village shop in La Up.
107	West turn 4 kilometres to Karen village of **Pankhor**. Easy to get lost in a maze of lanes. A very small and ordinary Karen village.

MAE SARIANG - CHIANG MAI (198 kilometres - 3.5 hours) Map page 171-172

Kilometres

100	**Mae Sariang** ✓✓✓For details see page 198.
98	North turn up metalled road 1 kilometre to **Mae Sariang Resort** ✪✪✪ (see page 201)
88	North turn to exceptionally friendly Karen village of **Ba Djee** ✓✓(2 kilometres).
86	North turn up dirt road to Karen village of **Mae Sawan** ✓✓. Keep to the track for 2 kilometres beyond the village. At the end, a footpath leads to **Mae Sawan Noi waterfall** ✓, a small but pretty waterfall surrounded by a pocket of lush jungle in the hill tribe fields.
76	Large Karen village of **Mae Lai** ✓on south side of road. Snacks and drinks in car park beside road.
73	Dirt road south by police post and bus stop to several villages, including three Pwo Karen villages, **Khong Pae** ✓✓✓(8 kilometres), **Ton You** (17 kilometres) and **Huai Mo** ✓ (23 kilometres). Pwo Karen wear very interesting costumes - unmarried men wear much

65	jewellery and the girls are weighed down with bronze and silver bangles and bracelets. South turn to **Pan House** ❶❷ (10 kilometres), a small guest house in the small farming town of Mae Pae. Pan is a trekking guide. He and his brother (also called Pan!) run this guest house as a base for treks to the many completely unspoiled hill tribe villages in the area. Very basic facilities in a traditional teak Thai house. Address: Pan House, Mae Pae, Hot, Chiang Mai Price:30 Rooms:2 (dorms) Comfort:☆Bathroom:0(cw outside) Design:☆☆☆☆ Location:☆☆☆☆ Position:central Quietness:☆☆☆ Restaurant: communal meals 15-25 *baht* Tours/treks:50 *baht*/day
59	North turn to two Karen villages, **Ban Dok Den** (7 kilometres), **Mae On Long** (9 kilometres)
56	North turn past bus stop to Hmong village of **Mac Toc** (17 kilometres) and **Chang More** ✓✓(26 kilometres) - a very traditional Lawa village where all women wear colourful traditional costume.
60-40	The main road traverses a high cool plateau largely given over to pine forest. There is a large experimental station where different species of pine are cultured. The area is known locally as the Sweden of Thailand for obvious reasons. To the north, good views of Thailand's highest mountain in the distance - Doi Inthanon.
28	Start of **Obluang National Park** ✓✓. The main road drops sharply from the plateau in a series of long winding bends through rocky scenery.
22	North turn along Rte 1088 to **Mae Chaam** (48 kilometres). A poor dirt road, difficult in places, but an alternative route back to Chiang Mai via Doi Inthanon (Mae Chaam - Chiang Mai see page 114). Rte 1088 passes through pleasant mountain and plateau scenery with several rural Thai villages on route. At kilometre 15 there is a hot spring.
18	**Kaw Krai Rat Resort** ❶❷❸❹❺ In lovely gardens on the edge of Obluang gorge, luxury bungalows and tree houses. The resort was formerly part of the Borneo Logging Co., and later a Japanese concentration camp. Address: (for booking)6/147 Soi Amorn Phan, Nak 6, Sukhaphiban 2 HD Bungkhum, Bangkok 10230. Tel; (17)8243. Price:700 Rooms:7 A/C:5 Fan:2 Bathroom:7(hw) Comfort:☆☆☆☆ to ☆☆☆☆☆ Design:☆☆☆☆☆ Location:☆☆☆☆☆ Quietness:☆☆☆☆☆ Restaurant:☆☆☆☆ Facilities Free transfer Chiang Mai airport (1.5 hrs)
18	300 metres after resort, path on north of road to gorge and river. The gorge is small but lovely, swimming possible from small sandy beaches at rivers edge. Nice walks along the gorge.
4	**Hot Resort** ❶❷❸ On north of road on banks of Mae Chaam river. A lovely site, but overpriced for the facilities. Address: Hot-Mae Sariang Road, Hot, Chiang Mai Price:600 Rooms:16 A/C:0 Fan:0 Bathroom:16(hw) Comfort:☆☆☆ Design:☆☆☆ Location:☆☆☆☆ Quietness:☆☆☆☆☆ Restaurant:☆☆
0	**Hot**. a small, dull Thai town with not much of interest. The town is new - the old site of Hot now being at the bottom of Bhumipol reservoir. There is one hotel at the crossroads, closed for decoration at time of writing. At T-junction in Hot turn north on Rte 108, signposted Chiang Mai.

DISTANCES ON KILOMETRE POSTS NOW MEASURED FROM CHIANG MAI

83	West turn along good dirt road 1 km to small Thai village. Here fork left onto surfaced road, which winds along the flat bottom of a narrow forested valley. through high cliffs ending at a small and exceedingly beautiful Buddhist **convent** ✓✓. There is a small cave containing a Buddha image in the southern cliff face used for meditation by the nuns.

Mae Sariang - Chiang Mai

	The stream in the forest is surrounded by nuns' cabins. The convent and its extensive grounds have a wonderful feeling of peace and harmony. The abbess welcomes visitors who are genuinely interested in meditation - if there is room they can stay indefinitely.
68	**Ban Mong ap Chang ✓✓.** This village specialises in the production of natural dyed cotton cloth. Several open air rural factories are signposted (small wooden signs), at which the entire process from cotton plants and boiling herbal dyes to the weaving on hand looms can be followed.
65	**Moon Duan Duang Resort ✪✪✪** On the east side of road - attractive and well furnished wooden cabins in a lovely wooded setting on the west bank of the Ping river. **Address:** Chom Thong, Chaing Mai **Price:** 350-500 (150 dorm) **Rooms:** 11 **Fan:** 11 **Bathroom:** 11(hw) **Comfort:** ☆☆☆ **Design:** ☆☆☆☆☆ **Location:** ☆☆☆☆☆ **Quietness:** ☆☆☆☆☆ **Restaurant:** ☆☆☆
59	**Chom Thong.** Small busy town and market centre for Karen and Hmong hill tribe villages. In the centre of the town, on the east side of the road, is perhaps the most beautiful temple in northern Thailand - **Wat Phra That Chom Thong ✓✓✓**. All good Buddhists in the north make a pilgrimage to this temple once a year, which is of great religious importance. The main *chedi*, dating form the 15th century, is very impressive, completely sheathed in brass plates. The *wiharn* was rebuilt in 1817, but has been little changed since then. It is an elegant building, filled with votive offerings and wood carvings, many of great antiquity. The grounds shaded by tall palm trees contain many primitive sculptures.
57	West turn on Rte 1009 (metalled road) to Doi Inthanon (details page 114). One kilometres along this road turn south on road signposted **Mae Ya waterfall**, the biggest and most beautiful waterfall in Torthern Thailand. The road deteriorates to a dirt track (4wd may be needed in wet season) From the car park it is a 1.5 kilometre walk to the falls along a densely forested valley. There is a well made footpath which crosses a rushing boulder strewn stream before the waterfall is reached. A wide curtain of water dropping 50 metres to the stream. The falls have many ledges and steep cascades along their length, and this is a scene of very great natural beauty. Since the falls face east, they are best visited in the morning, when the light shines on the water.
24	**San Pa Tong Market ✓✓** The largest market in Northern Thailand (Saturdays only). It was originally a livestock market, but now sells everything from lightbulbs to ox carts. Within the market area is a small lake with boating and fishing.
22	**San Pa Tong.** Mid sized Thai town. West turn on Rte 1013 leads back to Doi Inthanon through several Thai and Karen villages. A pretty but difficult route. At kilometre 17 there is a small elephant camp where elephants can be rented for 200 *baht* per hour. The road is only metalled for 8 kilometres, then poor dirt road.
11	**Hang Dong ✓✓** A town famous for the production of wooden sculptures - many to be sold as "antiques" in Chiang Mai and other tourist centres. Shop names such as "modern antiques" rather give the game away! In the centre of this small town, turn east down a gravel road to the village of **Bantawe**, where every house is a wood carving factory.
10	East turn to village of **Muang Kung**. This village specialises in the production of pots made under the house on primitive wheels.
10	West turn to mountain town of **Samoeng ✓✓** (38 kilometres) - a lovely drive into the hills (details page 109)
10-0	Very fast 4 lane highway from Hang Dong to Chiang Mai. At traffic lights turn left for airport (1 kilometre) or straight on for town centre.

WEST TOWNS

PAI

A small town on the west bank of the sizeable Pai river with a very pleasant sleepy atmosphere. At an altitude of 700 metres, Pai has a near perfect climate - rarely too hot in summer and delightfully cool in the winter, when each day dawns chilly and misty until the sun burns through in mid morning. Temperatures at dawn can be close to freezing in December and January, when daytime temperatures rarely exceed 27° C.

The Pai river has its origins in the hills to the north of Pai and flows west through Mae Hong Son and into Burma where it joins the Salween river. It provides opportunities for swimming, rafting and boating. The valley around Pai is a flat patchwork of rice paddies closely rimmed by the mountains which dominate the scenery. The population are mainly Shan, also known as *Tai Yai*, and speak a dialect of Thai not easily understood by other Thais. Their temples, of which there are several good examples, although Buddhist, differ markedly from other Buddhist temples, with filigreed tiers of pagodas above a large communal devotional wooden floor, usually on stilts.

The Pai area has a large number of Lisu, Lahu and Karen villages nearby, whose exotically dressed inhabitants are commonly seen shopping in the large market, and to whose villages several companies in Pai arrange treks at a standard price of 250 *baht*/day, all inclusive.

Although low key, tourism has started to blossom in Pai. There are now over 15 guest houses, mostly with very spartan facilities and several good cheap restaurants offering basic Thai and some western food. One - Own Place - specialises in Middle Eastern and Israeli food. Around Pai there are several sights to see including waterfalls, hot springs and temples, hill tribe villages and an interesting Chinese Kuomintang village.

TRANSPORT

BY BUS

Chiang Mai-Pai (4 hours):	07.00, 08.00, 11.00, 14.00
Pai- Mae Hong Son (2 hours):	07.00, 11.00, 14.00
Mae Hong Son - Pai:	06.30, 08.00 (A/C), 09.00, 11.00, 14.00
Pai-Chiang Mai:	06.30, 08.00, 14.00

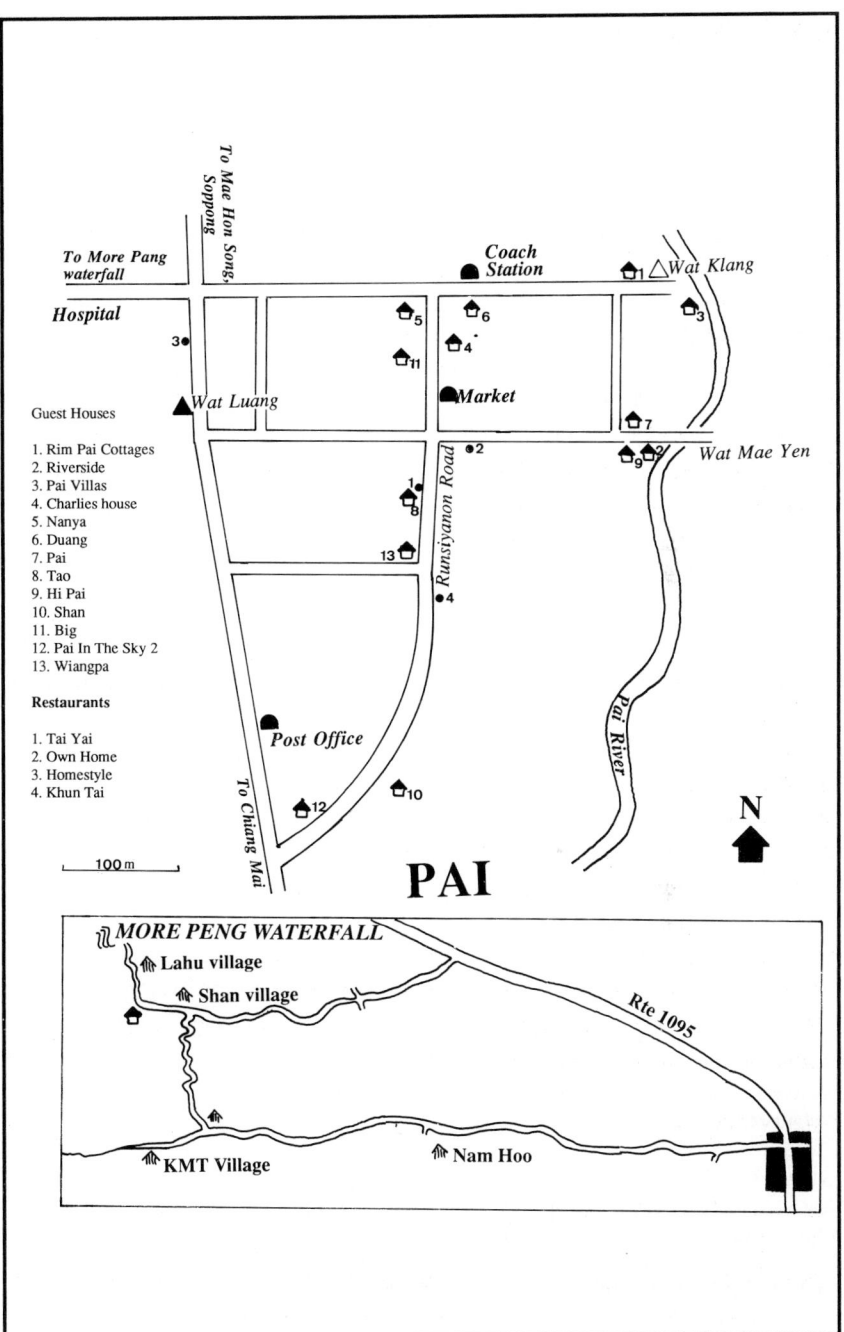

HEALTH
There is a good, well equipped clinic one block west of the bus station, and a small hospital 500 metres west along the same street.

MONEY
There is a branch of Krung Thai Bank on Runsiyanon Street, where money and travellers cheques can be exchanged.

ACCOMMODATION

Rim Pai Cottage ❁❁❁❁
Comfortable A frame huts and chalets in a pretty garden on the river bank.
Address: 17 Moo 3, Pai, Mae Hong Son.
Price:300 **Rooms:**13 **Fan:**13 **Bathroom:**13(hw0) **Comfort:**☆☆☆ **Design:**☆☆☆☆
Location:☆☆☆☆ **Position:**central **Quietness:**☆☆☆☆☆ **Restaurant:**☆☆☆

Riverside ❁❁❁
Nicely situated clean chalets with basic facilities on banks of Pai river looking across to mountains on opposite bank. Manager speaks English.
Address:115 Moo 4 Pai, Mae Hong Son
Price:609-120 **Rooms:**10 **Fan:**10 **Bathroom:**10(cw) **Comfort:**☆☆☆ **Design:**☆☆☆
Location:☆☆☆☆ **Position:**Central **Quietness:**☆☆☆ **Restaurant:**☆☆☆
Facilities swimming and rafting in Pai river **Tours/treks:** local.

Pai Villas ❁❁❁
Basic brick built chalets with palm leaf roof in large field near river. Nice views, peaceful location
Address:89 Moo 3 Ban Pa Khan vieng Tai, Pai, Mae Hong Son
Price:100 **Rooms:**7 **Fan:**7 **Bathroom:**7(cw) **Comfort:**☆☆ **Design:**☆☆☆ **Location:**☆☆☆☆
Position:central **Quietness:**☆☆☆☆☆ **Facilities** swimming/rafting

Charlies House ❁❁❁
New concrete bungalows and dorms behind main street. Friendly and clean. Some rooms very well equipped.
Address: Runsiyanon Street, Pai, Mae Hong Son
Price:60-200 **Rooms:**10 (2 dorms) **Fan:**10 **Bathroom:**3(hw)(hw outside)
Comfort:☆☆ to ☆☆☆☆ **Location:**☆☆ **Position:**centre **Quietness:**☆☆
Restaurant: bkfst/snacks **Tours/treks:**local

Nanya ❁❁❁
New clean rooms in well designed block in small pretty garden.
Address: Runsiyanon Street, Pai, Mae Hong Son
Price:60-100: **Rooms:**7 **Fan:**7 **Bathroom:**3(hw) **Comfort:**☆☆☆ **Design:**☆☆☆ **Location:**☆☆
Position:central **Quietness:**☆☆ **Restaurant:**bkfst, snacks

Pai

Duang ✿✿✿
Quite well furnished comfortable rooms, pleasant garden.
Address: Runsiyanon Street, Pai, Mae Hong Son
Price:30-150 **Rooms:**22 (3 dorms) **Fan:**23 **Bathroom:**3(hw)(hw outside) **Comfort:**☆☆ to ☆☆☆☆ **Design:**☆☆☆ **Location:**☆☆ **Position:**central **Quietness:**☆☆ **Restaurant:**☆☆ **Treks:**local

Pai ✿✿
Primitive but pleasant huts in grass field close to river.
Address: 80/3 Moo San Vieng Tai, Pai, Mae Hong Son
Price:60 **Rooms:**10 **Fan:**10 **Bathroom:**0(hw outside) **Comfort:**☆ **Design:**☆☆☆ **Location:**☆☆☆ **Position:**central **Quietness:**☆☆☆ **Tours/treks:**local

Tao ✿✿
Very basic accommodation but pleasant atmosphere.
Address: Runsiyanon Street, Pai, Mae Hong Son
Price:80 **Rooms:**8 **Bathroom:**0 (hw outside) **Comfort:**☆ **Design:**☆☆☆ **Location:**☆☆ **Position:**central **Quietness:**☆☆ **Tours/treks:**local

Hi Pai ✿✿
Primitive bamboo huts in shady garden near river.
Address:97/1 Vieng Tai, Pai, Mae Hong Son.
Price:60 **Rooms:**7 **Bathroom:**0(hw outside) **Comfort:**☆ **Design:**☆☆☆ **Location:**☆☆☆ **Position:**central **Quietness:**☆☆☆ **Restaurant:**☆☆

Shan ✿✿
Basic huts in field. not a good location but friendly and helpful
Address:140 Vieng Tai, Pai, Mae Hong Son.
Price:80 **Bathroom:**0(cw outside) **Comfort:**☆ **Design:**☆☆☆ **Location:**☆☆ **Position:**central **Quietness:**☆☆.**Tours/treks:**local.

Big ✿✿
Basic facilities in concrete ranch style building garage. Characterless but adequate. Pretty restaurant.
Address: Runsiyanon Street, Pai, Mae Hong Son.
Price:60-100 **Rooms:**9 **Fan:**9 **Bathroom:**5(4hw) **Comfort:**☆☆ **Design:**☆☆ **Location:**☆ **Position:**central **Quietness:**☆☆ **Restaurant:**☆☆☆

Pai In the Sky Two ✿✿
(No 1 closed down). Clean well equipped rooms but bad location and characterless.
Address:150 Vieng Tai, Pai, Mae Hong Son
Price:80-120 **Rooms:**26 **Fan:**26 **Bathroom:**10(cw)(hw outside) **Comfort:**☆☆☆ **Design:**☆☆ **Location:**☆☆ **Position:**central **Quietness:**☆☆ **Restaurant:**☆☆☆

Wiang Pai ✿
Old, dirty teak hotel with cement outbuildings
Address: Runsiyanon Street, Pai, Mae Hong Son
Price:50-100 **Rooms:**18 **Bathroom:**4(cw) **Comfort:**☆ **Design:**☆☆☆ **Location:**☆☆☆ **Position:**central **Quietness:**☆☆ **Restaurant:**☆☆☆

RESTAURANTS

Tai-Yai. Excellent food at cheap prices in small restaurant with very pleasant atmosphere. Scottish chef who bakes wonderful pastry dishes and great bread. A must for breakfast. **Own Home.** Thai, western and Middle East food at reasonable prices. **Home Style.** Extensive Thai menu specialising in local Shan food. Fascinating collection of local arts and crafts on walls.Decor and design of typical Shan house. **Khun Thai.** Nicely decorated Thai design bar and restaurant.

TREKKING.

Treks can be arranged through most guest houses, at a standard price of 250 *baht* per day inclusive. Duang and Charlies House have their own guides.The best treks are said to be from Home Style Restaurant.

WHAT TO SEE

IN PAI
Wat Luang ✓ A typical large Shan style temple.

AROUND PAI
1.5 kilometres over bridge to east of Pai **Wat Mae Yen ✓✓**. The temple is approached by 353 steps (although a road goes to the temple entrance). The temple is a centre for the teaching of Pali, the language of Buddhist ceremony. Lovely wooden carved doors to the temple, one which depicts nature, the other human life. Wat Mae Yen is built on a hill looking out over the town. A further 4.5 kilometres along the road at the base of the temple leads to **Mae Yen waterfall**. There are several places of interest on the dirt road leading west from Pai. 1.3 kilometres to north of road, small Shan temple of **Wat Houna**.
3.6 kilometres Shan village and temple of Nam Hoo. 5.0 kilometres turn off south, Chinese KMT village with dried mud houses with central doorway protected by Chinese good luck symbols. 5.4 kilometres Lisu village. Through village road narrows (4wd), uphill for 3 kilometres to Shan village. Turn left here, pass Lahu village (10 kilometres) to **More Pang waterfall**.

SOPPONG

Not so much peaceful as catatonic, Soppong is a very small town with an atmosphere of calm that makes speech above a whisper seem intrusive. Perched in a high valley surrounded by mountain peaks, the area has been described as a tropical Switzerland. People tend to come for a day and stay a month, beguiled by soporific Soppong. Its a wonderful place to do nothing, but if you want to, there is plenty to do in the area.

Soppong itself has nothing of great interest. It is a market town for the surrounding hilltribe villages, of which there are many. The town has a high Lisu population, but in the area there are also Lahu, Karen and Shan villages. There is a very small new Thai temple, a large school and police station, a hilltribe development office, several shops, two guest houses, two petrol stations and a bus stop. Government offices are found at Pang Mapha, three kilometres north of Soppong. Many maps show Pang Mapha as Soppong, an occasional source of confusion.

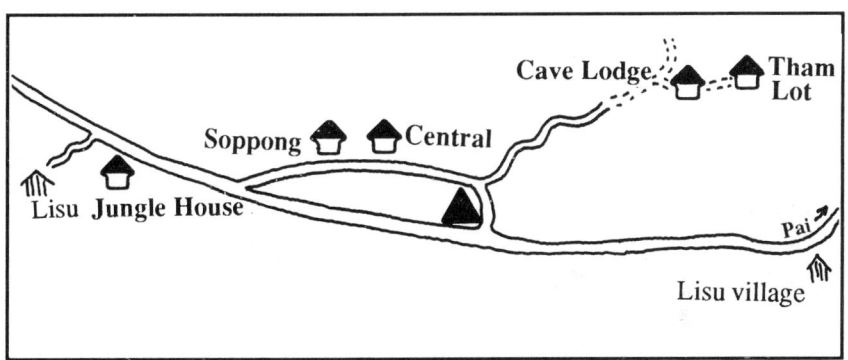

TRANSPORT

BUS (ORDINARY)
Soppong-Mae Hong Son (2 hours): 10.30, 12.30, 15.00, 18.00
Soppong-Pai (1.5 hours): 08.30, 11.00, 13.00, 16.00
Mae Hong Son-Soppong (2 hours): 06.30, 09.00, 11.00, 14.00
Pai-Soppong (1.5 hours): 07.00, 09.00, 11.30, 14.30

MINIBUS
Soppong-Pai-Chiang Mai: 07.00, 09.00, 15.00
Mae Hong Son - Soppong - Pai: 07.00, 09.00, 11.00

WHAT TO SEE

Lod Cave ✓✓✓ is the main attraction in the area. One of the largest cave systems in Asia, it stretches for several kilometres underground. Eroded out of the limestone by the small river of Huay Nam Lang running through it, it has caverns and passageways at several levels. The caverns are filled with sculpted shapes, stalactites and stalagmites carved out by the water. This is fascinating and beautiful of itself, but there is more. The caves have a large population of cave swifts and bats. At dusk the lower entrance has a 'rush hour' when birds come back to roost and the bats head out. The air is thick and the sky at the entrance is blackened by millions of tiny flying bodies.

In one of the upper levels are the wooden remains of large, six metre coffins from an unknown civilisation.

> "In the Soppong district there are at least 50 caves that contain prehistoric wooden coffins. The locals believe they were left by 'Pea-men' - malicious cave spirits. The coffins are hollowed logs, usually of teak, split in half lengthways. At each end are handles, sometimes carved out of a pigs head. Coffins are commonly six metres long, the longest recorded being 9.5 metres, and supported on big posts and cross beams two metres off the cave floor. In drier caves human bones and possessions remain, including cord impressed pottery, iron tools, bracelets, bronze objects and glass beads (some Roman). They are believed to be at least 2000 years old. Archaeological exploration has been very sparse. In the 1960s Gorman found evidence of human habitation going back 14,000 years. He dated carbonized seeds which indicate the earliest known cultivation in the world. The coffins are later remains."
>
> John Spies, Cave Lodge.

A guide is essential for a trip to the caves. The best is Ta, based at Cave Lodge. An elderly Shan, he is known as 'Slowly'. As he guides you through the caves, his continual advice 'lowly, lowly, mine or hea, tae i eessy' (slowly, slowly, mind your head, take it easy) gives a clue to his nickname. If Slowly is not available there are many guides who will offer themselves to you complete with hurricane lamp in the cave car park or village nearby. Allow two hours for the complete trip, and be prepared for some deep wading in the sometimes very cold water. Ask if you wish to see the coffins, which involve a steep climb up rickety ladders. The average price paid to the guides is 100 *baht*.

It is also sometimes possible to take an elephant ride through the caves. The elephants wade through the river, a trip taking 1.5 hours for *250 baht* per elephant. A unique experience.

Soppong

Hill tribe villages. Within easy walking distance from Soppong there are several pretty, interesting and friendly villages. Start at Jungle house, 1.5 kilometres north of Soppong. Walk 100 metres north, turn left. After one kilometre is a large Lisu village. Turn south here, walk eight kilometres passing through a Lahu and another Lisu village before reaching the, main road and walking back to Soppong. From the second Lisu village there is a path leading west to a remote Karen village. Ask at Jungle House for details. Their guide, Sunny, speaks excellent English and is very helpful.

ACCOMMODATION

Jungle House ✿✿✿
Basic but very pretty bamboo huts in a lovely garden close to the stream. Good food and very helpful, friendly staff.
Address: Soppong, Mae Hong Son
Price: 35-80 **Rooms:** 5 (dorm) **Bathroom:** 0(cw outside) **Comfort:** ☆ **Design:** ☆☆☆☆
Location: ☆☆☆☆ **Position:** 1.5 kilometres north of Soppong on west of main road.
Quietness: ☆☆☆☆☆ **Restaurant:** ☆☆☆ **Tours/treks:** local

Cave Lodge ✿✿✿
Nicely designed large Thai style teak house with big communal eating and living area in near perfect surroundings. 8 huts in grounds.
Address: Tham Lot, Soppong, Mae Hong Son
Price: 35-80 **Rooms:** 11 (dorms) **Bathroom:** 1(hw)(cw outside) **Comfort:** ☆ to ☆☆
Design: ☆☆☆☆ **Location:** ☆☆☆☆ **Position:** 7 kilometres north of Soppong (see map).
Quietness: ☆☆☆☆☆ **Restaurant:** ☆☆(vegetarian food eaten communally and limited menu)
Tours/treks: none organized, some guides available for caves and walks.

Soppong ✿✿
Reasonable huts near centre of town.
Address: Soppong, Mae Hong Son
Price: 80 **rooms:** 8 **Bathroom:** (cw outside) **Comfort:** ☆ **Design:** ☆☆ **Location:** ☆☆☆
Position: central **Quietness:** ☆☆☆

Tham Lot ✿✿
Huts by the stream by Tham Lod cave. Beautiful but primitive.
Address: Tham Lod, Soppong, Mae Hong Son
Price: 60 **Rooms:** 5 **Comfort:** ☆ **Design:** ☆☆☆☆ **Location:** ☆☆☆☆☆
Position: by stream near caves. **Quietness:** ☆☆☆☆☆

Central guest house ✿
Small dirty rooms above Muslim restaurant.
Address: Soppong, Mae Hong Son
Price range: 60 **Rooms:** 2 **Bathroom:** 0(cw outside) **Comfort:** ☆ **Design:** ☆☆ **Location:** ☆☆
Position: opposite bus stop **Quietness:** ☆☆☆ **Restaurant:** ☆

MAE HONG SON

In the far north west of Thailand, close to Burma to the west, and almost surrounded by high mountains, Mae Hong Son has long been an almost forgotten city and province. The first road to reach there only did so in 1965, and even then it was a long haul from anywhere else. Now, with very recent surfaced road and air links, Mae Hong Son is emerging from its medieval cocoon to face the present. The area is known as "the land of three mists" - the early morning mist which envelops the ground in the cool season every morning until the sun burns it off, the smoke of burning stubble and hill forest in the hot season, and the frequent mist of fine rain in the wet season.

Although in Thailand, Mae Hong Son is not really very Thai. A large majority of the population are Shan or hill tribe with their roots in Burma, and for most Thai is a second language. The temples are more influenced by Burma than Thailand, and many of the festivals and customs are unique to the area.

The city was first settled in 1831, when the Prince of Chiang Mai found himself in need of elephants. An expedition was sent into the wilderness and discovered a wealth of animals in the Mae Hong Son area. The corral to house these wild elephants grew into a village and attracted Shan people who settled here. The settlement grew so quickly that it was declared a city in 1874, and in 1893 the area became a province, with Mae Hong Son as its capital.

Mae Hong Son is a very pretty town. It has several lovely Shan temples, two built on the edges of a beautiful lake surrounded by tall palm trees. The area, very close to the centre of Mae Hong Son, and in many ways the towns spiritual centre, has recently been turned into a "fitness park" where modern health conscious locals jog in the early morning mists. The town centre has grown rapidly in the last few years, but most of the buildings are still the traditional two storey teak buildings - so attractive and practical in the tropical climate but in most Thai cities all too quickly being pulled down to make way for modern concrete constructions.

In the cool season Mae Hong Son really is cool - downright cold in the early mornings, commonly close to freezing point. The dawn mists are a feature of the town, but burn off mid morning giving warm sunny afternoons. Despite its altitude, Mae Hong Son is very hot in March and April, with afternoon temperatures close to 40° C., and in the wet season rainfall is heavy and frequently continuous for two or three days in August and September. The permanently

Mae Hong Son

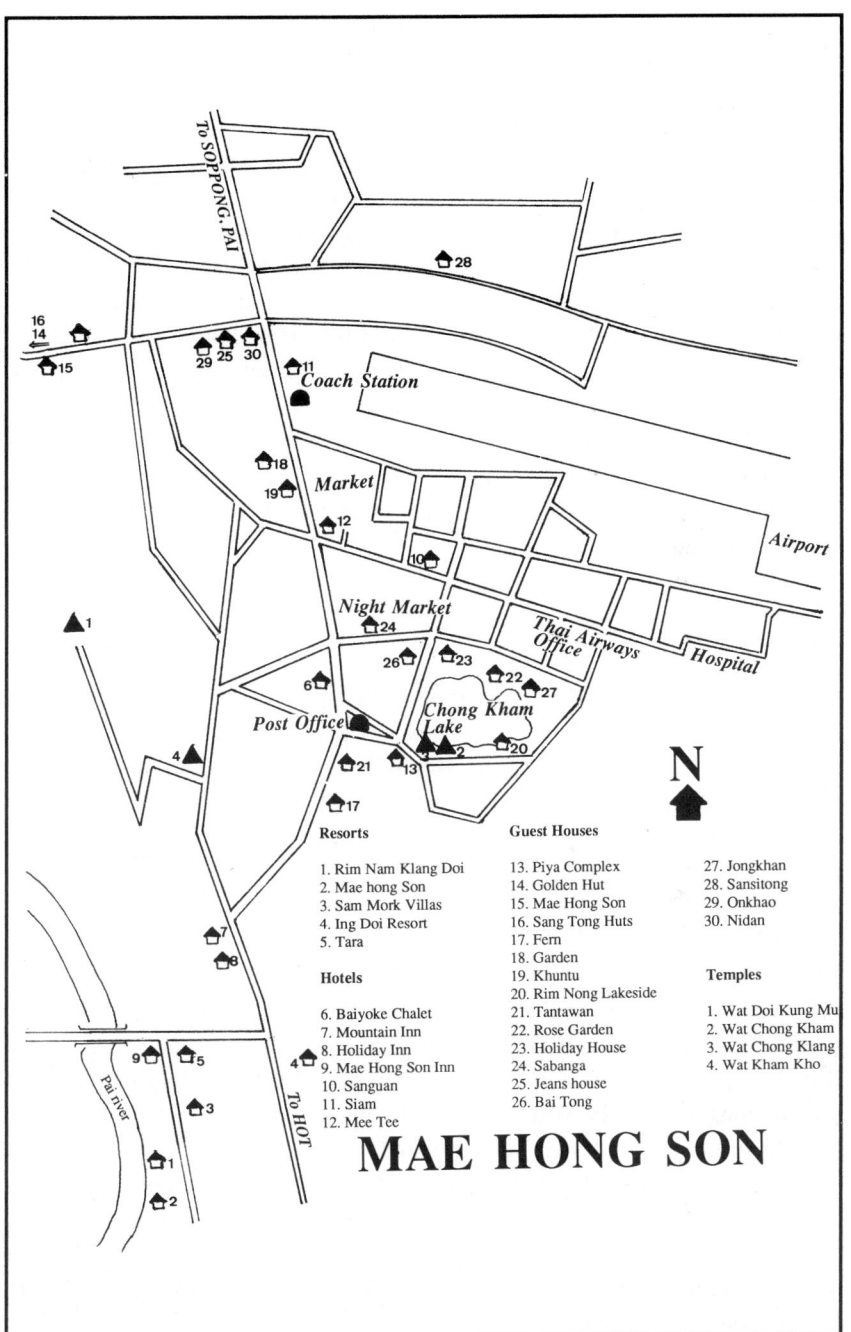

Resorts

1. Rim Nam Klang Doi
2. Mae hong Son
3. Sam Mork Villas
4. Ing Doi Resort
5. Tara

Hotels

6. Baiyoke Chalet
7. Mountain Inn
8. Holiday Inn
9. Mae Hong Son Inn
10. Sanguan
11. Siam
12. Mee Tee

Guest Houses

13. Piya Complex
14. Golden Hut
15. Mae Hong Son
16. Sang Tong Huts
17. Fern
18. Garden
19. Khuntu
20. Rim Nong Lakeside
21. Tantawan
22. Rose Garden
23. Holiday House
24. Sabanga
25. Jeans house
26. Bai Tong
27. Jongkhan
28. Sansitong
29. Onkhao
30. Nidan

Temples

1. Wat Doi Kung Mu
2. Wat Chong Kham
3. Wat Chong Klang
4. Wat Kham Kho

MAE HONG SON

high humidity and temperature make the slow pace of life here even slower.

Mae Hong Son is a market town for many surrounding villages. Lisu, Lahu, Hmong and Karen people are a usual sight shopping in the large markets, coming into town packed into the back of one of the ubiquitous pick ups which ply a bumpy and overloaded trade between country and town. The hills to the west of Mae Hong Son are not always completely safe. There are occasional skirmishes between opium warlords, rebel and official Burmese armies and Thai troops and police. Border incidents have occurred when Burmese troops crossed the border in pursuit of some rebel band or other, or when a drug shipment is intercepted. It is therefore advisable, if intending to visit any of these areas, to either take a guide from the town, or check with one of the travel agencies which areas are safe at that time.

Travel in the hills around Mae Hong Son is not easy at any time, and particularly in the wet season when 4wd is needed for most unsurfaced roads. Some pick up drivers charge more for female passengers, since the men have to get out and push!

THINGS TO SEE

Wat Doi Kung Mu ✓✓✓ This impressive Shan temple, built on a hilltop overlooking the town in 1860, is not only beautiful and fascinating, but provides wonderful views of the town of Mae Hong Son and the surrounding mountains. Take your camera. It is reached by a surfaced road - turn right 250 metres south of the town centre on the main road to Mae Sariang and drive two kilometres up the hill to the temple. Alternatively there is a long (800 metre) and very steep new staircase from the bottom of the hill.

Wat Chong Kham and **Wat Chong Klang** ✓✓✓ These two temples are adjacent to each other on the south side of the lake and make a stunning site with their pagodas mirrored on the still surface of the water. Wat Chong Klang has a collection of thirty-three 200 years old dolls, most about one metre high. They were brought from Burma in 1857 and represent characters from the previous incarnations of Buddha. Wat Chong Kham has a five metre statue of a sitting Buddha of brick and plaster, much revered.

Wat Kham Kho ✓✓ At the base of Doi Kung Moo, and interesting for the extraordinary amount of intricate iron filigree on the tiers of the pagodas and around its covered walkway. Inside is a large and cluttered collection of Buddha images, paintings, photographs and a multitude of objets d'art. It is like an overstocked religious antique shop.

Chong Klan Lake ✓✓ Perhaps the prettiest lake in Thailand. Surrounded by tall slender palm trees and two perfect temples, its shores have been converted into a landscaped garden with profuse blooms, at their best in February. With a backdrop of high, jungle covered peaks, a walk through the park and perhaps a drink at one of the small cafes is a must. In mid morning, watch the mist rise off the water and the sun break through the clouds over the hills as the temperature rises.

AROUND MAE HONG SON

```
CAUTION: BORDER PROBLEMS MAKE SOME AREAS TO THE WEST
OF MAE HONG SON OCCASIONALLY UNSAFE TO VISIT. CHECK
WITH TOUR GUIDES OR AGENCIES BEFORE TRAVELLING, OR
TAKE AN ORGANIZED TOUR.
```

Pha Sua Waterfall ✓✓✓, **Na Pha Pak** ✓✓ (Hmong village), **Kings Palace** ✓, **Mae Aw** (KMT)✓✓✓. All these are along the same road. Turn west off Rte 1095 17 kilometres north of Mae Hong Son along road signposted Pha Sua waterfall. The first 17 kilometres of road are part surfaced and in good condition. Two large Shan villages are passed through, **Khang Mai Sat** at 3 kilometres and **Mork Jon Pae** at 13 kilometres. Five kilometres further, the first of two Karen villages are passed, **Po-oh**, Two kilometres after this **Top Sok**. After Top Sok the road becomes very steep and rutted, impossible in the wet season without 4 wheel drive. However, it's only a 1.5 kilometre walk to the waterfalls.

Pha Sua Waterfall ✓✓✓ A steep path of earth steps leads from the car park (with small cafe) to the falls below. They are impressive, with a wide continuous curtain in the wet season, twelve separate torrents in the dry. To the west of the main falls is a lovely tranquil pool for swimming - but beware of swimming in the top pool - the undertow has swept tourists to their deaths here.

Na Pha Pak ✓✓ (Hmong village). Reached by continuing another ten kilometres uphill from the waterfall. A very bad stretch of road, but giving great views of the mountains and valleys. The village is at the start of a high altitude plateau. A large and friendly village surrounding a grass meadow (perfect for cricket). The village has a small guest house (see page 175). Continue along the road through the village, after two kilometres, to the west of the road on a small hill is **Pang Tong Kings Palace** ✓ Not at all palatial, it resembles a typical house on a prestigious housing estate in England. Beautifully manicured gardens. An odd sight in this wild countryside. Continue north a further six kilometres to the end of the road at Mae Aw.

Mae Aw ✓✓✓ A large Kuomintang village very close to the Burma border. The population are all Chinese, refugees from the communist Chinese revolution of 1949, followers of China's previous nationalist government. The houses are built of dried mud and bamboo, with a central doorway protected by 'spells' in Chinese characters around the door. The village is on the shores of a small lake from which drowned trees emerge. There is a small cafe serving Chinese food and drinks - but beware the flocks of killer turkeys which patrol the village pecking knee-caps.

The desolate landscape of deforested hills and the chill wind at this altitude give the village an eerie and alien atmosphere.

Pai river ✓✓ Drive two kilometres south of Mai Hong Son on route 108 (Mae Sariang road). Turn west on good road (Rte 1250) signposted Pong Daeng. Before the river turn south, 500 metres after Mae Hong Son resort is a Karen organization who have elephant rides and trips down the river, including the Karen long neck village very close to the border.

Karen Long Neck ✓✓ A branch of the Karens called the *Padong* whose women are fitted with neck rings at an early age. These are added to every year, with the result that the neck becomes extremely long, incapable of supporting the head if the rings are removed. There are several Padong villages in Burma, but until recently none in Thailand. A group of three long neck women were imported into Thailand purely as a tourist attraction a few years ago. Recently another three have been procured. The people who control tourism to the village charge 400 *baht* for transport and 300 *baht* to see and photograph these 'exhibits'.

Pla (fish) cave ✓✓ Much touted as of interest, but rather disappointing to most (details page 175).

iew of Mae Hong Son from Wat Doi Kung Mu   Pha Sua waterfall, Mae Hong Son

Wat Chong Kham, Mae Hong Son

Hmong child with opium poppies, Doi Pui, Chiang Mai

Lisu girl at New Year festival, Soppong, Mae Hong

Lawa village, La Up, Mae Sariang

Teak being ferried across the Salween river from Burma, Mae Sam Laep, Mae Sariang

Karen village, Doi Inthanon National Park

Doi Chiang Dao, to the east of the Mae Tang Valley

Lawa grandmother, Mae Sariang area

WHERE TO STAY

RESORTS

Golden Pai Resort ●●●●●
Beautifully designed and furnished bungalows in a peaceful location on the Pai river.
Address: (reservations) 277 Thapae Road, Chiang Mai 50000 **Tel:** (053) 273198 **Fax:** 279260
Price range: 300(dorm)-850(standard double)-1200 luxury) **Rooms:** 30 **A/C:** 30
Bathroom 30(hw) **Comfort:**☆☆☆☆☆ **Design:**☆☆☆☆☆ **Location:**☆☆☆☆
Position: 6 kilometres north of Mae Hong Son, 2 kilometres west of route 1095
Quietness:☆☆☆☆☆ **Restaurant:**☆☆☆☆ **Facilities:** swimming pool, TV in room

Rim Nam Klang Doi ●●●●
In a near perfect landscaped setting, well furnished rooms at reasonable prices.
Address: 70/75 Khunlumprapat Road, Mae Hong Son **Tel:** (053)611086
Price:400-750 **Rooms:**40 **A/C:**3 **Fan:**37 **Bathroom:**40(hw) **Comfort:**☆☆☆ to ☆☆☆☆☆
Design:☆☆☆☆ to ☆☆☆☆☆ **Location:**☆☆☆☆☆ **Position:**4 kilometres south of Mae Hong Son on Pasi river. **Quietness:**☆☆☆☆☆ **Restaurant:**☆☆☆☆ **Facilities:**pool, boat trip,
Tours/treks: to Karen Long Neck village (700 *baht*) by boat.

Mae Hong Son Resort ●●●●
Pleasant well equipped bungalows on the banks of the Pai river. Popular but expensive.
Address:(reservations)560-52 Thapae Road, Chiang Mai 50000 **Tel:** (053)249391
Price:970-1300 (bkfst inc.) **Rooms:**50 **A/C::**50 **Fan:**50 **Bathroom:**50(hw) **Comfort:**☆☆☆☆
Design:☆☆☆☆ **Location:**☆☆☆☆ **Position:**5 kilometres south of Mae Hong Son.
Quietness:☆☆☆☆☆ **Restaurant:**☆☆☆☆ **Tours/treks:** elephant/boat treks to Long Neck Karen village (700 *baht*/day)

Sam Mork Villas ●●●
Attractive wood and brick chalets in lovely gardens with central swimming pool.
Address: 28/1 T. Duang, Mae Hong Son **Tel:** (053)611478
Price:550-650 **Rooms:**35 **Bathroom:**35(hw) **Comfort:**☆☆☆ **Design:**☆☆☆☆
Location:☆☆☆☆☆ **Position:**3 kilometres south of Mae Hong Son **Quietness:**☆☆☆☆☆
Restaurant:☆☆ **Facilities:**pool

Ing Doi Resort ●●●
Palm and bamboo A-frame huts on steep hill side above main road. Huts rather crowded together but good value for facilities offered.
Address:109/1 Moo 8 T. Bang Mu, Mae Hong Son **Tel:** (053)611074
Price:200 **Rooms:**19 **Fan:**19 **Bathroom:**19(hw) **Comfort:**☆☆☆ **Design:**☆☆☆
Location;☆☆☆ **Position:**100 metres above main road 2 kilometres south of Mae Hong Son
Qietness:☆☆☆☆ **Restaurant:**☆☆☆

Tara Resort ●●●● ?
At time of writing not yet complete, but beautiful modern resort providing luxurious accommodation in wooded setting. Likely to be expensive, 1000 *baht* or more. To west of main road 2 kilometres south of Mae Hong Son.

HOTELS

Baiyoke Chalet ❂❂❂❂
Well decorated and furnished hotel with lovely Thai teak furniture and all facilities. Live music in restaurant makes some rooms noisy until 1 am.
Address: 90 Khunlumprapas Road, Mae Hong Son Tel: (053)611486
Price:650-10000-1200 Rooms:40 A/C:40 Bathroom:40 (hw) Comfort:☆☆☆☆☆
Design:☆☆☆☆ Location:☆☆☆ Position:central Quietness:☆☆ Restaurant:☆☆☆
Facilities: TV/video Tours/treks: wide range

Mountain Inn ❂❂❂❂
New, well designed modern hotel on outskirts of Mae Hong Son. Large popular Thai restaurant with cabaret. Rooms well equipped and comfortable but lacking charm
Address:112 Khunlumprapas, Mae Hong Son
Price:600-800 Rooms:81 A/C:81 Bathroom:81(hw) Comfort:☆☆☆☆☆ Design:☆☆☆☆
Location:☆☆ Position: 1 kilometre south of Mae Hong Son Quietness:☆☆ Restaurant:☆☆☆☆

Holiday Inn ❂❂❂❂
Uncompleted at time of writing. 200 metres south of Mountain Inn. Presumably with the usual Holiday Inn standards and prices.

Mae Hong Son Inn ❂❂❂
Quite well equipped rooms in a strangely designed hotel reminiscent of the Costa Brava. Small paddling pool occupied by piranhas.
Address: Bang Moo, Mae Hong Son.
Price:300 Rooms:20 Bathroom:20(hw) Comfort::☆☆☆☆ Design:☆☆☆ Location:☆☆☆
Position:2 kilometres south of Mae Hong Son Quietness:☆☆☆ Facilities:bar

Sanguan ❂❂
Old, very traditional teak hotel on noisy main street. nice architecture. All essential facilities.
Address: 35 Singhanna Banrung Road, Mae Hong Son
Price:80-120 Rooms:18 Fan:18 Bathroom:18(9(cw)9(hw) Comfort:☆☆ to ☆☆☆
Design:☆☆☆ Location:☆ Position:central Quietness:☆

Siam ❂❂
Large, airy, reasonably clean rooms in characterless 60s built block.
Address:23 Kuhunlumprapas Road, Mae Hong Son Tel: (053)611519
Price:180-350 Rooms:26 A/C:8 Fan:18 Bathroom:26(hw) Comfort:☆☆☆ to ☆☆☆☆
Design:☆ Location:☆ Position:central Quietness:☆

Meetee ❂❂
Concrete hotel in centre of town. Reasonably well equipped rooms but soulless and in need of renovation.
Address:53 Khunlumprapas Road, Mae Hong Son .
Price:140-400 Rooms:38 A/C:5 Fan:33 Bathroom:38(5hw) Comfort:☆☆☆ Design:☆
Location:☆☆ Position:central Quietness:☆ Restaurant:☆☆ Tours/treks:wide range.

GUEST HOUSES

Piya Complex ✪✪✪✪
Large guest house by the lovely Chang Klang lake with clean bamboo huts on lagoon to the side. Main building has pleasantly furnished rooms.
Address: 1 Soi 3 Kunlumprapas, Mae Hong Son **Tel:** (053)0611260
Price: 40 (dorm) 80-300 **Rooms:** 11, 6 huts) (3 dorms) **A/C:** 11 **Fan:** 3 **Bathroom:** 11(hw)
Comfort: ☆☆ to ☆☆☆☆ **Design:** ☆☆☆ **Location:** ☆☆☆☆ **Position:** lakeside **Quietness:** ☆☆
Restaurant: ☆☆☆ **Tours/treks:** wide range

Golden Hut ✪✪✪✪
Well equipped bamboo and palmleaf huts on lightly wooded hillside.
Address: 253 Moo 1 Pratcha-udit Road, Mae Hong Son **Tel:** (053)611544
Price: 100-150 **Rooms:** 25 **Fan:** 25 **Bathroom:** 25 (5hw) **Comfort:** ☆☆ to ☆☆☆ **Design:** ☆☆☆☆
Location: ☆☆☆☆ **Position:** 2kilometres west of town. **Quietness:** ☆☆☆☆
Restaurant: snacks/bkfst **Tours/treks:** wide range.

Mae Hong Son ✪✪✪
In pleasant countryside attractive buildings(ranch style house and 6 palm leaf huts) and a nice atmosphere.
Address: 195 Moo 11 T. Makasanti, Mae Hong Son
Price: 80 **rooms:** 12 **Fan:** 12 **Bathroom:** 0(cw outside) **Comfort:** ☆☆ **Design:** ☆☆☆☆
Location: ☆☆☆☆ **Position:** 1.5kilometres west of Mae Hong Son **Quietness:** ☆☆☆☆
Restaurant: ☆☆☆(limited menu) **Tours/treks:** good but difficult treks.

Sang Tong Hut ✪✪✪
Poor facilities but a lovely position on a landscaped hilltop looking over rivers, valleys and mountains. Expensive but worth it for many for its location.
Address: Mae Hong Son 58000
Price: 120-240 **Rooms:** 10 **Fan:** 3 **Bathroom:** 0(cw outside) **Comfort:** ☆ to ☆☆ **Design:** ☆☆☆☆
Location: ☆☆☆☆☆ **Position:** 2.5 kilometres west of town **Quietness:** ☆☆☆☆☆
Restaurant: bkfst/dinner only(except Sunday) **Facilities:** boating, elephant rides, rafting
Tours/treks: local

Fern ✪✪✪
Pretty house behind the excellent Fern Restaurant.
Address: 87 Khunlumprapas Road **Tel:** (053)611374
Price: 80-120 **Rooms:** 7 **Fan:** 7 **Bathroom:** 1(cw)(9hw outside) **Comfort:** ☆☆ **Design:** ☆☆☆☆
Location: ☆☆ **Position:** central **Quietness:** ☆☆☆ **Restaurant:** ☆☆☆☆

Garden ✪✪✪
Teak and bamboo rooms in coconut grove 50 metres behind main road. Cheap rooms tatty, new ones very pleasant.
Address: 44/1 Khunlumprapas Road, Mae Hong Son
Price: 70-150 **Rooms:** 20 **Fan:** 10 **Bathroom:** 10(hw) **Comfort::** ☆ to ☆☆☆ **Design:** ☆☆☆
Location: ☆☆ **Position:** central **Quietness:** ☆☆ **Tours/treks:** motor bike tours, trekking.

Khun Tu ✿✿✿
Lovely varnished teak rooms on busy main street.
Address: Khunlumprapas Road, Mae Hong Son
Price: 80-250 **Rooms:** 6 **A/C:** 1 **Fan:** 5 **Bathroom:** 1(hw) **Comfort:** ☆☆☆ to ☆☆☆☆
Design: ☆☆☆ **Location:** ☆☆ **Position:** central **Quietness:** ☆☆ **Tours/treks:** local

Rim Nong Lakeside ✿✿✿
Attractive building in lovely location on lake, but spartan and cramped rooms. Friendly staff.
Address: 4/1 Chamnansatid Road, Mae Hong Son
Price: 80-120 **Rooms:** 5 **Fan:** 4 **Bathroom:** 0(h w outside) **Comfort:** ☆☆ **Design:** ☆☆☆
Location: ☆☆☆☆☆ **Position:** lake **Quietness:** ☆☆ **Restaurant:** ☆☆
Tours/treks: motor bike and others.

Tantawan House ✿✿
New clean comfortable rooms in a characterless block.
Address: Khunlumprapas Road, Mae Hong Son
Price: 300 **Rooms:** 10 **Fan:** 10 **Bathroom:** 10(hw) **Comfort:** ☆☆☆☆ **Design:** ☆☆
Location: ☆☆ **Position:** central **Quietness:** ☆☆☆

Rose Garden ✿✿
Few facilities but pleasant location on lake.
Address: Chang Klang lake, Mae Hong Son
Price: 80 **Rooms:** 8 **Fan:** 2 **Bathroom:** 0(cw outside) **Comfort:** ☆ **Design:** ☆☆☆
Location: ☆☆☆☆ **Position:** lake **Quietness:** ☆☆ **Facilities:** Thai massage

Holiday house ✿✿
Small bamboo ranch style guest house near lake. Basic but clean and friendly.
Address: Chang Klang lake, Mae Hong Song
Price: 100 **Rooms:** 5, **Fan:** 5 **Bathroom:** 0 (hw outside) **Comfort:** ☆ **Design:** ☆☆☆
Location: ☆☆☆ **Position:** lake **Quietness:** ☆☆ **Facilities:** car and bike hire
Tours/treks: Range of treks

Sabang-Nga ✿✿
Basic but very clean guest house in small shady garden.
Address: Singhanna Bamblung Road, Mae Hong Son
Price: 80 **Rooms:** 8 **Fan:** 8 **Bathroom:** 0(hw outside) **Comfort:** ☆☆ **Design:** ☆☆☆ **Location:** ☆☆☆
Position: central **Quietness:** ☆☆☆

Jeans House ✿✿
Characterless concrete rooms (owner has plans for new pretty rooms) in rather unattractive part of town.
Address: 6 Prachautith Road, Mae Hong Son
Price: 40-80 **Rooms:** 15 **Fan:** 15 **Bathroom:** 0(hw outside) **Comfort:** ☆☆ **Design:** ☆
Location: ☆☆ **Position:** central **Quietness:** ☆☆ **Restaurant:** ☆☆☆ **Tours/treks:** local

Baitong House ❋❋
Spartan accommodation but friendly staff in pretty location by lake.
Address: Chang Klang Fitness Park, Mae Hong Son
Price:80 **Rooms**:4 **Fan**:4 **Bathroom**:0(cw outside) **Comfort**:☆ **Design**:☆☆ **Location**:☆☆☆☆
Position:lake **Quietness**:☆☆☆ **Tours/treks**: local treks.

Jongkhan ❋❋
Pretty location but small rooms (upper rooms better)
Address: Chang Klan Fitness Park, Mae Hong Son
Price:120 **Rooms**:8 **Fan**:8 **Bathroom**:0 (cw outside) **Comfort**:☆ **Design**:☆☆ **Location**:☆☆☆☆
Position:lake **Quietness**:☆☆☆ **Restaurant**: snacks only

Sansitong ❋
Address: Sansitong Road, Mae Hong Son
In a lane near town centre, a traditional Thai teak house on stilts. Interesting but very primitive.
Price:120 **Rooms**:6 **Bathroom**:0 (cw outside) **Comfort**:☆ **Design**:☆☆☆ **Location**:☆☆
Position:near centre **Quietness**:☆☆☆

Onkhao ❋
Wooden ranch style buildings in longon orchard. Small rooms.
Address: 2 Prachuatith Road, Mae Hong Son
Price:90-100 **Rooms**:8 **Fan**:8 **Bathroom**:0 (cw outside) **Comfort**:☆☆ **Design**:☆☆
Location:☆☆ **Position**:central **Quietness**:☆☆ **Restaurant**:☆☆

Nidan ❋
Rooms in cement block.
Address: 30/1 Khunlumprapas Road, Mae Hong Son
Price:80 **Rooms**:5 **Fan**;5 **Bathroom**:0(h woutside) **Comfort**:☆ **Design**:☆ **Location**:☆
Position:central **Quietness**:☆☆

MAE SARIANG

A smallish town on the banks of the Yuam river, Mae Sariang has two interesting Shan temples, a large mosque and a lovely street of teak houses which back onto the river. It has had long associations with Burma, and is now a staging post for teak and livestock imported from Burma across the Salween river which marks the border 35 kilometres to the west. Look out for large depots of teak in fields around the town.

The population are a mixture of Thai, Shan, hilltribe (mainly Karen) and refugee Chinese and Burmese (mostly Muslim, hence the mosque). **Wat Utthayarom** ✓ was built in 1896 AD and the more impressive **Wat Sri Boonruang** ✓✓ in 1939. They are both strongly influenced by Burmese temple design, and are in a most attractive compound. As with all Burmese influenced temples, they drip with tiers of iron filigree.

AROUND MAE SARIANG.

Mae Sam Laep ✓✓✓ (44 kilometres). A very large Karen village on the Salween river bordering Burma.

Not typically Karen, but a fascinating place to watch border activities - the huge teak logs ferried across the river by long tail boats whose powerful engines can barely cope with the fast current, the probably shady deals going on in the cafes built precariously on the shifting sands at the rivers edge, the big, new 4 wheel drive pick up on some dubious errand surging through the waters with spray flying - there are even rumoured to be some Karen long-neck women living in the village.

To get there drive west over the Yuam river bridge in Mae Sariang. For 14 kilometres the metalled road winds through the wide valley with a backdrop of the mountains south of Mae Sariang. Then the road turns into the hills, the hard surface peters out and the road eventually becomes horrendous. It follows a large stream down to the village, and in the last 15 kilometres this stream has to be forded (sometimes deeply) 58 times. Allow one hour for the last ten kilometres. Along the road Karen herders can be seen driving water buffalo and cattle to trucks which take them to Bangkok for slaughter, and every few kilometres there are juggernauts carrying teak logs and travelling at below walking pace along the almost impossible road.

Mae Sariang

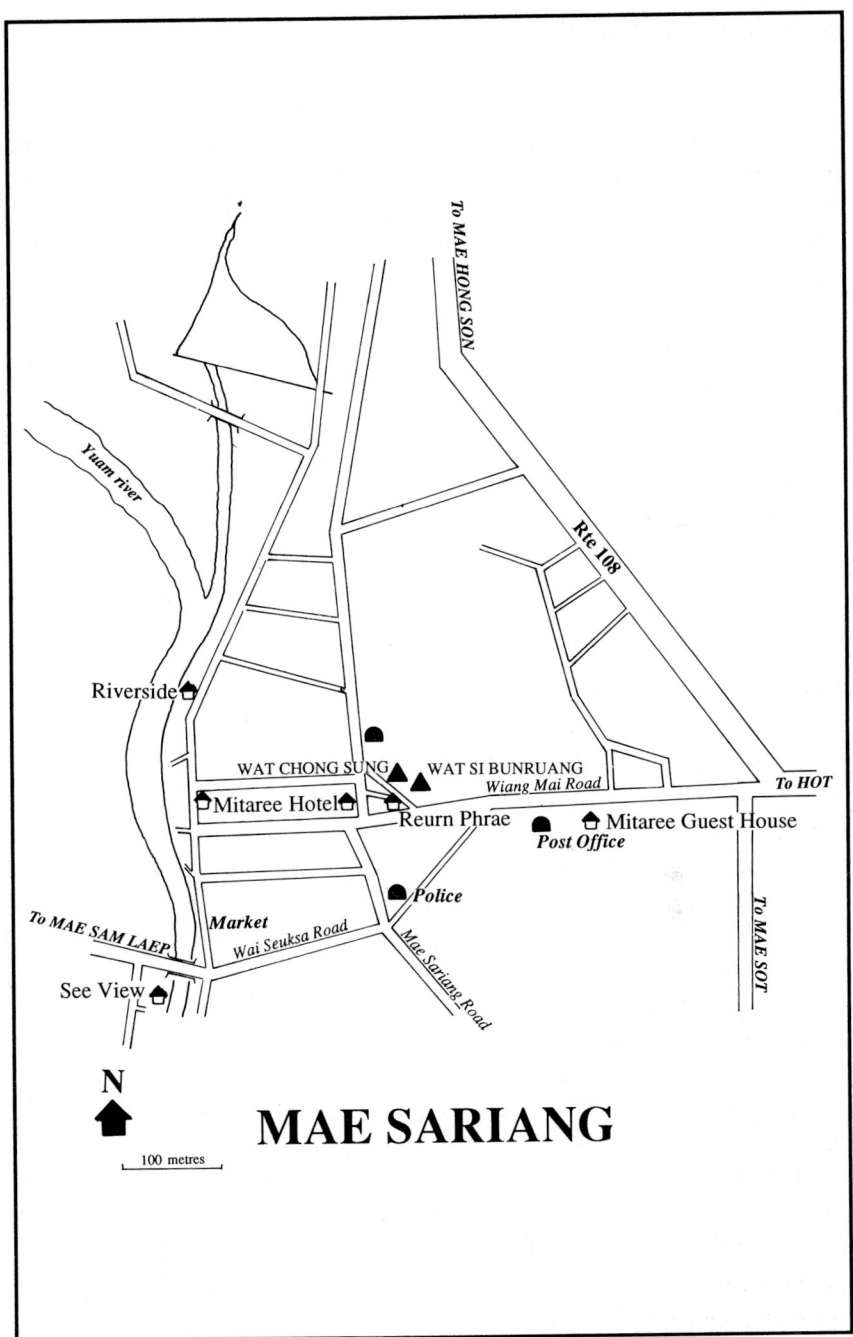

Mae La Up ✓✓✓ East turn from Rte 108 200 metres south of Mae La Noi, 30 kilometres north of Mae Sariang, along Rte 1266. Details page 177.

Hilltribe villages ✓✓ to **✓✓✓**. The hills around Mae Sariang contain a large number of villages - mostly Karen (Pwo and Sgaw) but a few interesting Lawa villages as well. Lawas are the only hilltribe to have inhabited Thailand for very long - the Thais took over most of their territories between 700 and 1000 years ago. Check the 'mapguide' section for directions to a number of accessible villages.

WHERE TO EAT

Reurn Prae Chef has won awards in Bangkok for his traditional food. Not to everyone's taste, but authentic and not expensive. Small restaurant in pleasant position.
Bakery House Wonderful cakes and breakfasts, nicely presented.
Inthara Good Thai food in cheap and very popular restaurant with fast, efficient service.
Roj Thip Thai and western food at reasonable prices and good quality.

TREKS AND TOURS

Riverside Guest House organises the most ambitious treks and tours to the Burmese border by 4 wheel drive vehicles. The **Mitaree Hotel** has tamer trips.

WHERE TO STAY

RESORTS

Mae Sariang ✪✪✪
Large chalets but basic facilities in lovely position on banks of river in unspoilt countryside.
Address: 334 Ban Mea, Mae Sariang, Mae Hong Son
Price range: 200 Rooms: 10 Bathroom: 10(cw) Comfort:☆☆ Design:☆☆☆
Location:☆☆☆☆☆ Position: 1 kilometre north of Mae Sariang - Hot Road 2 kilometres east of Mae Sariang. Quietness:☆☆☆☆☆

HOTELS

Mitaree ●●
Medium sized fairly new cement hotel in front of ancient wooden building (the old hotel). New rooms clean, large and airy but rather soulless, old rooms very basic and tatty.
Address: Mitaree Hotel, Mae Sariang Road, Mae Hong Son.
Price range: 100-350 **Rooms:** 32 **A/C:** 18 **Fan:** 14 **Bathroom:** 32 (18hw, 16cw)
Comfort: ☆ to ☆☆☆☆ **Design:** ☆ **Location:** ☆ **Position:** town centre **Quietness:** ☆☆
Restaurant: ☆☆ **Tours/treks:** 1 day tours from 150 *baht*.

GUEST HOUSES

See View ●●●●
Pleasant, large, clean, well furnished rooms in ranch style cement building and new wooden bungalows on Yuam river near lovely teak house with bar and small restaurant.
Address: See View, Mae Sariang, Mae Hong Son.
Price range: 120-140 **Rooms:** 18 **Fan:** 18 **Bathroom** 18 (4hw) **Comfort:** ☆☆☆ to ☆☆☆☆☆
Design: ☆☆☆☆ **Location:** ☆☆☆☆ **Position:** 1st south turn on west side of river bridge.
Quietness: ☆☆☆ **Restaurant:** ☆☆.

Riverside ●●●
Basic but clean and lovely rooms in a beautiful teak house overlooking river with large terrace. New bungalows on opposite bank.
Address: 85/1 Langparich Road, Mae Sariang, Mae Hong Son.
Price range: 100-120 **Rooms:** 17 **Bathroom:** 0 (hw outside) **Comfort:** ☆☆ **Design:** ☆☆☆☆
Location: ☆☆☆☆ **Position:** 300 metres from town centre **Quietness:** ☆☆☆ **Restaurant:** ☆☆
Tours/treks: to Burmese border, hilltribes, boating on Salween river.

Mitaree ●●●
Comfortable rooms with most facilities but lacking character.
Address: 34 Wiang Mai, Mae Sariang, Mae Hong Son
Price range: 120-350 **Rooms:** 70 **A/C:** 26 **Fan:** 44 **Bathroom:** 70 (55hw)
Comfort: ☆☆☆ to ☆☆☆☆☆ **Design:** ☆☆ **Location:** ☆☆
Position: 600 metres east of town on road to Hot. **Quietness:** ☆☆☆ **Restaurant:** ☆☆.

Reurn Prae ●●
Rooms in Thai private house with pretty gardens.
Address: 174/1 Wiangmai Road, Mae Sariang, Mae Hong Son.
Price range: 125-250 **Rooms:** 2 **A/C:** 1 **Fan:** 1 **Bathroom:** 2(cw) **Comfort:** ☆☆ to ☆☆☆
Design: ☆☆☆ **Location:** ☆☆☆☆ **Position:** in small lane to temple compound
Quietness: ☆☆☆☆☆ **Restaurant:** ☆☆☆☆

Mae Sariang ●
Small and basic rooms.
Address: 1 Moo 2, Langpanich Road, Mae Sariang Road, Mae Hong Son
Price range: 80-100 **Rooms:** 16 **Bathroom:** 8(cw) **Comfort:** ☆☆ **Design:** ☆ **Location:** ☆☆
Position: near river, 250 metres from town centre. **Quietness:** ☆☆.

Chapter Six

The South

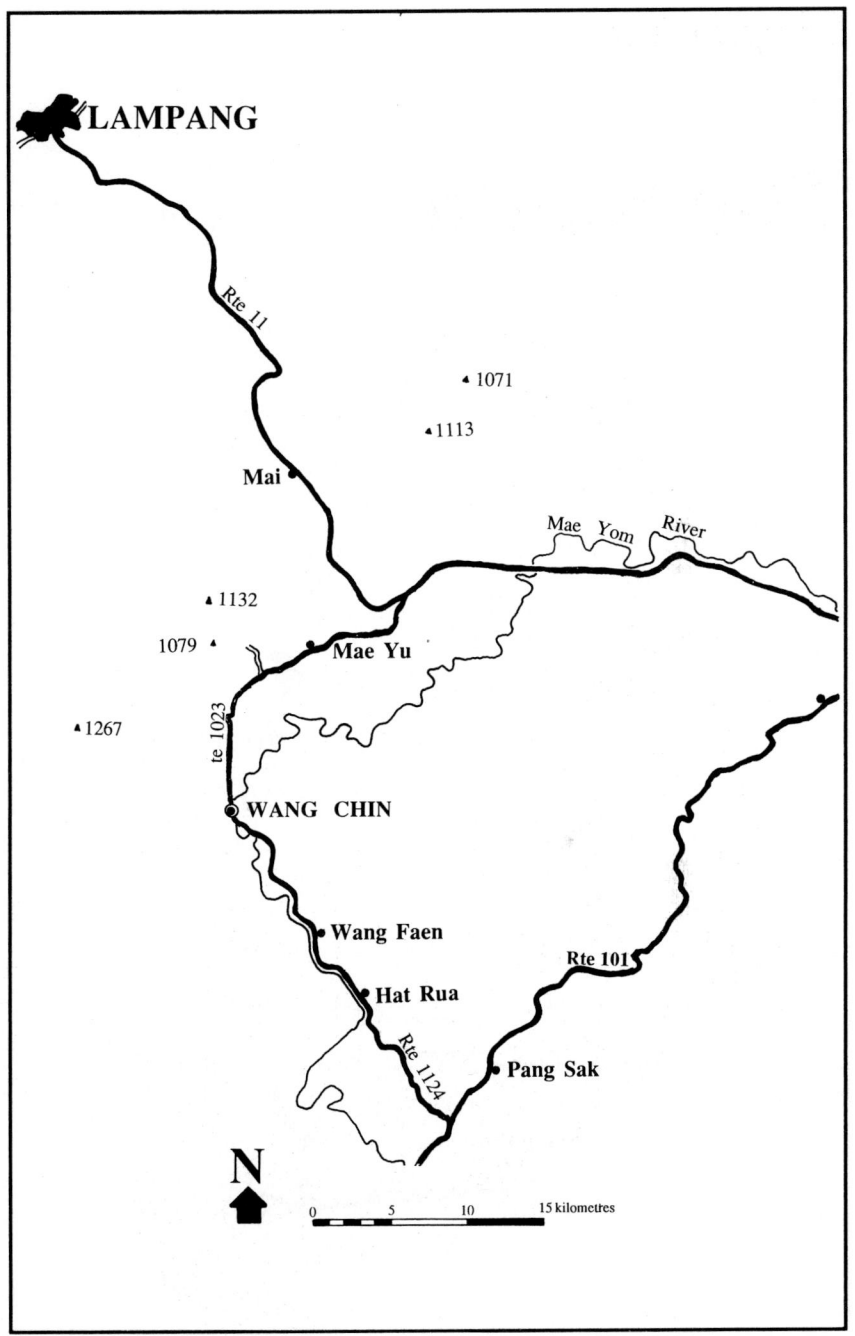

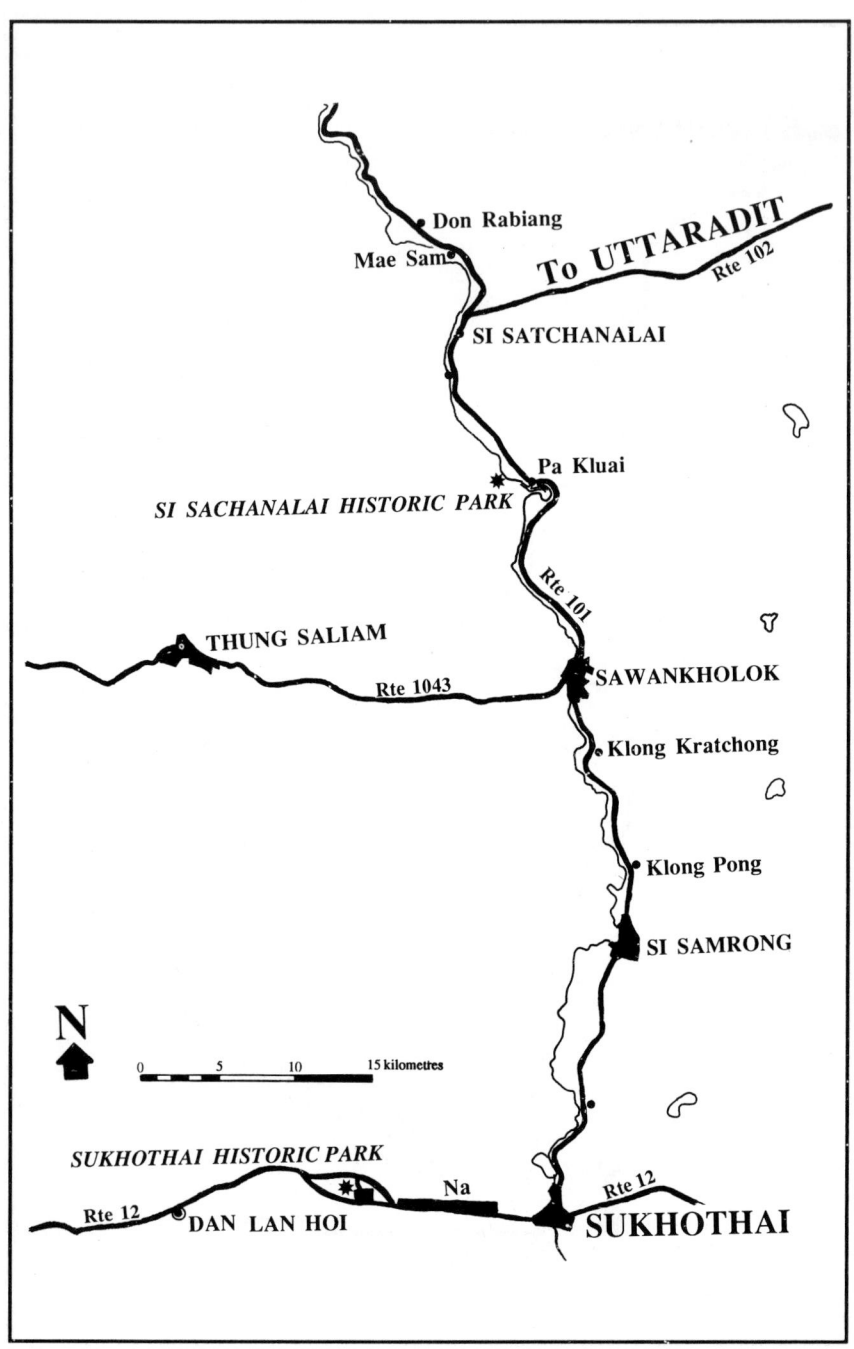

Sukhothai - Tak

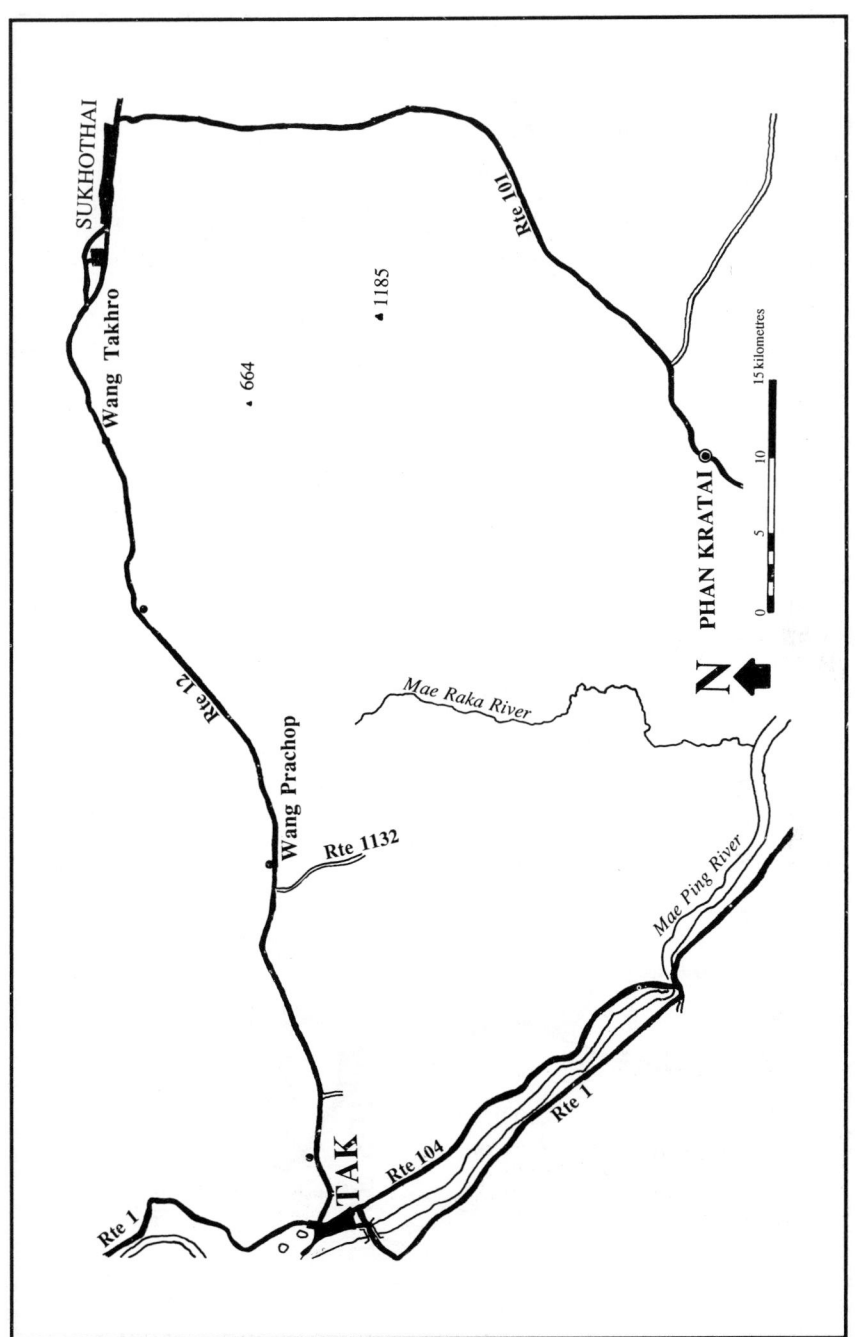

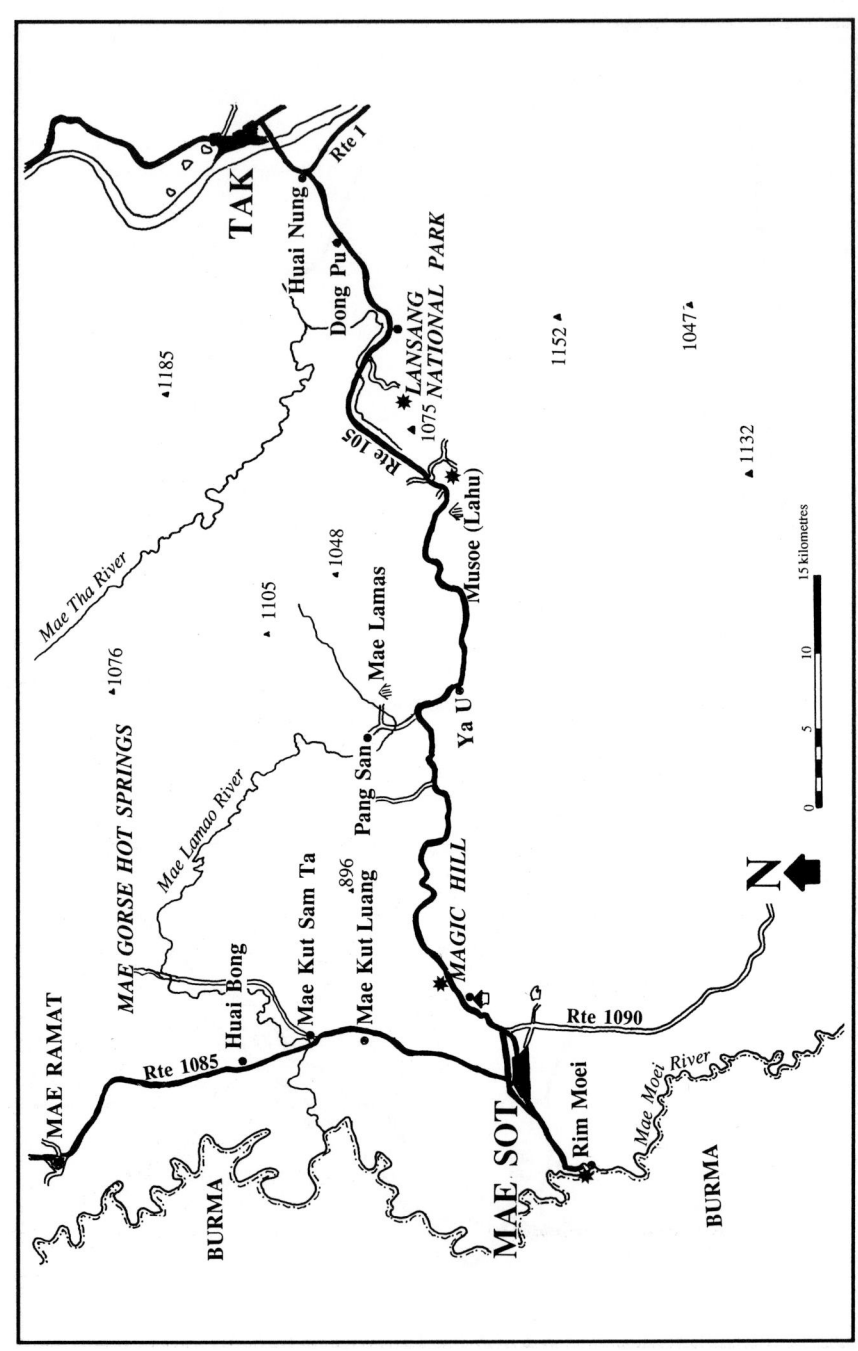

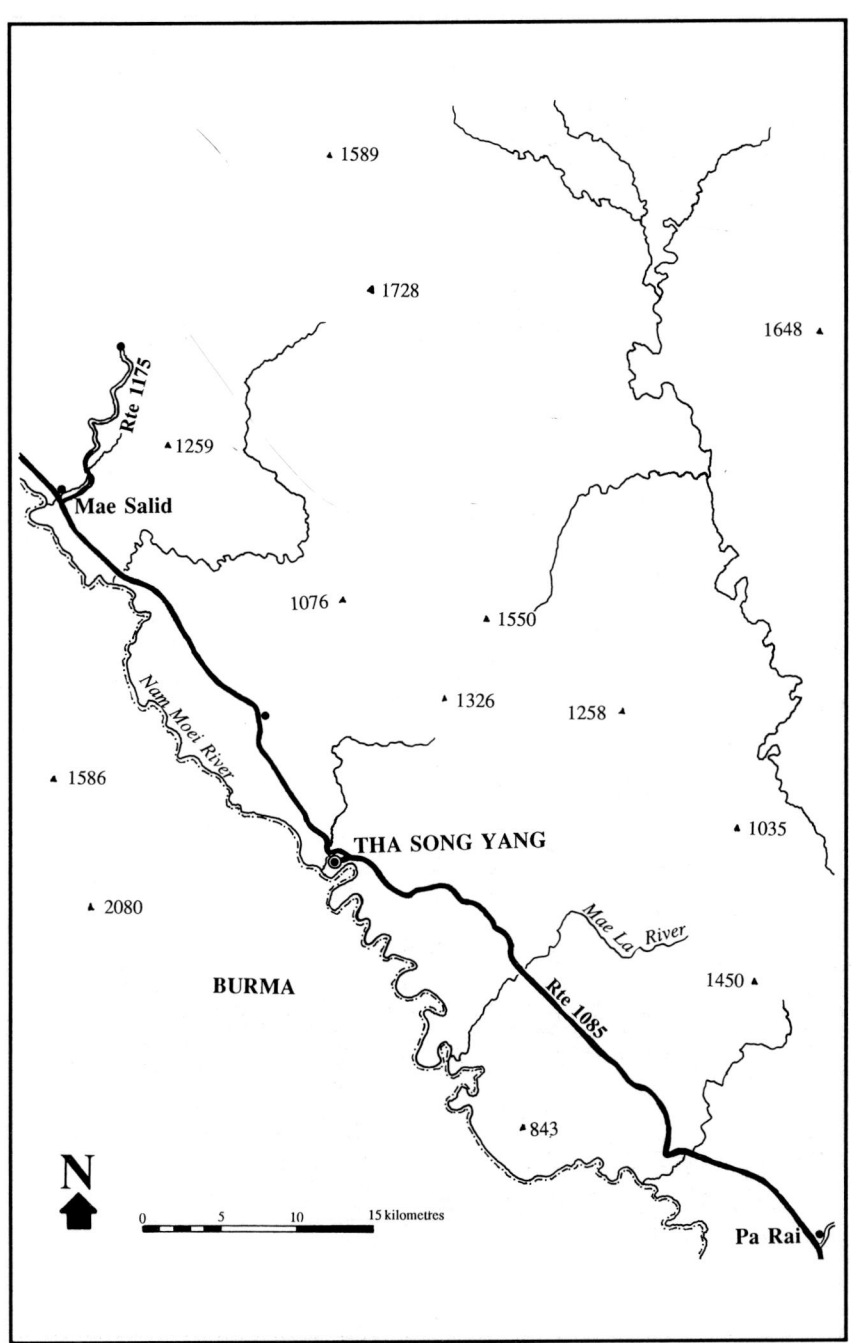

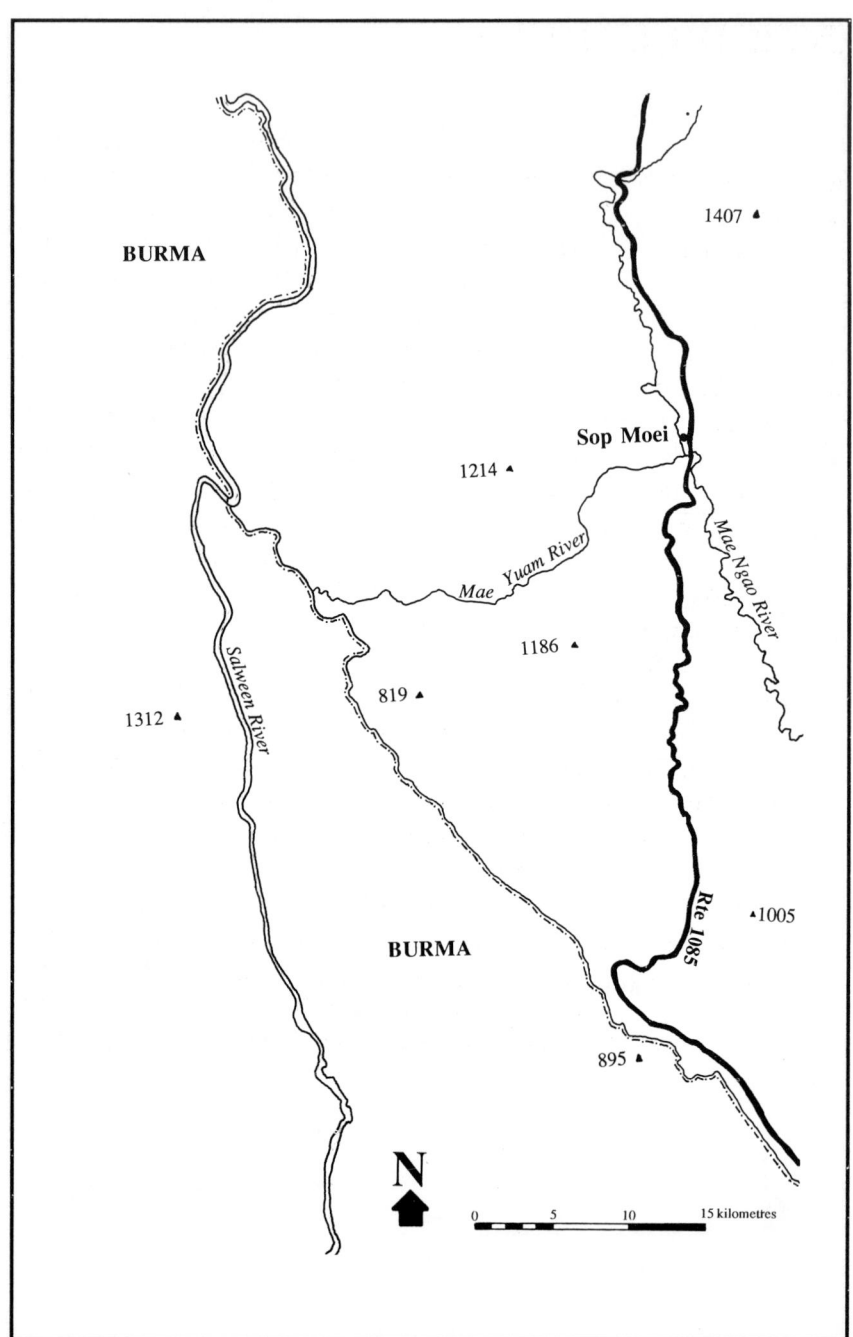

INTRODUCTION

THIS ROUTE includes the most interesting and attractive archaeological sites in Thailand, with an extension westwards to the Burmese border, then north along a road only completed in 1991 through some of the loneliest and wildest countryside in the north. Driving south from Lampang the steep hillsides and narrow fertile valleys typical of the north give way gradually to the flat plains of central Thailand. 1000 years ago this was the westernmost bastion of the Khmer empire. The large Thai minority in the Khmer city of Sukhothai rose up in 1238 AD to overthrow their Khmer masters, thus creating the first independent Thai state and building a new Sukhothai of great architectural beauty. Although now partly ruined, the site of Sukhothai has been beautifully restored to something of its former glory, and is an awe inspiring testament to the history of the remarkable Thai race. A few kilometres north of Sukhothai the second city of the Sukhothai empire - Si Satchanalai - has also been well restored. Although less impressive, it is an equally beautiful site, perhaps more authentic in feel and easier to identify with than Sukhothai.

Driving west from Sukhothai, over the Ping river at the ancient city of Tak, one is really at the border of Lanna Thai and central Thailand. The people here look rather darker and larger featured than the generally delicate Lanna Thais, and the northern Thai dialect is almost unknown here. The climate is noticeably warmer, particularly at night in the cool season. In the far west, Mae Sot was until recently considered too dangerous a town for tourism. Near an active part of the Burmese border, with frequent drug running and guerrilla incidents, the town had a "wild west" atmosphere, and still has a polyglot of different peoples living, working and moving through it. The road from Mae Sot to Mae Sariang follows the Burmese border closely. Only completed in mid 1991, it passes through wild and beautiful but almost uninhabited countryside. For those of a nervous disposition it might be wiser to drive north from Tak back to Chiang Mai.

CHIANG MAI - LAMPANG (99 kilometres - 1.5 hours)

For details of this, the first part of the route, see page 242.

LAMPANG - SUKHOTHAI (177 kilometres - 3 hours) Map page 203

Follow signs to Denchai from Lampang by-pass south east of town centre. Distances from beginning of Rte 11.

Kilometres

1	Large Chinese cemetery to west side of road.
10	Area of pineapple fields, many pineapple vendors on roadside.
12	Camp site to east of road by stream.
29	Mai. A pretty Thai town in a lovely green and fertile valley.
33	Spirit house to creatures of jungle whose statue surround it.
34	Area of coffee plantations.
37	Top of mountain pass, lush primary jungle.
43	South turn on Rte 1023 via Wang Chin. This is a pretty road, well surfaced with little traffic, which cuts out the busier, less attractive road through Denchai.

NB KILOMETRE POSTS NOW ON ROUTE 1023

68	Lovely traditional Thai *wat* with delicate wood carvings on doors and eaves.
70	Dirt road north 7 kilometres to hot springs.
76	**Wieng Ka Soi National Park** ✓✓Dirt road 3 kilometres to lovely series of waterfalls suitable for swimming. Highest fall with 50 metre drop (1kilometre walk). The jungle is reputedly inhabited by monkeys, gibbons, sambur deer, hornbills and wild cats.
76	Pleasant roadside restaurant.
90	Small town of **Wang Chin**, turn east here on new road Rte 1124. No kilometre posts. After about 20 kilometers turn south at junction with Rte 101.

DISTANCES NOW ALONG ROUTE 101

50	East turn Rte 102 to **Uttaradit** (35 kilometres). 500 metres: **59 Bungalows** ●●● Pleasant rooms in small hotel with numbers of 'short time' clients. Address: Kilometre 1, Rte 102, Si Satchanalai, Sukhothai Price range:300-500 Rooms: 16 A/C:6 Fan:10 Bathroom:16(hw) Comfort::☆☆☆ Design:☆☆☆ Location:☆☆ Position: 2 kilometres north of Si Satchanalai Quietness:☆☆.
48	**Si Satchanalai** Small town with wide main street, large restaurant 1 kilometre north. The old town is 11 kilometres south of here.
37	**Si Satchanalai Historic Monument** ✓✓✓ Turn west over the river, then after 100 metres north 1 kilometre to the entrance to the historical park. The best way to tour the park is by elephant. The 1.5 hour trip costing 200 *baht* per person. Touring by car costs 50 *baht*, by foot 20 *baht*. There is a beautifully situated resort less than 1 kilometre from the ruins **Wang Yom Resort** ●●● Address: Pa Kluai

Chiang Mai - Lampang

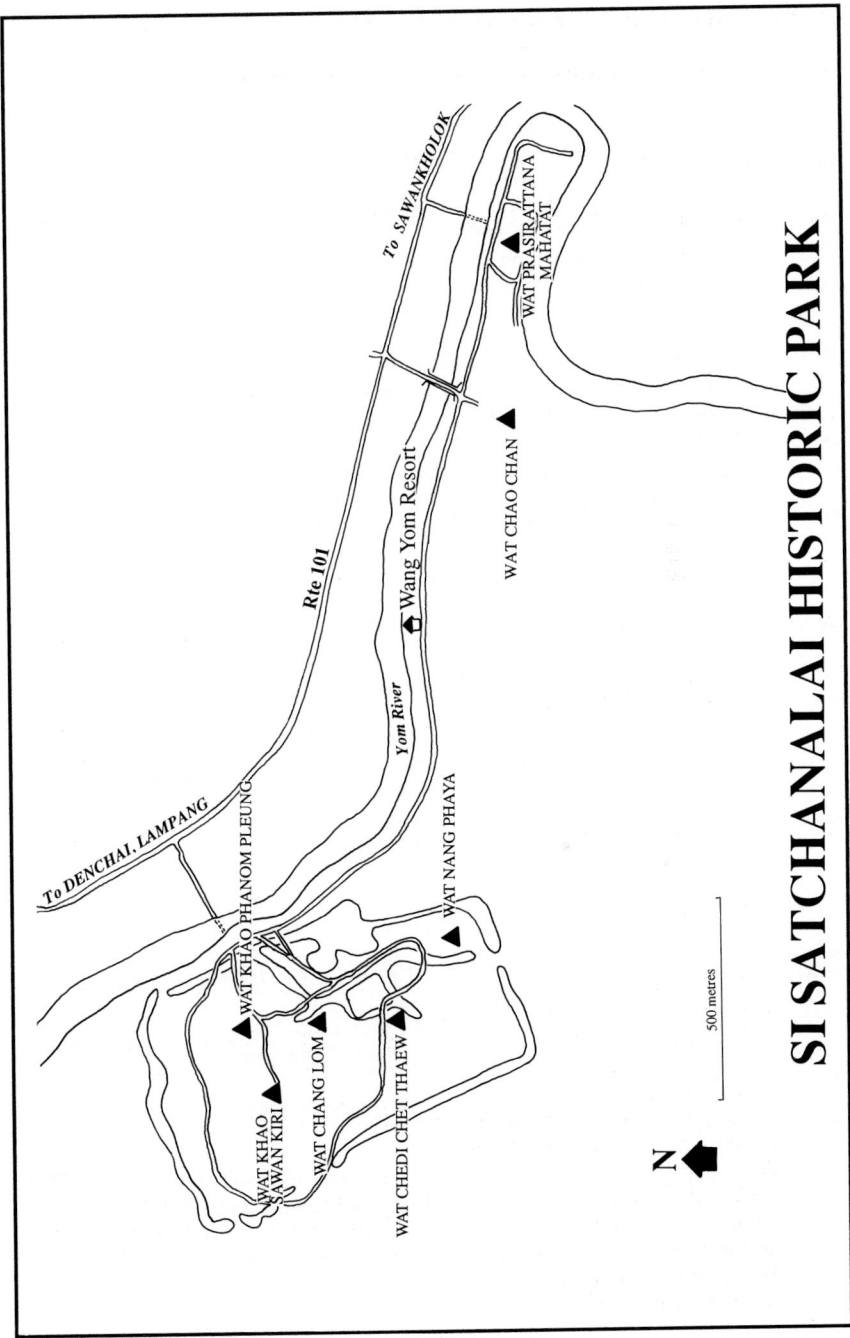

Price range: 400-1200 (including breakfast) **Rooms:**25 **Fan:**8 **Bathroom:**8 **Comfort:** ☆ to ☆☆☆ **Design:**☆☆☆☆ **Location:**☆☆☆☆ **Position:**1.5 kilometre north of bridge over Yom river **Quietness:**☆☆☆☆☆ **Restaurant:**☆☆☆(exp) **Facilities:** displays and demonstrations of local arts and crafts - spinning , weaving, folk dancing. The park encloses most of the old town, which was the second city of the Sukhothai empire, at its heyday between 1250-1400AD. It was the most important centre for the production of Celadon stoneware, and several of the old kilns have been excavated. Pieces of pottery can be found all over the area, particularly around the unexcavated parts of the city walls. The site of the city is quite picturesque. On the west banks of the Yom river, the walls enclose an area of 1 kilometre , surrounded by gently rolling countryside of rice fields and orchards. The area inside the walls contains two well defined low hills. After the entrance, the first and most impressive temple seen is **Wat Chang Lom** ✓✓✓. This was built by King Ramakhampaeng (see page 23) in 1290. Behind the ruins of the *wiharn* stands the oldest bell shaped *chedi* in Thailand, supported by 39 elephant statues, many still in good repair. Amongst the other temples, **Wat Khao Phanom Pleung** ✓✓ and **Wat Khao Suwan Kiri** ✓✓ are on top of a small hill, with imposing statues of Buddha and good views of the city and its environs. **Wat Chedi Chet Thaew** ✓✓ is an imposing collection of *chedis* of different shapes, sizes and styles. This was built in the 14th century by King Lo Tai..

3 kilometres south of Si Satchanalai on the west bank of the river is the small village of Chalieng, which is dwarfed by the most remarkable monument in the area - **Wat Prasirattanamahatat Chalieng** ✓✓✓. This temple was built by King Ramkhamhaeng around 1286 AD. The enormous pineapple shaped *prang* (Khmer version of a *chedi*) was built a little later, in the 15th century, by which time Si Satchanalai had become a province of Ayutthaya.

Five kilometres north of the old city, a road leads to the old kilns of **Ban Ko Noi** ✓. Well over 200 kilns have been excavated so far. There is also a small but interesting museum in the village.

0   **Sawankholok.** A large and busy town, the northernmost settlement of the central plains with several cheap and interesting restaurants and a reasonably comfortable hotel:
The Muang Inn ●●●
Address:21 Kasemrat Road, Sawankholok **Tel:** (053)642622
Price:120-220 **Rooms:**46 **A/C:**12 **Fan:** 34 **Bathroom:**46(12hw)
Comfort:☆☆☆ to ☆☆☆☆ **Design:**☆☆☆ **Location:**☆☆ **Position:**central **Quietness:**☆☆ **Restaurant:**☆☆ **Facilities:**cocktail lounge, singers.

NB KILOMETRE POSTS ON ROUTE 102 NOW MEASURED SOUTH FROM SAWANKHOLOK

3   East side of road, cottage industry producing sugar cakes. Sugar cane juice is boiled and distilled in large bamboo vats over clay ovens stoked with cane waste.
14 Large *wat* with golden seated Buddha.
17 Very large temple enclosing a school, extensive sports grounds and a very ornate crematorium.
31 Junction with Sukhothai-Tak road (Rte 12).
33 **Sukhothai new town** ✓ There is nothing of great interest in Sukhothai, although it does have a very good selection of hotels and guest houses at a range of prices, but most offering good value for money. Details page 220. From Sukhothai, Rte 12 leads east to Phitsanulok (55 kilometres, a fast, straight road passing through a completely flat landscape of rice paddies). Details of Phitsanulok page 222.

SUKHOTHAI - TAK (66 kilometres - 1 hour) Map page 205

46	To continue the southern circuit, take route 12 west out of Sukhothai signposted Tak. West side of the village of Ban Na, the luxurious: **Pailyn Hotel:** ●●●● Exceptionally comfortable and luxurious rooms built around a large swimming pool in a very new and impressive hotel. Address:10 Moo 1 Jarodvithitong Road, Sukhothai 64210 **Tel:** (055)613310-5 Fax: 613317 Price:800-2500 **Rooms:**238 A/C:238 Bathroom:238(hw) **Comfort:**☆☆☆☆☆ **Design:**☆☆☆☆☆ **Location:**☆☆ Position:4 kilometres east of old Sukhothai. **Quietness:**☆☆☆☆ **Restaurant:**☆☆☆☆☆ Facilities: two pools, bar, minibar, fridge, TV,video. **Tours/treks:**range of local tours
46	Rte 12 bypasses Old Sukhothai archaeological remains - this adds several kilometres to the trip to no good purpose. Turn north here for bypass, west to Old Sukhothai.
48	**Sukhothai cultural centre.** Demonstrations of local arts and crafts, singing and dancing, large restaurant and bar. Part of this complex is: **Thai Village House** ●●●● Very comfortable well equipped teak cabins in a small park of Thai culture. Address: 214 Jarodwithitong Muang Kho, Sukhothai, Tel:(055)611049 Fax:612583 Price:350-700 **Rooms:**70 A/C:70 Bathroom:70(hw) **Comfort:**☆☆☆☆☆ **Design:**☆☆☆☆☆ **Location:**☆☆☆☆ Position:1 kilometre east of Old Sukhothai**Quietness:**☆☆☆☆ **Restaurant:**☆☆ Facilities: Handicraft centre, bar, **Tour/treks:**local.
50	Restored ruins of **Old Sukhothai** ✓✓✓in a splendid park of lakes and woods. Unforgettable. Details page 216. If not visiting the sight, it is possible to drive straight through without paying for entry.
57	Junction with Old Sukhothai to north.
60-90	Low rolling hill country, sparsely cultivated, of open jungle and brush. Rather bleak and exposed.
5	**Lan Hoy.** Small town with a large number of lovely old teak houses, a small market and a number of food stalls.
103	South turn Tak airport one kilometre.
112	**Tak** ✓ A large town on the banks of the Ping river. Tak has an ultra-modern and unattractive town centre with wide streets and big markets, a few hotels and restaurants and little else to recommend it. Details page 228.

TAK - MAE SOT (80 kilometres - 1.5 hours) Map page 206

Leave Tak on Rte 1 which crosses the Ping river 2 kilometres south of Tak. 3 kilometres after the bridge at km post 414 turn west on Rte 105 signposted Mae sot.

7	To south of road, a large secondary school, funded by the Thai Royal Family for poor hill tribe children.
12	South turn to **Lansang National Park** ✓✓The centrepiece is a lovely series of waterfalls which have eroded interesting channels through the very ancient pre-cambrian rocks. From turn-off one kilometre to National Park headquarters, two kilometres to the waterfall, three kilometre to a large Lahu (Mussur) village. There is a car park and information centre with maps and photographs 200 metres from the first waterfall and a footpath along the stream for two kilometres to the highest and most spectacular falls.

12-26	The road climbs steeply through mountain jungle until a high, cool plateau is reached, dotted with peaks and steep sided valleys.
25	**Ban Musoe** ✓✓. South turn to a string of resettled Lisu, Hmong and Lahu hill tribe villages. This is a government run project providing funding for the development and marketing of alternative cool climate crops. Hill tribe workers are trained in the production of flowers, french beans, avocado pears, coffee, tea, citrus fruits and many others. The scenery in this area is particularly lovely and the villages recently moved from remote locations are traditional and extremely interesting.
25	North turn along metalled road to **Taksin National Park** ✓This mountain top park has been recently established to try to hold back the large scale deforestation of the area.There is a surfaced road(but with many difficult, unsurfaced sections) encircling the park. The headquarters with displays and photographs is 1.5 kilometre, from the turn off. Fork right here and drive two kilometres to a vertical waterfall reached by a precipitous footpath from the small car park. Excellent evergreen mountain jungle with much wildlife in this wild valley.
26	South turn one kilometre (poor dirt roads to the large Black Lahu village of **Sompuey** ✓✓ The Black Lahu (Mussur dam) wear very striking costumes. Most villages are very shy of strangers, but this village, although traditional, is also very friendly.
27	On the north side of the road is a car park and rest area with several stalls selling local products. Many of the stalls are run by beautifully dressed girls from the nearby Lahu village.
41	North turn along good dirt road to several large Thai villages, and in the hills a large Karen village (8 kilometres).
62	To north of road, large shrine in an area of sharp peaked limestone cliffs, mountains and ridges.
68	**Magic Hill** ✓✓. A very strange phenomenon. The road descends a long hill, then ascends again. At the bottom of the hill is a sign saying "Magic Hill" in Thai and English, and a white line has been painted across the road. If a car is parked on this white line, then the brake released with the engine off or in neutral, then the vehicle moves 200 metres, apparently uphill.
70	To south of road: **Taweechailand** ●●●●Comfortable wooden cabins in large park of manicured trees, lakes and gardens. There is a well stocked aviary and zoo, and piped music and news, giving the feel of an upmarket holiday camp. Address: 457 Intharakiri Road Tel: (055)531287 Price:300-600 Rooms:22 Fan:22 Bathroom:22(hw) Comfort:☆☆☆ Design:☆☆☆☆ Location:☆☆☆☆ Quietness:☆☆☆☆☆ Restaurant:☆☆☆☆ Facilities:boating, zoo.
80	**Mae Sot** ✓✓✓ A cosmopolitan rumbustious uninhibited town on the Burma border. Details page 231.

MAE SOT-MAE SARIANG (234 kilometres, 4 hours) Map page

This road (Rte 1085) has only been completely surfaced during 1991. It is a wild and lonely road, of beautiful and utterly unspoilt countryside, passing close to the Burmese border for most of its length. There are few villages, only one small town (with the only petrol station for 200 kilometres) and one guest house between Mae Sot and Mae Sariang. During the day the road is quite safe, but at night there is a risk of robbery. Make sure you have enough petrol, oil and water for the journey. Those of a nervous disposition might consider driving back to Tak and taking the much busier Rte 1 back to Chiang Mai. Leave Mae Sot by heading north to the by-pass.

Kilometres

79	North turn Rte 1085, signposted Mae Ramat.

NB DISTANCES ON KILOMETRE POSTS NOW FROM MAE SOT

13	East turn to **Mae Gorse Hot Springs** ✓ 7 kilometres along poor road.
34	East turn to **Mae Ramat**, a town largely of Karen refugees, many refugee camps in the area.
35	East turn Rte 1175 - interesting mountain road back to Tak.
45	The road this far has been through farmland and scrub - of little scenic interest. From this point the road climbs into lovely mountain scenery of peaks, tall mountain jungle and fast flowing streams.
59	West turn on poor dirt road 300 metres to impoverished Karen village at the foot of steep limestone cliffs.
84	West turn 1 kilometre to **Pa Sa Tong** ✓ a very sleepy Thai town on the Burma border. Pretty houses and a few petrol stations and shops. Apparently peaceful, but a major centre for Karen guerrillas.
93	Large Karen village with a small cafe on the west of the road.
108	Lovely river valley with several good spots for swimming.
114	East turn surfaced road to **Om Koi**, **Mae Ramaeng** (32 kilometres). A very steep road leading into high mountains with wonderful views, particularly at dawn when the valleys are filled with mist. **Monkrating Resort** ●●●● Large bungalows in beautiful mountaintop garden with spectacular views. **Address:** Monkrating, Mae Salid, Tak. **Price:** 300 per person including bkfst and dinner **Rooms:**53 **Bathrooms:** 53(cw) **Fan:** 53 **Comfort:** ☆☆☆ **Design;** ☆☆☆☆ **Location:** ☆☆☆☆ **Quietness:** ☆☆☆☆☆**Restaurant:**☆☆☆ **Tours\treks:** Range of local tours. **Chao Doi house** ●●● Bamboo and palm leaf huts in a near perfect mountain setting. **Address:** Monkrating, Mae Salid, Tak. **Price:** 250 per person including all food and treks. **Rooms:**20 **Bathroom:**20(cw) **Comfort:** ☆☆ **Design:** ☆☆☆☆ **Location:** ☆☆☆☆**Quietness:** ☆☆☆☆☆ **Restaurant:** ☆☆☆**Tours/treks:** Local treks included in price of room.
114	100 metres past the Om Koi, Monkrating turn, 300 metres to the east of the road: **Mae Salid** ●●● New teak guest house in remote, newly settled area. **Address:** Mae Salid, Tak **Price:** 100 **Rooms;**10 **Bathroom:**10(cw) **Comfort:** ☆☆ **Design:** ☆☆☆☆**Location:** ☆☆☆☆**Quietness:**☆☆☆☆ **Restaurant:**☆☆☆ **Tours/treks:** local.
165	Steep turn along poor dirt road to a small but pretty waterfall.
172	Large Karen village to west of road.
188	Bridge over the wide **Mae Pon river**. Karen village to east of road, whose inhabitants fish and raft on the river.
206	Administrative centre of **Sop Moei**.
228	To east of road, huge white Buddha in a small temple that looks over the town of **Mae Sariang** to the west.
230	Junction with Rte 108. turn west for **Mae Sariang**, east for **Hot** and **Chiang Mai** (details of this route page 177)

SOUTH TOWNS

SUKHOTHAI

There are now two Sukhothais. Modern Sukhothai is an unexceptional but pleasant enough large town, with a good choice of hotels and restaurants, but nothing remotely interesting architecturally. Twelve kilometres to the west along Rte 12 is the cultural park of Old Sukhothai.

OLD SUKHOTHAI

Deservedly the most famous archaeological site of Thailand, Old Sukhothai was the power base from which the Thais first forged an independent, unified nation. Northern Thais might protest that the kingdom of Lanna predated Sukhothai, but it was only when Lanna's King Mengrai and King Ramkamphaeng of Sukhothai forged a pact to unite their peoples against common threats from Burma, Laos and Cambodia that Thailand really came about, and Sukhothai was undeniably, in material terms, the dominant partner - and in Lanna Thailand there was never anything to compare with the glorious city of Sukhothai.

Sukhothai was originally a Khmer kingdom. The Khmers had their power base in Cambodia, although their culture was primarily Indian influenced. The Thai population of the city, one of many groups who had drifted south from China, rebelled against their overlords, whose autocratic, despotic ways and disciplined manners were anathema to the (even then) easy going Thais. They established a new social system, the antithesis of the Khmers, and quickly spread from this important power base throughout Central Thailand and beyond - as far as parts of Malaysia, Laos and Burma.

The first writing in Thai comes from Sukhothai. On a tablet dated 1292 AD, the then King Ramakhampaeng, perhaps the most significant figure in Thai history, declared his wish for a free, fair, compassionate and happy society. "Whoever wants to play, plays: whoever wants to laugh, laughs" he wrote. Sukhothai was not pre-eminent for long. In the 14th century, after less than 100

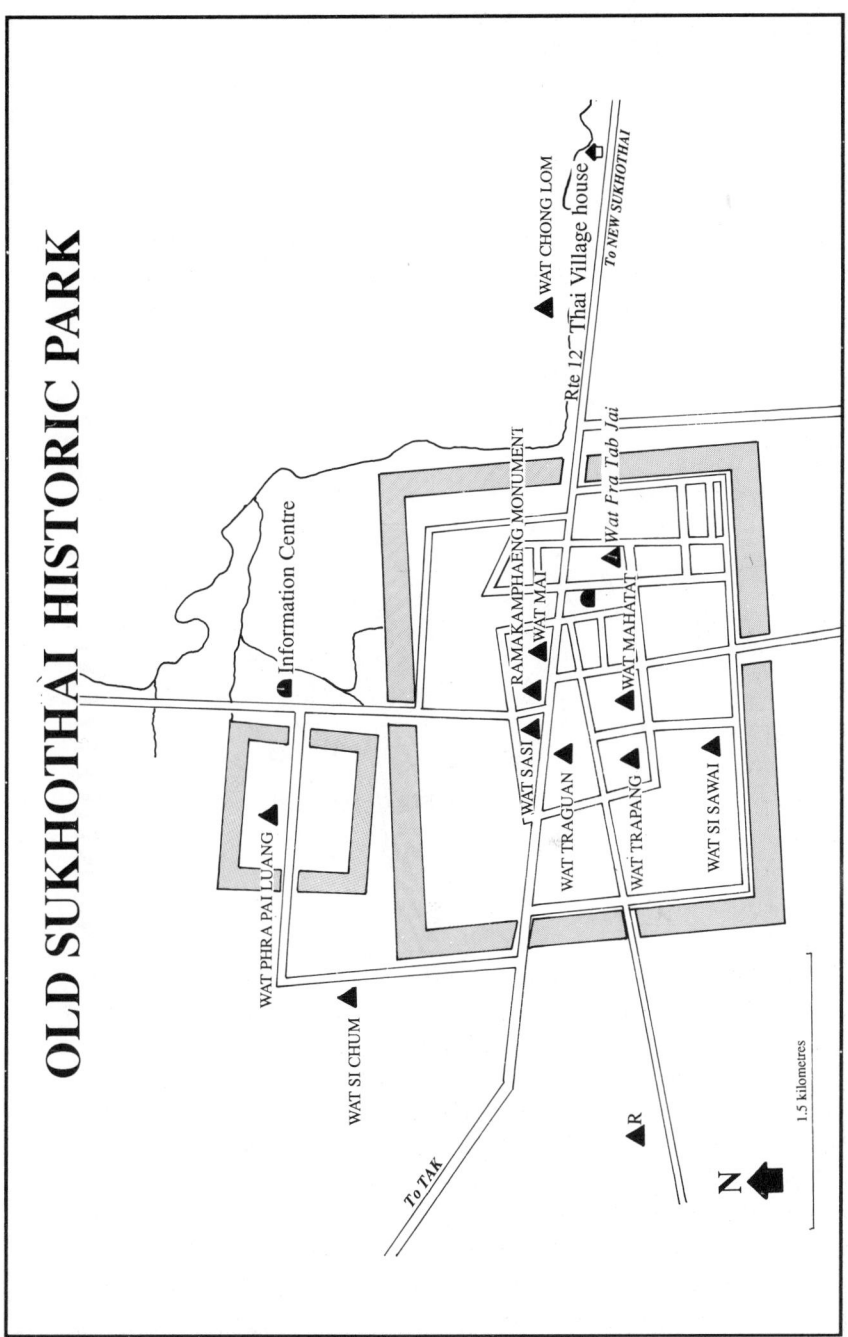

The South

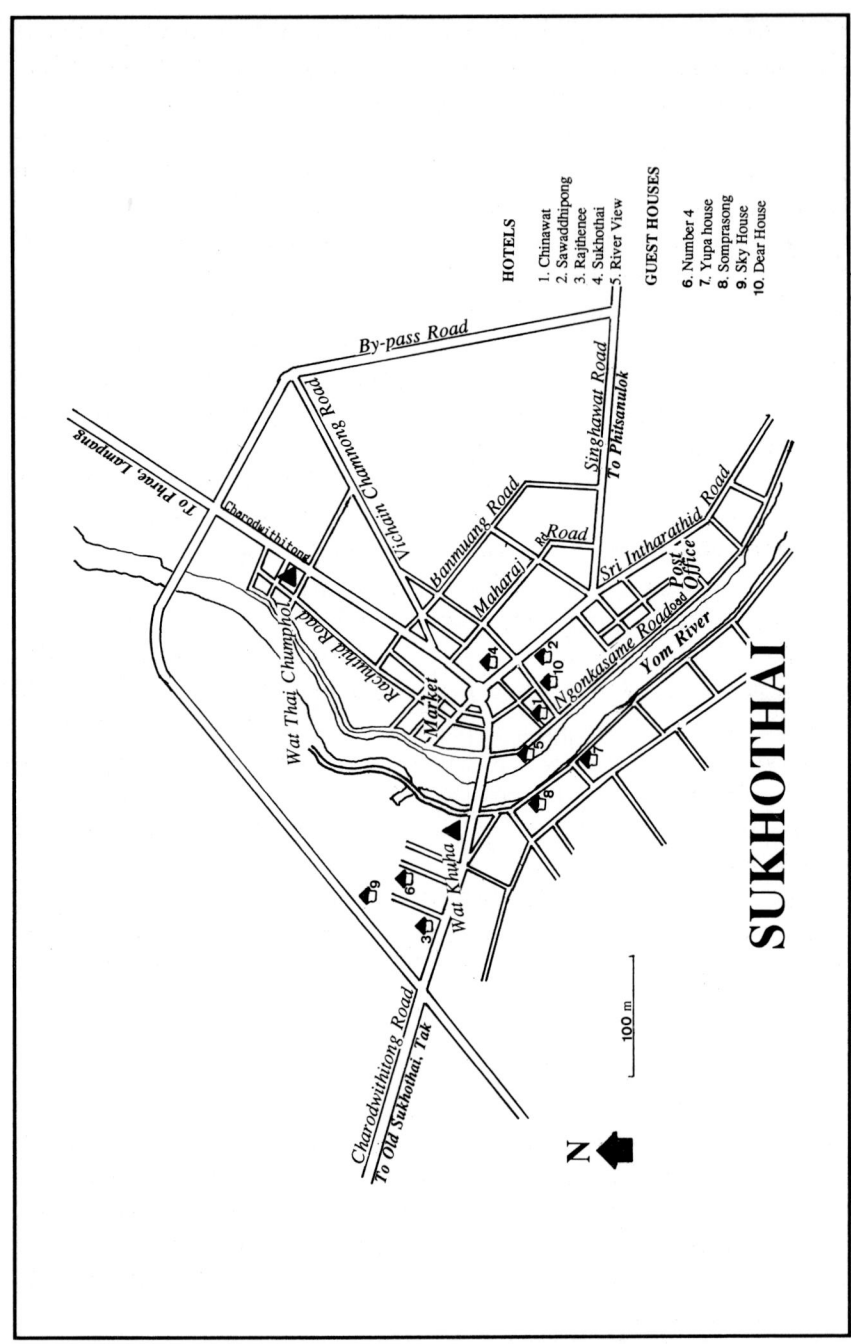

years, the kings of Ayutthaya, 300 kilometres to the south, conquered Sukhothai to establish a new Thai kingdom which lasted until defeat at the hands of that ever present threat to the Thais throughout history - the Burmese.

It was, though, a vital 100 years for Thai culture. Theravada Buddhism became the official religion, Thai script was developed from South Indian writing and the Thai people were made to feel part of a free nation. Artists of all types were encouraged and sponsored, establishing the tenets of design for buildings, paintings and sculptures that still survive today. It is likely that in the 12th century Sukhothai was the largest city in the world, with a population estimated at 300,000. The few Europeans who visited it were, by their own account, awed by what they saw. The city had a central area of three square kilometres, surrounded by triple fortifications through which four main gates pierced. At its centre was the royal palace and **Wat Mahatat**, the principal shrine of the kingdom which still today draws pilgrims to worship before its imposing sitting Buddha. Within the walls were ponds of unpolluted water, broad boulevards and large markets. Unlike Ayutthaya, Sukhothai was never sacked by an invading army, but nevertheless its buildings had deteriorated and been taken over by the jungle or demolished for local use. In 1977, the government decided that the significance of the site was such that it should be fully restored. The work took over 10 years to complete, and even now only the central part of the old city within the walls has been excavated. In the countryside all around strange shaped mounds and piles of laterite bricks hint at what else can be done. Nevertheless, the restoration is breathtaking in its scale, and it is not difficult to feel the power and beauty of what must have been. Sixty buildings have been restored, eighty -five archaeological sites have been excavated and most city moats and reservoirs have been cleared. The main road which used to pass through the middle of the park has been re-routed to the north, and a well designed restaurant and information centre have been built.

TOURING THE PARK

The best time to see the park is in the very early morning, before the heat of the day, or in the evenings when the sunsets are spectacular. Bicycles can be hired from several shops for 30 *baht* per day, probably the ideal way to tour the park. The entrance fee is 100 *baht*, payable at the gate on the main road at the eastern side. The park is very well kept by a team of gardeners, and the overall impression is of beautiful ancient temples, *chedis* and giant trees floating on a sea of lotus flowers.

Wat Mahatat ✓✓✓ The first buildings on the south side of the road. The largest and most important temple group, founded in the mid 13th century by King Intarakit and extended in 1240 AD by King Lo Tai to house a neckbone and a lock of hair from Buddha, brought from Sri Lanka. The central *chedi* (once covered in gold) is on a high platform, ending in a lotus bud. Around the base of the *chedi* is a frieze of walking monks. It is surrounded by eight towers in the shape of *prangs* - the elongated pineapples typical of Khmer architecture. This configuration represents the beneficent power of the king. There are also the remains of several *wiharns* and *salas*.

Wat Si Chum ✓✓✓ 1500 metres north of Wat Mahatat. A huge *mondop* housing a massive seated Buddha 15 metres high and eleven wide. The walls of the *mondop* are three metres thick and hide a passageway to the top, whose ceiling is composed of engraved slabs.

Wat Phra Phai Luang ✓✓✓ This *wat* is one kilometre north west of the main gate, surrounded by a complex of moats, which include the main reservoir for the town. It was built by King Jayavarman, one of the later Khmer kings, in 1200 AD, and later remodelled as a Buddhist temple. It has three Khmer *prangs* of great beauty and complex engraved decoration.

Wat Trapang Traguan ✓✓ 300 metres west of Wat Mahatat, its *wat* is in the middle of a large lake fringed with lotus flowers.

Wat Sa Si ✓✓ North of Wat Trapang Ngoen. Built on an island in a lake, with a pond inside it, and an exquisite bell shaped *chedi*. In front of this is a large chapel housing plaster Buddha images.

Wat Si Sawai ✓✓ 300 metres south of Wat Mahatat in a perfect setting. It has three Lopburi style *prangs* fronted by two chapel bases. Many metal religious objects have been excavated here.

NEW SUKHOTHAI

PLACES TO STAY

HOTELS

Northern Palace ✪✪✪✪
(formerly Bua Luang) Old Thai hotel given massive facelift, converted into luxury hotel with all facilities and large pool. Good value.
Address: 43 Singhawat Road, Sukhothai Tel: (055)611193-4 Fax: 612038
Price:650 Rooms:67 Bathroom:67(hw) Comfort:☆☆☆☆ Design:☆☆☆☆ Location:☆☆☆
Position:central Quietness:☆☆☆☆ Restaurant:☆☆☆☆ Facilities:snooker, TV, bar, video.

Chinawat ●●●
Clean and pleasant rooms in comfortable, western oriented hotel
Address: 1-3 Nikhomkasem, Sukhothai **Tel:** (055) 611385, 611689
Price range: 80-170 **Rooms:**46 **A/C:**8 **Fan:**38 **Bathroom:**46 (8hw) **Comfort:**☆☆ to ☆☆☆
Design:☆☆☆☆ **Location:**☆☆☆ **Position:** central **Quietness:**☆☆
Restaurant:☆☆☆(Thai and western) **Tours/treks:** range of tours, some treks.

Sawaddhipong ●●●
Clean and comfortable modern rooms, pleasant friendly atmosphere.
Address: 56/2-5 Singhawat Road. **Tel:** (055) 612268, 611567
Price:120-300 **Rooms:**54 **A/C:**12 **Fan:**42 **Bathroom:**54 (12hw) **Comfort:**☆☆☆ **Design:**☆☆☆
Location:☆☆☆ **Position:**central **Quietness:**☆☆ **Restaurant:**☆☆☆ **Tours/treks:** wide range.

Rajthanee ●●●
Fairly luxurious rooms in a recently renovated hotel, but in a rather poor location.
Address: 229 Charodvithitong, Sukhothai 64000 **Tel:** (055)611308,611031 **Fax:** 612878
Price:380-650 **Rooms:**81 **A/C:**81 **Bathroom:**81(hw) **Comfort:**☆☆☆ to ☆☆☆☆
Design:☆☆ **Location:**☆☆ **Position:** 1 kilometre west of Sukhothai **Quietness:**☆☆☆
Restaurant:☆☆☆ **Facilities:**TV,video, bar, fridge .

Sukhothai ●●
Acceptable but unexceptional accommodation in typical Thai hotel.
Address:15/1 Singhawat Road Sukhothai **Tel:** (055)611133, 611540 **Fax:** 612028
Price:140-220 **Rooms:**42 **A/C:**2 **Fan:**40 **Bathroom:**42(cw) **Comfort:**☆☆ to ☆☆☆ **Design:**☆☆
Location:☆☆ **Position:**central **Quietness:**☆ **Restaurant:**☆☆

River View ●●
Fading Thai hotel, cheap rooms dirty, expensive quite luxurious.
Address: 93 Nikhornkasem Road. Sukhothai **Tel:** (055)611656, 611516 **Fax:** 613373
Price:140-650 **Rooms:**45 **A/C:**20 **Fan:**25 **Bathroom:**45(20hw) **Comfort:**☆☆ to ☆☆☆☆
Design:☆☆ **Location:**☆☆☆ **Position:**central **Quietness:**☆☆☆ **Restaurant:**☆☆☆

GUEST HOUSES

Number 4 ●●●
Rooms in lovely teak house with pleasant gardens and terrace. Full of character with an excellent atmosphere.
Address: 234/6 Charodwithitong Road, Soi Panitsia, Sukhothai **Tel:**(055)611315
Price:80(dorm 30) **Rooms:**5 **Fan:**5 **Bathroom:**0(cw outside) **Comfort:**☆☆ **Design:**☆☆☆☆☆
Location:☆☆☆☆ **Position:** 1 kilometre west of town **Quietness:**☆☆☆ **Restaurant:**☆☆☆
Tours/treks:wide range.

Yupa House ✪✪✪
Large traditional Thai house with good sized but simple rooms near river. Exceptionally helpful service.
Address: 44/10 Prave Inakorn Road, Soi Mekapatana, Sukhothai **Tel:** (055)612578
Price: 60-80 (dorm 30) **Rooms:** 10 **Fan:** 10 **Bathroom:** 10(cw) **Comfort:** ☆☆ **Design:** ☆☆☆☆
Location: ☆☆☆☆ **Position:** central **Quietness:** ☆☆☆ **Restaurant:** ☆☆☆
Tours/treks: wide range.

Somprasong ✪✪✪
Clean, simple and pretty teak rooms in a pleasant house by the river.
Address: 31-32 Prawenakorn **Tel:** (055)611709
Price: 50-100 **Rooms:** 20 **Fan:** 20 **Bathroom:** 0(h outside) **Comfort:** ☆ to ☆☆ **Design:** ☆☆☆☆
Location: ☆☆☆ **Position:** central **Quietness:** ☆☆☆ **Restaurant:** ☆☆☆

Sky House ✪✪
New clean rooms in characterless building by the side of the bypass. Helpful staff. Range of prices and standards, from basic to well equipped and comfortable.
Address: 58/1-7 Bypass Road **Tel:** (055)612237
Price: 300 (A/C: dorm 50) **Rooms:** 45 **A/C:** 27 **Fan:** 18 **Bathroom:** 45(29hw)
Comfort: ☆☆ to ☆☆☆☆ **Design:** ☆ **Location:** ☆☆ **Position:** 1.5 kilometres north of town
Quietness: ☆☆ **Restaurant:** ☆☆☆☆ **Tours/treks:** wide range, free bikes, lifts to town

Dear House ✪✪
Simple but clean and pleasant tiled rooms above nice restaurant.
Address: 7 Nikhonkaset, Sukhothai. **Tel:** (054)611474
Price: 80 **Rooms:** 2 **Fan:** 2 **Bathroom:** 0(hw outside) **Comfort:** ☆☆ **Design:** ☆☆☆
Location: ☆☆ **Position:** central **Quietness:** ☆☆ **Restaurant:** ☆☆☆

PHITSANULOK

A big, busy, brash and friendly city: dynamic, ugly and very alive, with much to see and do, good hotels and excellent restaurants, and perhaps the most beautiful Buddha image in Northern Thailand.

GEOGRAPHY

Phitsanulok is on a wide stretch of the Nan river. It is the only city apart from Bangkok which allows dwellings to be built on the river, consequently crowded with houseboats and floating restaurants, which periodically get swept downstream in the wet season. It is geographically more a part of the central plains

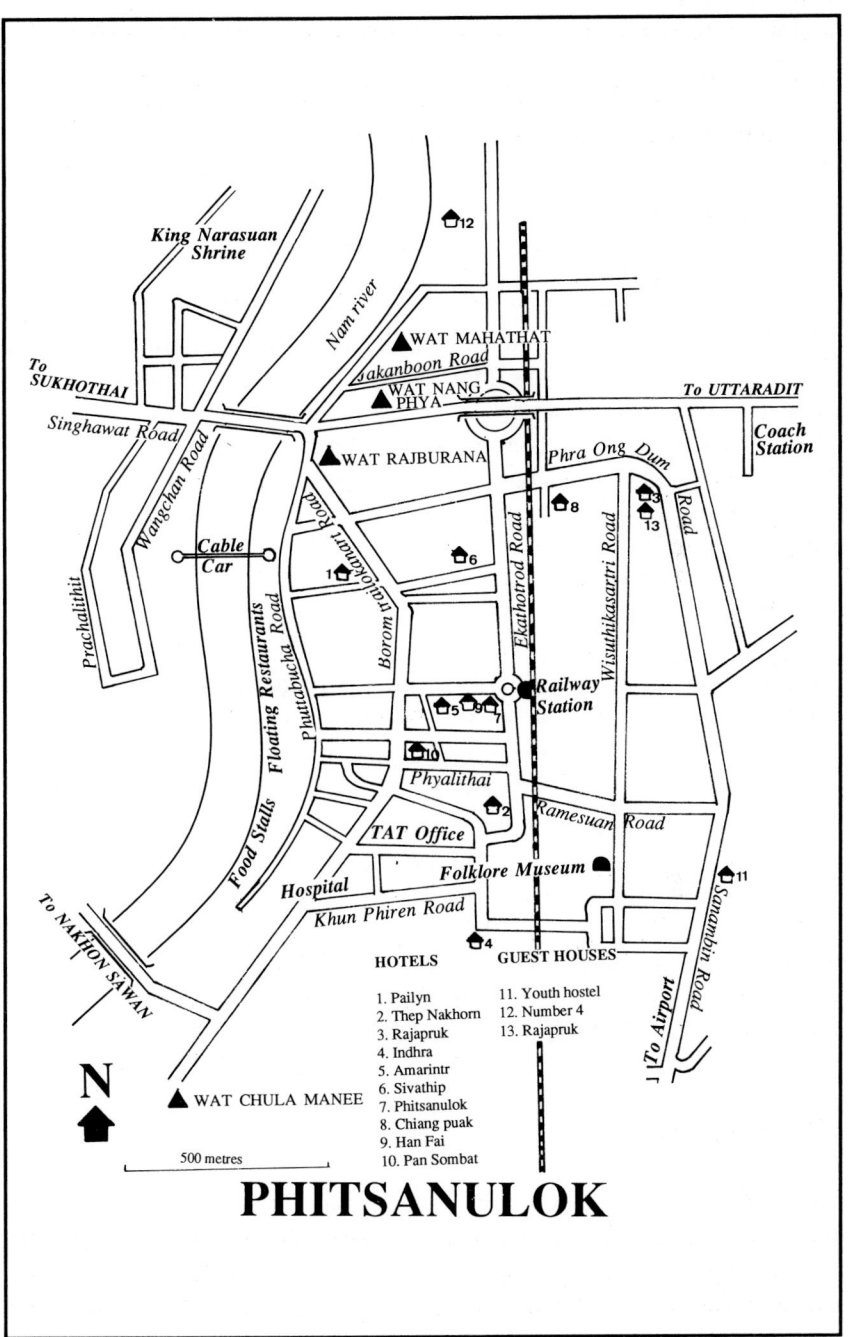

than the north - the only town in this book where flat plains stretch to the far horizons.
The city has a proud history. It was the spearhead of the attack on Burmese occupied Lanna Thailand in the late 18th century, which finally reunited the country.

TRANSPORT

The railway station is in the centre of the city, and is roughly the halfway point between Bangkok and Chiang Mai. Phitsanulok, for this reason, is a good jumping off point for the north.
There are air con buses between Phitsanulok, Nan, Sukhothai and Chiang Rai. The airport, linked with Bangkok, Chiang Mai and Nan, is to the south east of town.

PLANE TIMETABLE
Bangkok - Phitsanulok: 13.55 (Monday, Tuesday, Friday, Saturday)
15.30 (Wednesday, Friday, Saturday)
18.30 (Thursday, Saturday)
Phitsanulok - Bangkok: 11.05 (daily) 17.10 (daily)
Chiang Mai -Phitsanulok: 13.55 (Monday, Tuesday, Thursday, Saturday)
15.35 (Wednesday, Friday, Sunday)
18.30 (Thursday, Saturday)
Phitsanulok - Chiang Mai: 08.35 (Monday, Tuesday, Thursday, Saturday)
10.45 (Wednesday, Friday, Sunday)
17.20 (Thursday, Saturday)
Phitsanulok-Nan: 10.45 (Wednesday, Friday, Saturday)
Phitsanulok-Lampang: 08.30 (daily except Friday, Sunday)
Lampang-Phitsanulok: 10.00 (daily except Friday, Sunday

A large fleet of unusual 4 seater *tuk-tuks* operate in the city, with a fare of 10 - 20 *baht*.

RESTAURANTS

The city is famous for the quality of its food, and the restaurants listed are locally considered the finest in the north.
Phun Si, Sanambin Road. Hot and spicy, inexpensive and superb Thai food.

Wat Phra Si Mahatat, Si Satchanalai, Sukhothai

Wat Prakaew Don Tai, Lampang

Si Satchanalai Historic Park, Sukhothai

Si Satchanalai, Wat Mahatat

Detail of murals from Wat Phumin, Nan.

The Wang river in Lampang

Phi Tong Luang hunter, Nan

Village blacksmith, Phrae

Song Anung, exactly opposite, is also excellent.
Deng, also on Sanambin Road 250 metres south, is a little more expensive, with a good atmosphere. On the east bank of the river are several **boat** restaurants - an interesting if somewhat expensive experience. Further south is the original **Flying Vegetables** restaurant. Specialising in Pak Boong Roi, quick fried morning glory plants which are hurled to the waiter across the street who catches it on your plate. If you want to bring joy to other diners, try to catch it yourself - succeed and you will be generously applauded, but they would rather laugh if you don't!

NIGHTLIFE

All the big hotels, but notably the Rajapruk, have nightclubs with the usual blend of Thai singers and dancers. The city is pretty lively generally. The **River Pub and Restaurant** on the east side of the river serves good food and has live music nightly. The **Yat Fon** is a boat restaurant that cruises down the river every evening.

THINGS TO SEE

TEMPLES

Wat Phra Si Mahatat ✓✓✓
The skyline of Phitsanulok is dominated by the magnificent gilded Khmer *prang* of this temple. Behind it is an enormous painted plaster standing Buddha. The famous Chinaraj gold plated Buddha image is in a lovely *bot* within the temple grounds. Made in the early 15th century, it is the best example of late Sukhothai style. Around the head and shoulders is a golden halo. Behind the statue is a beautiful scene of gilded flowers and angels. The huge doors to the *bot*, inlaid with mother of pearl, are most intricate and beautiful.

Buddha Factory ✓✓
Inconspicuous from outside, but beyond a green metal door directly opposite the Folklore museum on Wisuthikasartri Road.
    Thailand produces a huge number of Buddha images of all sizes and styles. Many of them come from this factory in Phitsanulok, and of course the Chinaraj Buddha is a favourite for casts. The factory uses the 'lost wax' method of casting, so that one mould can make an unlimited number of images, and old

statues can be copied exactly. First a mould of the original is taken using resin. Into this hot wax is poured, which cools to produce a copy in wax which is polished and finished by hand. This image is then covered in plaster. When this sets, bronze or whatever metal is to be used is poured into the wax which burns away allowing the metal to form a perfect copy. Finally this is polished. The factory has good explanations of the processes involved in photographs and displays. It is strange to see pieces of Buddhas, the objects of so much reverence, in such inelegant states - with arms, legs and heads strewn around looking like the results of a nasty massacre. There is a small shop where statues of various sizes can be purchased.

Folklore Museum ✓✓
At the southern end of Wisuthikasartri Road. A very large display (the largest in Northern Thailand) of traditional artifacts from the region - agricultural implements, kitchen utensils, pottery, musical instruments and weapons. Many weird and wonderful objects whose function can sometimes only be guessed at - the descriptions are not very clear.

PLACES TO STAY

HOTELS

Pailyn ✪✪✪✪
Big, busy, luxury hotel with all facilities.
Address: 38 Baramatoilokanart Road Phitsanulok **Tel:** (055)215711-2
Price range: 800-2500 (suite) **Rooms:** 243 A/C:243 **Bathroom:**243(hw) **Comfort:**☆☆☆☆
Design:☆☆ **Location:**☆☆☆ **Position:** central **Quietness:**☆☆☆ **Restaurant:**☆☆☆☆
Facilities: coffee shop, disco, sauna, massage, TV, VDO, **Tours/treks:** range of tours.

Thep Nakorn ✪✪✪✪
Large luxury international hotel.
Address: 43/1 Sri Thamtripidok Road. Phitsanulok **Tel:** (055) 251817, 251837
Price range: 500-700 **Rooms:**150 A/C:150 **Bathroom:** 150(hw) **Comfort:**:☆☆☆☆
Design:☆☆☆☆ **Location:** ☆ **Position:** central **Quietness:**☆☆☆ **Restaurant:**☆☆☆☆
Facilities: cocktail lounge, cabaret, bar, VDO, TV **Tours/treks:** local tours.

Rajapruk ✪✪✪✪
Large, international style hotel with all facilities
Address: 99/9 Pha Ong Dan Road, Phitsanulok **Tel:** (055)258477
Price range: 600-700 **Rooms:** 123 A/C:123 **Bathroom:**123(hw) **Comfort:**☆☆☆☆
Design:☆☆☆ **Location:**☆☆ **Position:** central **Quietness:**☆☆☆
Facilities: pool, coffee shop, night club, massage parlour. **Restaurant:**☆☆☆☆

Indrha ●●●●
Pleasant mid sized modern hotel with very comfortable, well furnished rooms.
Address: 103/8 Srithumtripidok, Phitsanulok **Tel:** (055)259188, 259638
Price:300 **Rooms:**49 **A/C:**48 **Bathroom:**49(hw) **Comfort:**☆☆☆☆ **Design:**☆☆☆
Location:☆☆☆ **Position:** 1 kilometre south of centre **Quietness:**☆☆☆ **Restaurant:**☆☆☆
Facilities: fridge, minibar.

Amarint Nakork ●●●
Big, busy, well furnished and appointed hotel.
Address:3/1 Chaophraya Road, Phitsanulok **Tel:** (055)258588
Price:300-500 **Rooms:**110 **A/C:**110 **Bathroom:**110(hw) **Comfort:**☆☆☆☆ **Design:**☆☆☆
Location:☆☆ **Position:**central **Quietness:**☆☆☆ **Restaurant:**☆☆☆☆
Facilities:night club, coffee shop.

Sivathip ●●
Clean, comfortable rooms in modern hotel.
Address:110/21 Pasongpasat Road, Phitsanulok **Tel:** (055)244933-4
Price:160-210 **Rooms:**47(cw) **A/C:**15 **Fan:**32 **Bathroom:**47(cw) **Comfort:**☆☆☆ to ☆☆☆☆
Design:☆☆ **Location:**☆☆☆ **Position:**central **Quietness:**☆☆☆ **Facilities:**coffee shop

Phitsanulok ●●
Fairly modern hotel which has seen better days, but still offering clean and spacious rooms.
Address:90 Nalesuan Road, Phitsanulok **Tel:** (055)258425
Price:80-160 **Rooms:**60 **A/C:**20 **Fan:**40 **Bathroom:**60(cw) **Comfort:**☆☆ to ☆☆☆
Design:☆☆☆ **Location:**☆☆☆ **Position:**central **Quietness:**☆☆

Chiang Puak ●●
Clean, comfortable rooms, friendly staff, close to railway line.
Address:63/18 Aygar Tossalot, Phitsanulok **Tel:** (055)252822
Price:140-200 **Rooms:**53 **A/C:**25 **Fan:**28 **Bathroom:**53(cw) **Comfort:**☆☆ to ☆☆☆
Design:☆☆☆ **Location:**☆ **Position:**central **Quietness:**☆☆ **Restaurant:**☆☆☆

Han Fai ●
Address:73/1 Phayalithai Road. Phitsanulok **Tel:** (054)258484
Price:90-170 **Rooms:**60 **A/C:**5 **Fan:**55 **Bathroom:**60(cw) **Comfort:**☆ to ☆☆ **Design:**☆
Location:☆ **Position:**central, opposite railway station **Quietness:**☆

Pan Sombat ●
Address:4/1 Sainithai Road, Phitsanulok **Tel:** (054)258174
Price:70-150 **Rooms:**23 **Fan:**23 **Bathroom:**6(cw) **Comfort::**☆ to ☆☆ **Design:**☆☆ **Location:**☆
Position:central **Quietness:**☆

GUEST HOUSES

Phitsanulok Youth Hostel: ●●●
Delightful old teak house and new outbuildings and restaurant beautifully designed. Basic but very pleasant and charming accommodation. Excellent service.
Address: 38 Sanambin Road. Phitsanulok **Tel:** (055)242060
Price:100-120 (dorm 40) **Rooms:**30 **Fan:**30 **Bathroom:**0(hw outside) **Comfort:**☆☆
Design:☆☆☆☆☆ **Location:**☆☆☆ **Position:**2 kilometres east of centre **Quietness:**☆☆☆
Restaurant:☆☆☆

No. 4 ●●●
Charming traditional teak house. Simple rooms of great character.
Address:11/12 Akathodsant Rd. Phitsanulok
Price:80(dorm 30) **Rooms:**5 **Fan:**5 **Bathroom:**0(hw outside) **Comfort:**☆ to ☆☆
Design:☆☆☆☆ **Location:**☆☆☆ **Position:** close to river **Quietness:**☆☆ **Restaurant:**☆☆☆
Facilities:free bikes

Rajapruk ●●●
Large, clean and pleasant rooms behind luxury Rajapruk Hotel, use of hotel facilities including pool.
Address:99/10 Phaongdin Road, Phitsanulok **Tel:** (054)259303
Price:180-280 **Rooms:**78 **A/C:**18 **Fan:**60 **Bathroom:**78(hw) **Comfort:**☆☆☆ to ☆☆☆☆
Design:☆☆☆ **Location:**☆☆ **Position:**central **Quietness:**☆☆☆

TAK

At first sight Tak is a disaster. It has a very new, modern city centre of identical white concrete buildings surrounded by wide, seemingly empty streets, producing a bleak, soulless atmosphere.

Sadly, this characterless concrete is built on the banks of the wide and beautiful Ping river, which produces a breeze sufficient to stir the litter in the baleful streets, but is ignored by the town. Behind the concrete jungle things improve. To the south of the centre is an area of very lovely high roofed teak houses of a design unique to this area, and the parts of the city still undergoing modernisation have the odd old house, rickety and lovable, to relieve the drabness.

Tak's only claim to fame is that it produced one king of Thailand - Taksin, who ruled in the 18th century. He is commemorated by a statue surrounded by murals depicting his life in a small shrine to the north of the town centre.

Tak is built on the east bank of the Ping river. At this point, the river is one kilometre wide, and separates the central plains to the east from the wild, mountainous country which extends all the way west to the Burmese border.

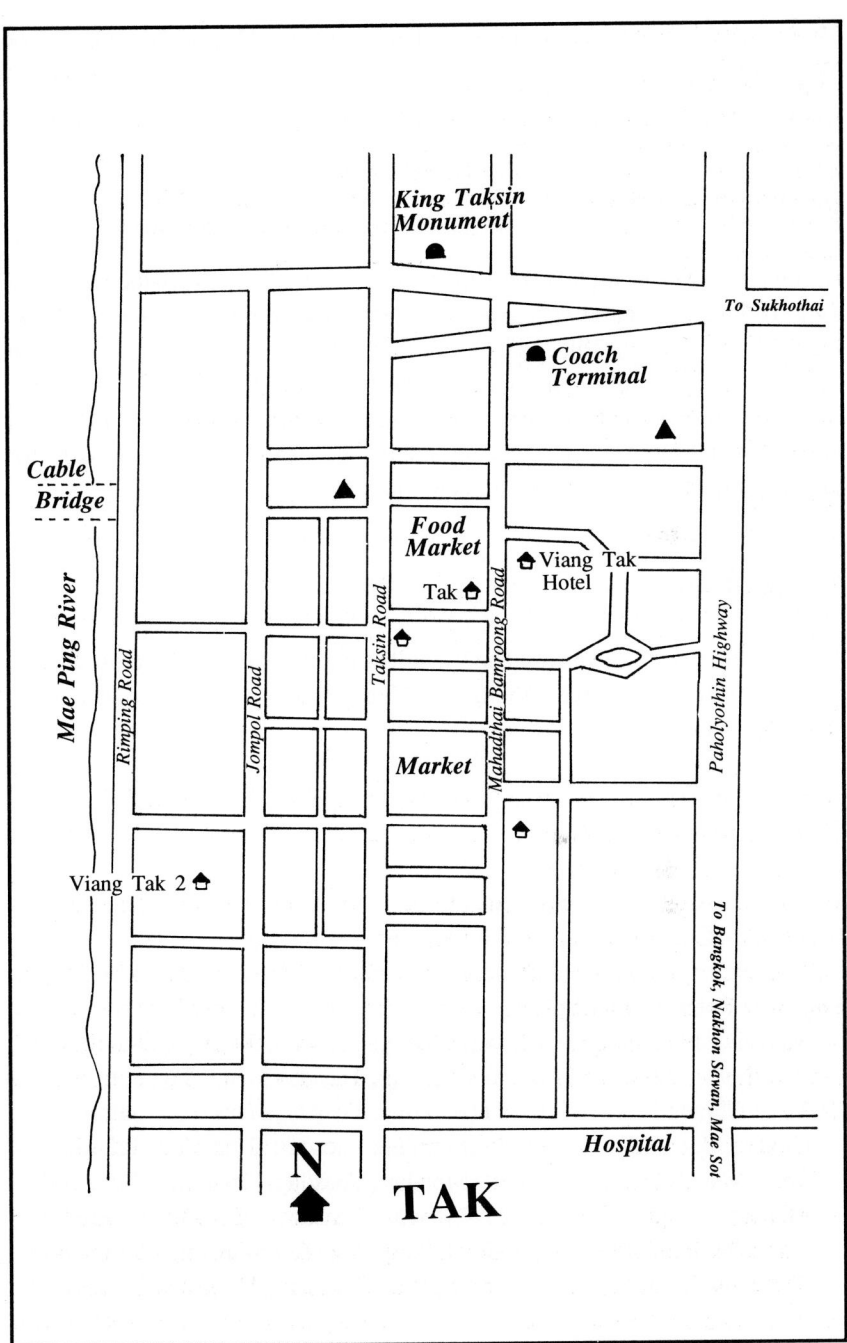

The countryside to the east is low scrubland, of no great beauty or fertility. Tak has the dubious honour of the highest temperatures in Thailand during the hot season, so is best avoided at that time of year.

RESTAURANTS

Excellent food in the night market opposite the Vieng Tak hotel, which itself has a good, though comparatively expensive, menu. Eating on the terrace overlooking the river at Vieng Tak 2 is pleasant. In the daytime, cheap, basic food can be had at the foodstalls in the market opposite the Mae Ping Hotel. Close to the river north of the centre are several nightime restaurants with low, traditional tables at which one eats sitting on tiny stools. These can be found by looking for the fairy lights on Rimping Road, near the river.

NIGHTLIFE

This is distinctly sparse in Tak. The Vieng Tak has the darkest nightclub suitable only for super sensitive bats. Vieng Tak 2 has a "cowboy bar" where decor and prices are wild west.

TRANSPORT

The coach station is at the north end of Paholyothin Rd. There are frequent buses to Mae Sot, Chiang Mai and Sukhothai.

The airport is 2 kilometres east of Tak. There are flights to Bangkok, Chiang Mai, Mae Sot and Phitsanulok.

Tak - Bangkok:	15.55 (Monday, Tuesday, Thursday, Saturday)
Bangkok - Tak:	07.10 (Monday, Tuesday, Thursday, Saturday)
Tak - Chiang Mai:	09.30 (Monday, Tuesday, Thursday, Saturday)
Chiang Mai - Tak:	13.55 (Monday, Tuesday, Thursday, Saturday)
Tak - Mae Sot:	09.30 (Monday, Tuesday, Thursday, Saturday)
Mae Sot - Tak:	15.05 (Monday, Tuesday, Thursday, Saturday)
Tak - Phitsanulok:	15.55 (Monday, Tuesday, Thursday, Saturday)
Phitsanulok - Tak:	08.35 (Monday, Tuesday, Thursday, Saturday)

PLACES TO STAY

HOTELS

Viang Tak ●●●●
Pleasant and very comfortable international standard hotel.
Address:25/3 Mahadthai R0ad. Tak Tel:(055)511910, 511910, 511095
Price:390-480 Rooms:100 A/C:100 Bathroom:100(hw) Comfort:☆☆☆☆ Design:☆☆☆☆
Location:☆☆☆ Position:central Quietness:☆☆☆☆ Restaurant:☆☆☆ Facilities:nightclub, coffee shop, cabaret, minibar, fridge, TV.

Viang Tak 2 ●●●●
Not so luxurious as its twin, but still very comfortable, overlooking the Ping river.
Address:25/3 Mahadthai Road, Tak Tel: (055)511910, 511910, 511095
Price:330-380 Rooms:150 A/C:150 Bathroom:150(hw) Comfort:☆☆☆☆ Design:☆☆☆
Location:☆☆☆☆ Position:central Quietness:☆☆☆ Restaurant:☆☆☆ Facilities:coffee shop.

Sangwan ●●
Old teak hotel with new annexe, new rooms utilitarian but comfortable.
Address:619 Taksin Road, Tak Tel: (055)511265
Price:120-200 Rooms:30 A/C:3 Fan:27 Bathroom:30(cw) Comfort:☆ t o☆☆☆ Design:☆☆
Location:☆☆☆ Position:central Quietness:☆☆ Restaurant:☆☆

Tak ●●
Clean rooms in a rather austere hotel building
Address:18/10 Mahathaibamlung Road. Tak Tel: (055)513422
Price:120-200 Rooms:23 Fan:23 Bathroom:23(cw) Comfort:☆☆ to ☆☆☆ Design:☆
Location:☆☆ Position:central Quietness:☆☆

Mae Ping ●
Address:231/46 Mahathaibamlung Road, Tak Tel: (055)511807
Price:40-140 Rooms:41 A/C:3 Fan:38 Bathroom:41(cw) Comfort:☆ to ☆☆ Design:☆☆
Location:☆☆ Position:central Quietness:☆☆

MAE SOT

Until recently regarded as a dangerous, wild and lawless town, Mae Sot has calmed down and is now as peaceful as any other Thai town. It is, though, different. Mae Sot is a cosmopolitan polyglot of Burmese, Thai and hill tribe peoples, all wearing their own costumes and getting on with life within their own cultures. Tourists feel invisible in Mae Sot. Elsewhere in Thailand tourists are special - from a cynical view point, at least partly for their importance to the local economy. In Mae Sot, there are so many races living there, and tourism is so low key, a western face is just another new variety. People watching in Mae Sot is interesting - Burmese Muslims in the male sarongs or *longyis*, Karen tribesmen, Chinese merchants, bearded Indians and Thai army rangers.

GEOGRAPHY

Mae Sot is in the valley of the Moei river which marks the Burmese border. Although a small river, the valley is wide. To the east, north and south are high mountain ranges, cutting off Mae Sot from the rest of Thailand. It is quite natural then, that the town should be more aligned with Burma economically, and the river just five kilometres to the east is a major international crossing point for goods, some imported legally, some illegally. Mae Sot, then, is a smuggling centre - mainly jade and other precious stones but also drugs, guns, timber and people. The Burmese side of the border is in Karen State, the bastion of the Karen National Army which has been fighting for independence for 40 years. Frequently, when the Karen are in control, it is possible (although dangerous) to cross into Burma.

TRANSPORT

There are frequent air conditioned buses to Bangkok, Chiang Mai, Phitsanulok and Tak.
From the airport, there are flights to Bangkok, Chiang Mai, Phitsanulok and Tak.

Tak - Mae Sot:	09.30 (Monday, Tuesday, Thursday, Saturday)
Mae Sot - Tak:	15.05 (Monday, Tuesday, Thursday, Saturday)
Bangkok - Mae Sot:	12.00 (Monday, Tuesday, Thursday, Saturday)
Mae Sot - Bangkok:	10.20 (Monday, Tuesday, Thursday, Saturday)
Chiang Mai - Mae Sot:	13.55 (Monday, Tuesday, Thursday, Saturday)
Mae Sot - Chiang Mai:	10.20 (Monday, Tuesday, Thursday, Saturday)
Phitsanulok - Mae Sot:	08.35 (Monday, Tuesday, Thursday, Saturday)
Mae Sot - Phitsanulok:	15.05 (Monday, Tuesday, Thursday, Saturday)

Mae Sot

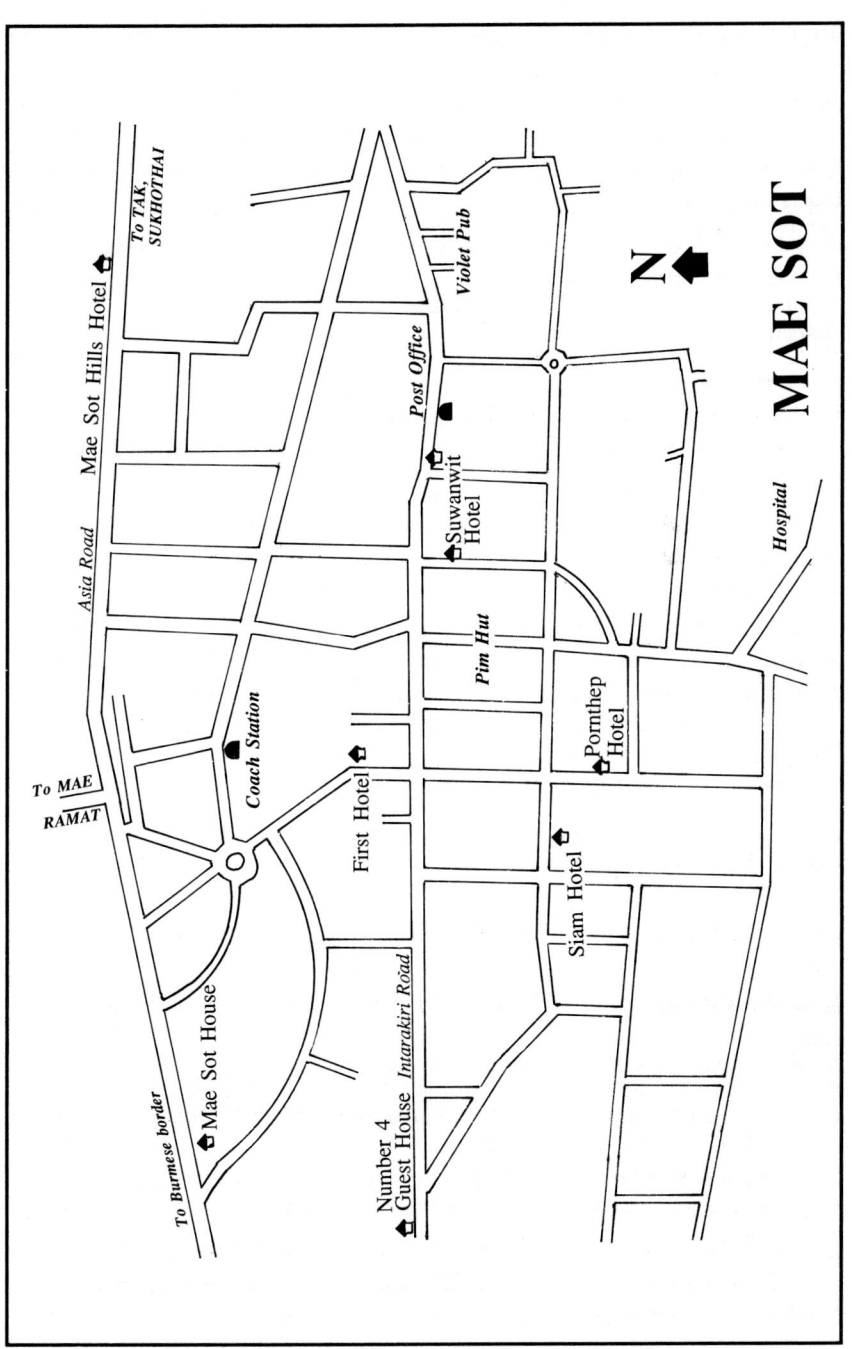

PLACES TO STAY

HOTELS

Mae Sot Hill ❋❋❋❋
International luxury hotel with all facilities.
Address:100 Asia Road, Mae Sot, Tak **Tel:** (055)532608
Price:800 **Rooms:**120 **A/C:**120 **Bathroom:**120(hw) **Comfort:**☆☆☆☆☆ **Design:**☆☆☆☆
Location:☆☆☆ **Position:**3 kilometres west of town **Quietness:**☆☆☆☆ **Restaurant:**☆☆☆☆
Facilities:pool, coffee shop, disco, night club, tennis courts, TV, video,
Tours/treks:range of tours.

Porn Thep ❋❋❋
Very clean and comfortable rooms in a large, friendly Thai hotel.
Address: 25/4 Soi Srivieng, Mae Sot, Tak **Tel:** (055)532590-4
Price:185-400 **Rooms:**148 **A/C:**80 **Fan:**68 **Bathroom:**148(80hw) **Comfort:**☆☆☆ to ☆☆☆☆
Design:☆☆☆ **Location:**☆☆☆ **Position:**central **Quietness:**☆☆ **Restaurant:**☆☆☆

Siam ❋❋❋
Recently renovated hotel. Cheaper rooms good value - quite clean and comfortable.
Address:185 Prasatwithi Road, Tak **Tel:** (055)531176
Price:120-350 **Rooms:**87 **A/C:**22 **Fan:**55 **Bathroom:**87(hw) **Comfort:**☆☆☆ to ☆☆☆☆
Design:☆☆ **Location:**☆☆☆ **Position:**central **Quietness:**☆☆ **Restaurant:**☆☆☆
Tours/treks:range of local tours.

Suvanavit ❋❋
Old, part teak hotel. Rather basic, but upper rooms not too bad.
Address: Soi Watluang, Mae Sot, Tak **Tel:** (055)531162
Price:60-100 **Rooms:**24 **Fan:**24 **Bathroom:**24(cw) **Comfort:**☆☆ **Design:**☆☆☆
Location:☆☆ **Position:**central **Quietness:**☆☆

GUEST HOUSES

Number 4 ❋❋❋
An unspoilt teak house with simply furnished but attractive rooms.
Address: Intarakiri Road, Mae Sot, Tak
Price:80 **Rooms:**5 **Fan:**5 **Bathroom:**0(hw outside) **Comfort:**☆☆ **Design:**☆☆☆☆
Location:☆☆☆☆ **Position:** 1kilometre west of town **Quietness:**☆☆☆☆ **Restaurant:**snacks

Mae Sot House ❋❋
Simple rooms in a pleasant complex. Excellent expert travel office.
Address: 82/8 Asia Road. Mae Sot, Tak
Price:60-200 **Rooms:**11 **A/C:**1 **Fan:**3 **Bathroom:**11(1hw) **Comfort:**☆ to ☆☆☆ **Design:**☆☆☆
Location:☆☆ **Position:**1 kilometre north of town **Quietness:**☆☆ **Restaurant:** ☆☆☆
Tours/treks: extensive range of treks and tours.

Chapter Seven

The East

INTRODUCTION

The east of Northern Thailand is largely unknown and unexplored by the tourist, although in the last three years this has begun to change. It is the most untouched, sparsely inhabited and traditional part of the north. For the visitor, it offers lovely scenery, some wonderful religious architecture, pleasant and peaceful towns, a glimpse of old fashioned Thailand and some excellent hotels with amazingly low prices.

The landscape is of high, jungle covered hills dissected by the valleys of four great rivers - the Wang, Yom, Nan and Wa. The hill ranges have occasional sharp peaks - over 2000 metres west of Phayao and east of Nan. The cities and towns of this region are all quite small, compact and widely scattered. Lampang is the largest, close to the southern limit of the hills. Nan, in the east of the region, was until recently isolated from the rest of Thailand by poor communications, and has links with nearby Laos. Phayao, on the shores of a large lake, is surrounded by the most fertile rice growing land in Thailand.

The temples of Lampang, notably **Wat Prakeo Don Tai** and **Wat Phra That Lampang Luang**, are amongst the most splendid in the north. Around Nan, the magical murals of **Wat Phumin** are in a temple area of great beauty. In Nan, the nomadic, pre stone age **Phi Tong Luang** peoples can be visited, as well as the wild, hill tribe country of the Laos border. Near Phrae, erosion has created some strange landscapes, widely believed to be inhabited by ghosts. Between Phrae and Lampang is the Elephant Training Centre, the only non tourist elephant camp in Thailand.

In the hills are many waterfalls and caves, unlike those of the Chiang Mai area little visited and sometimes stunningly beautiful. Communications were very poor until recently, when several new, well surfaced roads have been built, allowing easy travel between all major towns. However, off these roads almost all roads are dirt based and most make for a very bumpy, dusty or muddy ride.

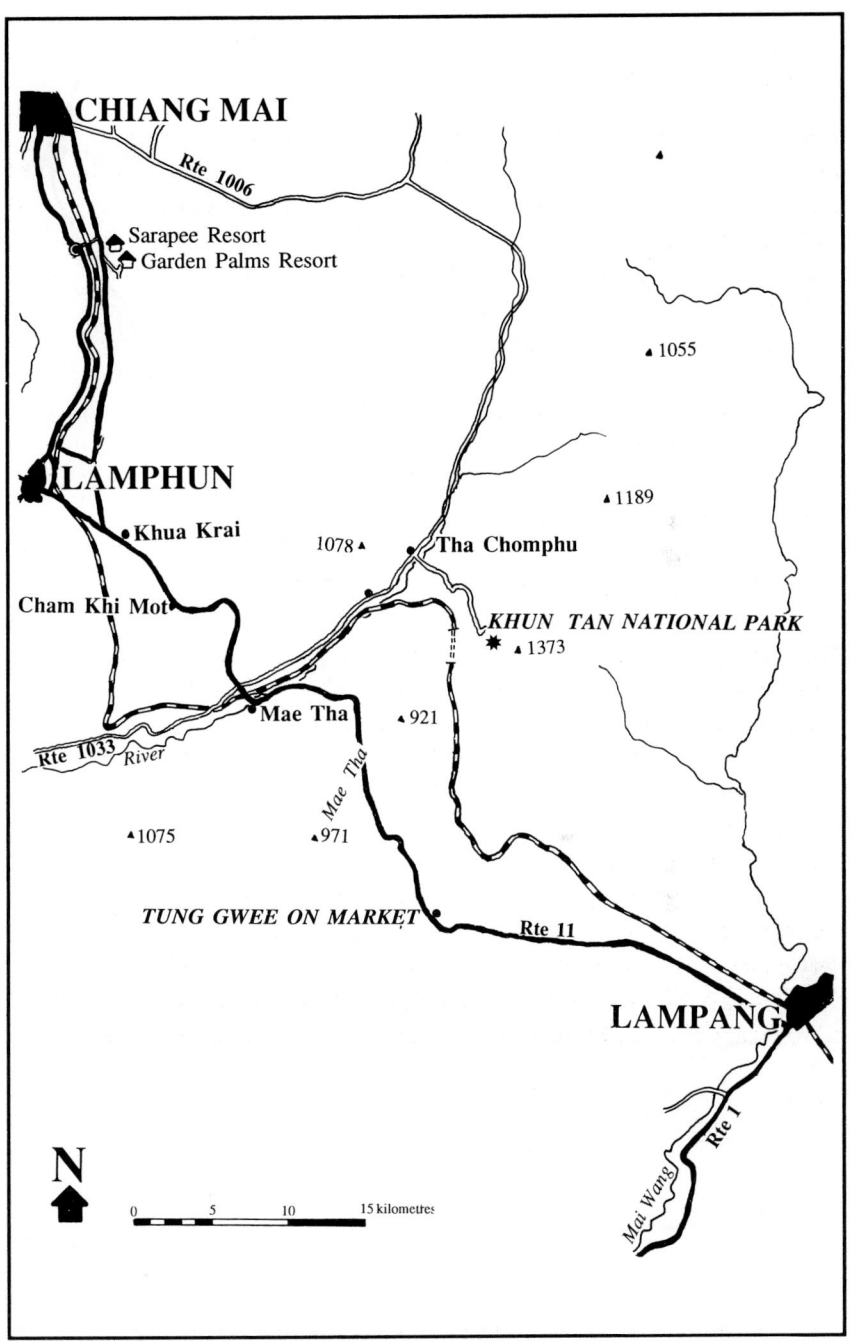

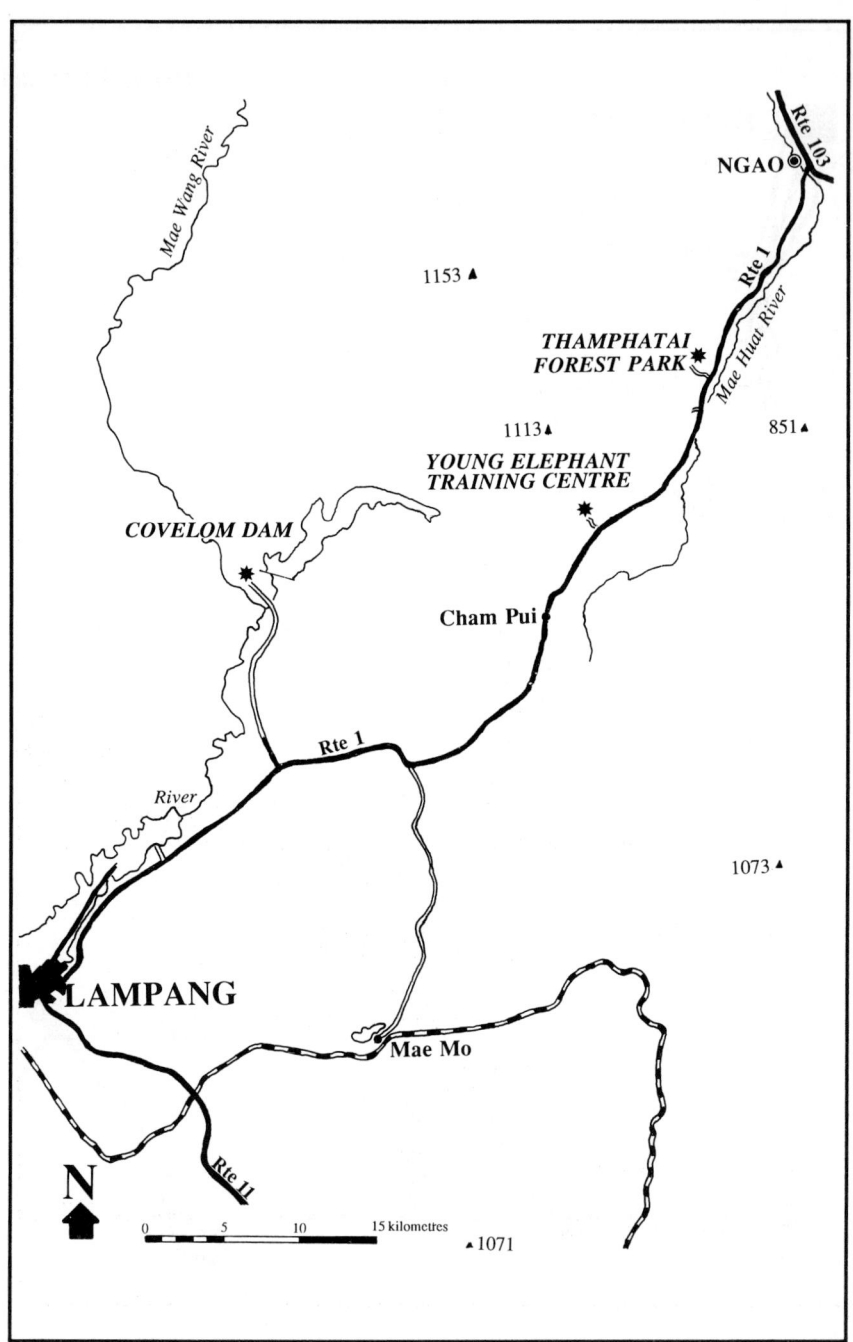

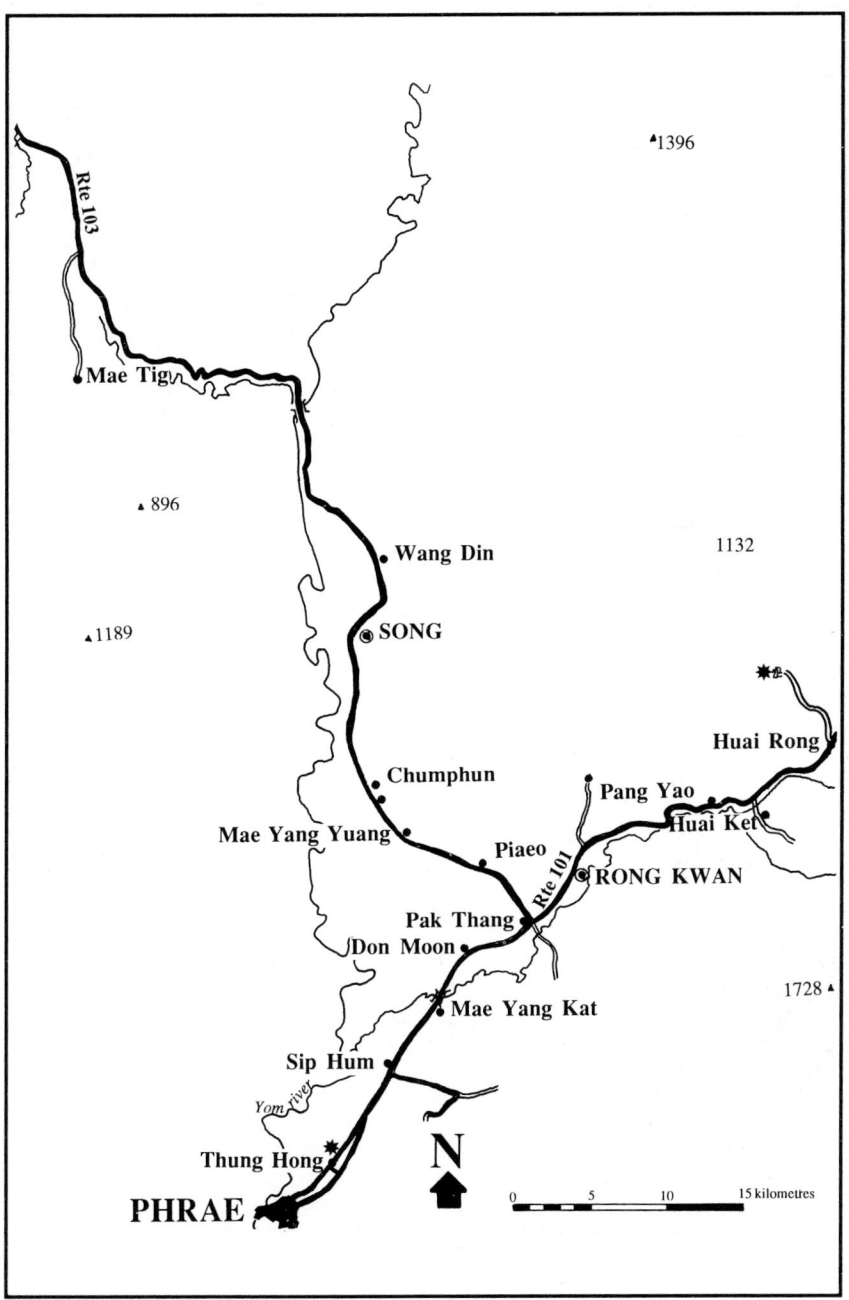

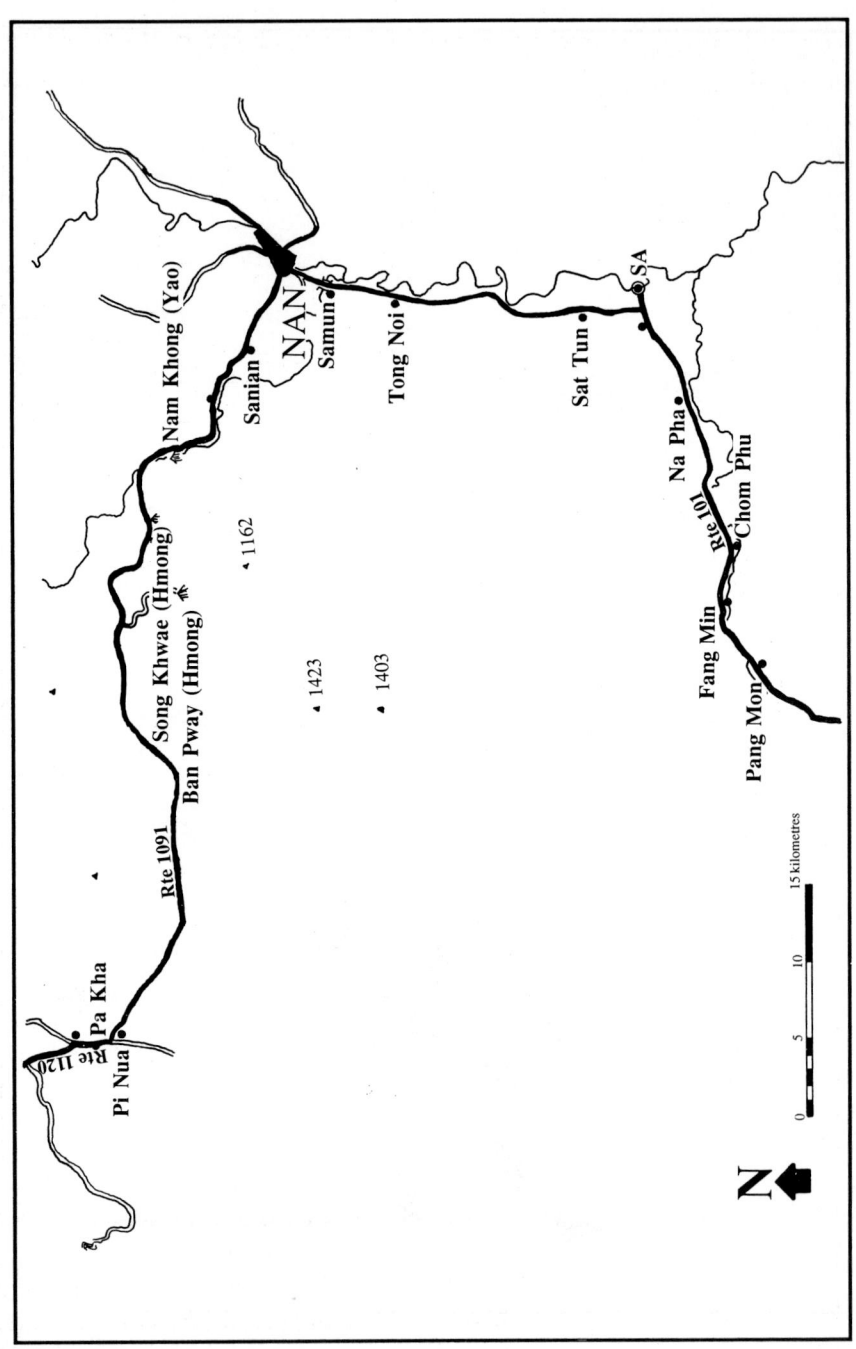

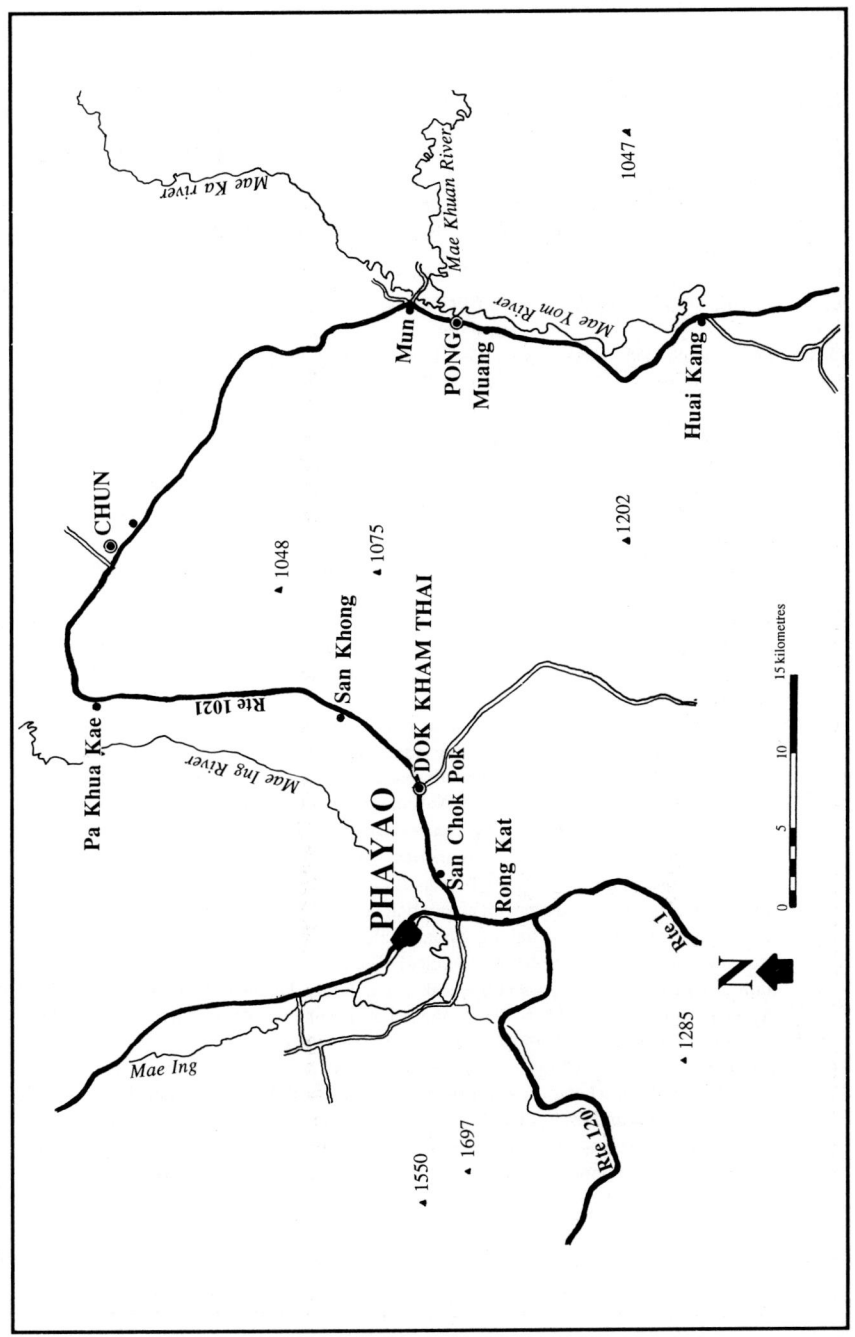

CHIANG MAI - LAMPANG (99 kilometres - 1.5 hours) Map page 237

Kilometres

0   Leave Chiang Mai by crossing east over Nawarat bridge, continuing straight to Superhigh way.
2   Chiang Mai railway station to west of road.
4   Junction with Superhighway. After traffic lights, turn south on Rte 11 signposted Lamphun-Lampang.

NB DISTANCES ON KILOMETRE POSTS FROM LAMPANG

95-65   Fast, straight road - wide and very busy. Beware of oncoming trucks and coaches, especially in early morning and evening. Most traffic from Bangkok arrives at Chiang Mai via this road.

81   **Sarapee** ❶❶❶ Large, well equipped and pleasantly furnished cabins on the shores of an artificial lake. Very attractive but some cabins close to main road.
Price:400-600 Rooms:23 A/C:4 Fan:19 Bathroom:23(hw) Comfort:☆☆☆ to ☆☆☆☆
Design:☆☆☆ Location:☆☆☆ Quietness:☆to☆☆☆ Restaurant:☆☆☆

81   Turn east 1.4 kilometres to:
Garden Palms Resort ❶❶❶❶ Large, comfortable and pretty cabins in a landscaped park with gardens, lakes and caged wildlife.
Address:133/1 Moo 7, Sarapee, Chiang Mai Tel: (053)248441
Price:800 Rooms:13 A/C:13 Bathroom:13(hw) Comfort:☆☆☆☆ Design:☆☆☆☆☆
Location:☆☆☆☆ Quietness:☆☆☆☆☆ Restaurant:☆☆☆
Facilities: pool, fishing, boating.

64   Road starts to climb out of the Ping valley, rice paddies and orchards give way to extensive teak plantations with young trees in low, scrubby jungle.

48   West turn Rte 1033 to **Wat Phra Phutthabaat** (32 kilometres). Details page 113.

48   West turn 18 kilometres to **Khun Tan National Park** ✓✓. Dirt road follows along the railway line, passing through the Thai villages of **Tha Chomphu** (8 kilometres), then turn south in **Tha Song Yang** (13 kilometres), five kilometres of poor and steep road to the National Park, passing the tiny railway station of Khun Tan en route. The park is a large area of mountain jungle with a very rich fauna and flora. There are chalets and houses for rent, but without any restaurant facilities (although cooking facilities are provided and food delivery can be obtained). The climate is cool and pleasant at this altitude (between 1000 metres to the peak of **Doi Khun Tan** at 1373 metres.)

37   Accident shrine to right of road - large number of spirit houses dedicated to those who have been killed in accidents along this road in Lampang province.

33   Rest area to west of road next to small shrine. Snacks and drinks available here.

21   **Tung Gwee-On market** ✓. A large market to the north of the road specialising in the sale of exotic animals and birds, including gibbons, giant monitor lizards and parakeets. During 1992 it is planned to move the Young Elephant Training Centre here.

2   **Lampang** ✓✓✓. A large and thriving city on the Wang river. Details page 246.

LAMPANG - PHRAE (141 kilometres - 2.5 hours) Maps pages 238 and 239

Rte 1 bypasses the middle of town to the south east. To continue to Nan and/or Phrae drive north east along the bypass through the Wang valley, past the airport to the south of the road.

NB KILOMETRE POSTS NOW MEASURED FROM BANGKOK

615	Orchid farm with good display to the west of the road.
617	West turn down metalled road through ornate gates to **Wat Pra That Sadit** ✓. A large and rich temple with a big brass covered *chedi*
623	West turn to **Covelom Dam** ✓(11 kilometres). Drowned valley surrounded by hills.
625-630	Teak plantations and pineapple fields in a landscape of low hills.
633	South turn to teak logging and storage area of Mae Mo (8 kilometres)
639	Road climbs into the hills with many rugged limestone ridges and outcrops on either side.
645	Army camp and teak conservation project to south of road.
648	**Champooy** ✓Thai/Yao village at crest of hills.
649	Large shrine surrounded by many offerings to the spirit of the mountains.
655	North turn 1 kilometre to **Young Elephant Training Camp** ✓✓✓. The only non commercial elephant camp left in Thailand, run by the government. Found in 1968, its function is to train young elephants for their duties in the forests of Thailand. Before the teak logging ban, they were used to haul the heavy logs, now used mainly against poaching. Elephants are still better than bulldozers in steep, rugged terrain. The number of elephants in residence varies between 30-60. Baby elephants go to school at three and finish at twenty years of age. The trainer or mahout - usually a Karen tribesman will stay with the elephant throughout its life. The setting of the centre is superb, in deep jungle surrounded by limestone cliffs to create a natural amphitheatre. Elephant shows take place between 8 and 11 am, everyday except Sunday and during April or May. There is no entrance charge, but short elephant rides are 30 *baht* per person. Sadly, there are plans to move the camp to **Tung Gwee-On**, 21 kilometres west of Lampang, and to convert it into a more tourist oriented attraction.
666	**Thamphatai Forest Park** ✓✓. From the car park to the north of the road, there is a well marked steep path to a large cliff in which is set a spectacular cave with a large Buddha sculpture besides a stalagmite. Just outside the cave is a stucco *chedi*. The cave is 400 metres long, lit by electric light, and ending in a cavern. There are other marked walks through the very pleasant mountain jungle.
668	North turn, dirt road 1.4 kilometres to **Forest Research, Demonstration and Extension Centre** ✓A large area of forest in which new tree species and hybrids for reafforestation are analyzed. There is a new, large display building.
673	**Wat Chang Kham** ✓✓. To north of road. A Burmese style new *wiharn* of exquisite taste and beauty. Painted black and red outside, polished teak inside, this large new temple building refutes the idea that only old temples can be beautiful.
681	Junction with Rte 103 1 kilometre south of **Ngao**, a small old town. Turn north here to Phayao, south for Phrae and Nan, to continue the eastern route.

NB DISTANCES NOW ALONG ROUTE 103

Route 103 passes through pleasant underpopulated countryside of low forested hills and narrow valleys. This area has a number of coal seams, whose mining is the major local occupation.

The East

63	Starting kilometre post on route 103.
50	West turn 5 kilometres down dirt road to coal mine and village of **Mae Tig**.
39	Coal mine 2 kilometres to west of road.
32	Forestry School to east of road.
30-0	Valley of the Yom river. Hills give way to rice paddies, road passes through several small prosperous agricultural villages.
0	End of route 103, junction with route 101. Turn south here to **Phrae** (25 kilometres) or north to **Nan**.

NB KILOMETRE POSTS READINGS NOW ALONG ROUTE 103

158	Kilometre post Rte 101 at junction with Rte 103
141	**Phrae ✓✓**. A large town with several good accommodations and a pleasant, friendly atmosphere. Details page 254.

PHRAE - NAN (110 kilometres - 1.8 hours) Map page 240

Drive north along Rte 101, signposted Nan.

138	**Thung Hong ✓** There are a number of villages in the Phrae area that specialise in the production of particular articles. This village is famed for the production of the blue denim shirts which are the traditional dress of the north Thai peasant. Every family is involved in the production or retailing of these shirts, and although the village is not particularly attractive, these shirts are very good value and hard wearing.
143	East turn 1.5 kilometres (dirt road), then south turn 1.7 kilometres (metalled) to **Muang Phi ✓**. This term means "land of ghosts", and is firmly believed by superstitious locals to be haunted. It is an area where a hard layer of rock caps soft sandstone. Erosion has produced a strange landscapes of rock pillars and strange shapes. There is a small cafe at the entrance.
164	West turn 11 kilometres along very bad road to cave and waterfall.
165-170	Lovely views of surrounding mountains (up to 1728 metres) as road climbs through jagged limestone mountains. Many large fields of cotton.
182	**Huai Kae**. Turn east here down metalled and dirt road (Rte 1216) three kilometres to a newly discovered and very remote cave - **Tham Huai Ki ✓**. Small signpost on north of road, steep climb one kilometre through jungle to easy to miss cave entrance. Torches and climbing gear needed.
187	**Huai Rong**. West turn to **Huai Rong Arboretum ✓✓** (4 kilometres), Five kilometres to **Huai Rong Waterfall ✓✓✓**. A very beautiful cascading waterfall into a clear stream in a lovely valley of tall jungle trees. Swimming in stream. A magical and little known place.
190	Teak preservation area to north of road.
210	The road leaves the mountains and enters the valley of the Nan river, swinging north.
225	**Sa ✓** A small sleepy town, bypassed by the main road, with a lovely old temple- **Wat Bun Yuen ✓**, with Laotian influence evident in its style. The recently restored *bot* has 3 tiers. The doors and guardian statues are especially fine.
249	Rte 1025 west to **Wat Phra That Khao Noi ✓**. This small temple on a hill gives good views of Nan and its valley. In the woods around the temple are scenes from Buddhist hell - primitive and gruesome statues of the fate in store for wrong doers in this world. Hell is not an intrinsic part of Buddhist philosophy, but seems to have been adopted in this part of Thailand.
251	**Nan ✓✓✓**. A large and prosperous town with many notable temples and the exquisite murals of Wat Phumin. (Details page 258)

NAN - PHAYAO (120 kilometres - 2.5 hours) Maps pages 240 and 241

Leave Nan on Rte 1091 west, signposted Phayao. A metalled but rather narrow and little used road. Few petrol stations or restaurants along the way.

NB KILOMETRE POSTS MEASURED FROM NAN

14	**Nam Khong** ✓ A Yao village, mixture of traditional Yao and Thai houses. Older women wear traditional costume.
19	**Song Khwae** ✓✓ Large Hmong village, well integrated and Thai-ised. To the west of the village is Doi Luang (1162 metres). This is the area where the **Phi Tong Luang** (Spirits of the Yellow Leaves) people have most of their settlements (details page 47). Frequently they work for Hmong villagers in their fields, so may be seen working here.
20	Pretty, winding mountain road with good views of surrounding country. Note high degree of deforestation to south of road.
24	Dirt road south to Hmong village of **Pway** 3 (5 kilometres) Traditional Hmong village, Phi Tong Luang frequently employed here.
35	Large sign and grass hut "Phi Tong Luang contact here" in English. No sign of anyone, but shows how these people have become a tourist attraction.
65	Junction of Rte 1091 and Rte 1120. Turn north here for Phayao.
66	Large petrol station with restaurant - good food.
67	Junction. Kilometre posts now show reducing numbers.
60	South turn 18 kilometres to **Tarnsawan waterfall** ✓. Very remote location, poor road.
35	**Wat Phra That Doi Yuak** ✓✓ In the small village of Muang, a perfectly lovely temple with chunky country *wiharn* with engraved eaves, gilded *chedi* and tall palm trees.
0	Junction with Rte 1021. Turn north here to Chiang Kham, south to Phayao.
25-0	Fast straight road through some of the most fertile rice paddies in Thailand.
29	**Wat Phra That Johm Krai** ✓✓. A large and splendid temple on a hill towering over the surrounding farmland paddies of the valley.
0	Junction with Rte 1, 4 kilometres to east of Phayao. Follow signs to Phayao - a town on the shores of a large lake with several good hotels and interesting temples. (Phayao details page 262)

PHAYAO - CHIANG MAI (115 kilometres - 2 hours) Map page 241

Drive south of Phayao on Rte 1, signposted Lampang.

727	West turn Rte 120, signposted Chiang Mai. This is an exceptionally pretty new road (not marked yet on most maps) which passes over high mountains to connect up with Rte 1019 at Mae Kha Jahn.

NB KILOMETRE POSTS NOW FROM THIS JUNCTION

20	Scenic high altitude lay-by with excellent views of undisturbed forest. Snacks and drinks for sale in the car park. No deforestation or hill tribe settlement in this area.
26	Dramatic limestone cliffs on either side of the road.
0	**Wang Nua Town**. Junction with Rte 1035 which continues south to Lampang, north west to link with Chiang Mai - Chiang Rai road. Kilometre post 105 on Rte 1035.
110	Limestone outcrops on high hills to west of road topped with yucca palms.
118	Junction with Rte 107 at Mae Kha Jahn. Turn south here to Chiang Mai or north to Chiang Rai. For details on these routes see page 131.

EAST TOWNS

LAMPANG

The second largest city in Northern Thailand, Lampang is noted for ceramics, brightly coloured horse drawn carts, a plethora of temples in different styles and a long history, much of it somewhat independent of the rest of Thailand.

HISTORY

Originally, in the 8th century, Lampang was the second city of the Mon empire of Haripunchai. This Indian influenced culture stretched across Burma, Thailand and Cambodia at one time, but Haripunchai was its northernmost kingdom, with Lamphun as its capital. Lampang was called Kelang Nakorn - a name seen in many places in the town.

Following abrasive wars with the Lanna empire of King Mengrai to the north in the 13th century, Lampang eventually succumbed, but held out several years longer than Lamphun. From then on it shared the fortunes of Lanna, including 300 years as a vassal state of the mighty Burmese empire. Lampang is proud of its leader in the 17th century, Tip Chang, who forced the Burmese from the city. For these reasons, Lampang has always had slight differences from the rest of Lanna Thailand. House and temple design still show the independent origins of Lampang, and although the Mon people as an ethnically distinct group have long been submerged in the mainstream of the Thai race, traces still remain.

At the end of the 19th century, Lampang became a very important teak logging centre, largely controlled by the British, who imported large numbers of Burmese artisans, adding to a Burmese community which had existed here since the 18th century.

GEOGRAPHY

Lampang is situated in the valley of the Wang river, which rises south of Chiang Rai and flows into the Ping river 200 kilometres to the south west. A high

Lampang

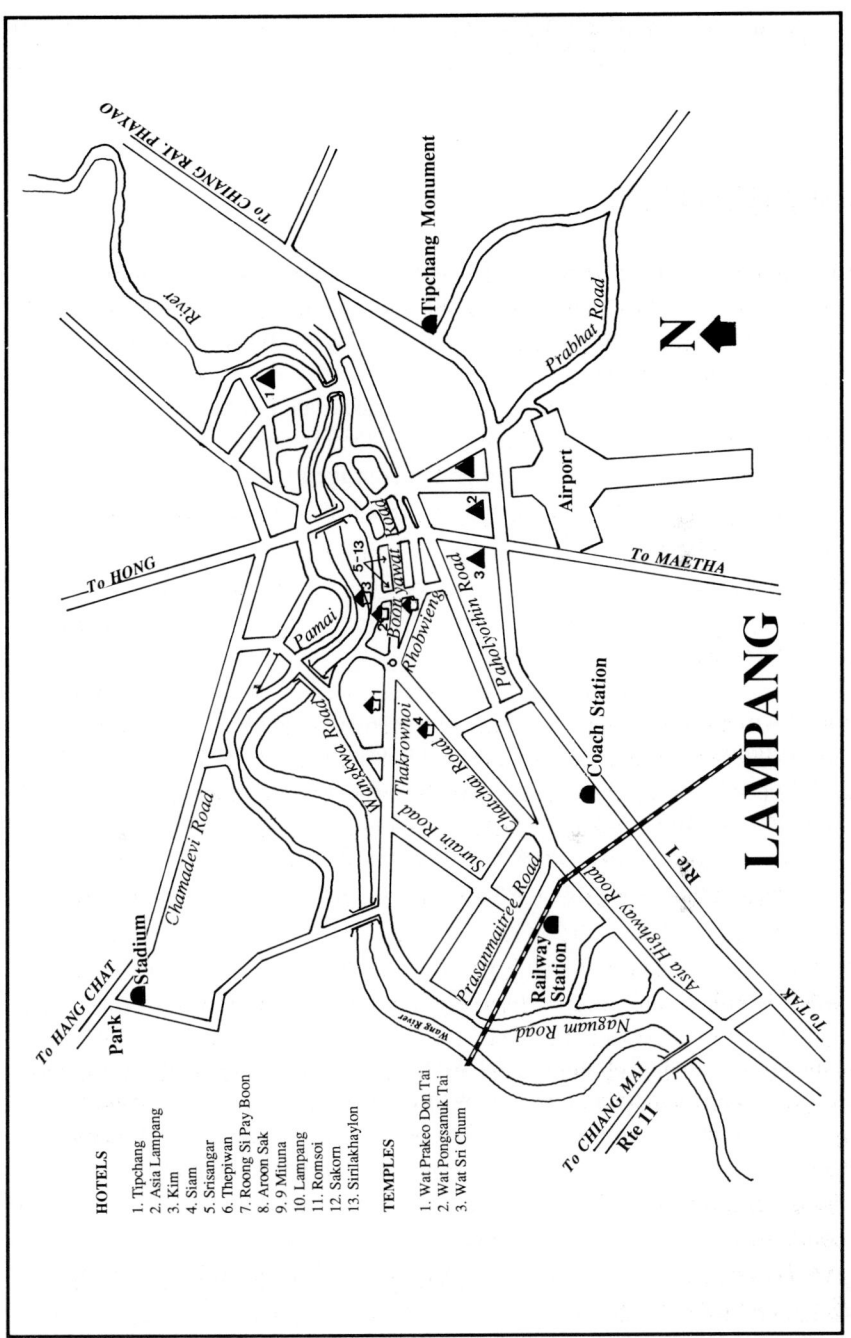

mountain range, of which Doi Khun Tan is a member, separates Lampang from Chiang Mai and the west. The city is similarly isolated by high hills from the east and north.

AGRICULTURE

The valley is fertile, growing, in addition to the usual rice, fruits such as lychee, longon, mango, papaya and breadfruit. Tobacco fields with their large green cabbage like leaves are seen throughout the area, and on slightly higher ground cotton is a productive crop.

The forests, once extensive, have been decimated in the last twenty years, and with the banning of teak logging, once the raison d'etre for the city, reafforestation is actively researched and encouraged in the area. The climate is similar to that of Chiang Mai, but with slightly warmer cool seasons and a marginally lower rainfall.

INDUSTRY

Lampang is a major market centre for the densely populated lowlands around it. The production of good quality wooden furniture still continues, and the local cotton production has led to a clothes manufacturing business. Local clay has similarly created a large ceramics industry. Traditional Lampang styles and colours - blue and white - are seen throughout Thailand. There are several kilns in town, and numerous stalls, where the attractive pieces are very inexpensive.

LAY OUT

Lampang is situated straddling the Wang river, which flows roughly north-east to south-west. The river is crossed by three bridges. The main centre has moved over the centuries from north to south of the river. At the heart of the city is a huge clock tower on a roundabout, from which roads fan out in all directions. To the south is a small public path with a giant aviary and a small sad zoo containing depressed looking poorly housed animals. The main shopping area and day market is at the west end of Boonyawat Road. Carry on down here for the municipal offices.

TRANSPORT

PLANE
The airport is one kilometre south of the city, reached via Paholyothin Road. There are links with Bangkok and Phitsanulok.
    Bangkok - Lampang: 09.05 (daily except Friday and Sunday)
                                  12.40 (Friday and Sunday)
    Lampang - Bangkok: 10.00 (Daily except Friday and Sunday)
                                  15.05 (Friday and Sunday)
    Phitsanulok - Lampang: 08.30 (daily except Friday and Sunday)
    Lampang - Phitsanulok: 10.00 (Friday and Sunday)

TRAIN
The train station is 1.5 kilometres west of the town centre, but *samlors* and pick ups wait the arrival of every train. Trains leave for Bangkok at 08.54, 17.50, 19.29, 21.37 and 23.01. Trains leave for Chiang Mai at 03.00, 05.10, 06.01, 09.40 and 17.08. Lampang - Bangkok is a 10-12 hour journey, Lampang - Chiang Mai is about 2 hours.

BUSES
The main coach station is on the Asia Highway 1.5 kilometres south west of town. Air con buses go to Chiang Mai, Nan, Phayao, Chiang Rai, Uttaradit and Phrae.

LOCAL TRANSPORT

HORSE DRAWN CARRIAGE
These brightly coloured, exotically decorated carriages pulled by manicured horses are about 100 years old. They were introduced for the benefit of the teak merchants, and most still belong to the families who originally built them. Today's driver will probably be the grandson of the original builder. They seat four, and a trot around town of 30 minutes costs about 50 *baht* - an idyllic if comparatively expensive way to see the sights.

SAMLOR
The bicycle rickshaw is the main means of transport. The standard fare is 5 to 10 *baht*. There are no *tuk-tuks* in Lampang, and few taxis, so choice is limited.

SONGTHAEW

Pick ups travel around town (5 *baht*) or can be caught outside the train station or south of Boonyawat Road to most destinations within 30 kilometres.

SHOPPING

The day market is at the western end of Boonyawat Road. This is also where most of the bigger shops are. The night market, which has a wide variety of goods of all descriptions on sale is behind the Siam Hotel between Chatchai and Thakrownai Road.

ENTERTAINMENT

For its size, Lampang has a disproportionately high number of sleazy night clubs and sleazier massage parlours, both patrolled by overdressed young ladies of dubious intent. The main night club area is close to the night market, between Chatchai and Thakrownai Road. All the bigger hotels have singers in their "coffee bars", and west of Thakrownai Road are several garden restaurants surrounded by fairy lights, where the food is less important than the alcohol and attractiveness of the singers.

The **Riverside** bar, Tipchang Road: a large teak building with seats and stairs at several levels over the river, is a very relaxed and pleasant place for a drink, popular with tourists and locals.

RESTAURANTS

There are many good restaurants in Lampang. The best Thai food, in atmospheric restaurants, can be had at the **Sri Wang** on Thakrownia Road and the **Wiang Lakon** on Paholyothin Road. Sukiyaki is popular in Lampang. The best is the **Poppy** restaurant opposite the Siam Hotel on Chatchai Road - a spotlessly clean restaurant giving excellent value. East of the Asia Lampang Hotel on Boonyawat Road are a number of small, open restaurants serving very tasty Thai noodles and other basic dishes. The Asia Lampang and Tipchang Hotel restaurants serve western food.

TEMPLES

Lampang has many temples - almost every *soi* is likely to hold some colourful *wat*. Its long history and cosmopolitan past has resulted in a range of styles, and

the richness of the citizens in the past has produced the finances to commission the finest artists, the most beautiful icons and most splendid decorations.
Wat Prakeo Don Tai ✓✓ Is the most important and interesting temple in the city. It is said to have been built by the founder of the city, although nothing from the 8th century survives. Its medieval importance can be judged by the fact that in the 15th century it housed both the famous Emerald Buddha, now in the Grand Palace in Bangkok, the most revered Buddha image in Thailand, and a similar image, also made in jasper, called the Prakeo Don Tao, now in Wat Phra That Lampang Luang. This is said to have been found inside a water melon by a lady called Suchada, who then had an affair with a monk and was put to death, bringing ruin on the town.

The *chedi* is 50 metres high, the only original structure left. The *wiharn* and the hall of the reclining Buddha were built in the 1930s by the venerated monk Srivijaya. Next to the *chedi* is a very beautiful *mondop*, with a roof in nine tiers of exquisitely carved teak, built by Burmese woodcarvers and presented by a Thai prince in 1909. The Buddha image within is a Mandalay style bronze.

Wat Pongsanuk Tai ✓✓ The loveliest temple in Lampang, built in the late 18th century in pure Lanna style. The shady new monastery surrounds the old one, entered by four flights of stairs. The Lanna *chedi* is encased in copper, and next to it is a *mondop* containing a cage with four Buddha images around a *bothi* tree.

Wat Sri Chum ✓✓ This is the most beautiful of the three Burmese temples in Lampang. It was built at the turn of the century by devout carpenters as a place for them to worship. The large building is made entirely of teak, with the usual Burmese style tapering tiers of dripping teak filigree reaching to the topmost point. Inside, up a flight of stairs with a red lacquered roof, is the main devotional area, with heavily lacquered inlaid walls depicting life in Lampang 100 years ago. In one corner, behind glass, is a silver, Burmese style modern Buddha lit by green neon lights, Strange. The abbot speaks good English, and is most happy to answer questions.

AROUND LAMPANG

Wat Phra That Lampang Luang ✓✓✓ 18 kilometres south west of the city, signposted off Rte 1. The most interesting temple in Northern Thailand. In the 8th century a Haripunchai fort enclosed by three earthwork fortifications, it has since that time been a place of pilgrimage and beauty. The temple complex is in a large village. The main buildings were built in 1496 AD, and are within a walled square, the walls roofed and four metres high. There are two entrances, the main one approached by a large *naga* staircase leading to a heavily (and very beautifully) ornamented main gate. Behind this is an ancient and lovely *wiharn*, with a three tiered roof sweeping gracefully almost to ground level. The walls are decorated with paintings of local noblemen dating from the late 18th century. To the left of the *wiharn* is a smaller one, exquisitely decorated with mosaics and inlaid lacquerwork. To the right of the main *wiharn* are two smaller ones. One of these - **Wiharn Nam Tan**, is believed to be the oldest surviving wooden building in Thailand, with 16th century murals just visible on panels below the roof. The *chedi* is tucked close behind the main *wiharn*. It is 45 metres high, and is believed to contain a lock of Buddha's hair. There are three *bodhi* trees in the compound, believed locally to be the abode of animist spirits who, for example, can cure mental disease. The building containing the **Prakeo Don Tai** is outside the main compound. This jasper Buddha, equal in beauty to the Emerald Buddha, has been much coveted over the centuries by princes, and the cause of more than one battle.

PLACES TO STAY

HOTELS

Tipchang ✪✪✪✪
Standard international class luxury hotel, lacking character but extremely comfortable.
Address: 54/22 Tarkrao Road, Lampang **Tel:** (054)226501
Price:780-1100 **Rooms:**130 **A/C:**130 **Bathroom:**1309hw) **Comfort:**★★★★★ **Design:**★★★★
Location:★★★ **Position:**central **Quietness:**★★★ **Restaurant:**★★★★
Facilities:TV, video, bar, coffee shop.

Asia Lampang ✪✪✪✪
Very well furnished and equipped rooms in a luxury hotel of some character.
Address: 229 Boonyawat Road, Lampang **Tel:** (054)217844
Price:330-400 **Rooms:**72 **A/C:**72 **Bathroom:**72(hw) **Comfort:**★★★★★ to ★★★★★
Design:★★★★ **Location:**★★★ **Position:**central **Quietness:**★★★ **Restaurant:**★★★★
Facilities:fridge, minibar, coffee shop **Tours/treks:** local tours

Kim ✪✪✪
Comfortable modern hotel, but lacking atmosphere.
Address: 168 Boonyawat Road, Lampang **Tel:** (054)217721
Price:260 **Rooms:**45 **A/C:**45 **Bathroom:**45(hw) **Comfort:**★★★★ **Design:**★★★
Location:★★★ **Position:**central **Quietness:**★★

Siam ✿✿✿
Friendly, wclean and comfortable rooms in modern Thai hotel. Well organized, pleasant service.
Address: 260/26029 Chatchai Road, Lampang **Tel:**(054)217277
Price:129-223 **Rooms:**50 **A/C:**28 **Fan:**22 **Bathroom:**50(28hw) **Comfort:**☆☆ to ☆☆☆☆
Design:☆☆☆ **Location:**☆☆ **Position:**central **Quietness:**☆☆ **Restaurant:**☆☆
Facilities:cocktail lounge, cabaret.

Srisangar ✿✿
Simply furnished but reasonably clean, good sized rooms at very low prices.
Address: 213-215/1-5 Boonyawat Road, Lampang **Tel:** (054)217070,217811
Price:60-100 **Rooms:**34 **Fan:**34 **Bathroom:**34(cw) **Comfort:**☆☆ to ☆☆☆
Design:☆ **Location:**☆☆ **Position:**central **Quietness:**☆

Thepiwan ✿✿
Large, fairly clean rooms at a low price on a busy main street.
Address: Charoenmuang, Lampang **Tel:** (054)511003
Price:70-120 **Rooms:**52 **Fan:**52 **Bathroom:**52(cw) **Comfort:**☆☆☆ **Design:**☆☆ **Location:**☆
Position:central **Quietness:**☆ **Restaurant:**☆☆☆

Roong Si Pay Boon ✿✿
Spartan, but clean and adequate rooms in newish Thai hotel.
Address: 88 Yangtarakitgorson Road, Lampang **Tel:** (054)511011
Price:120-180 **Rooms:**64 **A/C:**5 **Fan:**59 **Bathroom:**64(cw) **Comfort:**☆☆ to ☆☆☆ **Design:**☆☆
Location:☆☆☆ **Position:**central **Quietness:**☆☆

Aroon Sak ✿✿
Fairly clean and well looked after Thai hotel. Cheap but unattractive rooms.
Address:90/9 Boonyawat Road, Lampang **Tel:** (054)217344, 217532
Price:80-200 **Rooms:**50 **A/C:**7 **Bathroom:**50(cw) **Comfort:**☆ to ☆☆☆ **Design:**☆☆
Location:☆☆ **Position:**central **Quietness:**☆☆☆

9 Mituna ✿✿
Adequate rooms around a courtyard in a fairly modern but rather neglected hotel.
Address: 285 Bunyawat Road, Lampang **Tel:** (054)222261
Price:120-260 **Rooms:**48 **A/C:**7 **Fan:**41 **Bathroom:**48(7hw) **Comfort:**☆☆to ☆☆☆ **Design:**☆☆
Location:☆☆ **Position:**central **Quietness:**☆ **Restaurant:**☆☆

Lampang ✿✿
Basic accommodation in a faceless concrete hotel.
Address:696 Suan Dok, Lampang **Tel:** (054)227311-2 **Fax:**227313
Price:100-280 **Rooms:**52 **A/C:**9 **Fan:**43 **Bathroom:**52(9hw) **Comfort:**☆☆to ☆☆☆
Design:☆☆ **Location:**☆☆ **Position:**central **Quietness:**☆☆

Romsoi ✿✿
Ageing rather ugly hotel with sparsely furnished rooms.
Address: 142 Boonyawat Road, **Tel:** (054)217054
Price:80-200 **Rooms:**40 **A/C:**2 **Fan:**38 **Bathroom:**40(cw) **Comfort:**☆☆to☆☆☆ **Design:**☆☆
Location:☆☆ **Position:**central **Quietness:**☆☆

Sakorn ⬤
Spartan rooms in a prison like characterless compound.
Address:139/11 Paholyothin Road, Lampang **Tel:** (054)217573
Price:100-240 **Rooms:**60 **A/C:**10 **Fan:**50 **Bathroom:**60(10hw) **Comfort:**☆☆ to ☆☆☆
Design:☆ **Location:**☆☆ **Position:** 1 kilometre south west of town **Quietness:**☆☆
Restaurant:☆☆ **Facilities:**cocktail lounge

Sirilakhaylon ⬤
Basic, austere hotel.
Address:240-242 Passatmaida Road, Lampang **Tel:** (054)217197
Price:50-60 **Rooms:**30 **Fan:**30 **Bathroom:**25(cw) **Comfort:**☆☆ **Design:**☆ **Location:**☆
Position:central **Quietness:**☆

PHRAE

A relaxed and pleasant city with good food and some excellent hotels, Phrae has nothing of any great note - no exquisite temples or dramatic landmarks. It is merely a nice place to be.

The town is situated on the east bank of the Yom river. Its transport links with cities further north were difficult before the recent road building programme, separated from Lampang and Nan by high mountain passes, so culturally it is closer to the cities of north central Thailand - Sukhothai, Uttaradit and Phitsanulok.

It is a prosperous city. Apart from the fertile valley producing rice, cotton, pineapples, tobacco and fruit, the area has several open cast coal mines and, until recently, profitable teak forests.

Phrae is most famous within Thailand for the production of the heavy duty blue denim shirts and baggy trousers which are the traditional dress of the working Thai. Most are produced in the village of **Thung Hong** just north of the centre (see page 244). Wood carving, rattan furniture making and steel production are other local, mainly cottage industries.

The city is built around the old fortifications which enclose the original town. The walls have gone, marked only by flower gardens, except for the area near Pratu Mai, where a portion of the old moat and walls can still be seen. The main shopping area is at the western end of Charoenmuang and Rasdamnern Roads. Along the *soi* linking these two roads are a number of food stalls and restaurants serving an interesting range of local food not seen elsewhere (taste it and you will know why!)

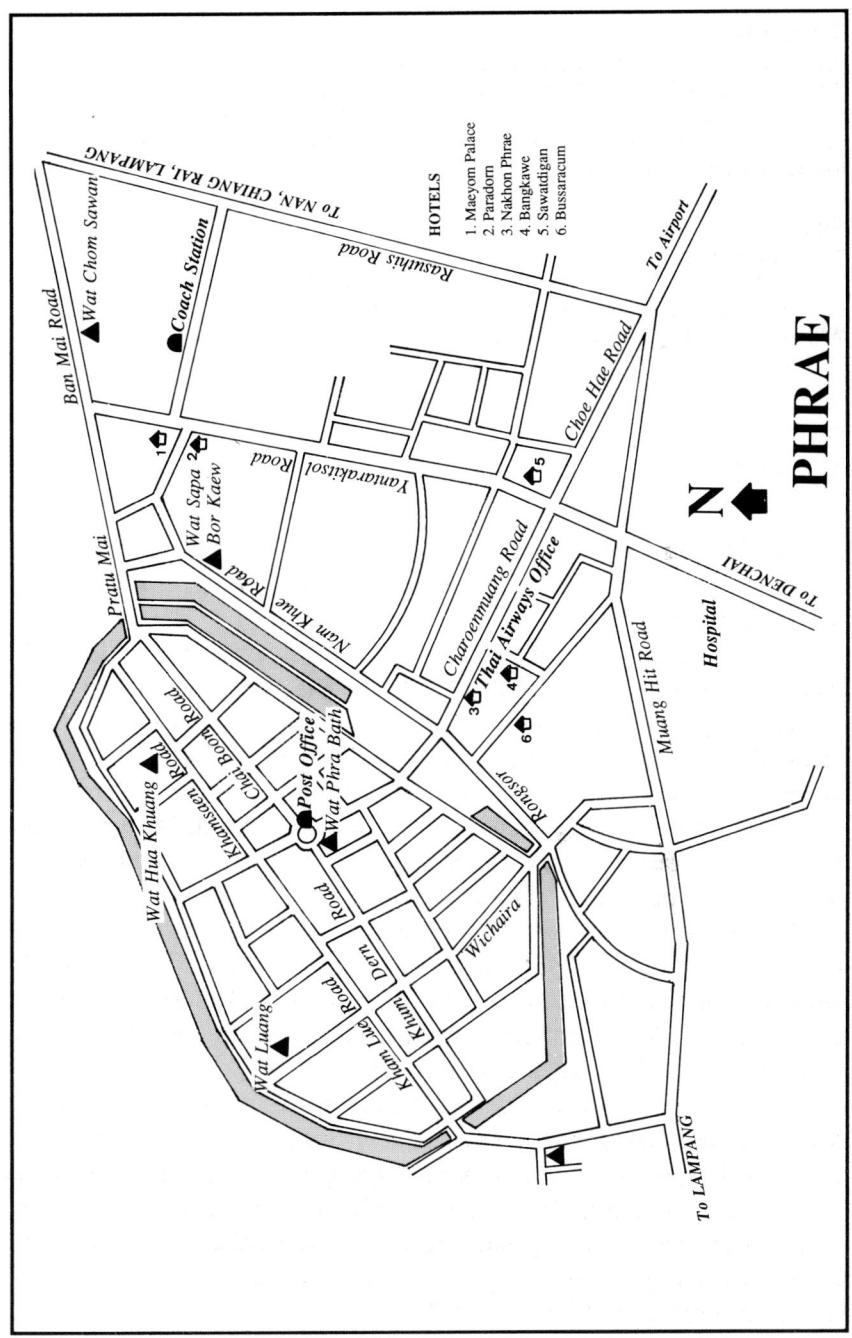

NIGHTLIFE

The Maeyom Palace is much the classiest place in town for an evening's entertainment, with a near perfect restaurant and nightly cabaret. Next door, the Paradorn Hotel also has a pleasant nightclub. Between the two is a busy but rather tasteless bar.

TRANSPORT

Phrae is only 23 kilometres north east from the railway station at Denchai, with which frequent pick-ups connect.

The bus station is behind the municipal stadium between Yantarakiti and Rasuthis Roads. There are frequent air con buses to Chiang Mai, Nan, Lampang, Sukhothai, and Uttaradit.

PLANE
The airport has connections with Bangkok and Nan

Bangkok-Phrae:	07.20 (daily)
Phrae-Bangkok:	10.50 (daily)
Nan-Phrae:	10.00 (daily)
Phrae-Nan:	09.00 (daily)

TEMPLES

There are Burmese and Laotian influences visible in the temples of Phrae. Best of the Burmese style is **Wat Chom Sawan** ✓, with a large, ornate teak *wiharn* and a small collection of caged animals behind. Within the old citadel, **Wat Phra Bath** ✓ shows Laotian influences.

PLACES TO STAY

HOTELS

Maeyom Palace ✪✪✪✪✪
Luxurious accommodation in a lovely new hotel at low prices for standard of service. Unbeatable value for money.
Address: Yankrakijsol Road, Phrae **Tel:** (054)522906
Price: 480-700 **Rooms:** 104 **A/C:** 104 **Bathroom:** 104(hw) **Comfort:** ☆☆☆☆☆ **Design:** ☆☆☆☆
Location: ☆☆☆ **Position:** central **Quietness:** ☆☆☆☆☆ **Restaurant:** ☆☆☆☆☆
Facilities: pool, coffee shop, fridge, video, cabaret.

Paradorn ✿✿✿✿
Well furnished, comfortable rooms in a big, modern, hotel.
Address:177 Yankrakijsol Road, Phrae **Tel:** (054)413112
Price:140-250 **Rooms:**55 **A/C:**21 **Fan:**34 **Bathroom:**55(21hw) **Comfort:**☆☆☆☆ **Design:**☆☆☆
Location:☆☆☆ **Position:**central **Quietness:**☆☆☆ **Restaurant:**☆☆☆ **Facilities:**night club

Nakhon Phrae ✿✿✿
Large, comfortable, modern and friendly hotel.
Address: 29 Rasdamnern ROad, Phrae **Tel:** (054)511122,511024
Price:350-500 **Rooms:**260 **A/C:**110 **Fan:**150 **Bathroom:**260(hw) **Comfort:**☆☆☆ to ☆☆☆☆
Design:☆☆☆ **Location:**☆☆☆ **Position:**central **Quietness:**☆☆☆ **Restaurant:**☆☆☆☆
Facilities:coffee shop **Tours/treks:** local

Bankawe ✿✿
Luridly coloured spartan hotel in quiet *soi*.
Address: Charoenmuang Soi 1, Phrae **Tel:** (054)511372
Price:90-150 **Rooms:**30 **A/C:**6 **Fan:**24 **Bathroom:**30(cw) **Comfort:**☆ **Design:**☆☆
Location:☆☆☆ **Position:**central **Quietness:**☆☆☆☆

Sawatdigan ✿✿
Very basic hotel.
Address:76 Kantarakitkosol, Phrae **Tel:** (054)511032
Price:70-130 **Rooms:**25 **Fan:**25 **Bathroom:**25(cw) **Comfort:**☆ **Design:**☆ **Location:**☆
Position:central **Quietness:**☆☆

Bussaracum ✿✿
Reasonably clean and adequate accommodation.
Address: Lathamloen, Phrae **Tel:** (054)511437
Price:100-180 **Rooms:**24 **A/C:**3 **Fan:**21 **Bathroom:**24(cw) **Comfort:**☆☆ **Design:**☆☆
Location:☆☆☆ **Position:**central **Quietness:**☆☆☆

GUEST HOUSES

Number 4 ✿✿✿
Simple but pleasant accommodation.
Address:22 Soi 1 Yantarakitkosane, Phrae
Price:70-100(dorm 50) **Rooms:**5 **Fan:**5 **Bathroom:**0(hw outside) **Comfort:**☆☆ **Design:**☆☆☆☆
Location:☆☆☆ **Position:**central **Quietness:**☆☆☆

NAN

Until recently officially declared a "remote province", Nan has only in the last few years become completely integrated with the rest of Thailand. In the last five years good new roads have at last been built to link with the rest of the country. Before that, the area was a hotbed of revolution and guerrilla activity - much of it fomented by the nearby communist state of Laos.

HISTORY

Nan was a semi independent principality until the beginning of this century. The city was founded in the late 14th century as a vassal of the emergent Sukhothai Kingdom. It then fell under the control of the Chiang Mai based Lanna Kingdom, and was colonised by the Burmese in the late 16th century until they were expelled in 1786. From then Nan nominally owed allegiance to Bangkok, although the geographic isolation of the area made this fairly meaningless.

GEOGRAPHY

Nan is at the northern edge of a small upland valley which widens out for a few kilometres to provide fertile rice growing land. High mountains with altitudes of more than 1500 metres encircle Nan in all directions. To the east and north, the hills rise up to the Laos border fifty kilometres away. To the west, around the mountain of Doi Luang, live the primitive and little known **Phi Tong Luang** or Mlabri people. South, the fertile valley ends near the small town of Sa. The province is very sparsely inhabited. A large proportion of the population is hill tribe. There are many Hmong and Yao villages in the hills, but restricted to the Nan area are Kha-mu and H'tin villages. Nan province is a particularly interesting area for exploration, but is not suitable for independent travelling without a guide.

LAY OUT

The town is built on the west bank of the Nan river. The centre is architecturally unattractive, most teak buildings having been replaced by tatty modern concrete constructions. The exception is the area of temples between Suriyapong and Mahaprom Roads, around which there are many old teak houses and well kept gardens.

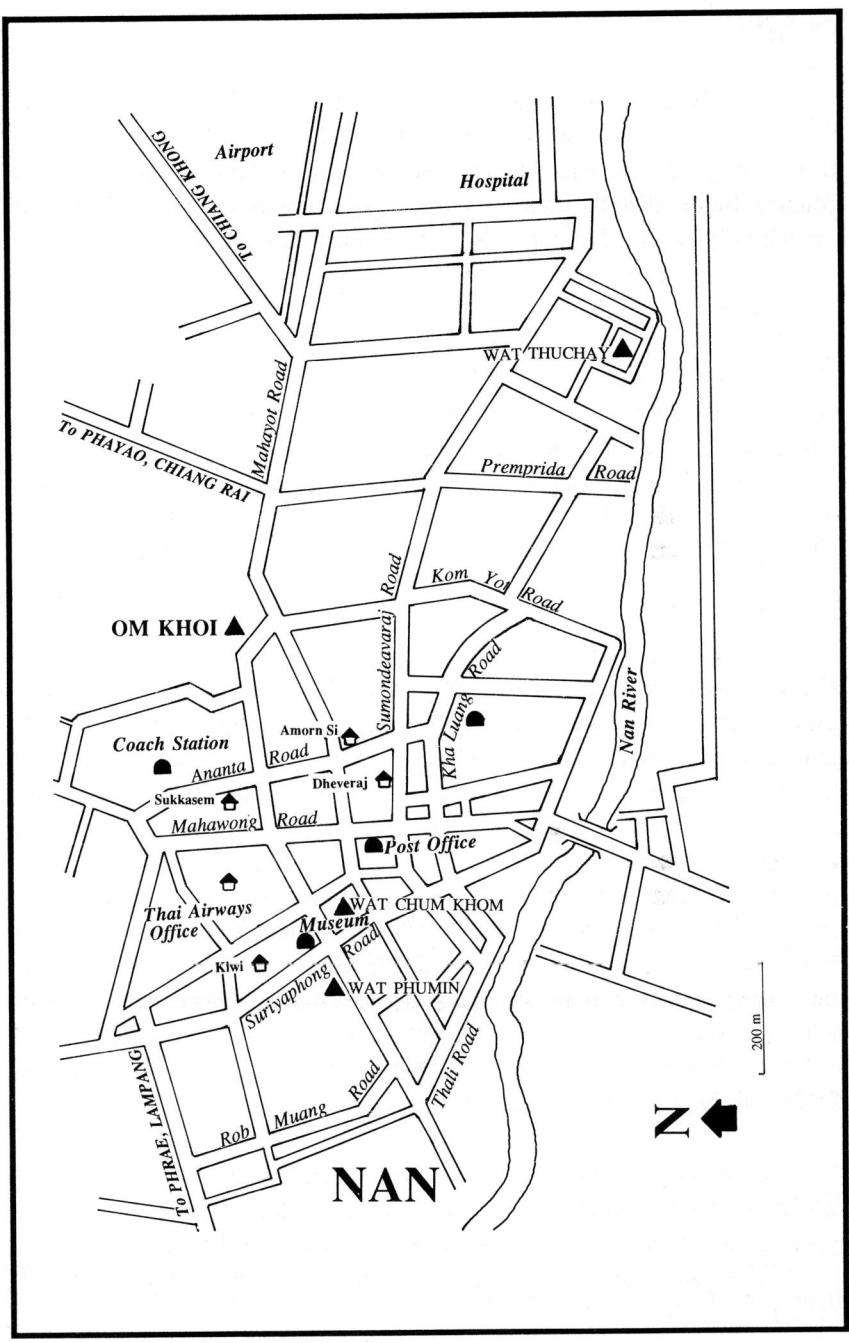

TRANSPORT

There are daily air con buses (5-6 hours) between Nan and Chiang Mai via Phrae or Phayao. The city also has connections with Chiang Rai (4 hours).

FLIGHTS
There are flights to Bangkok, Chiang Mai, Phitsanulok and Phrae.

Nan-Bangkok:	10.00 (daily)
Bangkok-Nan:	07.20 (daily)
Nan-Chiang Mai:	12.00 (Wednesday, Friday, Sunday)
Chiang Mai-Nan:	15.35 (Wednesday, Friday, Sunday)
Nan-Phitsanulok:	16.40 (Wednesday, Friday, Sunday)
Phitsanulok-Nan:	11.40 (Wednesday, Friday, Sunday)
Nan-Phrae:	10.00 (daily)
Phrae-Nan:	09.00 (daily)

TRAVEL AGENT

FHU Travel service. Nan is at present developing its tourist potential, and this is an excellent, well organized travel agency with good local knowledge and experience. Tours are available from half day to one week to the Laos border country and to view the Phi Tong Luang.

RESTAURANTS

The best Thai food is to be had at the **Suriya Garden** at the north end of Sumondeavaras Road - live music too. The **Dheveraj Hotel** has a good air conditioned restaurant with acceptable western dishes as well as better Thai food. The **Tip-top** restaurant has an Italian chef who serves good pasta and pizzas, and a good range of Thai food. On the corner of Komyot and Khaluang Road is an excellent cheap Thai restaurant.

ENTERTAINMENT

Nan is not a good city for night life. There are one or two insalubrious "coffee shops", but the Dheveraj Hotel has an interesting disco and night club.

LOCAL EVENTS

Nan is famous for its boat races, held every October-November, when each village in the region enters a large Naga prowed boat with 50 oarsmen per vessel. Everyone gets wildly excited. Great fun.

TEMPLES

Nan has some extremely beautiful temples and art, much influenced by nearby Laos.
Wat Phumin ✓✓✓ 100 metres south of Suriyaphong Road opposite the museum and Wat Cham Khang. This exquisite small temple has recently been completely restored, and of all the temple sights in the north, this is possibly the most interesting. The white coloured temple, built in 1596 AD, is cross shaped, with steps leading to the open interior. In the centre is a structure of four large bronze Buddhas facing the cardinal points of the compass. What is so exceptional are the exquisite murals completely covering the inner walls. In lovely pastel colours and in great detail, are delicate but primitive paintings on a number of themes, including daily Thai life, the arrival of westerners, a vision of heaven and hell and stories from the life of Buddha. What makes them so special, apart from their beautiful simplicity, are the wry observations of human relations - couples flirting, people casually lolling about, reading books etc. They were made probably about 100 years ago by local peasant artists, whose identity is sadly unknown.
Wat Cham Khang ✓✓ A graceful *wiharn* with tall roof and pleasingly decorated walls. Behind it is an unusual *chedi*, built in 1406 AD and resembling closely one at Si Satchanalai. It is tiered, and on the second tier there are tusked elephant statues on the corners. To the right of the *wiharn* and *chedi*, in the monks building, is a three metre high walking Buddha in solid gold.
National Museum ✓✓ An interesting but quite small collection of local area objects, including a 300 year old one metre black elephant tusk. There are good displays, in English and Thai, giving accounts of Nan's history, art and culture.
Wat Suan Tan ✓✓ Little remains of the original wiharn, but it houses a lovely Sukhothai style bronze Buddha four metres high. An eye catching landmark is the temple's white *prang*, like an elongated pineapple forty metres high, more typical of central Thailand than the north.

PLACES TO STAY

HOTELS

Dheveraj ✿✿✿✿
International standard luxury hotel - fraying a little at the edges.
Address: 466 Sumon Dheveraj Road, Nan **Tel:** (054)7100212
Price: 600-1000 **Rooms:** 154 **A/C:** 120 **Fan:** 34 **Bathroom:** 154(hw) **Comfort:** ☆☆☆
Design: ☆☆☆☆ **Location:** ☆☆ **Position:** central **Quietness:** ☆☆ **Restaurant:** ☆☆☆
Facilities: night club, disco **Tours/treks:** local, including Phi Tong Luang

Amorn Si ✿✿
Basic accommodation but clean and well run.
Address: 97 Mahajut Road, Nan **Tel:** (054)710510
Price: 80-150 **Rooms:** 22 **Fan:** 22 **Bathroom:** 22(cw) **Comfort:** ☆☆ **Design:** ☆☆ **Location:** ☆☆
Position: central **Quietness:** ☆☆

Sukkasem ✿✿
Average but adequate concrete hotel.
Address: 29/31 Ananworaritded Road, Nan
Price: 120-220 **Rooms:** 28 **Fan:** 28 **Bathroom:** 28(8hw) **Comfort:** ☆☆ **Design:** ☆☆ **Location:** ☆☆
Position: central **Quietness:** ☆☆

GUEST HOUSES

Kiwi ✿✿✿
New Zealand management. Simple accommodation in a pretty teak house. Great atmosphere, knowledgeable staff.
Address: 32 Mahawong Road, Nan.
Price: 60-80 **Rooms:** 5 **Fan:** 5 **Bathroom:** 0(cw outside) **Comfort:** ☆ **Design:** ☆☆☆☆
Location: ☆☆☆ **Position:** central **Quietness:** ☆☆☆ **Tours/treks:** interesting local treks.

Nan ✿✿
Old teak house in quiet corner of Nan near temples. clean and pleasant but spartan rooms.
Address: 57/16 Mahaphom, Nan **Tel:** (054)771148
Price: 70-100 **Rooms:** 10 **Fan:** 10 **Bathroom:** 09cw outside) **Comfort:** ☆ to ☆☆ **Design:** ☆☆☆
Location: ☆☆☆☆ **Position:** central **Quietness:** ☆☆☆☆

PHAYAO

A pleasant city with great, but as yet largely unexploited, tourist potential, and several good value hotels.

GEOGRAPHY

Phayao is situated on the south east bank of a large lake - Kwan Phayao, six kilometres by three kilometres. To the west of the lake the mountain of Doi Bussaracum (1856 metres) broods. The city is at the southern end of a large and exceedingly fertile valley, which produces more rice per year than anywhere else in Thailand. Phayao is separated from Chiang Mai and the Ping valley by two ranges of mountains with altitudes of up to 2000 metres. A new and beautiful mountain road now links the two cities, via the small town and valley of **Wang Nua**.

HISTORY

Phayao was first inhabited in the bronze age. In the 12th century it was an independent city state. The kings of Lanna and Sukhothai, the main kingdoms, needed the agreement of little Phayao before the first independent Thai state could be formed in 1285AD. As a result of repeated Burmese incursions, the city was abandoned until 1840AD, when it was resettled from Lampang. The new city was enclosed within walls, which have since disappeared. Phayao this century was within Chiang Rai province until 1977, when it became a province in its own right. Geographically in a low basin, the city is exceptionally hot in March, April and May.

LAY OUT

The centre of Phayao is a rabbit warren of small streets on a promontory extending into the lake. Most municipal offices are a few hundred metres north of this area.

RESTAURANTS

Phayao has one outstanding restaurant, the **Bua**, a lovely teak building looking out over the lake and serving the best Thai food at low prices. Other than this,

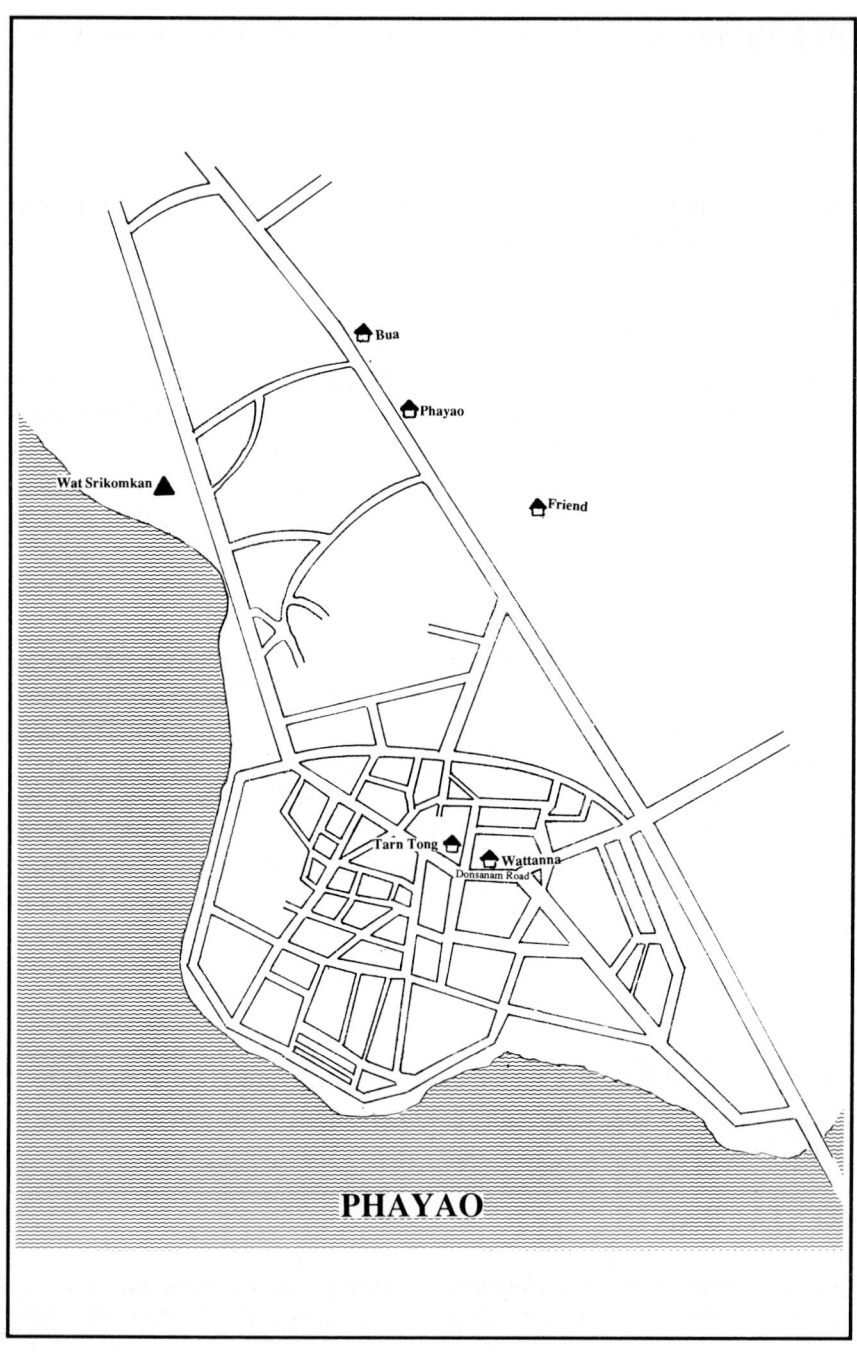

apart from the hotels, there are a number of stalls which serve good and very cheap basic Thai food.

ENTERTAINMENT

The **Wattanna** and **Than Tong** hotels have night clubs with live music, as does the **Phayao** on Paholyothin Road.

TEMPLES

Wat Srikomkan ✓✓✓ Two kilometres north of the town centre on the edge of the lake, this is a fascinating complex. The modern *wiharn* houses the largest Buddha image in the north of Thailand, covered in gold leaf and 16 metres high. Around the *wiharn*, in a covered walkway, are thirty-eight Buddha heads, from the 14th century AD onwards, in the local Phayao style. Just outside the temple walls to the south is a magnificent new *wiharn* built over the waters of the lake, looking like a more oriental Brighton pavilion. It has been decorated in Lanna style with murals by Thailand's leading artist. To the north of the temple is a small museum of religious objects from all over Phayao. Two hundred metres north of this is a weird collection of macabre sculptures depicting hell. The figures are all suffering the consequences of their actions on earth - the woman with her belly ripped out, was guilty of having an abortion. The figures caught on the tree covered in sharp spines with hungry wolves below and cobras in the branches above are guilty of adultery. The man with his tongue extending to the ground was a liar. There is a large pot containing boiling sinners, and various gods and demons to ensure that everything is running satisfactorily.

WHERE TO STAY

RESORTS

Bua ✪✪✪✪
Extremely comfortable and spacious houses with private garages in landscaped gardens.
Address: 262 Superhighway Thawangthong, Phayao **Tel**: (054)481596,481855
Price:600-800 **Rooms**:14 **A/C**:14 **Bathroom**:14(hw) **Comfort**:☆☆☆☆ **Design**:☆☆☆☆
Location:☆☆☆☆ **Position**:4 kilometres from town centre **Quietness**:☆☆☆ **Restaurant**:☆☆☆

Friend ✿✿✿
Pleasant cabins in small garden. Clean, quiet and comfortable.
Address: Superhighway, Phayao **Tel:** (054)431309, 481556
Price:300(100 dorm) **Rooms:**12 **Fan:**12 **Bathroom:**12(hw) **Comfort:**☆☆☆ **Design:**☆☆☆☆ **Location:**☆☆☆☆ **Position:**4 kilometres east of town **Quietness:**☆☆☆☆ **Restaurant:**☆☆☆

HOTELS

Phayao ✿✿✿✿
comfortable but rather characterless accommodation. More expensive rooms quite luxurious.
Address: 445 Paholyothin Road, Phayao **Tel:** (054)481970-3
Price:680-840 **Rooms:**75 **A/C:**75 **Bathroom:**75(hw) **Comfort:**☆☆☆☆ to ☆☆☆☆☆
Design:☆☆☆ **Location:**☆☆☆ **Position:**4 kilometres **Quietness:**☆☆☆

Wattanna ✿✿✿
Modern Thai hotel - clean, comfortable and good value.
Address: Dansanam Road, Phayao **Tel:** (054)431203
Price:80-200 **Rooms:**36 **A/C:**2 **Fan:**34 **Bathroom:**36(17hw) **Comfort:**☆☆to☆☆☆
Design:☆☆☆ **Location:**☆☆ **Position:**central **Quietness:**☆☆

Tarn Tong ✿✿
Clean and well organized hotel. Rooms in new wing very comfortable.
Address: 55/59 Donsanam Road, Phayao **Tel:** (054)431302,431342 **Fax:**481252
Price:150-320 **Rooms:**124 **A/C:**30 **Fan:**94 **Bathroom:**124(hw) **Comfort:**☆☆☆ to ☆☆☆☆
Design:☆☆☆ **Location:**☆☆☆ **Position:**central **Quietness:**☆☆
Facilities: "Boom Boom" night club.

Appendix One

Thai Wordlist

Word List

For those who wish to speak Thai correctly, a Thai phrase book is recommended. Included here is a list of a few useful words and short phrases. The system used is not phonetic, but is as simple to use as possible, and should produce results which, without being perfect Thai, will be generally understood. In the list below, Thai words are given as a combination of English words, and should be pronounced as those English words. Where Thai words or syllables are found only within English words, that English word is given in brackets next to the Thai word, with the relevant part underlined. For example, the Thai word for fish is "pla". The word in brackets following "pla" is the English word (plaque), with the section of the word that corresponds to the Thai word underlined.

All words in brackets, then, are English words.

Hyphens indicate that syllables so linked should be spoken as one word. It is important to speak Thai without gaps between words - try to make sentences flow. Remember to clip the ends of words which end in consonants, and extend those ending in vowels. The correct tone is not indicated in this list - it is very difficult to pronounce correctly, overcomplicates communication for the novice, and for single words or short phrases is not usually esssential for comprehension.

Unless otherwise indicated by the above method, vowel sounds are pronounced thus:

A	as in *apple*
E	as in *end*
I	as in *it*
U	as in *up*
EE	as in *deep*
OO	as in *moon*
AA	as in *army*
OU	as in *ought*

POLITE EXPRESSSIONS

It is polite in Thai to finish any statement with the use of the word "crap" if the speaker is a male, "car" if a female. "Crap" and "car" can also mean "yes" or "I understand" to interrogative questions.
Similarly, "I" or "my" vary with the sex of the speaker - "deechan" is feminine, "Pom" is masculine.

Hello	Sa(sad)-what dee crap/car.
How are you?	Sa(sad)-by dee my.
I'm fine thanks	Sa(sad)-by dee crap/car.
Please	Crap/car.
Thank you	Crap coon crap/car.
Never mind	My pen lie.

ESSENTIALS

Yes	Chai (chime)
No	My chai(chime)

NB. There are several ways of saying YES or NO - the above are the commonest.

Can you speak English?	Poot paas-at Ang-rit die my crap/car
I cannnot speak Thai	Poot Thai my die
What is your name?	Coon chew ari(arise) cap/car.
My name is	Pom/deechan chew ..... cap/car.
Do you have?	Me .... my crap/car.
Do you have a room?	Me hong my crap/car.
Like	Chorp
Do not like	My chorp
I want	Pom/deechan tong-an
I do not want	My ou(ounce) crap/car
Delicious	Alloy crap/car
When?	Myrrh-ari(arise)
Where?	Tea-nigh
How many?	Key
What is this?	Knee-ari(arise)

I understand	Cow-jai(gyrate) crap/car
I do not understand	My cow-jai(gyrate)
To go	By
Where are you going?	By-nigh(night) crap/car.
How much?	Tow(town)-lye crap/car
The bill, please	Check bin crap/car
Expensive	Peng(penguin)

NUMBERS

0	Sum	11	Sip et
1	Nung	12	Sip song
2	Song	13	Sip sam
3	Sam	14	Sip sea
4	Sea	20	Ea(each) sip
5	Har(hard)	30	Sam sip
6	Hock	100	Loy (loyal)
7	Jet	1000	Pan
8	Bet	10000	Moon
9	Cow	100000	Cen (central)
10	Sip	1000000	Lahn (lance)

TIME

Yesterday	Myrrh one-knee
Today	One-knee
Tomorrow	Proong-knee
Hour (o' clock)	Mong(mongrel)
Morning	Chow
Afternoon/evening	Yen

GETTING AROUND

Where is...?	....you tea-nigh
Station	Sat-annie
Taxi	Taxi
Bus	Rot me
Train	Rot fi(fight)
Airport	San-am bin
Police	Tam roo-at
Post office	Pay-sunny
Telephone	Too-ra-sap
Bank	Ban
Market	Tal(talc)-at
Village	Barn
Town	Chang
Street	Tan-on
Lane/side street	Soy
Mountain	Doy
Kilometre	Key-low

TOURING

Car	Rot
Jeep	Rot jeep
Motor bike	Moto-by
Petrol	Ben-seen
Diesel	Dee-sen
Oil	Nam manrot
Fill up	Tim
Litres	Leat
Petrol station	Pam-nam-man
Garage	Oo-sam-rot
Broken down	Rot sear

Word List

AT THE HOTEL

Hotel	Roo-ng(gnarl)-rem(remove)
Room	Hong
Do you have a room?	Me hong my crap/car.
Single room	Hong tea-ang(anger) dee-oh.
Twin room	Hong song tea-ang(anger).
Room with double bed	Hong tea-ang yai.
Bathroom	Hong-nam
Restaurant	Ran-a-han
Hot water	Nam lawn
Cold water	Nam yen

AT THE RESTAURANT

NB. For details of Thai Cuisine, see the Food and Drink section.

Waiter/waitress (to call)	Nong
The menu please	Men-oo cap/car
Have you a table?	Me dough my crap/car
Spicy	Pet
Not spicy	My pet
Drinks	Derm(dermis)
Water	Nam
Orange juice	Nam som
Coke	Coo-laa
Tea	Char lawn
Iced tea	Char yen
Coffee	Caff-ay
Iced coffee	Caff-ay yen
Milk	Nom
Beer	Beer
Whisky	Lou(loud)

Meat	Gnu-a
Chicken	Guy
Duck	Bet
Pork	Moo
Beef	Gnu-a
Prawns	Goo-ng
Crab	Poor
Fish	Pla (plaque)
Vegetables	Pack
Rice	Cow
Potatoes	Man far-rang
Cabbage	Gall(gallon)-am pea
Cauliflower	Gall(gallon)-am door
Beans	Tour
Corn	Cow port
Tomato	Mac-ewer tet
Aubergine	Mack-ewer
Mushrooms	Het

HEALTH

Sick	My sa-by
Hospital	Roong payer barn
Doctor	More
Ambulance	Rot roong payer barn
Chemist	Lan-ky-yaa
Medicines	Yaa

Appendix Two

List of Maps

Map Index

ROUTE MAPS

Northern Thailand   10,11
Chiang Mai Area   102

THE FAR NORTH

Chiang Mai to Mae Kachan   117
Mae Kachan to Chiang Rai   118
Chiang Rai to Doi Mae Salong   119
Doi Mae Salong to Chiang Dao   120
Chiang Dao to Chiang Mai   121
Maekhong River   122
Thoeng to Chiang Rai   123

THE WEST

Chiang Mai to Huay Nam Dam   166
Huay Nam Dam to Soppong   167
Soppong to Mae Surin   168
Mae Surin to Mae La Noi   169
Mae La Noi to Hot   170
Hot to Chiang Mai   171

THE SOUTH

Lampang to Si Satchanalai   203
Si Satchanalai to Sukhothai   204
Sukhothai to Tak   205
Tak to Mae Ramat   206
Mae Ramat to Mae Salid   207
Mae Salid to Sop Moei   208

THE EAST

Chiang Mai to Lampang   237
Lampang to Ngao   238
Ngao to Phrae   239
Phrae to Pakha   240
Huai Kang to Phayao   241

TOWN PLANS

Central Chiang Mai   78-79
Chiang Mai District   80
Chiang Rai   133
Chiang Saen   164
Doi Mae Salong   164
Khun Yuam   176
Lampang   247
Lamphun   110
Mae Hong Son   189
Mae Sariang   199
Mae Sot   233
Nan   260
Pai   180
Phayao   264
Phitsanulok   223
Phrae   255
Si Satchanalai   211
Soppong   185
Sukhothai   217
Sukhothai Historic Park   218
Tak   229
Thaton   **164**

Index

Index

A
Administration 66
Agriculture 50
Akha 44-45, 124
Amphur 66
Animism 32
Ayutthaya 7, 23, 24

B
Bala 145
Ban 66
Ban Musoe 214
Banks 61
Ban Soppong Hot Springs 126
Bantawe 179
Beer 41
Bhumipol (King) 24
Birds 58-59
Borsang 103, 105
Bot 33
Bothi (Bo) tree 33
British Council 83
Buddhism 8, 27, 32, 34
Burma 9, 21, 24, 25 27, 83, 124, 132, 155, 156, 172, 216
Business hours 64

C
Cambodia 48, 216
Car hire 74
Cham Bong Bang 124
Champooy 243
Chang More 178
Changwat 66
Chao Phrya river 83
Character 26
Chedi 33
Chiang Dao 130, 131
Chiang Dao caves 130

Chiang Khong 23, 157-158
Chiang Mai 9, 20, 23, 24, 43, 45, 51, 52, 77-100, 172, 209, 210, 215, 242
    Accommodation 96-100
    Bars 93
    Bookshops 94
    Discos 94
    Geography 83
    History 82
    Hospitals 95
    Massage 94
    Post Offices 95
    Restaurants 90
    Shopping 89
    Transport 85
    Temples 86-87
Chiang Rai 20, 22, 34, 45, 52, 82, 124, 127, 132-143
    Accommodation 137
    Bars 136
    Geography 132
    History 134
    Restaurants 135
    Transport 136
    Temples 134
Chiang Saen 22, 24, 146, 153-155
Chillis 37
Chom Thong 103, 114, 179
Chulalongkorn (King) 2, 25
Climate 19
Coach travel 62, 136
Cobra 71
Consulates 67
Cooking 36
Covelam reservoir 243
Cow Soy 38
Culture 7

D

Denchai 210
Desserts 39
Doi Arng 129
Doi Bussaracum 263
Doi Inthanon 7,113
Doi Khun Tan National Park 242
Doi Laan 126
Doi Mae Salong 52, 125, 128, 158-160
Doi Pui 83, 106-107
Doi Saket 125
Doi Sutep 82, 83, 101, 106-107
Doi Tung 34, 144, 145
Drink 40
Driving 72

E

Eating 36
Economy 67
Electricity 68
Elephant 58
Etiquette 27

F

Family 28
Fang 22, 83, 129, 162-164
Fang National Park 163
Flora 58
Food 35-40
Fruit 40

G

Golden Triangle 132, 155-157
Government 66

H

Haad Khrai 148
Hang Dong 103, 179

Haripunchai 22
Health 69-71
Hilltribes 25-54
Hillltribe Research Centre 88
Hmong 43-44, 172
Hongse 34
Hot 48, 178, 215
Huai Kae 244
Huai Muang Ngam 129
Hua Mo 177
Huay Luk 130
Huay Mai Sai 143
Huay Nam Dam 174
Huay Rong waterfall 244
Huay Sai 157

I

India 8

J

Joe-kher 173

K

Kala 34
Kaew Satai 128
Karen 32, 44, 49, 50, 88, 172
Karen long neck (Padong) 192
Kinnari 34
Khao Hwai Nang Po 176
Khmer 23, 209, 218
Khong Pai 177
Khong Sai 113
Khue Garn 147
Khun Gorn waterfall 126
Khun Klang 115
Khun Sa 173
Khun Tan National Park 85
Khun Yuam 176
Kuomintang 56, 180
Kumkarn 23

L

La Up   177, 200
Lahu   46, 172
Lampang   22, 29, 209, 210, 242, 243, 246-252
Lamphun   22, 82, 107, 111
Landscape   18
Lan Hoi   213
Language   30
Lanna   22-25
Lansang National Park   213
Laos   22, 132, 148, 155, 156, 157, 216
Lao Sip   128
Lawa   23, 48, 82
Lisu   45, 172, 187
Lon Jai   128
Luang Prabang   23, 24, 82

M

Mae Aw   175, 191, 192
Mae Cam Mai   144
Mae Chaam   178
Mae Chan   127
Mae Gnao reservoir   131
Mae Ha   109
Mae Kha Jahn   126, 245
Mae Kanin   109
Mae Klang waterfall   115
Mae Hong Son   9, 20, 21, 45, 48, 51, 172, 175, 180, 188
Maekok river   83, 132, 134
Maekhong river   25, 124, 155
Mae La Luang   177
Mae La Na   174
Mae La Noi   177
Mae La Up   177, 200
Mae Ma   146
Mae Malie   131, 173
Mae Ramat   215

Mae Rim   131, 173
Mae Sae   124, 144, 146, 149-152
Mae Sa valley   103
Mae Sam Laep   198
Mae Sakua   177
Mae Sariang   9, 48, 51, 172, 177, 198-201, 214, 215
Mae Salid   215
Mae Sawan   177
Mae Sawan Noi waterfall   177
Mae Set   173
Mae Sot   209, 213, 231-234
Mae Suai 1   26, 129
Mae Surin   176
Mae Surin waterfall   176
Mae Taman Elephant Camp   131
Mae Tang river   131
Mae Ya waterfalls   115, 179
Magic Hill   214
Mai   210
Mai Ai   129
Matrathorn waterfall   106
Mengrai (King)   22, 82, 162
Meo (Hmong)   43-44, 172
Mien (Yao)   46-49
Mlabri   47
Mon   22
Money   61
Mongkut (King)   25, 82
Monks   31
More Pang waterfall   184
Mosques   31
Motor bike renta   175
Muang Kung   179
Muang Ngai   130
Muang Phi   244
Musser (Lahu)   46, 172

N

Naga 33
Nam Khong 175, 245
Nam Prik 38-39
Na Pha Pak 175, 191
Nam Rin 274
Nan 52, 244, 245, 258-262
Nan Chao 21
Natural History 57-59
Ngao 243
Nong Lum 115
Nong Heng 177

O

Obluang Gorge National Park 178
Om Koi 215
Opium 19, 54-56, 124, 132
Orchids 18

P

Pa Heo 113
Pa Klua 145
Pa Sao 113
Pa Sa Tong 215
Pai 51, 52, 172, 180-185
Pai river 180, 192
Pan Baek 174
Pang Mapha 185
Pasang 111
Pegu 24
Petro 173
Pha Bong Hot Springs 175
Pha Sua waterfall 175, 191
Pha Tang 149
Phayao 9, 21, 126, 245, 262-265
Phi Tong Luang (Mrabri) 47, 245
Phitsanulok 212, 222-227
Photography 68
Phuping palace 101

Phrae 243, 244, 254-257
Phrao 130
Ping river 83, 88
Pla (fish) Cave 192
Plane 68, 85, 136
Police 66
Pong Na Cam Elephant Camp 143
Post 65
Pyongyang 109

R

Reptiles 57
Railways 63
Ramakamphaeng 23, 216
Religion 31-35, 49
Restaurants 36-37

S

Sa 244
Sai Thong 149
Sala 33
Salween river 198
Samoeng 103, 109, 179
Sam Laek 128
Samlor 64
San Jaroen 126
San Pa Tong 179
Sanitation 71
Sankamphaeng 103, 104-106
Sarapee 113
Sawankholok 212
Shaman 50
Shan 21, 25, 172
Singha 34
Sipsong Panna 22
Si Satchanalai 209, 210
Slash and burn 50
Social life 25
Sonpuey 214
Songthaew 64

Sop Moei 215
Sop Ruak 124, 146, 155-157
Soppong 185-187
Soup 38
Sri Lanka 21
Sukhothai 209, 210, 213, 216-222, 262
Sukhothai Historical Park 213, 216-219
Szechuan 21
Spirit Houses 31

T

Tai Yai (Shan) 21, 25, 172
Tak 20, 24, 209, 213, 215, 228-231
Taksin (King) 229
Taksin National Park 214
Tarnsawan waterfall 245
Telecommunications 65
Thaat 129
Tha Chomphu 242
Tham Lot 186-187
Tham Luang 145
Tha Song Yang 242
Tham Ku Kaeo 145
Tham Pla 145
Thamphatai Forest Park 266
Thaton 83, 124, 129, 161-162
Thoed Thai 128
Thoeng 148-149
Thonburi 24
Thung Hong 244, 254
Tiger 7
Tilokarajah (King) 23
Tipping 37
Ton You 177
Tours 51
Trains 63
Tung Gwee On 242-243

Tub Tao Cave 130
Tuk-tuk 64

U

Uttaradit 210

V

Vatchirathin waterfall 115
Vehicle rental 74
Vietnam 24
Visas 67

W

Wang Lao 146
Wang Nua 245
Wang Chin 210
Wang Pa Pao 126
Wang River 248
Wat 32
Wat Chamadevi 112
Wat Chedi Luang 154
Wat Phraa That Haripunchai 111
Wat Phra Singh 86
Wat Suan Dok 87
Water 40
Weights and measures 68
Whisky 41
Wiang Chai 148
Wiang Kaen 148
Wieng Ka Soi National park 210
Wiharn 33
Wine 41

Y

Yang (Karen) 32, 42-43, 49, 50, 88, 172
Yao 46, 49
Young Elephant Training Centre 242-243
Yunnan 82